Managing Cash Flow

An Operational Focus

Rob Reider
Peter B. Heyler

John Wiley & Sons, Inc.

This book is printed on acid-free paper.

Published by John Wiley & Sons, Inc., Hoboken, New Jersey
Published simultaneously in Canada.

JK

For general information on our other products and services, or technical support,
please contact our Customer Care Department within the United States at 800-762-2974,
outside the United States at 317-572-3993 or fax 317-572-4002.

Wiley also publishes its books in a variety of electronic formats. Some content that
appears in print may not be available in electronic books.

Library of Congress Cataloging-in-Publication Data:

Reider, Rob, 1940–
    Managing cash flow / by Rob Reider, Peter B. Heyler.
        p. cm.
ISBN 0–471–22809–5 (acid free)
    1. Cash management.   I. Heyler, Peter B.   II. Title.
    HG4028.C45 R453 2003
    658.15'244 – dc21

                                                                    2002012147

Printed in the United States of America.
10 9 8 7 6 5 4 3 2 1

Contents

About the Authors   v

Acknowledgments   viii

Introduction   1

Chapter 1: Understanding Cash Management   9
- Cash Flow Basics 12
- History, The Fed, and Float 21
- Bank Issues and Concerns 28
- Conclusion 33

Chapter 2: Managing Cash Flow—Receipts and Disbursements   35
- Using the Balance Sheet 36
- Cash Receipts 39
- Cash Disbursements 58
- Conclusion 67

Chapter 3: Planning and Budgeting   69
- Relationship between Planning and Budgeting 71
- Strategies for Competitive Advantage 74
- Strategic Planning Process 76
- Short-Term Planning 81
- Conclusion 94

Chapter 4: Analyzing the Sales Function   95
- Cash Management Study 95
- Purpose of the Sales Function 96
- Conclusion 122

Chapter 5: Cost Reduction Analysis Procedures   123
- Benchmarking Strategies 124
- Activity Based Costing Principles 152
- Conclusion 174

Chapter 6: Analyzing Non-Value-Added Functions   176
- Looking at the Accounting Function 177
- Choosing What to Analyze 179
- Identifying Goals and Basic Business Principles 182
- Prioritizing Activities 184

Financial Reporting   185
Developing the Cash Management Analysis Survey Form   188
Compiling the Data   188
Analyzing the Data   192
Organizational Issues   198
Budget Analysis   200
Analysis of Functional Costs   202
Analysis of Accounting Operations   206
Activity Based Costing Applications   211
Developing Recommendations   213
Specific Recommendations   214
Organization Recommendations   233
Other Areas for Review   235
Conclusion   237

Chapter 7: Investing, Financing, and Borrowing   **239**
Investing Excess Cash   239
Financing Sources for the Business   250
Borrowing for Cash Shortfalls   251
Conclusion   262

Chapter 8: Planning Cash Flow   **263**
Cash Flow Planning   263
Managing Cash Balances   276
Cash Planning Approaches   279
Conclusion   282

Chapter 9: Controlling and Analyzing Cash Flow   **285**
Brief Look at FASB 95   285
Cash Flow Projections—Methodology   287
Cash Flow Reporting and Controls   293
Interpretation and Analysis of Cash Flow   300
Conclusion   322

Afterword   **323**

Appendix A—Cash Study: Managing Cash Flow   **325**

Appendix B—Cash Conservation Checklist   **341**

Index   **347**

ABOUT THE AUTHORS

Rob Reider, CPA, MBA, PhD, is the president of Reider Associates, a management and organizational consulting firm located in Santa Fe, New Mexico, which he founded in 1976. Prior to starting Reider Associates, he was a manager in the Management Consulting Department of Peat, Marwick in Philadelphia. His areas of expertise encompass planning and budget systems, managerial and administrative systems, computer processing, financial and accounting procedures, organizational behavior and theory, management advisory services, large and small business consulting, management information and control techniques, and management training and staff development.

Rob has been a consultant to numerous large, medium, and small businesses of all types in the aforementioned areas (in both the private and public sectors). In addition, he has conducted many and varied operational reviews and benchmarking studies and has trained both internal staff and external consultants in these techniques.

He is the course author and nationally sought after discussion leader and presenter for more than 20 different seminars that are conducted nationally for various organizations and associations. He has conducted more than 1,000 such seminars throughout the country and has received the AICPA Outstanding Discussion Leader of the Year award.

Considered a national expert in the areas of operational reviews and benchmarking strategies, Rob provides specific consultation in the areas of general business management, development of internal and external consulting practices, organizational and management systems, and the development and conducting of continuing professional education (CPE) and other training programs.

Rob is the course author of nine Reider Associates self study courses marketed nationally. He is also the author of the following books published by John Wiley & Sons, Inc.

- *The Complete Guide to Operational Auditing*
- *Operational Review: Maximum Results at Efficient Costs*

- *Benchmarking Strategies: A Tool for Profit Improvement*
- *Improving the Economy, Efficiency, and Effectiveness of Not-for-Profits*

Rob has also been a presenter at numerous professional meetings and conferences around the country and has published articles in professional journals. He has been a frequent commentator on the educational video programs produced by Primemedia Workplace Learning such as The CPA Report, The Governmental Update, and the Accounting and Financial Managers Network

Rob has earned the degree of Bachelor of Science (B.S.) in Business Administration and Master of Science in Business (MBA) from Drexel University as well as Doctor Of Philosophy (Ph.D) in Organizational and Management Psychology from Southwest University. He is currently listed in Who's Who In The East and West, Who's Who In The World, Who's Who In Finance and Industry, Personalities In America, International Biography, Who's Who of Emerging Leaders In America, and Who's Who In Executives And Businesses.

For more information about Rob Reider and Reider Associates, visit his web site at www.reiderassociates.com/otp/ or e-mail him at hrreider@reiderassociates.com.

Peter B. Heyler, CPA, MBA, is president of his own consulting firm, PBH Executive Services, based in Missoula, Montana. He specializes in the areas of strategic, financial, and business development planning for small and medium-sized clients in a variety of businesses. He has experience and expertise in general management, accounting, finance, business strategy, personnel management, and international business.

Mr. Heyler has conducted CPE programs for the AICPA and many state CPA societies. He also presents seminars, workshops, and training programs for educational and private organizations. He has been a full-time and/or adjunct faculty member of Rider College, Beaver College, Ursinus College and Bucks County (PA) Community College. Involvement in international consulting and management education with the United Nations Industrial Development Organization (UNIDO), Global Volunteers, the U.S. Agency for International Development (AID), and the University of Pennsylvania Wharton School's Applied Research Center has also been part of his past experience. He has had teaching and/or consulting experience in Ghana, Zambia, India, Pakistan, Thailand, Singapore, Hong Kong, Indonesia, Egypt, Albania, Poland, Ukraine, Sri Lanka, China, Vietnam, Romania, Spain, and England.

Mr. Heyler is course co-author and seminar facilitator of the following CPE programs presented by Reider Associates:

- How to Evaluate Capital Investment Opportunities
- Managerial Accounting: A How-To Guide for Management Decisions
- Strategic Budgeting and Planning for Competitive Advantage
- Effective Controllership for the Smaller Business

- Cash Flow: Managing the Lifeblood of the Organization
- Financial Statement Analysis for Profit Improvement
- Communicating Financial Information to Operations

With nearly 15 years prior experience as an executive in private industry, Mr. Heyler assumed a variety of financial management responsibilities for three manufacturing companies, including Vice President of Finance and Administration, Treasurer, and Chief Financial Officer. Previously he was a Senior Accountant and Consultant with Arthur Young & Co. in New York and Philadelphia where he provided services to many clients in widely diverse industries.

Mr. Heyler earned a BA degree in Economics/Mathematics from Yale University and an MBA degree from Harvard Business School. He also received his CPA certificate from New York and Pennsylvania. He is a member of the American Institute of Certified Public Accountants, the Pennsylvania Institute of Certified Public Accountants, the Montana Society of Certified Public Accountants, the Institute of Management Consultants, and the National Association of Corporate Directors, and has served on the boards of several for-profit and not-for-profit organizations.

For more information about Peter Heyler or PBH Executive Services, the e-mail address is pheyler@montanaheylers.com.

Rob and Peter have been seminar partners for over twenty years. In this capacity, they have co-developed, authored, and presented numerous professional seminars and self study courses.

> *IT IS A GOOD AUTHOR*
> *WHO KNOWS HIS OWN MATERIAL.*

ACKNOWLEDGMENTS

The authors wish to acknowledge assistance from several people in assembling information for this book: Mark Lyons, president of Community Bank in Missoula, Montana, along with John Giuliani and Anne Robinson from Community Bank; and Neil Kyde of Neil G. Kyde, Inc. of Holicong, Pennsylvania. Their input and assistance in checking accuracy of certain parts of the book are greatly appreciated. However, the authors wish to absolve them all from any errors that may appear. Any such errors, of either commission or omission, are totally the responsibility of the authors.

We also recognize that much of the value of this book has been the result of seminar participants who over the years have added comments and suggestions about the material that have found their way into the book. While we cannot explicitly thank them by name, we do acknowledge the value of their participation.

It would be improper and ungrateful not to recognize the patience and stamina of our respective wives, Barbara Reider and Gingy Heyler. Without their willingness to put up with our frustrations, deadlines, and often aggravating behavior, the project would never have been completed.

INTRODUCTION

CASH IS KING! Cash availability is the lifeblood of the organization. With it, assuming there is proper management and economical, efficient, and effective operations, the company can grow and prosper—without it the organization perishes. Like the absence of water to anything living, the absence of cash to the business means death—slow, torturous, physically painful, and mentally agonizing.

Business owners, managers, shareholders, and many others have become enamored with sales and revenue increases, reported profits, earnings per share, price–earnings ratios, cost reductions, and related concepts that focus on the market capitalization of the business and its related stock price per share. Such sales and revenue increases calculated on accrual-based accounting principles may be unrealistic when it comes to real sales to quality customers that can be collected in a timely fashion that ensure a real profit to the business. While these new yardsticks may be significant and even elegant scorekeeping measures for determining how well the enterprise is doing financially, they have minimal significance for the business without cash—unable to meet payroll, pay vendors, or—horror of horrors—make requisite tax payments. Profit is a periodic measure, calculated monthly, quarterly, and annually. Cash, however, is a daily concern. The eager search of the daily mail for incoming checks is not just greed or lust—it is often a survival issue.

This book concentrates on cash management, the lifeblood of any business enterprise. The purpose of these materials is to help readers understand how to manage, plan, and analyze cash flow for their organizations. General focus is on helping the reader understand:

- Cash flow and management techniques necessary for the business to function economically, efficiently, and effectively
- How to recognize and manage effectively the principal factors affecting cash receipts and cash disbursements in the organization
- The impact of operations on the cash flow of the company
  - Organizational planning

1

- Sales
- Operating costs
- Non-value-added activities
- Effective principles for investing excess cash and borrowing to cover cash shortfalls
- Practical planning techniques and procedures for managing the cash flow of the organization
- Some techniques and measures to analyze the cash flow of the organization

Profit can be thought of as a figment of the accountant's imagination, especially since there is so much room for legitimate interpretation, judgment, and flexibility in determining exactly the organization's net income for the period. Cash, however, is cash. It is precisely measurable, tangible, and absolute. Having enough cash allows the business manager to concentrate on other more enjoyable aspects of the business—growth, development, new customers, new products, new processes, and so on. Not having sufficient cash forces the business to fixate on getting more cash any way possible, sometimes to the exclusion of effective management and proper growth and development for the organization. Cash management is an indispensable element in the success and continuity of the business. Remember that each situation is unique, but cash management concerns are the same for every business.

HAPPINESS IS POSITIVE CASH FLOW.

At a personal level, while cash cannot buy happiness, it can alleviate a lot of anguish. For the business, understanding cash, managing it, and controlling it are essential to long-run success.

WHY THE BUSINESS EXISTS

When a company considers effective cash management, it must keep in mind that there are four overriding issues that must always be kept in mind as to why it exists.

1. *Customer Service.* To provide goods and services to satisfy desired customers, clients, patients, and so on so that they will continue to use the organization's goods and services and refer it to others. A successful organizational philosophy that correlates with this goal is "to provide the highest quality products and service at the least possible cost." Clearly, this is essential in any business, but thinking needs to be expanded to include all those who have a stake in the company. Stakeholders to consider include:

- Customers—present and prospective
- Owners and shareholders
- Management and supervision
- Employees and contractors
- Vendors and suppliers
- Special interest groups (unions, environmentalists)
- Government (FDA, EEO, EPA, FAA, IRS, legislative)

> **THEY ARE ALL CUSTOMERS; WE MUST RESPECT THEIR POINTS OF VIEW AND EARN THEIR RESPECT FOR OURS.**

2. *Cash Conversion.* This dictates that the company provide desired goods and services so that the investment in the business is as quickly converted to cash as possible, with the resultant cash inflow exceeding the cash outflow, ensuring long-run profitability, positive return on investment, and positive cash flow. The correlating philosophy to this goal can be stated as follows: "To achieve desired organization results using the most efficient methods so that the organization can optimize the use of limited resources."

> **IF THE COMPANY DOES NOT GENERATE POSITIVE CASH FLOW, IT WILL NOT STAY IN BUSINESS.**

3. *Making Money.* The easiest and most obvious reason that most businesses use as the reason for existence is to make money. While certainly a legitimate and essential goal, it is not by itself enough without the others.

> **MAKING MONEY IS NECESSARY, BUT HOW WE MAKE MONEY IS MORE IMPORTANT.**

4. *Survival.* To live and fight another day! This is arguably the overarching goal of any business that is not liquidating or shutting its doors. The business must first survive to be able to achieve its other goals.

> **SURVIVAL IS ATTAINABLE ONLY WITH ADEQUATE CUSTOMER SERVICE, CASH CONVERSION, AND REAL PROFITS.**

This means that the company is in business to stay for the long term – to serve its customers and grow and prosper. A starting point for establishing cash management goals is to decide which businesses the organization is really in so that cash management efficiencies and effectiveness can be compared to such overall company goals.

BUSINESSES AN ORGANIZATION IS NOT IN

Once short-term thinking is eliminated, managers must realize they are not in the following businesses, and cash management decision making becomes simpler:

- *Sales business.* Making sales that cannot be collected profitably (sales are not profits until the cash is received and unless all the costs of the sale are less than the amount collected) creates only numerical growth.
- *Customer order backlog business.* Logging customer orders is a paperwork process to impress internal management and outside shareholders. Unless this backlog can be converted into timely sales and cash collection, there is only a future promise, which may never materialize.
- *Accounts receivable business.* Get the cash as quickly as possible, not the promise to pay. True, customers are the company's business and keeping them in business keeps the company in business. However, the company has already put out its cash to vendors and/or into inventory. Therefore, it must focus on getting its money back. Get out of the accounts receivable business to the extent possible—ideally altogether—by moving toward cash sales.
- *Inventory business.* Inventory does not equal sales. Keep inventories to a minimum—zero if possible. Procure raw materials from your vendors only as needed, produce for real customer orders based on agreed delivery dates, maximize work-in-process throughput, and ship directly from production when the customer needs the product. To accomplish these inventory goals, it is necessary to develop effective organizational life stream and cash management procedures that include the company's vendors, employees, and customers.
- *Property, plant, and equipment business.* Maintain at a minimum—be efficient. Idle plant and equipment result in inefficient use. If the assets are there, they will be used. Plan for the normal (or small valleys), not for the maximum (or large peaks); network to outsource for additional capacity and insource for times of excess capacity.
- *Employment business.* Get by with the lowest number of employees possible. Never hire an additional employee unless absolutely necessary and unless there is value added; learn how to cross-train and transfer good employees. Not only do people cost ongoing salaries and fringe benefits, but they also require attention and supervision, which can result in empire building.

- *Management and administration business.* The more an organization has, the more difficult it becomes to manage its business. It is easier to work with less and be able to control operations than to spend time managing the managers. Too much of management results in getting in the way of those it is supposed to manage and meeting with other managers to discuss how to do this. Management as an end rather than as a means is toxic to the organization.

If an organization does both of these successfully—that is, pays attention to its reasons for existence and stays out of the businesses it should not be in, it will more than likely (outside economic factors notwithstanding) grow and prosper through well-satisfied customers, and it will keep itself in the positive cash conversion business.

Of course, an organization also has to stay out of the pure numbers business—looking only at-short term reporting criteria such as the amount of sales, backlog, locations, employees, and the big devil, "the bottom line," that others judge as success.

> ## *KEEP YOUR EYE ON THE CASH,*
> ## *NOT ON RECORDED PROFITS.*

The organization must decide which of the preceding factors it wishes to embrace as cash management goals, which ones it will not include, and which additional criteria it will include. These criteria become the overriding conditions upon which the organization conducts its operations and against which it measures effective cash management.

> ## *KNOW THE BUSINESS THE COMPANY IS IN,*
> ## *FOR THE WRONG BUSINESS*
> ## *WILL DO THE COMPANY IN.*

SOME BASIC BUSINESS PRINCIPLES

Each organization must determine the basic principles that guide its operations. These principles become the foundation on which the organization bases its desirable cash management goals. Examples of such business principles include:

- Produce the best quality product at the least possible cost.
- Set selling prices realistically so as to sell all the product that can be produced within the constraints of the production facilities.

- Build trusting relationships with critical vendors; keeping them in business keeps the company in business.
- The company is in the customer service and cash conversion businesses.
- Don't spend a dollar that doesn't need to be spent; a dollar not spent is a dollar to the bottom line. Control costs effectively; there is more to be made here than by increased sales.
- Manage the company; do not let it manage the managers. Provide guidance and direction, not crises.
- Identify the company's customers and develop marketing and sales plans with the customers in mind. Produce for the company's customers, not for inventory. Serve the customers, do not just sell them.
- Do not hire employees unless they are absolutely needed; only do so when they multiply the company's effectiveness and the company makes more from them than if they did the work themselves (i.e., there is value added).
- Keep property, plant and equipment to the minimum necessary to satisfy customer demand.
- Plan for the realistic, but develop contingency plans for the unexpected—positive and negative.

> ## *BASIC BUSINESS PRINCIPLES GUIDE CASH MANAGEMENT DIRECTION.*

PURPOSE OF THIS BOOK

This book is not intended to be a financial text; rather, we will be looking at cash management with an operational focus that considers the above principles in an effort to maintain the company in the most economical, efficient, and effective manner possible. In this regard, the company must keep in mind those businesses it should not be in. With these principles in mind, operations can be analyzed to identify areas for improvement in which best practices can be implemented that maximize cash inflow and minimize cash outflow.

Although the primary focus of ongoing cash management and continual operational analysis is on the manner in which cash is used by the organization, considering the sources and uses of cash and the policies and procedures used to deal with over- and undercash conditions, there are other operational areas—due to their direct impact on cash flow—that will need to be addressed as well, including:

- *Sales of products or services*
  - Are sales made to quality customers with the right products at the right time?
  - Does each sale make a contribution to profits?

- Are sales compared to all relevant costs such as product costs (i.e., direct material and labor), assignment of product related activity costs (e.g., manufacturing processes, quality control, shipping, receiving, etc.), functional costs (e.g., purchasing, accounts payable, billing, accounts receivable, etc.), and customer costs (e.g., marketing, selling, support services, customer service, etc.)?
- Do sales relate to an agreed upon sales forecast? Is the company selling the right products to the right customers?
- Do sales integrate with an effective production scheduling and control system?

- *Manufacturing or production of services*
  - Are sales orders entered into an effective production control system, which ensures that all sales orders are entered into production in a timely manner to ensure on-time, quality deliveries?
  - Is work-in-process kept to a minimum so that only real customer orders are being worked on rather than building up finished goods inventory?
  - Are the most efficient and economical production methods used to ensure that the cost of the product is kept to its realizable minimum?
  - Are direct materials and labor used most efficiently so that waste, reworks, and rejects are kept to a minimum?
  - Are nondirect labor (and material) costs such as quality control, supervision and management, repairs and maintenance, materials handling, and so on kept to a minimum?

- *Billing, accounts receivable, and collections*
  - Are bills sent out in a timely manner—at the time of shipment or before?
  - Are accounts receivable processing procedures the most efficient and economical?
  - Is the cost of billing, accounts receivable processing, and collection efforts more costly than the amount of the receivable or the net profit on the sale?
  - Is the number and amount of accounts receivable continually analyzed for minimization?
  - Are any customers paying directly or through electronic funds transfer at the time of shipping or delivery?
  - Are bills and accounts receivable in amounts exceeding the cost of processing excluded from the system?
  - Has consideration been given to reducing or eliminating these functions?

- *Inventory: raw materials and finished goods*
  - Are raw material and finished goods inventories kept to a minimum?
  - Are raw materials delivered into production on a just-in-time basis?

- Are finished goods completed in production just in time for customer delivery?
- Is the company working toward getting out of these inventory businesses altogether?

- *Purchasing, accounts payable, and payments*
  - Are all items that are less than the cost of purchasing excluded from the purchasing system—with an efficient system used for these items?
  - Are all repetitive high-volume and -cost items (e.g., raw materials and manufacturing supplies) negotiated by purchasing with vendors as to price, quality, and timeliness?
  - Does the production system automatically order repetitive items as an integrated part of the production control system?
  - Has consideration been given to reduce these functions for low- and high-ticket items leading toward their possible elimination?
  - Does the company consider paying any vendors on a shipment or delivery basis as part of its vendor negotiation procedures?

- *Other costs and expenses: general, administrative, and selling*
  - Are all other costs and expenses kept to a minimum? Remember that an unnecessary dollar not spent is a dollar directly to the bottom line.
  - Are selling costs directed toward customer service and strategic plans rather than maximizing salespeople's compensation?
  - Is there a system in effect that recognizes and rewards the reduction of expenses rather than the rewarding of budget increases?
  - Are all potential non-value-added functions (e.g., management and supervision, office processing, paperwork, etc.) evaluated as to reduction and elimination?

There are many other operational areas and concerns that could be listed. Those listed above are only meant as examples of areas that should be considered in the company's management of cash. Effective cash management may result in the analysis of many of the company's major operations as cash affects every function and activity. To ensure that the company operates with effective cash management procedures, it must understand that every dollar expended and every dollar collected must be evaluated as to its appropriateness to the company's plans and operations.

Benjamin Franklin once said, "There are three faithful friends – an olde wife, an olde dog, and ready money." The first two shall pass without comment, but the third assuredly is as relevant today as it was in Franklin's time.

> ## *CASH IS THE FUEL*
> ## *THAT POWERS THE COMPANY.*

CHAPTER 1

Understanding Cash Management

**MANAGING THE COMPANY
MEANS MANAGING ITS CASH FLOW.**

We will be discussing the crucial subject of managing cash flow, the lifeblood of the organization—a vital element in the success and continuity of the business. The emphasis of the materials is on the principal components of cash management—what company management must know to better understand the organization's cash flow and what can be done to enhance its overall cash position. We will be looking at cash management from the operational viewpoint of one who manages the cash of the organization rather than strictly from the typical accountant's viewpoint of recording cash receipts and disbursement transactions. Our focus will be on a pragmatic and simple approach to cash management appropriate to organizations of any size—from the large to the medium-sized and smaller. The basic techniques should be applicable to all organizations, not just large organizations using sophisticated technical techniques to move and manage millions of dollars daily. Remember that each situation is unique, but cash management concerns are the same for every business.

As mentioned in the Introduction, profit can be thought of as an imaginary number created by accountants. Having enough cash allows company management to concentrate on growth, finding new businesses, acquiring new customers, locating new business partners, developing new products, installing new processes, and so on. Not having enough cash forces the company to fixate on getting more, sometimes to the exclusion of growth and development.

An early step in successful cash management is for the organization to clearly define its desired criteria for success as related to such factors as reasons for existence, basic business principles, mental models, belief systems, performance drivers, and so on. Many of these criteria can be articulated in the company's mission statement, vision statement, credo, or other such statement of purpose. This thinking can also result in probing deeper into the inner workings of the organization. These organizational criteria typically relate to the company as an entity as well as to its major functions. An example of such an organizational results criteria structure is as follows:

- *Organization-wide criteria*
  - Operate all activities in the most economical, efficient, and effective manner possible.
  - Provide the highest-quality products or services to customers at the lowest cost consistent with the level of quality targeted.
  - Satisfy customers so that they will continue to use the company's products or services and refer the company to others.
  - Convert the cash invested in the business as effectively as possible so that the resultant cash exceeds the cash input to the maximum extent possible.
  - Achieve desired results using the most efficient methods so that the company can optimize the use of its limited resources.
  - Maximize net profits without compromising ethical standards, quality of operations, customer service, or cash requirements.

- *The Sales Function*
  - Make sales to customers that will be collected profitably.
  - Develop realistic sales forecasts that result in real present or future customer orders.
  - Sell company products or services to the right customers at the right time in the right quantities.
  - Ensure that actual customer sales correlate directly with management's long- and short-term plans.
  - Assure that sales efforts and corresponding compensation systems reinforce the goals of the company.
  - Integrate customer sales with the other functions of the company, such as manufacturing, marketing, merchandising, engineering, purchasing, finance, and so on.

- *Manufacturing or service provision*
  - Operate in the most efficient manner with the most economical cost structure.
  - Integrate manufacturing or service processes with sales efforts and customer requirements.
  - Manufacture or provide services in the most timely manner considering processes such as customer order entry, timely throughput, and customer delivery demands.
  - Increase productivity of all manufacturing and service operations on an ongoing basis.
  - Eliminate, reduce, or improve all facets of the manufacturing/service operation including activities such as receiving, inventory control, production control, storeroom operations, research and development,

quality control, packing and shipping maintenance, supervision and management, and so on.
  - Minimize the amount of resources such as personnel, facilities, and equipment assigned to manufacturing or service operations.

- *Personnel*
  - Provide only those personnel functions that are absolutely required as value-added activities.
  - Maintain the levels of personnel at the minimum required to achieve results in each functional area.
  - Provide personnel functions such as hiring, training, evaluation, and advancement in the most efficient and economical manner possible.
  - Develop an organizational structure that coordinates all functions in the most efficient manner to achieve their purposes.
  - Minimize the hiring of new employees by such methods as cross-training, interdepartmental transfers, and other best practices.
  - Implement compensation and benefit systems that provide for effective employee motivation and achievement of company goals.

- *Purchasing*
  - Use a system of central purchasing for those items in which economies are achievable.
  - Implement direct purchase systems for those items that the purchasing function does not need to process, such as low-dollar-value and routine recurring purchases.
  - Simplify systems so that the cost of purchasing is the lowest possible.
  - Effectively negotiate with vendors so that the company obtains the right materials at the right time at the right quality at the right price.
  - Maintain a vendor analysis system so that vendor performance can be objectively evaluated.
  - Develop effective computerized techniques for economic processing, adequate controls, and reliability.

- *Accounting*
  - Analyze the necessity of each of the accounting functions and related activities such as accounts receivable, accounts payable, payroll, budgeting, and general ledger.
  - Operate all accounting functions in the most economical manner.
  - Implement effective procedures that result in the accounting functions focusing on analytical rather than mechanical activities.
  - Develop computerized procedures that correlate accounting activities with operating requirements.
  - Create reporting systems that provide management with useful operating data and indicators that can be generated from accounting data.
  - Eliminate or reduce all unnecessary accounting operations that provide few or no value-added benefits.

CASH FLOW BASICS

> ### *CASH IS THE LIFEBLOOD*
> ### *OF THE ORGANIZATION.*

What Is Cash Flow?

Effective cash flow management is essential to the survival of the business. It may be even more important than producing goods or services or generating a sale. Most businesses can lose a sale or a customer and still continue operations. However, miscalculate the availability of cash when needed, for example, for payroll or taxes or a critical vendor, and the company may very suddenly be out of business. Cash flow management helps to avoid such operational crises by applying some basic principles to the business.

The company needs cash to pay its bills—business expenses (i.e., service or manufacturing costs, selling expenses, general and administrative costs)—and to pay off scheduled liabilities (e.g., loans, accounts payable, taxes, etc.) on time. Cash comes from only four generic sources:

1. *Sale of equity.* In the form of company stock or ownership of the business
2. *Borrowing.* From a variety of sources such as financial institutions, friends and relatives, customers, vendors, or owners
3. *Conversion of assets to cash.* Sale of idle or unneeded facilities or equipment, reduction of excess inventory, or collection of accounts receivable
4. *Reinvesting profits.* Those resulting from real cash collections, not just from recorded sales that may or may not be collected

Keep in mind that every business has to be continuously in *the cash conversion and expansion business*. The process starts with a cash infusion, produces products or services for customers, sells and delivers the product or service, bills, collects payment, and adds the resulting cash to the business coffers. A successful business collects more cash from customers than it expends for providing and servicing its products and services. When the business ultimately liquidates, profit and cash are the same. But during its existence, the business calculates periodic income statements and balance sheets, based on accrual accounting, that serve as a measure of performance. It also calculates a cash flow statement to measure sources and uses of actual cash.

Because of timing differences, profits and cash flow move differently. Good cash flow with inadequate profits means short-term survival but long-term problems. Good profits without adequate cash flow means immediate trouble. Even if the company generates a profit, it must be concerned with managing its cash and minimizing the gap between cash outflow and cash inflow. This *cash gap* can be considered the number of days between when it pays for materials and services and when it receives payment for the sale of the product or service. The longer this gap, the more time the company is out of pocket for cash. The cash gap needs to be financed, preferably from prior sales. Otherwise, cash must come from outside sources with the attendant costs of borrowing or equity, which have a negative effect on profits.

If the company is successful, ending cash will exceed starting cash by more than enough to cover the time value of the cash injection(s). The company cannot be in the business of selling to nonpaying customers or selling products that generate less cash than their costs. Furthermore, investing in accounts receivable, sales backlog, or inventory should be avoided since these cannot be spent or reinvested until they are converted back into cash. Inadequate cash is often the principal limiting factor in the growth of the business, and the company's goal should be to accelerate the cash conversion process as much as possible.

Effective cash management maximizes cash generation for the business. This means, in effect, generating positive cash flow by applying effective techniques for collecting cash due to the company, expending no more cash than necessary, and delaying (within limits) the payment of cash due others. For the business to survive, it must have cash when it needs it. In addition, a positive cash buffer provides a safety net against unforeseen business crises, emergencies, or management errors and allows the company to take advantage of opportunities that may arise. Sufficient cash availability is also necessary for the business to grow and survive. Businesses fail not from lack of growth or lack of profitability, but from lack of cash to pay the bills.

Also keep in mind that an overinvestment in cash can impose opportunity costs on the business by loss of earnings on that "excess" cash that would be available from investment in profitable alternative opportunities. However, excess cash does not normally lead to serious business problems, while insufficient cash is always a problem. Effective cash management allows the company to control its cash and manage its business economically, efficiently, and effectively. In this way, the company can reduce business disruptions, operate in a smooth and efficient manner, and provide for ongoing growth and profitability.

Understanding and managing cash flow is not nearly as difficult a process as it may at first seem. There are a finite number of places where cash comes from and where it goes. We are not dealing with an inordinately complex process. To show this, a schematic, "Flow of Funds in a Business," is depicted in Exhibit 1.1. It illustrates that cash comes from only a limited number of business sources and is used for only a limited number of activities. Therefore, there are only a limited number of areas to which company management can look to find opportunities to generate more cash inflows or reduce cash outflows. This is not intended to oversimplify the cash flow management process, but it is necessary for management to understand that the process need not be made more complicated than necessary.

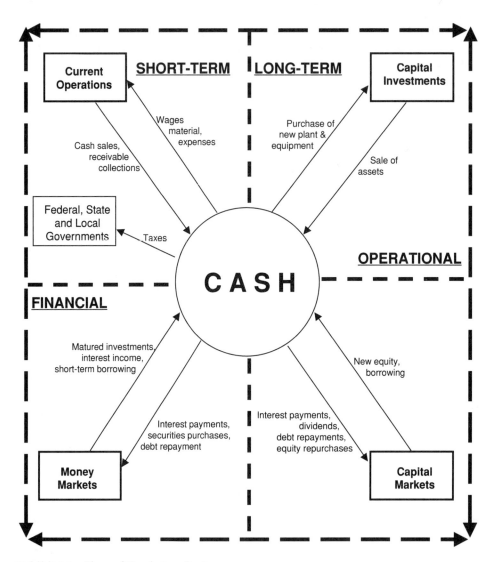

Exhibit 1.1   Flow of Funds in a Business

> ## *MANAGING CASH FLOW*
> ## *IS A MANAGEABLE ACTIVITY.*

Cash Flow Process

Any business—manufacturing, service, financial, not-for-profit, government, and so on—begins with an infusion of cash. The fundamental operating cash flow process within the business then operates in a continuous loop of short-term asset transformation as shown in the "Cash Generation Cycle" in Exhibit 1.2.

> ## *FROM CASH TO CASH ... AS QUICKLY AS POSSIBLE.*

This is the process for a manufacturing business. A service business, a retail store, or even a not-for-profit organization goes through the same series of activities. The only adjustment is that the descriptors will be different. A retail store will purchase inventory, but will not do any manufacturing; instead, it will incur merchandising costs to make the items available for sale in an appealing manner. A service or not-for-profit establishment may not purchase inventory or do any manufacturing but will have to incur costs to ready the services for their clients' benefit. In any business, cash will have to be expended prior to receiving a return from customers or clients. Having sufficient cash available to allow that to happen is essential to both short-term survival and long-term success.

A business starts with cash—the owner's investment and usually some borrowed funds. The purchase of goods or services, together with the manufacturing activities or service provision, transforms the cash into inventory or services to be delivered. As the goods or services are provided to the customer, they are converted to accounts receivable or cash receipts. The collection process then transforms the accounts receivable back into cash. If the business process works properly, the cash received is greater than the cash laid out, and the resulting excess provides the business with additional funds to reinvest and grow. The process then needs to repeat itself in an ever-increasing continuous cycle. A major

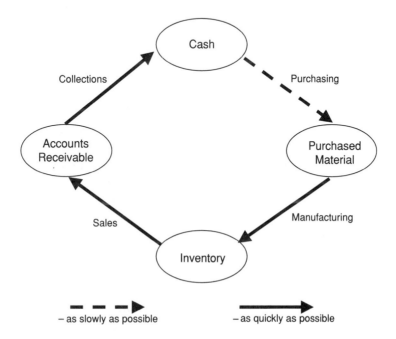

Exhibit 1.2 Cash Generation Cycle

planning step must always be to have sufficient cash available to allow this series of activities to continue unabated.

The schematic in Exhibit 1.2 is, of course, a simplistic representation of a typical cash generation process. Factors such as accounts payable, outside financing, asset conversion, and profits from operations typically increase the amount of cash resources available. However, accounts receivable increases, inventory investment, debt repayments, dividends, and operating losses decrease the level of cash. In addition, most businesses require periodic purchases of property, plant, and equipment in order to maintain or expand their business activities. These are not part of the cash generation cycle, but do require an additional outlay of cash, often quite significant.

In reality, the cash flow process does not operate simply or smoothly, but is subject to numerous disruptions. Changes in the level of inventory retard or increase the flow of cash as do changes in the level of accounts receivable and accounts payable. Payables are free short-term loans from vendors or suppliers that represent a source of cash for the business. Inventory and accounts receivable, however, are idle assets reducing cash availability until they can be converted into sales and collected. Chronically high levels of inventory or accounts receivable can easily threaten the survival of the business. While cash itself contributes only minimally (through possible interest earnings) to profitability, it does make possible the acquisition of the goods and/or services that create profitability.

The problems associated with too little cash are obvious. But is it possible to have too much cash? At first glance, it would seem not. But having too much cash on hand means that the company is not utilizing its cash in the most effective manner. Cash in the form of money on hand cannot generate the kind of potential return required of a business. The cash needs to be invested appropriately in the business to generate an adequate return. If the business is able to generate a greater return on its cash than it can get from the business, there is a problem with that business. Except in unusual and generally short-term instances, returns on cash will be less than can be generated in a flourishing business. Therefore, having too much cash on hand represents an inefficient utilization of resources and a flawed investment strategy.

What, then, are we saying? Too little cash means problems of survival, while too much cash can result in lost opportunities and inefficient utilization of limited resources. Cash flow management is a continual effort to smooth out fluctuations and focus on the Goldilocks Cash Management Principle: "not too much; not too little; but just the right amount." What, however, is the right amount? There is no formula to make this determination, but there are several factors that need to be considered:

- There needs to be enough cash to pay the company bills.
- There needs to be enough cash to meet any requirements such as compensating balances, minimum cash balances to cover service charges, or loan covenants.

- There needs to be enough cash to handle unanticipated opportunities or emergencies.
- There needs to be enough cash to provide the owners of the company, company management, and/or the cash manager with sufficient "sleep insurance"—that is, to provide a sufficient margin to meet the safety needs of the business and its management personnel.

The first two of these are relatively easy to calculate; but the latter two are totally subjective and will have to be determined by each company and each cash manager individually.

HOW MUCH CASH IS ENOUGH? HOW MUCH IS TOO MUCH?

Objectives of Cash Management

Cash management focuses on making the asset transformation process of the business work smoothly. To accomplish this, the company needs to be aware of the objectives of cash management:

- Control and track cash flows.
- Optimize sources and uses of cash.
- Maximize revenues and minimize expenditures.
- Collect for sales as quickly as possible.
- Expend cash only where necessary (i.e. for value-added functions and activities only).
- Pay creditors no sooner than necessary, and minimize the costs associated with vendor purchases and payments.
- Provide for adequate external sources of funding.
- Properly manage external short-term borrowing and/or investment activities.
- Effectively utilize any excess differential cash generated.
- Keep the cash conversion gap at a minimum.

Effective cash management is necessary due to a lack of synchronization between incoming and outgoing cash flows, a lack of reliable forecastability of cash inflow amounts and timing, and costs of holding cash balances or borrowing to cover cash shortfalls. What the cash management system should be designed to do is shorten the cash generation cycle by effectively managing the assets, liabilities, revenues, and costs of the business.

Cash flow can be maximized, borrowing minimized, and return on assets enhanced by:

- Selling profitable products or services to quality customers who pay on time
- Speeding collection of accounts receivable or collecting in advance of or at time of delivery of the product or service
- Getting material and purchased parts inventory into production and out the door as quickly as possible or getting out of that inventory business entirely by letting suppliers carry the inventory
- Maintaining work-in-process inventory at minimum levels by effective production scheduling and control techniques that ensure maximization of real customer orders into production, minimizing production time, eliminating rework and rejects, and minimizing production costs
- Reducing or eliminating finished goods inventory by shipping immediately from production to the customer
- Reducing expenditures wherever possible
- Taking maximum advantage of accounts payable or other interest-free loans by not paying sooner than required
- Avoiding accounts payable entirely where payable costs exceed the amount of the invoice or where vendor price reductions for fast payment exceed the cost of processing the payments
- Operating the business efficiently by keeping costs and non-value-added activities to a minimum
- Managing the cash of the business by minimizing investment in facilities and equipment, or by increasing results with use of fewer such resources
- Operating with the smallest number of personnel possible
- Diligent management of the cash assets of the business by incurring costs and expenses for only necessary value-added functions and activities
- Maximizing sales to real quality customers, which can be produced and delivered at real cash profits

Profitability versus Liquidity

We have all heard the outcry, "If I'm making so much money, why don't I have any cash?" This exemplifies the difference between profitability and liquidity. Profitability has to do with making an adequate return on the capital and assets invested in the business. Liquidity is having an adequate cash flow that allows the business to make necessary payments and ensure the continuity of operations. Investors, and therefore management, have become somewhat obsessed with profitability in terms of return on investment (ROI) (e.g., return on assets [ROA] or return on equity [ROE]) as the primary method to judge business success.

The main reason profitability does not always ensure liquidity is the system of accruals used in accounting for profit and loss. The accrual accounting system records revenues and expenses as they are incurred, sets up accounts receivable and inventory, establishes accounts payable, capitalizes and amortizes assets, and so on to arrive at profit or loss based on the timing of the economic event, not on the flow of cash. Because of accounting judgments required and flexibility permitted, profit can be determined in part by the accountant's imagination and legitimate creativity; but cash is cash—it is real and precisely measurable. Cash flow management looks at actual cash receipts and disbursements to arrive at the amount of cash available. Business survival is much more a matter of adequate cash flow than that intangible thing called profit. Cash, not profit, is used to pay the bills.

> ## *RECORDING PROFITS IS NOT THE SAME AS COLLECTING CASH.*

Profit versus Cash Flow Example

Jack B. Nimble had been an employee with ABC Machining for nearly 20 years. When the owners decided to sell, Jack seized the opportunity. He knew he could be more successful than his bosses, and this was his chance—he bought the company. ABC Machining had reached a plateau of about $1 million monthly sales with operating profits of about 9 percent of sales. Jack, upon taking over, set up an expansion program with a goal of increasing sales almost immediately by 50 percent with an operating profit margin of 20 percent. In his first year as owner, Jack's program began showing success. Annual sales increased to more than $15 million and resulted in over $2.3 million in operating profit (15 percent of sales) as shown below:

($$ in 000s)	Prior Year	Current Year	Next Year (projected)
Sales	$ 12,002	$ 15,073	$ 20,292
Cost of goods sold	8,436	10,290	13,877
Other expenses	2,474	2,480	2,875
Operating profit	$ 1,092	$ 2,303	$ 3,540
% of Sales	9.1%	15.3%	17.4%

Despite reaching his sales and profitability goals, Jack found himself with a $92,000 cash deficit by the end of the current year. Jack had assumed that a profitable and growing operation would automatically provide for enough cash.

Had Jack understood cash management, he would have carefully studied his cash flow situation, which, in fact, looked like this:

Beginning cash in bank	$ 208,000
Collections	13,110,000
Addition to long-term debt	500,000
Inventory purchases	(5,029,000)
Payroll	(1,975,000)
Other manufacturing expenses	(2,101,000)
Selling & administrative expenses	(2,257,000)
Capital equipment purchases	(1,608,000)
Taxes, interest and debt principal	(940,000)
Cash position at end of year	$ (92,000)

Obviously, the cash flow deficit was not the result of voodoo or black magic, but developed predictably from normal business operations—payments being made on a different timing schedule from actual cash receipts. However, the cash deficit came as a complete surprise to Jack. He did not understand the significance of income statement profits being based on accrual accounting—sales recorded when made, not when accounts receivable are collected; and expenses recorded as incurred, not when paid. And some expenses handled via accounting entries such as depreciation, amortization, and prepaid items are recorded currently, but represent prior cash disbursements, while expenditures for fixed assets, inventory, and other "deferred" expenses are paid for but do not immediately appear on the income statement.

Accrual accounting is essential for effective financial management. It allows the business to evaluate performance over a defined but arbitrary period (e.g., month, quarter, year) by correctly matching revenues and expenses for that period. However, the sales recorded are not normally the same as cash receipts, nor are expenses recorded the same as cash disbursements because of timing differences. Thus, a profit of $2.3 million turns into a cash deficit of $92,000 in our example above—exemplifying the difference between profitability and liquidity and accrual versus cash flow accounting. Had Jack understood cash flow management, he could have avoided a cash deficit by deferring payments, accelerating collections, or getting external financing through debt (his actual solution) or equity investment.

*THE BALANCE SHEET AND INCOME STATEMENT
DO NOT TELL THE CASH STORY.*

HISTORY, THE FED, AND FLOAT

Historical Perspective

Why all the interest in cash flow management that has developed in the last 25 years or so? A number of factors have brought serious attention to the importance of cash flow management:

- Swings in interest rates on both borrowed and invested funds—short-term interest rates moved from 1 to 3 percent in the 1950s, to around an average of 4 percent in the 1960s, 4 percent to 10 percent in the 1970s, all the way up to nearly 20 percent in the 1980s, back down to about 3 percent through the early 1990s fluctuating in the mid single digits through the balance of the 1990s, and back in the early twenty-first century to the low single digits of the 1950s. The lofty interest rates of the late 1970s and early 1980s were a big factor in making the management of cash an important issue.
- General economic conditions—from the boom of the 1960s, which tended to get business away from basics and into a go-go mind set with the temptation to make big money through stock issues; to the economic malaise of the 1970s when businesses had to scratch harder to make money; then to the merger mania, junk bond, easy money attitude of the 1980s; to the hard economic times of the early 1990s where cost cutting and downsizing (or "right-sizing") became the standard; followed by the major stock market boom times to the end of the century; and then another downturn exacerbated by the events of September 11, 2001.
- Return to fundamentals in the 1970s with the wilting of the stock market boom and easy money times of the 1960s. Return on investment measures again became fashionable as earnings per share and price/earnings ratios fell. Since cash is part of the investment base, it is expected to create a return just as inventory, receivables, and fixed assets are expected to generate a return.
- Financial institutions, many troubled by problems in the 1980s, have aggressively marketed cash management services that were previously beneath their dignity or capability. Examples are cash collection lockbox services, electronic (cashless) payment services, online transaction capability, and sophisticated cash investment programs.

Federal Reserve System

To understand how cash management techniques can work and to determine which options are relevant to the business, one needs to understand the process of money movement through the Federal Reserve System (Fed). The Fed is the nation's central banker and in its own words:

It attempts to ensure that growth in money and credit over the long run is sufficient to encourage growth in the economy in line with its potential and with reasonable price stability. In the short run the Federal Reserve System seeks to adapt its policies to combat deflationary or inflationary pressures as they may arise. And as a lender of last resort, it has the responsibility for utilizing the policy instruments available to it in an attempt to forestall national liquidity crises and financial panics. (Board of Governors of the Federal Reserve System, *The Federal Reserve System: Purposes and Functions,* 7th Ed. [Washington, D.C.: Publication Services, Division of Support Services, Board of Governors of the Federal Reserve System, 1984], 1-2.)

Among its myriad functions, the Fed is responsible for:

- Establishing monetary policy
- Supervising and regulating the nation's banking system
- Providing a variety of services to banks and the U.S. Government such as:
  - Clearing checks
  - Providing currency and coin
  - Acting as fiscal agent for the government

The Federal Reserve System consists of 12 Federal Reserve Banks located in Boston, New York, Philadelphia, Cleveland, Richmond, Atlanta, Chicago, St. Louis, Minneapolis, Kansas City, Dallas, and San Francisco. There are branch banks in 25 other cities. As the bankers' bank, the Fed acts as a depository and lending institution for member banks as well as a funds transfer agent to move large sums of money rapidly within the banking system. As the fiscal agent of the government, the Fed maintains the U.S. Treasury's checking account, clears Treasury checks, issues and redeems government securities, and so on. It performs similar functions for other federal agencies and is the receiving agent for tax deposits from individuals and businesses. The Fed also handles the mechanics of selling Treasury securities, servicing outstanding issues and redeeming maturing issues, as well as getting involved in international money transactions and dealing with U.S. foreign currency operations.

The Fed establishes and implements U.S. monetary policy through several areas of activity:

- *Regulating the money supply.* By increasing or decreasing the supply of money in the economy, the Fed can effectively increase or decrease economic activity by making more or less money available to financial institutions for lending purposes.
- *Prescribing reserve requirements.* An increase in reserve requirements for banks serves to reduce their supply of funds available for lending. Conversely, a reduction in reserve requirements expands the banks' lending capacity.

- *Setting the discount rate.* The loan discount rate is the interest rate charged to banks for borrowing from the Fed. The higher the rate, the more expensive it is to borrow and the higher will be the interest rates charged by banks to their customers. This will, of course, reduce the total amount of borrowing and will act as a damper on business activity. The reverse is true if the discount rate is lowered—lower bank interest rates, increased borrowing, and business stimulation.
- *Handling government securities transactions.* Buying or selling U.S. government securities enables the Fed to add to or reduce the amount of overall money in the economy. A reduced amount of money slows economic activity while an increase in money supply increases activity.

In addition to supplying the requisite currency and coin to the economic system consistent with monetary policy guidelines established, the Fed also provides the principal mechanism for processing and clearing checks through the nationwide banking system. While some financial institutions clear checks directly, most banks use the Fed to deposit their out-of-town checks and pay out against their own bank's checks that have been deposited at out-of-town banks. This check-clearing service provides a timely and accurate mechanism for getting checks charged against proper accounts regardless of where they were deposited (at least within the United States). The check-clearing process is depicted in Exhibit 1.3.

As a natural adjunct to the check-clearing system, the electronic transfer of funds within the banking system is another activity the Fed handles through two types of services:

1. Transfers by wire between the Fed offices, depository institutions, the Treasury, and various government agencies
2. Automated clearinghouses (ACHs), which significantly speed the clearing and settlement of electronically originated transactions. This concept is a precursor of the so-called checkless society, which continues to evolve.

Concept of Float

> ## *FLOAT IS THE STATUS OF FUNDS IN TRANSIT.*

The existence of a clearing process as handled by the Federal Reserve System contributes to what is called "float." Float can be simply defined as the "status of funds in transit." There are basically two kinds of float:

1. *Disbursements float.* This is represented by the dollar amount of checks issued by a company that have not been processed by the banking system and cleared through its disbursements account. Essentially, this money is

1. Check drawn on your bank clears same day:

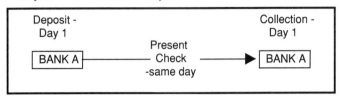

2. Check drawn on nearby bank clears in one day

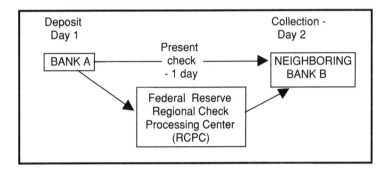

3. Check drawn on out-of-state bank
   Federal Reserve makes funds available in no more than
   two days when check is deposited to RCPC (2-day rule)

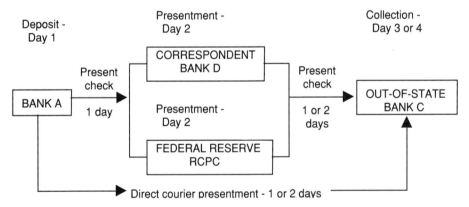

Exhibit 1.3   Check-Clearing Process

floating in the banking system, the payees' processing systems, or the mail
system.

  2. *Collection or availability float.* This is the status of funds waiting to clear the
  system during the time until the funds from a deposited check are available for use by the depositor.

It would be logical to think that the company's disbursements float should
be offset by an equal amount of collection float for another company and vice

versa. However, two factors destroy this concept of an even-up relationship. First is the mail time from delivery by the payer to receipt by the payee; second is the fact that the Fed has a second-day availability rule, which gives every bank availability of funds within three days of presentation, regardless of how long actual clearance takes. Any differences between the second-day availability and actual clearance is "eaten" by the Fed.

It is worthwhile to examine the components of float so that the reviewer understands how it is created, how it can be measured, and how it can be managed. The initial component of float is *mail time*—that is, the amount of transit time in the U.S. Postal Service between the mailing of the check and the receipt by the payee. This can be fairly lengthy (up to five days, or even longer) let's say from Yuma, Arizona to Presque Isle, Maine, or very short (the next day, theoretically) for instance from Minneapolis to St. Paul. The standard actual mail transit time between any two places can be calculated by comparing postmark and receipt dates. Further information can also be obtained from the company's bank.

The second component of float is *processing time*, which is the company's internal time to receive, open, log, endorse, and deposit checks. This can be a matter of hours, days, or weeks, depending on how the company is organized to process checks received. Some of the factors that have an impact on processing time include:

- Post office location and processing procedures
- Frequency and time of mail delivery
- Company's processing procedures—clerical and audit
- Bank location (i.e., in or out of town)
- Company philosophy as to the degree of urgency in getting checks processed and deposited

The third component of float is *clearing time*, which is the amount of time to clear the check through the banking system and be collected from the drawee bank. The various bank clearing procedures having a direct effect on float time are as follows:

- *Internal transfer.* The check is drawn on and deposited in the same bank—there is no float.
- *Direct clearance.* Banks present their checks directly to a neighbor bank or another bank with which they have a direct clearing agreement—one-day clearing time.
- *Federal Reserve clearance.* Checks are cleared through regional Fed check processing centers—usually two to four days' float.
- *Correspondent bank clearance.* Certain large banks do the clearing job instead of the Federal Reserve, using essentially the same process—up to four days' float.

The amount of the company's disbursements float can be determined by sophisticated studies and analyses, or it can be done much more simply (though less precisely) by studying bank statements and determining over a period of several months the time between issuance and deduction from the account for large vendor payments, and the total amount of checks that remain outstanding at each month end. These procedures will give an order of magnitude to the ongoing and month-end amounts of float, which will be, if not precisely accurate, at least a close approximation of reality.

The amount of collection or availability float can be determined by talking with the depository bank to find out its policy on clearing time—that is, the time it takes before deposits are available for use. The time can vary from as little as immediate availability to as long as 10 days, two weeks, or possibly more. Each bank has its own policy. However, a company with a large enough account may be able to negotiate a faster availability time.

A summary of some of the principal features of float can be seen in Exhibit 1.4.

Economic or Total Business Float

For purposes of effective cash management, however, the float concept should be expanded. Exhibit 1.5 is a macro look at what might be called *economic float* or

---

I. DEFINITIONS:

    Float = status of funds in transit
            = items in process of collection (uncollected funds)

II. ELEMENTS OF FLOAT:

	Disbursements Float	Collection/Availability Float
1. Mail float	USPS delivery time	USPS delivery time
2. Processing float	Vendor procedures	In-house procedures
3. System float	Check clearing time	Check clearing time

III. COST OF COLLECTION/AVAILABILITY FLOAT:

Annual volume of credit receipts	×	Transit time in days/365	×	% cost of funds	=	Cost of float

Example:

$100 million	×	1/365	×	4%	=	$10,959/day

IV. ADVANTAGE OF DISBURSEMENTS FLOAT:

Annual volume of checks issued	×	# days outstanding/365	×	% cost of funds	=	Advantage of float

Example:

$75 million	×	1/365	×	4%	=	$8,219/day

Exhibit 1.4 Float Features

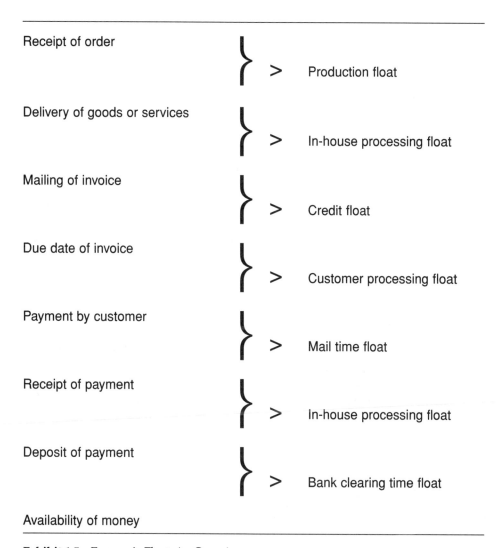

Receipt of order

> Production float

Delivery of goods or services

> In-house processing float

Mailing of invoice

> Credit float

Due date of invoice

> Customer processing float

Payment by customer

> Mail time float

Receipt of payment

> In-house processing float

Deposit of payment

> Bank clearing time float

Availability of money

Exhibit 1.5 Economic Float: An Overview

total business float for an organization—a summary of the components that cause the time difference between receipt of an order from a customer and availability of the money to the company for reinvestment or other use.

By understanding the entire company business operating process, this economic or total business float concept can be managed to help improve the company's overall cash flow. By shortening the production cycle (i.e., the time between the receipt of an order and the satisfaction of that order), production float can be reduced and cash will flow faster. By ensuring that the company's invoicing system is set up to get the invoice out upon delivering the product or service, the in-house processing float can be eliminated, and the clock will start sooner on the collection process. By reviewing whether a 30-day payment policy is necessary competitively, some of that time may be saved by reducing credit float and speeding up the time to collection. And by following up regularly on overdue accounts, the customer processing float time can be managed to keep customers from taking advantage of lax follow-up collection procedures.

As an example, if we look at a hypothetical company with annual sales volume of $100 million, we can see the effects of improvement in total business float as follows:

Assume $100 Million Annual Sales Volume

	Cash Gained
Save 14 days on production delivery	$ 3,836,000
Save 2½ days by invoicing daily rather than weekly	685,000
Process deposits daily rather than every other day	274,000
Collect in 40 rather than 45 days	1,370,000
TOTAL POTENTIAL CASH GAIN	$ 6,165,000

While it is arguably unlikely that any business will be able to accomplish all of these improvements, the example shows that any improvement can substantially add to the amount of cash available to a business. For any business of any sales volume, it is easy to calculate the amount of cash that can be generated by a one-day improvement in cash flow. This then becomes a useful number to determine the impact of any change in procedures to speed up the flow of cash in the business.

> *UNDERSTANDING AND MANAGING TOTAL BUSINESS FLOAT HELPS IMPROVE CASH FLOW.*

BANK ISSUES AND CONCERNS

Bank Services

The stability and constancy associated with the banking industry in the past are gone. Deregulation, expanded intra- and interstate banking, competition from nonbanking financial institutions, and online banking capability have all contributed to changes in dealing with cash and related financial transactions. Banking services have become increasingly varied and complicated in the past several years, and the control over and payment for these services have become more complicated as well. Banking services now available include such things as:

- *Interest-bearing options.* Certificates of deposit (CDs), interest bearing checking accounts, money market funds, and the like

- *Checking or demand deposit accounts.* Checking accounts, direct payroll deposit accounts, zero-balance accounts, wire transfer services, online access, and the like
- *Cash management services.* Lockboxes, sweep accounts, check reconciliation, automatic investment of excess cash, and the like
- *Investment services.* Treasury bill purchases, Eurodollar investments, commercial paper purchases, REPOs, bankers' acceptances, and the like
- *Other services.* Credit cards, money orders, retirement account management, safe deposit boxes, trust and investment services, estate planning assistance, travelers' checks, and the like

Understanding these services is part of the cash manager's responsibility in order to ensure that necessary services are available from the banking institution and that unnecessary services are not being charged for as part of the cost of bank services. Any bank can provide virtually any service, if not directly, then through correspondent bank relationships. For the occasional need, use of a correspondent bank is appropriate; but if the service is required on a regular basis, then it should be provided directly by the company's own bank. Paying for those services is appropriate, but paying for services that are not used is an unnecessary cost that should be avoided.

Bank Costs

In considering the use of these banking services, the company must recognize that there are costs associated with each. The bank will charge for any of these services that are used, one way or another. The service charges may be itemized monthly and charged directly to the account as service charges or fees; or they may be covered by the implicit earnings on non-interest-bearing accounts. Normally, if the account is not charged directly for such bank services, this means that balances are large enough to cover the costs of these services, which means that bank balances might be higher than necessary. Therefore, many companies prefer to maintain their excess funds in interest-bearing accounts and pay for service charges directly. This allows them to maximize their interest income and keep detailed track of the cost of bank service charges. Others prefer to maintain a sufficient balance in non-interest-bearing accounts to cover any service charges. The cash manager must select the option that best meets the company's needs.

Compensating balances are another way banks get paid for providing services. The earnings to the bank from these non-interest-bearing balances can be considerable and can cover quite a number of services. Typically, the account officer will look at the overall yield to the bank from the company's accounts to determine whether it meets bank profitability guidelines. This is done by comparing the costs of all services rendered, including interest payments on operating accounts, to the total dollars on deposit to see if the bank's earnings on the deposits offset the costs of services rendered and interest paid and generate an adequate yield. If they do not, the bank will attempt to increase its yield, by increasing the direct charges or by obtaining additional non-interest-paying or compensating balances.

Some of these bank service charges can be controlled by handling responsibility for certain tasks internally. For instance, packaging coins and currency, MICR encoding checks, and bank reconciliations are services that cost the banks and that a company could do on its own to save fees. The company must decide whether it is economically worthwhile to take on these tasks by comparing costs for performing these activities to the bank's service charges.

Bank Selection

In selecting a lead bank to meet the company's needs, the cost issues discussed above are only one element in making a decision, and they may be secondary or tertiary considerations. Other areas need to be looked at as well, including the following, which are listed in a typical order of importance to the banking customer:

- *Financial stability.* The company's bank, quite obviously, needs to be financially sound, or there is a risk of losing some assets. This issue is a much more visible one today than it was just a few years ago because of the disruptions that have occurred in the entire banking industry. Not only have savings and loans suffered—all banks are subject to financial distress if they are not properly managed, and it must be one of the factors to be reviewed in making a decision about which bank(s) to use. If the company maintains balances less than $100,000, losses will be covered by Federal Deposit Insurance Corporation (FDIC) insurance. But while this provides some sense of reassurance and safety, it is generally an undesirable event to have to cash in on insurance coverage. Automobile, home, and liability insurance coverage is there for protection in the event of some catastrophe. But it is far more desirable and cost-efficient to drive safely, have smoke detector systems, and take care of property than to have to cash in on the insurance policy. The same is true with regard to bank balances. Therefore, look for financially stable institutions for banking needs.
- *Size.* The lead bank should be large enough to handle the needs of the company's account, but not so large that the company will get lost in the bank system. The company should ideally be a large enough entity to the bank that its business is considered important. This provides some leverage in negotiating loans, determining compensating balances, charges for services, and so on. The prestige associated with dealing with a large bank does not offset the flexibility the company gets in its relationships with a bank that considers service as its most important advantage.
- *Services.* The bank must be able to provide the services needed. However, there is no need to choose a bank based on availability of services rarely

or never required. Most banks have the necessary connections to provide the services occasionally needed, even if they do not provide them directly.

- *Performance.* The bank needs to perform well. For instance, deposits need to clear quickly, checks must be processed properly, loan requests need to be responded to quickly and positively, reports and statements must be timely and accurate, transactions must be handled as requested, and the bank must show sincere interest and concern. Recurrent processing errors, inappropriate ISF (insufficient funds) stoppages, and the like. will be detrimental to the company's business image and should not be tolerated.
- *Location.* Dealing with a distant bank requires that deposits be mailed, running the risk of loss within the postal system. This will be a major aggravation from which to recover. A local bank means deposits can be made directly, saving time and potential irritation. Having a branch, at least, near the business can be a considerable time and aggravation saver, particularly with items such as deposits, payroll check processing and cashing, needs for cash, and general communication.
- *Costs.* In most geographic areas, the bank charges will be reasonably consistent due to competitive pressures. Therefore, many times, cost becomes a nonissue when deciding among competing banks. Typically, a single higher cost for a service will be offset by a lower cost for another service so that competing banks tend to equal out. While important to review carefully, costs tend typically not to be significant deciding factors.

Bank Relationships

There are no free lunches. The company's senior managers must recognize that bank services have costs associated with them and these must be factored into the costs of doing business. Historically, bank compensation was handled almost exclusively through the maintenance of balances in the bank. With low and relatively stable interest rates, the opportunity costs of these captive balances were minimal and no one paid much attention to them. But with the extraordinarily high rates that occurred in the late 1970s and early 1980s, interest costs were no longer insignificant. Even though rates have periodically returned to lower levels, bank costs have not moved back into obscurity – they must be identified, quantified, and monitored just as any other service cost. The simple expedient of trading banks and playing one off against another is effective only for a limited time. It is better to find the "right" bank and build a lasting and stable relationship. The mutual objective of the customer and the bank should be to assure a reasonable level of compensation for credit and noncredit services while not paying more than the going rate.

Another issue that must be managed is the determination of the number of banks with which to maintain relationships. The answer to this question will be dependent on the size of the business (i.e., larger businesses are far more likely to require a variety of banks to service their needs than are smaller businesses); the nature of the business (i.e., certain businesses because of geographic dispersion, requirement for diverse services, or other factors may require a greater number of banks to provide the requisite services than other businesses that can survive effectively and efficiently with only one banker); and on the attitude of the business management toward financial centralization versus decentralization (i.e., greater decentralization will likely lead to dealing with a larger number of banks). The latter is a management philosophy issue without a right or wrong answer, but has to be dealt with by company management to develop logical and consistent banking relationships.

In deciding on which banks to deal with, management should:

- *Look for a banker who understands* the company's industry and will work at understanding its specific business. A banker should be serving the company's best interests, and bankers who are more focused on selling their services than on serving customer needs will not adequately meet those needs.
- *Make inquiries and get referrals* about a new bank in the same way as for a new employee or any new supplier.
- *Get to know the bank account officer well.* The bank is likely to use its belief in the ability of company management as a principal criterion in deciding whether or not to lend money. Management's belief in the bank officer's ability to service company needs should be equally important. The people who represent the bank should be the most important criterion in deciding on which bank to use.
- *Understand the bank officer's authority.* The company should be dealing with an individual who has the authority to make decisions on his or her own. A junior level officer who has to go back to the office to get approval for nearly every action will be a frustration and a time-waster. Try to deal only with banks that provide account officers who have appropriate authority to decide and to act.

Finally, the effectiveness of the company's bank relationships will be determined in large measure by the following factors:

- *A clear understanding of responsibilities.* This encompasses the company's responsibility to the bank in terms of adhering to provisions and requirements agreed to in loan covenants, account balances, and any other agreements made, as well as the bank's adherence to commitments, services, and costs.
- *Providing information.* This, too, is a two-way street with regard to keeping the banker apprised of events relevant to the future of the organization; and the bank similarly keeping the company notified of information that

affects its relationship with them along with any general economic information that can affect future success. Successful banking relationships feature a regular flow of information in both directions.

- *Strong communications.* No one in business likes surprises, especially unpleasant ones. A good banker knows how to deal with negative events and recognizes that they do happen. However, a bank officer can be far more helpful and effective with early warning of unpleasant events along with an explanation of why they happened and what plans are in place to recover from them. Therefore, be sure to keep the bank officer informed about successes and failures as early as possible. Regular and reliable communications will go a long way toward developing the kind of stable and symbiotic relationship that will benefit both parties.

> *THE BANKING RELATIONSHIP*
> *SHOULD BE A PARTNERSHIP.*

CONCLUSION

Managing cash flow is not as difficult as managing profitability, working capital, or assets and liabilities because there are fewer factors to consider. However, just because it is simpler does not mean it is less important. Quite the contrary. Managing cash is arguably more important than the others, because having enough cash is a survival issue of immediate importance.

Some issues involved in cash management can be difficult to manage, including that of how much cash to maintain for operating purposes. Too little cash is an obvious problem, but maintaining too much is also problematic inasmuch as that means insufficient utilization of scarce company resources. Cash, like accounts receivable, inventory, and plant and equipment, needs to work for the company in order to optimize return on the investment in all assets of the organization.

It is also important for everyone in the organization to understand that strong sales and profits do not ensure good cash flow. The timing differences between accrual based profitability and cash flow means that even a company with growing sales and strong profits may run out of cash with ensuing disastrous results. This means that the company needs to understand and plan its cash flow just as carefully as it understands and manages its sales, profits, and investments.

Finally, the company needs to recognize the role its bank plays in the overall management of its cash. Banks have often been (sometimes justifiably) characterized as exploitative, self-centered, and unconcerned about their customers.

However, a solid banking relationship, where both parties understand and communicate with each other, can create a strong connection that benefits both. That is the goals toward which both the bank and the company should work.

> *SALES ARE GOOD.*
> *PROFITS ARE BETTER.*
> *CASH IS BEST!*

CHAPTER 2

Managing Cash Flow—Receipts and Disbursements

> ## *MAXIMIZE CASH IN,*
> ## *MINIMIZE CASH OUT.*

A workable cash management system needs to have several pieces in place before it can function effectively. The first of these is information—internal and external. Internal information consists of records of accounts payable, checks written, accounts receivable, cash balances, and other cash transaction information that affects the cash flow of the organization. It also includes forecast cash flow information with details about operating plans, capital needs, sales growth projections, personnel changes, merger/acquisition/divestiture strategies, and so on. External information, related principally to company banking procedures, includes such things as bank statements, check clearance times, funds availability data, transaction costs, cash balances, and the like.

A second series of needs relates to the internal systems of the organization, including:

- *Disbursements systems,* such as imprest accounts, prefunded or controlled disbursements accounts, zero-balance accounts, and so on, to handle payments
- *Collection systems,* such as lockboxes, concentration accounts, remote collection systems, and related programs that work toward getting money quickly into usable or interest-bearing status
- *Asset management systems,* designed to turn receivables and inventory into cash as fast as possible and/or to maintain a lean fixed asset base to prevent unnecessary tie-up of cash.

The third set of needs for a good cash management system is a sound system of controls—both management and audit controls. Management controls relate to the quality and operation of the entire system, not just the transactions. An effective management control system has the following objectives:

- To make sure there is enough cash available to pay the bills
- To identify the existence of any excess cash so that it can be invested to generate earnings for the company

- To account for all transactions so that correct information will be recorded
- To control cash so as to preclude theft or fraud

Meeting the first two objectives listed necessitates such tasks as comparing results to budget (often adjusted based on actual activity levels experienced, that is, in use of flexible budgeting) and investigating differences, reviewing and evaluating investment performance, and persistent searching for opportunities to improve the overall system.

Audit controls, which address the latter two objectives, are designed into the system to meet the needs of safety, security, and accuracy of transactions. These controls include such things as separation of duties, internal audit reviews, established and enforced policies and procedures, personnel controls, and the like. Audit controls relate to reacting to transactions that have already occurred, while management controls relate to proactive steps for creating improved results.

The fourth set of requirements for an effective cash management system is the need for banking facilities that are sufficient to support the company's demands. These bank facilities include the obvious processing capabilities for handling checks and deposits, the ability to service the company's investment needs for excess cash efficiently and rapidly, and the provision for short-term borrowing on a flexible and responsive basis to cover those times when cash is inadequate to meet immediate obligations.

USING THE BALANCE SHEET

Jack B. Nimble's success (see Chapter 1) in increasing sales by 25 percent and achieving an operating profit of 15 percent while simultaneously running a cash flow deficit reveals a primary principle of cash flow management: that accrual-based accounting results must be severed from related cash flow. Many businesses get themselves into financial troubles, just like Jack, by ignoring the cash flow side and winding up in an unanticipated cash squeeze. Previously, we saw the effect that using and relying exclusively on accrual-based income statements and ignoring cash flow realities had on Jack's situation. Let's now look at what purpose the balance sheet serves as a tool for cash management.

The balance sheet, like the income statement, is generally an accrual-based financial statement that provides a snapshot of the financial position and structure of the organization at a particular point in time. Jack B. Nimble's simplified balance sheets comparing the beginning and end of his first year are shown in Exhibit 2.1. The changes show how the balance sheet can be used as a financial tool to help identify cash flow problems.

The balance sheet at 12/31/x1 reflects Jack's financial position prior to taking over the business. The 12/31/x2 balance sheet reflects the changes in financial position resulting from his sales increases and other new initiatives. At the end of 12/31/x2, Jack B. Nimble Company had used up all of its cash and then some. In

	12/31/X2	12/31/X1	Change 20×2 over (under) 20×1
ASSETS			
Cash	$ 0	$ 200	$ (200)
Accounts receivable	2,000	100	1,900
Inventory	2,500	2,500	0
Other assets	3,300	2,000	1,300
Total Assets	$7,800	$4,800	$3,000
LIABILITIES			
Accounts payable & accrued expenses	$1,800	$ 800	$1,000
Other liabilities	1,900	1,300	600
Total Liabilities	3,700	2,100	1,600
STOCKHOLDERS' EQUITY	4,100	2,700	1,400
Total Liabilities and Equity	$7,800	$4,800	$3,000

Exhibit 2.1 Jack B. Nimble Company
Comparative Balance Sheets
($$ in 000s rounded to nearest $100,000)

addition, the increased sales volume's effect on the other areas of Jack's financial structure and its cash flow position can be seen by:

- The increase in accounts receivable of $1.9 million (which alone absorbed more than the increase of $1.4 million in equity and the $200,000 in beginning cash)
- The increase in accounts payable and accrued expenses of $1 million
- An additional $1.3 million used to invest in other assets (primarily plant and equipment)—a cash investment, not a direct function of sales volume

One might conclude that based on the negative effects on cash flow, further sales growth is needed to bring in more cash. In reality, additional sales increases often add to an already existing difficulty in cash availability and in meeting accounts payable, payroll, tax, and other business commitments. More sales generally require more investment in accounts receivable, inventory, personnel, and even facilities—all of which require the expenditure of still more cash. Jack has already delayed payments to vendors, and without external financing or accelerated collections of receivables, his cash position will deteriorate even more and accounts payable will fall so severely past due that his suppliers may refuse to provide additional materials or services.

Balance sheet analysis provides us with an understanding of the effect of sales, income, and cash flow on the organization's financial position. The company may have a positive cash flow and a profitable operation over a short-term period, while at the same time developing financial indications that foretell future problems. In this case, an increase in accounts receivable (uncollected cash) and fixed assets without sufficient cash reserves to handle them forced a delay in the payments of accounts payable and accrued expenses.

Cash Flow Costs

Cash flow problems can cause operational problems, which will ultimately result in real costs to the business. These costs can be direct cash costs—bad debt losses caused by failing to follow up on overdue receivables, storage and carrying costs of excess inventory, operating and insurance costs associated with excess fixed assets, and interest costs on borrowings necessitated by the cash flow problems. Or they might be indirect business costs, such as vendors refusing to deliver, an inability to secure additional financing for worthwhile long-term investments because of too much short-term borrowing, inadequate space caused by too much inventory or fixed assets, an inability to service customers adequately, and the like. Solving the company's cash flow problems normally accomplishes more than helping avoid financial embarrassment—it also helps to increase company earnings.

For instance, the Jack B. Nimble Company had a large increase in accounts receivable, which created the need to borrow money to get out of the cash flow deficit and allow for the timely payment of obligations. In this situation, we should look at the cost of borrowing about $800,000 to get payables down to an acceptable position and to continue to pay off other liabilities; and another $125,000 or so to pay off the line of credit and build up operating cash reserves. At a 9 percent interest rate, the cost per year would be nearly $85,000—money that could be better used in the business, particularly in a time of substantial growth and expansion. Had Jack held his investment in accounts receivable and fixed assets in line with his sales growth, which would have reduced the need for incurring debt, the interest cost saving would have flowed straight to the bottom line and his cash crisis could have been averted.

Operationally, it is necessary also to look at the quality of the receivables—that is, are they collectible or has Jack merely buoyed up sales by selling to less desirable credit-risk customers at less than favorable prices? Also, while borrowing provides the cash necessary to meet cash commitments and avoid a cash flow crunch in the short term, it does not solve the cash flow problem caused by burdensome investments. Borrowing, in this case, is only an expensive, and short-term, crisis delayer. In our scenario, Jack has avoided some of his cash flow problem by using vendors to finance his extra investment. He has thereby temporarily avoided the full cost of borrowing and its related interest costs. But has he protected his bottom line? No, because the excess investment is still a cash flow problem with an effect on earnings. He has an opportunity cost of lost potential earnings and growth. That is, he has lost prospective use of and earnings on cash, which could be used profitably elsewhere – to reduce other borrowing, expand the business, reduce other liabilities, earn interest on the excess cash, or even speed up growth by investing in compatible businesses.

CASH RECEIPTS

> *SPEED THE COLLECTION,*
> *SPEED THE CASH.*

Accounts Receivable

Accounts receivable has a significant impact on cash flow, as we have just seen in the case of Jack B. Nimble Company. It represents the results of the company's sales effort, except the cash hasn't been collected yet. Goods or services have been delivered in exchange for the customers' promises to pay at a later date (usually after 30 days). Most businesses, because of competitive necessities, must operate on credit, and payment of receivables represents their major source of ongoing operating cash. If customers pay late or not at all (bad debts), the company can wind up with insufficient cash to meet its current obligations.

Accounts Receivable Collection Period
Collection period defines the time between setting up the account receivable and the ultimate cash collection from the customer. The longer the collection period, the higher the investment in accounts receivable. The shorter the collection period, the more readily available is the cash flow generated. If at all possible, accounts receivable should be eliminated entirely. The cash manager may be able to convince management that the costs of billing, accounts receivable processing, and collection efforts are sufficiently high that passing them on to the customer may be worth investigating. In exchange for lower prices, the customer may be willing to pay at time of delivery, preferably through an electronic transfer that will make the funds immediately available to the company. Such opportunities should be pursued to maximize cash inflows, reduce cash conversion gap time, and eliminate unnecessary functions that do not add value.

It is important to know the average collection period for accounts receivable and to take measures to continually work toward keeping it at a minimum, consistent with good customer relations and competitive necessities. The most commonly used process for calculating the average collection period is:

Total annual credit sales / 365 = average daily sales

Accounts receivable balance / average daily sales =
average collection period, in days

For example, Jack B. Nimble Company's 20x2 calculation would be as follows (see Appendix A Case Study):

Average daily sales = $15,073,400 million/365 = $41,297 sales per day

Average collection period = $2,029,600/$41,297 = 49.1 days

However, for internal measurement purposes, it is better to use a shorter period of time to measure the collection period. Typically, the accounts receivable represent sales made in the last one to three months. Therefore, it would be more meaningful to determine the sales made in the last, say, two months, divide by 60 days, and divide that result into the accounts receivable balance. That will give a much more current look at the collection period relative to the actual sales that make up those receivables. The calculation for Jack B. Nimble would be:

Average daily sales (Nov/Dec) = $3,000,900/60 = $50,015 sales per day

Average collection period = $2,029,600/$50,015 = 40.6 days

This calculation can be made each month to provide an ongoing immediate evaluation of collections. The lower (in this case) collection period reflects the elimination of the lower level of sales in the early part of the year, which is no longer pertinent at the end of the year. As in all such cases of financial ratio analysis, the absolute number is less relevant than its changes over time.

Accordingly, each sales dollar stays in the form of accounts receivable for about 40 days. If this is quick enough to meet the company's cash flow needs, and if it is close enough to published collection terms, the decision may be to leave well enough alone. However, the cost of offering accounts receivable terms can be calculated. In our example, each day's reduction in the collection period frees up over $50,000 in cash that can be used for investment, liability repayment, or cash reserves. Reducing the average collection period improves cash flow by converting accounts receivable into cash more rapidly. This concept is described in Exhibits 2.2 and 2.3. Company management must determine an acceptable collection period and what to do about any roadblocks that might cause an overinvestment in accounts receivable.

> ## *ACCOUNTS RECEIVABLE ARE INTEREST-FREE LOANS TO CUSTOMERS.*

Accounts Receivable to Sales

Collection period analysis is one tool to help determine overinvestment in accounts receivable. However, if calculated on a 12-month basis, it may not pick up a recent change or buildup in receivables. Another tool to help identify

Avg. Collection Period (days)	Sales per Day				
	$ 1,000	$ 2,000	$ 3,000	$ 4,000	$ 5,000
	Investment in Accounts Receivable				
30	$ 30,000	$ 60,000	$ 90,000	$ 120,000	$ 150,000
35	35,000	70,000	105,000	140,000	175,000
40	40,000	80,000	120,000	160,000	200,000
45	45,000	90,000	135,000	180,000	225,000
50	50,000	100,000	150,000	200,000	250,000
55	55,000	110,000	165,000	220,000	275,000
60	60,000	120,000	180,000	240,000	300,000

Exhibit 2.2   Effect of Collection Period on Investment in Accounts Receivable

possible unfavorable changes in the accounts receivable level is the monthly accounts receivable to sales ratio. The formula is quite simple: ending balance of accounts receivable divided by sales for the month. For example, Jack B. Nimble Company's projected ratio at 12/31/x2 was:

$1,875,000 / $1,500,000 = 1.25 months sales in receivables

Looked at alone the ratio merely shows that receivables were 125 percent of monthly sales, which may or may not be satisfactory. However, comparing this ratio to other periods may help identify potential cash flow problems. Calculating the actual ratio for 12/31/x2, Jack's first year of operation, shows:

$2,029,600 / $1,256,100 = 1.62 months sales in receivables

which indicates that receivables increased more than sales between the projected and actual results, and Jack has tied up more cash than planned. Remember that normally a higher sales volume will result in a larger investment in accounts receivable, but a higher ratio of accounts receivable to sales means that investment in receivables has increased at a greater rate than sales. This upward change often

Reduction in Avg. Collection Period (days)	Sales per Day				
	$ 1,000	$ 2,000	$ 3,000	$ 4,000	$ 5,000
	Cash Generated				
1	$ 1,000	$ 2,000	$ 3,000	$ 4,000	$ 5,000
3	3,000	6,000	9,000	12,000	15,000
5	5,000	10,000	15,000	20,000	25,000
7	7,000	14,000	21,000	28,000	35,000
10	10,000	20,000	30,000	40,000	50,000

Exhibit 2.3   Effect of a Reduction in Average Collection Period on Cash Flow

indicates the initial signs of a potential cash flow problem. If the business is seasonal in nature, the cash manager may wish to compare ratios against comparable
months in the prior year. Then, if indicated, determining the specific cause of an
upward trend will become necessary.

A quick look at the ratio at 12/31/x1, before Jack took over the company
shows:

$$\$142,000 \ / \ \$1,000,000 \ = \ 0.14 \ \text{months sales in receivables}$$

Comparing this to the more current figure of 1.62 months shows dramatically how Jack's decision to offer 30-day terms has had a dramatic, and financially harmful, effect on this ratio and on his overall cash flow situation.

Accounts Receivable Aging
The accounts receivable aging schedule is a familiar tool, and someone in the company is likely to have prepared or reviewed one. It is another tool to help identify
cash flow problem areas in the early stages as well as the specific source of a problem. Jack B. Nimble Company's policy is to sell on a net 30-day basis with established credit limits for customers. The company expects to be paid, of course, in
30 days from date of the sale. However, based on the aging schedule shown in
Exhibit 2.4, the company is not effectively following up on collections, especially
regarding Customer DEF. Some of Jack's customers are taking advantage of him,
possibly as a remedy for their own cash flow problems. Customer DEF is the
worst offender.

The first thing to look at in the aging schedule is the customers causing the
collection period to extend beyond 30 days. They must be aggressively contacted, and if changes are not forthcoming, decisions need to be made regarding the benefits of ongoing sales to them—shipment holds, cash on delivery
(COD) shipments, or even order cancellations in some instances may become
necessary. Intelligent use of the aging schedule can also yield information about
recent changes in paying habits – slower payments resulting in more outstanding and older balances, credit limit breaches, failure to take cash discounts if
offered, and so on. These signals can be used as early warning indicators to
help ward off future problems and as signs of a possible critical cash management problem.

An aging schedule is also necessary to avoid harassing customers whose
accounts are not yet overdue. Persistent calls to customers who pay on time and
are not yet late can create serious customer relations problems. Occasional calls
regarding large payments to be sure that they will be remitted on time may be
acceptable, but repeated calls when not justified should be avoided.

In this case, Jack B. Nimble must pay immediate and energetic attention to
Customer DEF—a clear problem customer who should be dealt with now. The
aging schedule provides the information necessary to know where to look for
problems. The company cannot reasonably expect customers to pay earlier than
scheduled (it's nice if they do, but don't base any spending plans on that

happening—would you pay early?). So it is only the slow payers that can be legitimately chased. And the only way to know who they are is to have an accurate, timely aging schedule that can be used to maintain control over all accounts receivable.

An analysis of the aging schedule shown in Exhibit 2.4, together with historical and trend data of those specific customers, could disclose the following operational concerns:

- *Most customers take at least the full 30 days to make their payments.* The cash manager should consider whether the company's policy of net 30 days is cost-efficient and whether the cost of money for this period is included in the company's cost and sales price calculations. This should induce the company to look at the cost and revenue advantages of other payment policies, including payment at time of receipt of the goods or services (COD).
- *Customer analysis, including trends in purchase and payment history.* For instance, which customers are reducing their payment period, which customers are increasing their payment period (particularly those exceeding the 30-day payment period), which customers are increasing or decreasing their total amount of purchases, which customers have stopped purchasing or stopped payments, and so on?
- *Who are the company's major customers?* Those customers who make up approximately 80 percent of total sales. These are usually a handful of total customers. What are the trends for these customers? Are total sales going up or down? What products are these customers buying? Is the company really making money (i.e., net profit per sale) on each sale to these customers? Are all costs of doing business with these customers included in the company's reporting procedures?

Collection Systems

> ## MOVE CASH COLLECTIONS CLOSER TO THE SALE.

It would be ideal for businesses to be able to collect the cash due upon delivery of their goods and/or services. Even better would be to collect in advance of delivery. While a worthy goal of an effective cash management system, this is unlikely for most businesses. Therefore, the cash manager should concentrate on developing effective and efficient collection systems to increase cash flow and keep investment in accounts receivable at a manageable minimum level. Various factors have an impact on this goal, including:

- Credit policy
- Invoicing procedures
- Accounts receivable follow-up
- Cash discounts
- Finance charges
- Holding delivery

Credit Policy

While it would be best to be able to collect the cash at the time (or in advance) of the sale, almost all businesses offer credit terms or a grace period to pay for goods and services to be competitive. The company's credit policies should include the time period within which its customers are expected to remit cash. In addition, there normally is a set dollar amount or credit limit beyond which credit will not be granted. For instance, a customer with a credit limit of $3,000 and credit terms of 30 days is expected to pay within 30 days and not exceed a $3,000 balance outstanding at any time. Should the outstanding balance exceed $3,000, the company must decide whether to stop selling to the customer, sell on COD terms only, or increase the credit limit. Setting credit policies is only part of the system; enforcement and control to ensure adherence is also a necessary part so as to maximize cash inflow and minimize credit losses.

When customers purchase goods or services they agree to pay within the designated period of time stated in the credit policy, and the company agrees to carry them as a receivable. If all customers pay within the agreed-upon time period, the credit term period defines the collection period. In reality, this rarely happens. Some customers (not enough) pay early, while others (too many) take longer to pay. The company's credit terms and policies, however, are the starting point for reviewing and analyzing customers and their payment habits as well as the company's own cash flow requirements.

CREDIT IS A PRIVILEGE, NOT A RIGHT.

Having a well-defined credit policy also instills discipline into the sales activity. Credit is a privilege, not a right of customers. The credit policy should force the sales staff to review all customers as to whether or not they are entitled to credit. An effective screening process will help to eliminate problem customers before they become problems rather than after the sales have been made and they pay late or are unable to pay at all.

Invoicing

The starting point for accelerating cash receipts is the company's internal systems; and the starting point in the overall collection system is the customer's invoice. The quicker the company gets the invoice into the customer's hands, the sooner the payment process starts. Get invoices out on time! Customers will not start their payment process until they have both the product or service and an invoice. Their payment clock begins at the later of receipt of the invoice or receipt of the goods. So each day of delay in issuing an invoice extends the collection period and decreases the amount of cash available. One of the most effective systems of invoicing is to make the packing list part of the invoice set. This means that the invoice becomes part of the shipping packet and is available to send out when the product ships. Mail the invoice the same day as shipment or even a day or two earlier if the shipment is sure to go. This will help to ensure that the customer has the invoice when the goods arrive.

A second vital consideration is to make sure that the invoices are accurately prepared. An inaccurate invoice creates an all-too-easy opportunity for the customer to avoid payment. It is the company's job to prepare a correct invoice—not the customer's to fix it. Accurately prepared invoices eliminate another excuse not to pay.

Company management needs to consider present invoicing practices, noting any lack of economies or inefficiencies. Through a thorough knowledge of best practices (by use of an effective internal and/or external benchmarking study), the most effective invoicing procedures can then be developed and installed to help keep the cash flowing in as quickly as possible.

Accounts Receivable Follow-up

> ## THE SQUEAKY COLLECTION WHEEL
> ## GETS THE CHECK.

An accounts receivable aging schedule was shown in Exhibit 2.4. The next step is to use it as an analytical tool and as a collection trigger. With most small businesses now using microcomputers and sophisticated accounting software, they can get instantaneous accounts receivable aging schedules and can use the computer as an analytical tool. The company can define the criteria that meet its needs and correspond to its collection philosophy. For instance, the system could highlight on a weekly basis all receivables coming up to 30 days old and those over 30 days old and still unpaid, and on an every-other-day basis all receivables over 60 days old. This allows the company to stay current on all overdue invoices and take appropriate action regularly and persistently. The company may also wish to identify those bills that have been paid each day and

CUSTOMER	Total Balance Due	< 30 <days	31-59 days	60-89 days	90-120 days	>120 days
ABC Company	75,200	75,200	0	0	0	0
BCD Company	108,800	100,800	8,000	0	0	0
CDE Company	61,900	40,000	21,900	0	0	0
DEF Company	120,400	20,200	19,600	10,100	10,100	60,400
Other companies	1,663,300	1,492,900	170,400	0	0	0
Total	2,029,600	1,729,100	219,900	10,100	10,100	60,400
% of Total	100.0%	85.2%	10.8%	0.5%	0.5%	3.0%
Prior Month Total–$	1,856,600	1,627,300	158,800	10,100	10,100	50,300
Prior Month Total–%	100.0%	87.7%	8.6%	0.5%	0.5%	2.7%
GOAL %	100.0%	90.0%	8.0%	2.0%	0.0%	0.0%

Exhibit 2.4　Jack B. Nimble Company
Date: 12/31/32
Accounts Receivable Aging Schedule

earmark those for which it has been promised payment to increase the chances of timely follow-up.

Company management should establish collection policies regarding overdue notices (generally not very effective), phone calls, personal visits, and referrals to collection agencies, and follow them diligently. Credit policies should be tied in to each customer account (e.g., credit limits without sales department override capability) so that sales can be stopped or switched to COD or some other action whenever the policies are violated. If credit and collection procedures are not pursued aggressively, even ruthlessly, customers may love the company, but it will be paid last. One of the company's cash management rules may be to pay creditors as late as possible. Customers are likely to play by the same rules, but the company wants to put itself at the head of the payment line. A fair, clearly understood, and consistently followed collection procedure will help keep the company at the head of that line.

Cash Discounts

> # TERMS OF 1/10, NET 30 = 18.4 PERCENT ANNUAL INTEREST RATE

Many companies believe that offering a customer a cash discount for early payment (e.g., a 1 percent discount for payment in 10 days) is worth the cost. The company needs to determine if such a policy is necessary (to compete, maintain, or enlarge market share, or remain viable) and cost-effective, and then establish a policy as to what percentage discount to offer and for what period of time. Cash discounts will speed up collections to a certain extent, but they also have drawbacks. The most obvious is the cost of the discount itself, which can be easily calculated. A less obvious, but no less expensive drawback is the cost of the effort in following up on unauthorized discounts taken. Many customers will take discounts if offered regardless of when they actually make payment. The cost of following up and trying to collect these unauthorized discounts is high relative to the amount involved. Yet letting the customer get away with an unauthorized discount rewards negative behavior and ensures continuation of the practice. It can become a nasty lose-lose situation.

Allowing cash discounts for early payment is a tool used by many companies to encourage their customers to pay more quickly and increase their cash flow. Often, there is no real economic reason for cash discounts other than tradition or common practice. The cash manager should fully analyze any cash discount practices and recommend changes if justified, even though such policy changes might be strongly resisted by management. For example, the company might consider a 1 percent cash discount for payment within 10 days as an alternative to full payment in 30 days (this would be called terms of "1/10, net 30").

Before deciding whether cash discounts are good or bad for the business, the relevant costs and benefits need to be considered.

Inducing customers to pay in a shorter period using a cash discount has the benefits of:

- Shortening the average collection period
- Accelerating the company's cash flow
- Reducing investment in accounts receivable
- Reducing bad debts
- Decreasing the costs of carrying accounts receivable

However, there are costs involved in offering cash discounts, such as:

- The cost of the discount (unless the cost is included in the company's pricing structure)
- The effect on revenue expectations and earnings—that is, the revenue plan
- The indirect costs associated with following up on unauthorized discounts
- Processing costs needed to ensure that each customer is taking the correct discount for such things as partial payments, items in dispute, small purchases, and so on

Let's look at some alternatives for the Jack B. Nimble Company, assuming a sales volume of $18 million per year ($1.5 million per month) and further assuming that all customers pay on time:

Terms	Net 30 days	1/10, net 30	2/10, net 30
% taking discount	None	50%	100%
Accounts receivable balance	$ 1,500,000	$ 1,000,000	$ 500,000
Annual A/R carrying cost (4%)	$ 60,000	$ 40,000	$ 20,000
Annual discount cost	None	90,000	360,000
Total annual cost	$ 60,000	$ 130,000	$ 380,000

It is clear that Jack has the least cost when he offers no cash discount and that the total costs increase as the amount of the discount increases. The carrying costs saved by reducing the amount of accounts receivable is more than offset by the discount cost. However, in certain situations, limited cash resources may force the company to offer cash discounts. Typically, cash discounts help the company's cash flow at the expense of earnings. But if the company can reinvest the increased cash flow profitably, it may be able to minimize the cost or even increase net profits.

We can adjust the preceding calculation to bring more realism into the equation by revising the assumption that all customers pay on time. If we assume the same $18 million annual sales volume with a 50-day rather than a 30-day collection period, the analysis will look like this:

Terms	Net 30 days	1/10, net 30	2/10, net 30
% taking discount	None	50%	90%
Accounts receivable balance	$ 2,500,000	$ 1,500,000	$ 700,000
Annual A/R carrying cost (4%)	$ 100,000	$ 60,000	$ 28,000
Annual discount cost	None	90,000	324,000
Total annual cost	$ 100,000	$ 150,000	$ 352,000

Here we can see that the impact of the discount policy is somewhat mitigated or even reduced because of the potential for a more significant reduction in the accounts receivable balances. What this means, essentially, is that the longer it takes to collect accounts receivable, the more potential benefit there is from establishing a discount policy. An offset, of course, is that customers who take unauthorized discounts still need to be managed.

By allowing customers a cash discount for early payment (say 10 days), the company is actually paying for the use of its customers' money for the remaining period of 20 days that the company otherwise would have waited. Thus cash discounts can be looked at as an interest expense paid for borrowing funds from customers (or not lending to them). The formula for calculating the annualized interest rate that the business incurs from a cash discount policy is as follows:

$$\text{Annualized interest cost} \times \frac{\text{discount \%}}{(100 - \text{discount \%})} \times \frac{365}{(\text{total days} - \text{discount period})}$$

As an example, a company with 1/10, net 30-day terms incurs the following annualized cost:

$$\text{Annualized interest cost} = \frac{1\%}{(100 - 1\%)} \times \frac{365}{(30 - 10)}$$

$$= \frac{1\%}{99\%} \times \frac{365}{20} = 18.4\%$$

Thus, the actual cost incurred for a 1/10, net 30-day policy is the equivalent of an 18.4 percent annual interest rate. Costs associated with other plausible (and perhaps some not-so-plausible) discount terms are as follows:

Terms	Cost	Terms	Cost
1/2%/10, net 30	9.2%	1/2%/20, net 30	18.3%
1/10, net 30	18.4%	1/20, net 30	36.9%
2/10, net 30	37.2%	2/20, net 30	74.5%
3/10, net 30	56.4%	3/20, net 30	112.9%
1/10, net 60	7.4%	1/20, net 60	9.2%
2/10, net 60	14.9%	2/20, net 60	18.6%
3/10, net 60	22.6%	3/20, net 60	28.2%

Interestingly, if customers actually pay in 55 days, and a cash discount program gets them to pay in 10 days, the effective cost reduces to 8.2 percent as follows:

$$\text{Annualized interest cost} = \frac{1\%}{(100 - 1\%)} \times \frac{365}{(55 - 10)}$$

$$= \frac{1\%}{99\%} \times \frac{365}{45} = \underline{\underline{8.2\%}}$$

However, if they take the discount and still pay in 55 days, the company loses the entire discount cost with no offsetting benefit at all.

Note that the cost a customer incurs for missing a cash discount is the same as the business suffers for allowing it. Keep in mind that a customer is more likely to pass up a smaller discount than to strain its cash flow. Typically, the business can profit by eliminating cash discounts from its credit terms. However, other factors such as competitive conditions, customer expectations, historical practice, industry practices, and so on, need to be considered. If company management believes that it must offer cash discounts, it should look at them as normal business expenses to be factored into pricing. Elimination of cash discounts also will lead to an increase in accounts receivable causing a drain on cash resources and possibly on borrowing power. The costs of cash discounts may be more favorable than elimination in this instance.

In reality, not all customers will pay within the designated credit period, and this may cause cash flow problems. The company could, of course, refuse to sell on credit or at all to those who do not pay on time. This policy could prove expensive in terms of lost sales. Credit policy needs to consider sales and profit goals as well as cash flow concerns, even though the existence of a potential cash flow squeeze often may be the deciding factor in determining policies, regardless of the effect on profitability.

Finance Charges

> ## CASH DISCOUNTS ARE AN INCENTIVE TO PAY, WHILE FINANCE CHARGES ARE A PENALTY FOR NOT PAYING.

Cash discounts are an incentive for customers to pay early; finance charges (e.g., 1 percent monthly on the unpaid balance) are a penalty to customers who do not pay within established terms. A credit card company automatically hits cardholders with a finance charge if they do not pay within parameters—no ifs, ands, or buts. This process works well for them because it is accepted and they have a large volume of customers whom they can treat rather anonymously. For the typical smaller business, however, collecting finance charges can be a major headache. Some customers simply refuse to pay, and their persistence generally makes it easier to yield than to fight on. Others who do pay may not put up a major fight, but may simply take their business elsewhere. Either way, because it is a penalty rather than an incentive, the company instituting the finance charge is the loser, and for most smaller businesses finance charge procedures are not worth it. If a finance charge policy exists, the practicality of the policy should be considered. Should it be eliminated, and if so what better practice (e.g. adding expected late payment costs to the customer's price) could be instituted? If a finance charge policy remains in place or is added, the company needs to do it with its eyes open regarding the potential pitfalls.

Holding Delivery

> ## NO PAY ... NO WAY

If the company has customers—and they occur in every business—who are egregiously late with payments, it may be necessary to consider discontinuing further shipments or deliveries. For this to work fairly and effectively, the company's policies and procedures must be well established and consistently followed, and strong reporting and follow-up actions will have to be in place. Avoiding this kind of problem may not be possible with certain new customers since references and credit information will not always be accurate or current. However, for ongoing customers, the company should be able to identify the chronic slow- and no-pays. As discussed earlier, adequate systems should enable the company to spot adverse changes in payment practices and head off potential problems before they do too much damage.

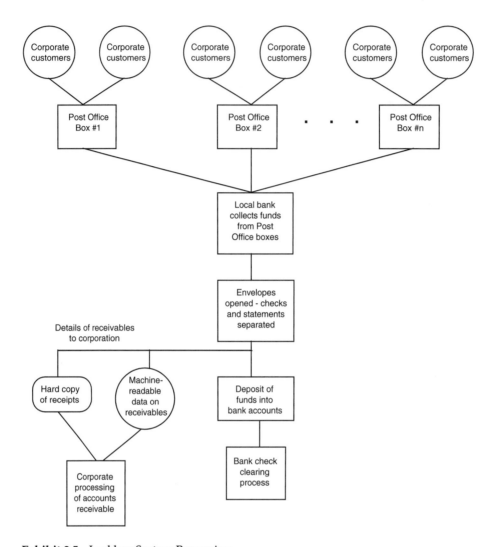

Exhibit 2.5   Lockbox System Processing

Cash Processing Systems

> ## *PUT THE CASH TO WORK AS QUICKLY AS POSSIBLE.*

Once the company has its internal systems for credit policy, invoicing, accounts receivable, and collections working smoothly, it can consider the various methods for speeding cash through the banking system and into an interest-bearing account. These methods include:

- *Remote collections.* If there are regional offices in different parts of the country, have customers send or deliver their payments directly to those

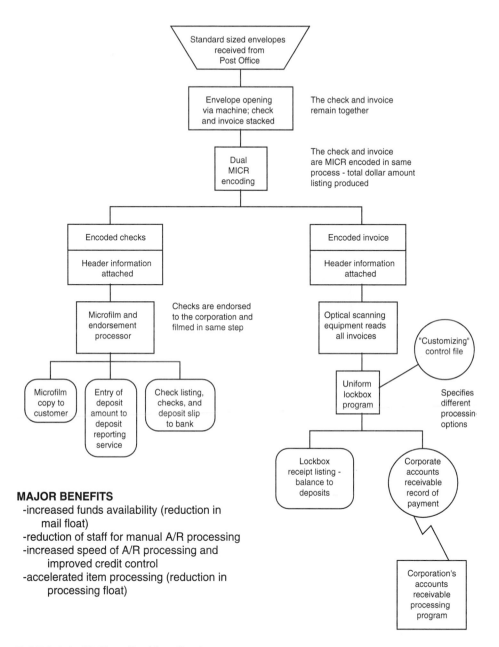

Standard sized envelopes received from Post Office

Envelope opening via machine; check and invoice stacked

The check and invoice remain together

Dual MICR encoding

The check and invoice are MICR encoded in same process - total dollar amount listing produced

Encoded checks

Header information attached

Encoded invoice

Header information attached

Microfilm and endorsement processor

Checks are endorsed to the corporation and filmed in same step

Optical scanning equipment reads all invoices

"Customizing" control file

Microfilm copy to customer

Entry of deposit amount to deposit reporting service

Check listing, checks, and deposit slip to bank

Uniform lockbox program

Specifies different processing options

Lockbox receipt listing - balance to deposits

Corporate accounts receivable record of payment

Corporation's accounts receivable processing program

MAJOR BENEFITS
-increased funds availability (reduction in mail float)
-reduction of staff for manual A/R processing
-increased speed of A/R processing and improved credit control
-accelerated item processing (reduction in processing float)

Exhibit 2.6 Uniform Lockbox Service

local offices closest to them. This process can save mail time and clearance time, but the control problems associated with this approach and the nuisance value to employees at the local offices may offset much or all of the benefit.

• *Lockboxes.* Lockbox systems are established by banks at central post offices to intercept remittances earlier in the mail cycle before they get sent

---

1. WHOLESALE LOCKBOXES
    - -Low volume levels, with high value per item
    - -e.g. 500 checks/month at $5,000/check

2. RETAIL LOCKBOXES
    - -High volume levels, with low value per item
    - -e.g. 100,000 checks/month at <$100/check
    - -Credit card payments, mail order business payments, utility bill payments, etc.

3. MANUAL LOCKBOXES
    - -Bank arranges with local postal service to reserve a post office box
    - -Mail is sorted by the postal service
    - -Bank picks up and processes checks for deposit in company account

4. AUTOMATED LOCKBOXES
    - -Same as above except that relevant customer remittance data captured in machine-readable form and transmitted electronically to the company for further processing (accounts receivable recording and management)

Exhibit 2.7   Types of Lockboxes

out to the company's location. The bank collects and processes the remittances and sends the company the remittance advices and/or copies of the checks. By the time the company knows the check has been received, it is already in the bank account. Lockbox systems can generally knock one or two days off collection time. If this two days is equal to an additional, say, $100,000 in cash availability, at an interest rate of 4 percent the company has achieved an additional earnings potential of $4,000 per year. Compare this to the cost of the lockbox system and its other benefits to see if it makes sense for the company. Lockbox system processing is shown in Exhibit 2.5, uniform lockbox service in Exhibit 2.6, and types of lockboxes in Exhibit 2.7.

- *Wire Transfers.* Wire transfers from customers (from their bank to the company's bank) increase cash availability markedly since they avoid mail, bank clearance, and internal processing time delays. However, customers may object to the cost of a wire transfer and to the loss of their own float.
- *Electronic Funds Transfers (EFT).* EFT systems are really debit card or preauthorized check (PAC) type transactions whereby funds are immediately transferred upon processing the transaction. Typically, the customer signs an authorization agreement with the company that allows checks to

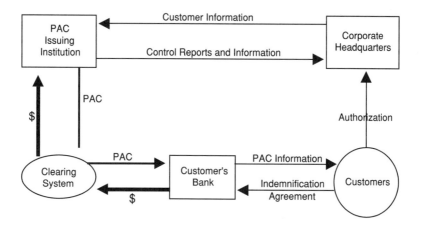

PROCESS

1. Customer signs authorization agreement with company allowing checks to be drawn against their account at specified intervals under specified conditions.
2. Corporation forwards to bank its file of customers and dates when PACs are to be produced.
3. Transactions for PAC applications are fixed amount, repetitive types of payments such as insurance, cable TV payments, mortgages, lease payments, rentals, etc.

ADVANTAGES TO RECEIVING COMPANY

1. Increased cash flow predictability.
2. Elimination of billing costs.
3. Elimination of lockbox costs and corporate accounts receivable handling costs.
4. Reduction of collection float, elimination of mail and company processing float.
5. Reduction of corporate collection expenses, late payments and forgotten remittances.

Exhibit 2.8   Pre-Authorized Checks (PACs) System

be drawn against their accounts. EFTs can be used for transferring cash from a customer's account at the time of shipment or delivery, eliminating the need for other billing, accounts receivable processing, and collection procedures. A schematic showing a typical PAC system and the advantages of PACs is shown in Exhibit 2.8.

- *Concentration Accounts.* Now that the money is in the company's cash system, company management may want to look at possibilities of getting it to work more quickly. For instance, a concentration account for cash receipts places all available cash in one location. This makes it easier to manage the cash and also gives the company the advantage of larger amounts to invest. Normally, the earnings potential of $100,000 is greater than 10 units of $10,000 or even two units of $50,000. To get its money into the concentration account as quickly as possible the company could consider wire transfers from its other banks or the use of depository transfer

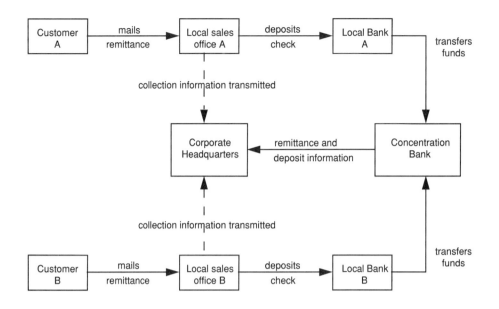

ADVANTAGES
-increased cash flow
-early notice of dishonored checks
-improved internal control (separation
  of duties)

DISADVANTAGES
-setting up collection functions at local
  sales offices
-communication links (possible delays in
  transmission of remittance information
  to headquarters)

Exhibit 2.9   Area Concentration Banking

checks (DTCs), which are preauthorized checks used by the concentration bank to move funds from a remote account. A schematic of area concentration banking is shown in Exhibit 2.9.

Credit Terms and Accounts Receivable Example

> ## THE REAL COST OF ACCOUNTS RECEIVABLE
> ## CAN BE CALCULATED.

Credit policy and terms have a definite effect on the level of sales and related accounts receivable. At one point, ABC Machining (now Jack B. Nimble Company) enjoyed a unique position in its industry—demand for its products exceeded its ability to supply. The company was able to sell all of its monthly production of about $1 million on a continuing basis. By requiring cash payment at time of delivery, they offered no credit terms and were still able to sell 100 percent of their output.

Before adopting a credit policy, Jack asked his controller to determine the effects of various credit terms on his cash flow and earnings based on the following conditions:

- Monthly sales volume of $1.5 million
- Interest cost, direct or opportunity, at 4 percent per year on accounts receivable
- Customers will pay within agreed-upon terms
- Options of 10-, 20-, or 30-day payment terms to be evaluated

The results of the controller's analysis were:

	Accounts Receivable	*Cost per Year (at 4%)*
Net 10 days	$ 500,000	$ 20,000
Net 20 days	$ 1,000,000	$ 40,000
Net 30 days	$ 1,500,000	$ 60,000

Obviously, the longer the credit terms, the higher the investment in accounts receivable and the higher the cost to the company in interest costs or opportunity costs. As Jack opts for longer credit terms to make himself competitively attractive, he must plan to find the cash to cover the $500,000 to $1.5 million that will become unavailable as he increases terms from 10 to 30 days—either from reserves, from borrowing, or from additional equity in the company. In our example we will assume Jack chose the 30-day terms in order to be maximally competitive. For the company under review, it may be able to be less generous; either way, it will have some degree of freedom to act in its best overall interests.

In establishing credit terms, keep in mind their significance on customers, and their impact on cash flow. Typically, the cost of carrying a reasonable investment in accounts receivable is a normal business expense, but the company should consider raising selling prices by an amount to cover all or part of this cost. The competitive situation faced in the marketplace will, of course, have a major effect on the feasibility of this approach. If the pricing situation is so competitive as to preclude a higher price to cover these costs, the company will have to look at other cost reductions or accept lower profitability.

The company's credit terms may also have an effect on its sales volume. The business probably has a number of competitors who provide similar goods and services. Other factors being equal, the company might consider lengthening its credit terms to increase volume. Longer terms will allow customers to hold onto their cash longer, which could make the company a more attractive vendor. The cost of this extra time needs to be balanced against the benefits of additional sales; but the company also needs to keep in mind that its competitors might match its moves, thus leaving everyone—except the customers—worse off. Sales could easily return to the old levels, resulting in no gain, but with an increase in accounts receivable investment and the resulting increase in expenses.

An analysis of Jack B. Nimble Company's situation disclosed the following for the future of the company, based on sales information provided by Jack's sales manager (and using a 360-day year):

	10-Day Terms	*20-Day Terms*	*30-Day Terms*
Expected sales volume (annual)	$ 18,000,000	$ 23,400,000	$ 28,800,000
Accounts receivable balance	$ 500,000	$ 1,300,000	$ 2,400,000
Operating profit (20% of sales)	$ 3,600,000	$ 4,680,000	$ 5,760,000
A/R carrying costs (4%)	20,000	52,000	96,000
Operating profit after carrying costs	$ 3,580,000	$ 4,628,000	$ 5,664,000
Adjusted operating profit % of sales	19.89%	19.78%	19.67%

Based on assumptions that longer credit terms will result in increased sales volume as shown and that customers will normally take the longer payment terms, it is clear that each projected increase in the credit period results in higher earnings (even after the carrying costs) because of the increase in sales volume. Return on sales, however, reduces marginally because of the carrying costs. This type of analysis should be done for all businesses, since every situation will be different. In too many instances a business will adopt a net 30-day credit policy without the benefit of analysis and will thereby have little or no idea of its cost.

The company should also take into account the fact that longer credit terms can easily lead to increased bad debt write-offs, and customers gained through more lenient credit policies may be financially weaker and less likely to pay on time—or at all. Remember, the goal is to convert sales into cash, not into accounts receivable— receivables are merely a way station. Before easing credit terms, consider all aspects of the situation, and keep in mind that it will be extremely difficult to tighten these policies once the more lenient ones have been in effect.

CASH DISBURSEMENTS

NO PAY BEFORE ITS TIME.

We have just discussed how to manage the collection and control of cash receipts more effectively, but it is also necessary to look at methods for disbursing cash so

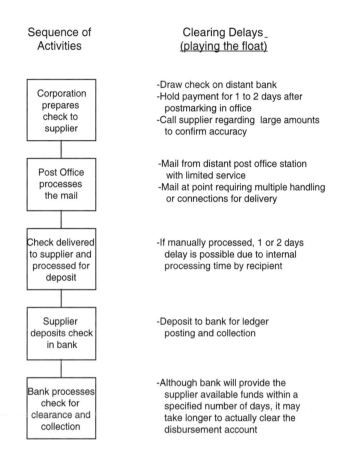

Sequence of Activities	Clearing Delays (playing the float)
Corporation prepares check to supplier	-Draw check on distant bank -Hold payment for 1 to 2 days after postmarking in office -Call supplier regarding large amounts to confirm accuracy
Post Office processes the mail	-Mail from distant post office station with limited service -Mail at point requiring multiple handling or connections for delivery
Check delivered to supplier and processed for deposit	-If manually processed, 1 or 2 days delay is possible due to internal processing time by recipient
Supplier deposits check in bank	-Deposit to bank for ledger posting and collection
Bank processes check for clearance and collection	-Although bank will provide the supplier available funds within a specified number of days, it may take longer to actually clear the disbursement account

COMMENTS
-Centralization is most efficient and effective method of controlling cash outflows
-Allows scheduling payments based on company-wide needs and cash availability
-Deceleration of payables may jeopardize supplier relationships

Exhibit 2.10 Centralization of Payables and Float

that the company can hang onto its money as long as possible while continuing to maintain proper relationships with suppliers. Large and small businesses need efficient and effective methods to control their cash outflows. One of the most efficient methods is to centralize the payment of accounts payable and then to schedule payments company-wide—paying as late as terms allow. As with accounts receivable, the company can also "play the accounts payable float." Float factors used to delay check clearing in the payables system include internal systems, mail, customer systems, and bank clearance float. A schematic depicting the float factors in a typical centralized disbursements system is shown in Exhibit 2.10.

Some of the factors for the company to consider in managing its cash disbursements include the following:

- Internal systems
- Payment policy
- Payment systems
- Managing the cash disbursement system
- Bank accounts

Internal Systems

The first thing to look at, as in the case of collections, is the company's internal system of managing disbursements. Rules 1, 2 and 3 are: Do not pay more than is owed. While this may seem painfully obvious, it is all too common for companies to pay bills that are incorrect or not really due. For example, if a purchase order calls for a price of 20¢ a unit and the invoice says 22¢, the 22¢ should not be paid without an investigation and a credible reason for the change. If the Receiving Department indicates that 22,000 units were received and the invoice is for 25,000 units, do not pay for more than the 22,000 units. Also make sure that procedures are in place for approval of all incoming invoices by an appropriate employee. There are too many miscreants out there who mail what seem to be invoices in hopes that someone will send them a check. Do not assume that the company is immune from this type of scam.

Rule 4 is: Do not pay early! If standard terms from the company's vendors are net 30 days, those suppliers expect to be paid in 30 days—there is neither need nor special benefit to be derived from paying earlier. If a particular supplier offers a discount, the pros and cons as previously discussed under cash receipts should be investigated. Cash discounts offered by suppliers can be reviewed as a form of interest earned for paying them earlier than required. Based on the present value of money and the company's present cash position, the cash manager should determine whether certain cash discounts are advantageous. Remember that 1 percent, net 30 day terms is equivalent to 18.4 percent annual interest and 2 percent, net 30 days is equal to 37.2 percent interest. Normally, a cash discount of 1/10, net 30 or better is worth taking advantage of—even by borrowing the money—while discounts less than that may not be economically justifiable.

A well-designed accounts payable system will ensure that:

- Bills are paid on time, but not before their time.
- Discounts taken have been determined to be economically advantageous to the company.
- Invoices are paid only once.
- The quantities and prices on vendor invoices are correct and appropriate.

Internal review of all invoices, particularly those of large amounts and/or charged to certain accounts such as capital improvements, should also be made to determine whether the goods or services were needed in the first place, and if less expensive alternatives could have been used. In many cases, such goods can be returned, but if not, the company can at least take steps to be sure that this kind of unnecessary spending is avoided in the future. These kinds of audit checks should be integrated into the company's purchasing procedures and performed at the time of purchase requisition processing in what is known as a value analysis system. An effective purchasing system should also be integrated with the company's planning and budgeting systems. In this way, all expenditures can be preapproved as part of agreed-upon plans, and unnecessary monies not spent will not only add to the company's cash flow but will also reflect directly on its bottom line.

With the capabilities of office computers, all sizes of business now have the ability to automate their planning, budgeting, purchasing, payables, and general ledger systems in an integrated manner. Systems can be easily installed with inexpensive packaged software and microcomputer hardware that are economically priced and have enhanced processing capability. An effective computerized accounts payable system enables control over payments to be made, when they will be made, and whether or not the cash is available to pay them all. This type of system helps to avoid unpleasant surprises and allows effective planning of cash needs.

If the company has a planning and budgeting system (or some other control system) in place, procedures should be implemented to review any variances in detail. Analysis of variances, particularly major ones, is a primary tool to help control company expenditures and to ensure that proper prices and quantities of goods are being paid for and received. Knowing what is and what should be works not only for controlling costs and profits, but also for controlling the company's cash flow.

Payment Policy

> ## *PAYING VENDORS LATE IS RISKY BUSINESS.*

The normal procedure for most companies regarding vendor payments is to pay on the due date, but not before. However, in a strapped cash position, the company could consider paying later than the date specified by the terms of the invoice. Before pushing this idea too far, remember that vendors want to get paid just as badly as the company wants to get paid by its customers. A slow pay factor may have been added to prices charged to certain customers, and company vendors may be making similar pricing adjustments. Slow-paying customers also tend to get less service when they have a need than do prompt-paying customers. For most businesses, good vendor relations with primary suppliers of goods and services are extremely important. If the company is forced to pay later than agreed-upon terms, be selective as to which vendors are placed in this category. Typically, it is the nonessential vendors (e.g., service providers) who are the first to get hit.

Many times, the company can manage to get some payment relief without hurting its relationships with vendors if it discusses the problem with them and gets their agreement to accept slower payments for a defined period of time. Even cold-hearted suppliers recognize that companies go through cash squeezes from time to time. A discussion in advance can often lead to a mutually satisfactory arrangement that will ease the cash flow problem and maintain good working relationships with the vendors. Their primary interest is likely to be keeping their customer base, and an open communications policy with them can keep the company's relationships on a solid footing. In fact, they might even think more highly of the company because it informed them about the problems and plans for resolving them.

Payment Systems

> ## CASH FLOW MANAGEMENT
> ## IS A ZERO SUM GAME.

There are a number of procedures available for managing disbursement activities. We have previously discussed the possibility of using dispersed collection locations to speed up the collection of funds. Conversely, remote payment locations can be used to slow the process of disbursing money through the system. For instance, drawing checks on banks in locations remote from the payee can add time to the check-clearing process and add float time to the company's cash flow system. The question of legality of these types of systems occasionally arises, but they are not illegal per se. In general, be cautious about using delaying tactics. The inconvenience and potential costs associated with them may well exceed their benefits. And also remember that cash flow management is a zero sum game— whatever benefit the company is able to attain comes at the expense of the other party to the transaction. Many delaying tactics will be transparent to suppliers and may harm the company's relationships with them.

Managing Cash Disbursement Systems

Managing cash disbursements systems can be handled in any one of several ways to control cash outflow and keep money in interest-bearing accounts for as long as possible. There are three types of funding systems available.

1. *Prefunding system.* The simplest, safest, but least effective from the standpoint of holding money back is a prefunding disbursements system. In

this system the amount of money needed to cover all checks written is already in the disbursements bank account at the time the checks are written. As the checks clear, the money is available to cover them, and there is no possibility, barring administrative or clerical error, of bounced checks. This system, however, removes money from interest-bearing potential prior to its actually being needed to cover checks written. Safety has its price.

2. *Estimated funding.* A more economical and efficient, but slightly riskier, cash disbursements system is estimated funding, in which checks are written at one time and the funds to cover those checks are deposited in the disbursements bank account based on estimates of when the checks will clear. This method is effective in situations such as dividend accounts or payroll accounts in which historical patterns of clearance can be studied and predicted with reasonable accuracy. The danger, of course, is predicting inaccurately in which case there is the possibility of bounced checks. This method should be entered into only after thorough analysis and careful consideration due to the greater possibility of inaccuracies and bounced checks, which is likely to be detrimental to the company's reputation.

3. *Controlled disbursements funding.* A method of disbursements cash management called controlled disbursements funding works in conjunction with the company's banking institution. The bank notifies the company each day about the amount of checks that have been presented for payment. The company then arranges to transfer just enough funds to the disbursements account to cover those checks. Use of float is maximized, the company's money remains in interest-bearing form for the maximum time, and the possibility of bounced or dishonored checks is virtually eliminated. The company's bank is likely to require a fee for this service, which will offset part of the savings generated, and the company may need to protect itself against potential overdrafts with a line of credit or other borrowing capability to cover possible shortfalls.

An analysis of these three types of funding systems is shown in Exhibit 2.11. Utilizing disbursements float is not illegal, but cash must be available to cover checks when they are presented to the bank for payment. In deciding how to set up the company's cash disbursements system, the cash manager should keep in mind company goals regarding disbursements—that is, to use float to the company's advantage by having the funds available to cover checks when presented for payment, not when written. The banking industry is very much in a state of flux at present. New and creative ideas arise on a regular basis. As a result, there might well be other kinds of programs and services available that we have not mentioned. The most sensible approach is to keep alert to banking industry services and best practices used by other companies. Good communications with the bank will help the company work out an arrangement that is agreeable to both parties and will prevent unpleasant surprises to either.

	DAY 0	DAY 1	DAY 2	DAY 3	DAY 4
a. PREFUNDING					
Checks written	100%	0%	0%	0%	0%
Estimate of checks to clear	0%	30%	50%	20%	0%
Funds deposited to cover checks	100%	0%	0%	0%	0%
b. ESTIMATED FUNDING	DAY 0	DAY 1	DAY 2	DAY 3	DAY 4
Checks written	100%	0%	0%	0%	0%
Estimate of checks to clear	0%	30%	50%	20%	0%
Funds deposited to cover checks	0%	50%	45%	5%	0%
c. CONTROLLED DISBURSEMENTS FUNDING	DAY 0	DAY 1	DAY 2	DAY 3	DAY 4
Checks written	100%	0%	0%	0%	0%
Actual checks cleared	0%	27%	51%	18%	4%
Funds deposited to cover checks	0%	27%	51%	18%	4%

Analysis

If an average $100,000 worth of checks are written on Thursdays and we can earn 4% on our excess cash, the following potential earnings can be calculated:

Exhibit 2.11   Cash Disbursements Systems

Estimated Funding vs. Prefunding

$100,000 saved for 1 day	=	$100,000
$ 50,000 saved for 4 days (incl. weekend)	=	200,000
$ 5,000 saved for 5 days (incl. weekend)	=	25,000
TOTAL	=	$325,000 × 4% / 365
	=	$35.62/week or $1,850/year

Controlled Disbursements Funding vs. Prefunding

$100,000 saved for 1 day	=	$100,000
$ 73,000 saved for 4 days (incl. weekend)	=	292,000
$ 22,000 saved for 5 days (incl. weekend)	=	110,000
$ 4,000 saved for 6 days (incl. weekend)	=	24,000
TOTAL	=	$526,000 × 4% / 365
	=	$57.64/week or $3,000/year

Exhibit 2.11 Cash Disbursements Systems (continued)

Bank Accounts

A key factor in determining what kind of disbursements system to establish for the company is to understand the amount of its disbursements and the balances it needs to service transactions, to cover transaction costs, and to meet compensating balance requirements. This will allow the company to calculate any excess balances it is able to generate and the amount of earnings potential they represent. This information will enable the cash manager to make intelligent estimates of the advantages and disadvantages of available systems.

Some of the types of bank accounts available include the following:

- *Demand deposit accounts.* These accounts are the basic no frills checking accounts that have been the staple of bank business for many years. A number of years ago, banks began paying interest on these checking accounts in certain instances. However, according to federal regulations, banks may not pay interest on corporate business checking accounts.
- *Imprest accounts.* These are accounts with fixed, usually small, balances that are reimbursed as checks are drawn against them. For example, payroll accounts, small vendor payment accounts, travel expense reimbursement accounts, and the like are appropriate.
- *Zero balance accounts.* These accounts are zeroed out, usually daily, by transferring any remaining balances to a concentration account, or by transferring from a concentration account sufficient funds to cover the checks that have been presented for payment. The transfers between the concentration and zero balance accounts can be handled automatically by the bank or by specific company authorization. These are also referred to as sweep accounts. Vendor payments are an appropriate use for zero balance accounts. A schematic appears in Exhibit 2.12.
- *Automatic balance accounts.* These accounts have receipts and disbursements processed through them and are automatically closed out daily to an agreed-upon amount by the bank by transferring money to or from an interest-bearing account. Automatic balance, zero balance, and imprest accounts are basically variations of the same theme.

In addition to the preceding types of accounts, there are other variations that have been established by banks to service their customers and try to gain a competitive advantage. If the company has a particular situation to deal with, it would probably be to its advantage to talk with the bank and some of its competitors to see what could be done to solve the problem or take advantage of the opportunity. The competitive situation in the banking and financial services market provides a real opportunity to develop creative solutions. In the development of effective systems to meet company needs, a disbursements system that maximizes the earnings potential of discretionary funds is necessary to minimize balances in non-interest bearing accounts and consolidate funds for maximum yields.

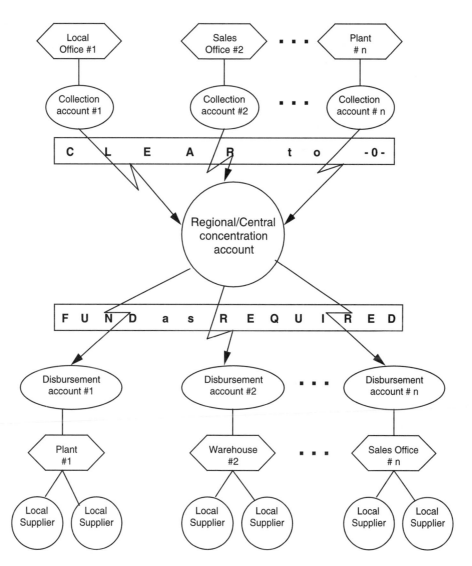

Exhibit 2.12   Zero Balance Accounts

CONCLUSION

In order to be able to effectively manage the cash receipts and disbursements of the organization, it is necessary to fully understand what those receipts and disbursements are, where they come from, and how they affect and are affected by company operations. Since the company's balance sheet and income statement both are intimately interwoven with the company's cash flow, a review of these basic financial statements is a good place to start for this management process.

Cash receipts primarily derive from collections from customers for sales made either from cash sales or accounts receivable collections. While we advocate the desirability of cash sales, most businesses will incur at least some accounts receivable because of competitive necessities. Controlling those receivables and ensuring their timely collection is one of the most effective methods of assuring positive cash flow for the organization. Good record keeping, strong credit and collection policies, and effective follow-up on overdue accounts will help ensure that the money flows into the corporate coffers on a timely basis. Once the money is on the way or has been received, it then becomes necessary to utilize those funds appropriately, either by temporarily investing them for short-term earnings or by reinvesting them back into the business to secure long-term benefits for company stockholders.

The other side of the cash flow coin is cash disbursements, and an effective cash management system will focus a lot of attention on keeping those disbursements under control. Paying only bills that are due when they are due is the most obvious and arguably most effective procedure to follow, but it is often short-circuited or overlooked. As in the case of cash receipts, understanding systems that are available to help manage those cash outflows are important as well, which requires a good working relationship with the company bank and awareness of the services the bank can offer the company.

> *ACCOUNTS RECEIVABLE ARE NOT CASH RECEIPTS.*
> *ACCOUNTS PAYABLE ARE NOT*
> *CASH DISBURSEMENTS.*

CHAPTER 3

Planning and Budgeting

> ## *PLANNING PROVIDES FOCUS FOR THE FUTURE, NOT A GUARANTEE OF RESULTS.*

Establishing good understanding of the organization's cash flow—cash needs and sources—requires that effective planning take place. Typically, this is thought of as a budgeting activity. While cash flow budgeting is necessary and desirable, there needs to be emphasis on overall strategic planning as well. Strategic planning does not usually devote a lot of specific effort to cash flow, but the results of the strategic planning process need to be examined in light of cash flow requirements. And, as mentioned earlier in this book, the operational activities of the organization, which are very dependent of the results of the strategic plans, represent the major sources and uses of cash. Therefore, spending time on strategic planning will have a major impact on the organizations' cash flow. (We will discuss cash flow planning and budgeting specifically in Chapter 8.) This chapter addresses the broader issue of general corporate planning. Its relevance to cash flow is that without proper planning techniques and processes in place, the organization will not be able to adequately foresee its cash requirements.

A good starting point in understanding the cash flow system of the company is to understand the organization, why it is in existence, and what it is trying to accomplish (its mission, goals, and objectives). To accomplish this, there needs to be understanding of the organization's long-term and short-term planning methods and related budgeting and control processes. Focus should be on the organization's approach to planning and its integration with the budgeting process. The planning and budgeting techniques should be a means of achieving improved organizational effectiveness, including healthier management of cash. Management should also be aware of the elements of an effective planning/budgeting system to compare with the practices of the organization under review.

Definitions of goals and objectives are presented in Exhibit 3.1. Note that goals are broad directions or targets toward which the organization or department desires to move. Goals are generally not achievable except in the long run. If a goal is established that in fact can be achieved, it does not sufficiently stretch the organization's abilities. Goals establish the route—they are a direction, not a destination.

GOALS
  –Statements of broad direction
  –That describe future states or outcomes of the organization to be attained
    or retained
  –That indicate ends towards which the organization's effort is to be
    directed

OBJECTIVES
  –Measurable, desired accomplishments related to one or more goals
  –Attainment is desired within a specified time frame and can be evaluated
    under specifiable conditions

CHARACTERISTICS OF OBJECTIVES
  • MEASURABLE – attainment (or lack thereof) can be clearly identified
  • EXPLICIT – clear indication of who, what, when, how
  • TIME-SPECIFIC – to be accomplished within a stipulated period of time
  • REALISTIC – capable of being attained within the time frame specified
    and with the expenditure of a reasonable and cost-effective amount of
    effort and resources

Exhibit 3.1   Planning Definitions

However, objectives are specific desired results, relating to one or more goals, that can be attained within a given time frame. Normally, short-term goals and objectives are developed for a specific planning cycle (usually a one-year annual cycle) for both the organization and each departmental unit. As top management is responsible for developing the long-term organizational goals, so operating managers and staff are responsible for developing and implementing the short-term goals and objectives within the framework of the overall long-term plans.

> *GOALS ARE STATEMENTS OF BROAD DIRECTION.*
> *OBJECTIVES ARE SPECIFIC RESULTS*
> *TO BE ATTAINED.*

There should be interaction and interdependence among the strategic (long-term) planning, short-term planning, detail planning, and budgeting and monitoring processes. The planning process should be an essential first step that leads ultimately to the preparation of an effective budget for the organization. By learning effective planning and budgeting procedures, management will be able more effectively to review and analyze such procedures as part of their organization-wide, departmental, or specific function cash management study.

RELATIONSHIP BETWEEN PLANNING AND BUDGETING

> *THE BUDGET DOES NOT DETERMINE THE PLAN;*
> *THE BUSINESS ENVIRONMENT AND NEEDS DO.*

Organizations may both plan and budget, and many consider them as separate activities. In reality, they should be one integrated process. Planning comes first until the organization defines its goals and objectives. Knowing where to allocate resources, including cash, is an essential part of the budget process. All organizations plan; all organizations budget. If management thinks about whether or not to hire a new engineer; if they evaluate the benefits of a new product line before starting it; if they have considered the advantages and disadvantages of a new building or computer system before laying out the funds, they are planning. If they think about whether they have the funds available to go to a trade show or buy a new vehicle, they are budgeting. Some organizations plan and budget formally, others informally (or even secretly); some are effective, others ineffective or even counterproductive in their methods. But all organizations plan and budget! They are essential to survival. The advantages of formalizing and opening the planning and budgeting process to lower levels of the organization are that they provide an open, integrated, and reasonably structured process that significantly benefits the long-term viability of the organization. It is for these reasons that planning is considered a critical activity to include in a company's evaluation of its cash management processes.

Every organization – whether a manufacturer, service provider, or not-for-profit – must plan its future direction if it desires to achieve its goals and objectives. The organizational plan is an agreed upon course of action to be implemented in the future (short- and long-term) and directed toward moving the organization closer to its stated goals and objectives. The planning process, if exercised effectively, forces the organization to:

- Review and analyze past accomplishments
- Determine present and future needs
- Recognize strengths and weaknesses

It also enables the organization to:

- Identify future opportunities
- Define constraints or threats that may get in the way
- Establish organizational and departmental goals and objectives
- Develop action plans based on the evaluation of alternatives
- Prioritize the selection of action plans for implementation based on the most effective use of limited resources

Early in the planning process the organization must determine why it is in existence. Once the organization has identified all of the reasons that it is in existence and has articulated them by means of an organizational mission statement, vision statement, or credo, it must then define related organizational goals, both long and short term. These organizational goals are typically formulated by top management, although, as previously stated, it is good practice to obtain feedback from lower-level managers, supervisors, and operating personnel within the organization as to the appropriateness, practicality, reasonableness, and attainability of the stated organizational goals. A good rule to keep in mind in the development of an effective organizational plan is that in most organizations the employees closest to day-to-day operations usually know most about present problems and what needs to be done to correct them. Accordingly, the organization that wishes to be successful over the long term must have "everyone" (i.e., representatives from many levels) in the organization involved in the planning process. Having lower-level employees involved in developing the mission statement may be inappropriate, but digging down deeper in the organization than may first be thought necessary should be seriously considered. Involvement is one of the best ways to get commitment, and this can be a very effective "involving" step. Many organizations have been unsuccessful in their planning efforts and their ability to survive because of lack of foresight and their inability or unwillingness to use employees' input creatively.

> ## *PLANNING INVOLVEMENT PERVADES THE ORGANIZATION.*

In addition, operating personnel need to know how to plan properly and operate according to such plans (putting the plans into action) in order to carry out their responsibilities successfully as part of an integrated organizational plan. Operations personnel cannot plan for their own areas effectively unless they understand and work with the organization's long- and short-term goals—and have had the opportunity to provide significant input to these plans. It is not sufficient, however, for operations personnel to be allowed merely to provide input; top management must also encourage that input, seriously consider it in the finalization of organizational goals, and provide appropriate feedback as to why any reasonable ideas were not implemented. The development of organizational goals must be institutionalized with top-to-bottom discussion for it to be most successful.

Yet personnel must also understand the principle that members of top management have the ultimate decision-making power and therefore may still make the final decision, regardless of operations personnel input. The result of such exclusive top management decision making, however, is organizational goal setting by directive rather than by participation. Because operations staff will see these organizational goals as top management's and not their own, they will not only be less inclined to direct their efforts toward achievement of those goals, but may also tend to work openly against or even sabotage the attainment of the goals. In an effective planning system, it is extremely important to have everyone in the organization working toward the same goals. In this manner, management and operations staff are far more likely to make decisions that are consistent with the organization's overall plans and direction.

Within this framework, how then does an organization plan effectively for its future? A schematic of the organizational planning process is shown in Exhibit 3.2. Note that in the development of long- and short-range plans, which includes

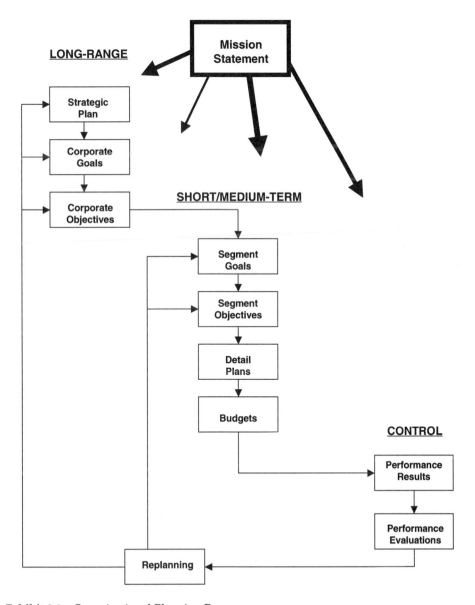

Exhibit 3.2 Organizational Planning Process

the development of detail plans and related budgets, a top-to-bottom approach is used. Top management, operations management, and staff interact and communicate, resulting in an agreed-upon set of organizational plans (strategic plans, corporate goals, and corporate objectives) and departmental/segment goals, objectives, detail plans, and budgets.

STRATEGIES FOR COMPETITIVE ADVANTAGE

> *STRATEGIC PLANNING HELPS PEOPLE*
> *UNDERSTAND WHAT TO DO.*

As can be imagined, there are many different strategies that an organization could adopt to achieve an advantage over the competition. However, many types of strategies share similar characteristics that drive the strategy and provide the competitive advantage. Among these differing strategies to be considered, many would fall into the following two categories (as depicted in Exhibit 3.3):

1. *Differentiation Strategy.* In differentiation strategy, the product or service to be provided is differentiated from the competition by various factors that increase the value to the customer/client, such as enhanced performance, quality, prestige, features, service, reliability, or convenience. Differentiation strategy is often, but not always, associated with higher price. The desire is make price a less critical factor to the customer.
2. *Low Cost Strategy.* Low-cost strategy achieves a sustainable cost advantage in some important element of the product or service. Low-cost leadership position can be attained through high volume (high market share, perhaps), favorable access to lower-cost raw materials or labor markets, or state-of-the-art manufacturing procedures. Low-cost strategy need not always be associated with charging lower prices, as lower product or service costs could also result in increased profits or increased marketing, advertising, promotion, or product development investment.

Although most planning strategies usually involve differentiation and/or low-cost strategy, there are many other kinds of strategy that could be exploited. Examples include specific organizational competencies such as creativity and innovation, global perspectives, entrepreneurialism, research capability, sophisticated systems, automation and computerization, and so on. Within this framework, the following three strategies (also summarized in Exhibit 3.3), which are not easily categorized as either differentiation or low-cost strategies, could be considered in formulating long-range plans:

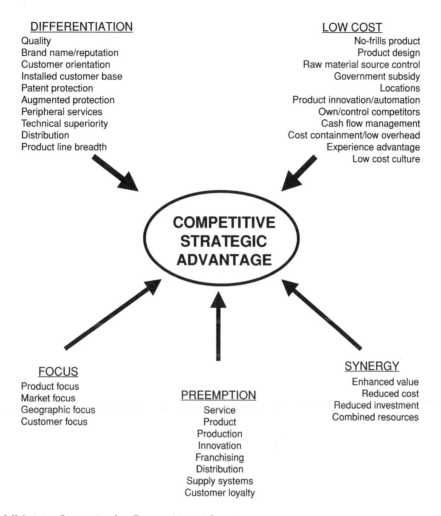

DIFFERENTIATION
Quality
Brand name/reputation
Customer orientation
Installed customer base
Patent protection
Augmented protection
Peripheral services
Technical superiority
Distribution
Product line breadth

LOW COST
No-frills product
Product design
Raw material source control
Government subsidy
Locations
Product innovation/automation
Own/control competitors
Cash flow management
Cost containment/low overhead
Experience advantage
Low cost culture

COMPETITIVE
STRATEGIC
ADVANTAGE

FOCUS
Product focus
Market focus
Geographic focus
Customer focus

PREEMPTION
Service
Product
Production
Innovation
Franchising
Distribution
Supply systems
Customer loyalty

SYNERGY
Enhanced value
Reduced cost
Reduced investment
Combined resources

Exhibit 3.3 Strategies for Competitive Advantage

1. *Focus*. This strategy involves organizations that focus on either a relative- ly small customer base or a restricted part of their product or service line. For example, a retailer selling to tall men or small women, or a CPA offer- ing personal financial planning services to highly compensated individu- als would be employing a focus strategy. The particular focus is usually the driving force in the planning effort, though differentiation and/or low cost may also be part of the strategy.

2. *Preemption*. A preemptive strategic move is the first implementation of a strategy into a business or service area that, because it was first, produces a distinct competitive advantage. Normally, for such a preemptive move to create an advantage, competitors should be inhibited or precluded from matching or countering the move. Some examples might be tying up the major distributors in a new market area before the competition can make a

move, becoming the sole source for a particular product such as a new computer software package, or being the only CPA firm in town that is a member of a professional practice management association (assuming such membership provides a distinct advantage). Being able to pull off such a preemptive move will put competitors at a substantial disadvantage.

3. *Synergy.* The benefits of synergy (where the total is greater than the sum of its parts) can occur when an organization has an advantage due to its connection with another organizational entity within or outside the firm. The two entities may share sales and marketing efforts, research and development capabilities, office and support staff and facilities, warehousing, and so on. With the element of synergy, the two or more entities may be able to offer the potential customer/client the products or services that are desired, which neither might be able to do alone. For example, a more traditional CPA firm might link together with a computer software development firm to provide clients with full computer systems development services. The combination could create a synergy that would not exist if each worked separately.

STRATEGIC PLANNING PROCESS

> ## *PROGRESS REQUIRES CHANGE;*
> ## *IF THE BUSINESS NEVER CHANGES,*
> ## *IT WILL NEVER PROGRESS.*

In addition to a discussion of the basics of strategic planning and some of the benefits that can accrue from its effective use, we should also deal with some of the mechanics of the strategic planning process. An overview of the strategic planning process is presented in Exhibit 3.4. It depicts the external and internal analyses that provide the inputs into strategy development, strategic decisions, and related strategic management. This can be referred to as a situational analysis, that is, a review of the existing situation of the organization in its environment today. Having a solid understanding of where the organization stands right now with regard to its external environment and its internal strengths and weaknesses is a good first step in the overall strategic planning process.

External Analysis

External analysis involves a review of relevant elements external to the organization, focusing on the identification of opportunities, threats, strategic questions, and alternatives. Inasmuch as there are many external factors that can be considered, it is important that the external analysis not be overdone, since this could

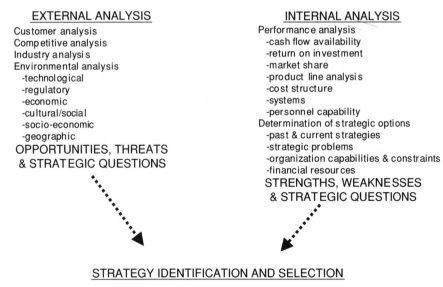

EXTERNAL ANALYSIS
Customer analysis
Competitive analysis
Industry analysis
Environmental analysis
-technological
-regulatory
-economic
-cultural/social
-socio-economic
-geographic
OPPORTUNITIES, THREATS
& STRATEGIC QUESTIONS

INTERNAL ANALYSIS
Performance analysis
-cash flow availability
-return on investment
-market share
-product line analysis
-cost structure
-systems
-personnel capability
Determination of strategic options
-past & current strategies
-strategic problems
-organization capabilities & constraints
-financial resources
STRENGTHS, WEAKNESSES
& STRATEGIC QUESTIONS

STRATEGY IDENTIFICATION AND SELECTION
1. Define the corporate mission
2. Identify the strategic alternatives
   -by product or service
   -by strategic investment thrust
   -by unique competitive advantage
3. Select the strategy
   -consider strategic questions
   -evaluate strategic alternatives
4. Implement the strategy
   -develop operating plans
5. Review the strategies and replan as required
   -install timely and accurate information
   & control systems

Exhibit 3.4 Overview of the Strategic Planning Process

result in substantial cost in terms of time and resources. Some elements that could be reviewed in an external analysis include the following:

- Customer analysis involves identifying the business's customer/client base and their needs. Particular emphasis should be placed on products/services desired, special requirements, quality and service considerations, and the like.
- Competitive analysis includes the identification of competitors, both existing and potential. Areas that could be included in competitive analysis are intensity of competition, competitors' performance, their objectives (i.e., are they the same as yours?), strategies employed, strengths, weaknesses, and so on.
- Industry analysis focuses on determining the potential of the industry in general and the products/services within the industry. For instance, will

the organization and others be able to earn sufficient profits, or is the industry or product/service so competitive that attractive profits are unlikely to be attained? Elements that can be included in the analysis are industry size or potential, growth prospects, competitive intensity, barriers to entry (or to exit), threat of substitution, the power of suppliers and customers, cost structure, distribution/marketing channels, industry/product/service trends, and key success factors (such as quality, service, customer relationships, etc.).

- Environmental analysis focuses on factors outside the organization that may create opportunities for or threats to the organization. This analysis must necessarily be limited so that it doesn't become excessive in terms of time and scope. Areas that could be included are technological changes (impact of new developments), regulatory issues (effect of new or pending legislative initiatives), economic factors (effects of general economic conditions), cultural/social considerations (what's "in" or "hot" in the market), demographic trends (age patterns, socioeconomic changes, population pattern shifts, etc.), or geographic factors (urban/suburban/rural changes, weather, transportation considerations, etc.).

Internal Analysis

Internal analysis involves achieving a detailed understanding of those areas of strategic importance within the organization. An examination of corporate strengths and weaknesses and their impact on the strategic issues is essential to this process. The appropriate considerations can be categorized as follows:

- *Performance analysis*, which evaluates the performance of the organization in terms of financial results (e.g., return on investment) as well as other performance measures such as market share, product line analysis and performance, cost information, product development, management systems, personnel capability, and so on.
- *Determination of strategic options*, which focuses on a review of those elements of the organization that influence strategy choices, such as past and current strategies; strategic problems which, if uncorrected, could cause significant damage (e.g. insufficient professional staff or other resources); organizational capabilities and constraints; financial resources/constraints; flexibility to change; strengths/weaknesses (build on strengths or neutralize weaknesses); and so on.

> *THE SITUATION AUDIT HELPS THE ORGANIZATION DETERMINE ITS STARTING POINT FOR PLANNING—THAT IS, ITS SITUATION RIGHT NOW.*

Once the organization has evaluated its current situation, the determination of strategic plans process can begin. The steps in this process are:

1. *Strategy Identification and Selection.* The recommended first step in an effective external and internal analysis is to *define the corporate mission:* Why are we in existence and what is our purpose? A good mission statement usually defines the areas in which business is conducted, how the business is conducted, and what makes it unique. In addition, the mission statement can state growth directions, organizational philosophy, behavioral standards and ethics, human relations philosophies, financial goals, and the like.

2. The second step, *identify the strategic alternatives*, could include the following considerations:
   - Strategic investment thrust (i.e., growth/expansion, stability, retrenchment/harvest or divestiture/liquidation)
   - Competitive advantage strategies, such as in functional areas (sales, service, quality), or use of assets and skills, differentiation, low-cost, focus, preemption, and synergy

3. Criteria to consider in the third step of the strategy identification and selection process, *select the strategy*, include:
   - Responsiveness to opportunities and threats
   - Use of competitive advantage
   - Consistency with mission statement and objectives
   - Feasibility and realism
   - Compatibility with the internal organization
   - Consistency with other company strategies
   - Organizational flexibility
   - Use of organizational synergy
   - Exploitation of organizational strengths and/or competitor weaknesses
   - Minimization/neutralization of organizational weaknesses and/or competitor strengths

4. Step four, *implement the strategy*, involves converting the selected strategies into operating plans. These operating plans consist of the organizational and departmental goals, objectives, and detail plans that are necessary to move the organization toward meeting their strategic goals and objectives. To support these operating plans, resources must be allocated that are sufficient (but not excessive) to ensure successful working of the operating plans. This is the process of budgeting.

5. Finally, the fifth step of the process, *review the strategies and replan as required*, requires development and implementation of an adequate and timely information system that allows management to measure progress

toward strategic plan and related operating plan goals, objectives, detail plan activities, and budgets.

Some potential pitfalls of planning systems are shown in Exhibit 3.5. These pitfalls are intended as warnings of things to be avoided, not excuses for avoiding the planning process altogether.

A. TOP-DOWN VS. BOTTOM-UP SYSTEMS

In a top-down system, top management creates strategy as well as departmental goals and objectives that they consider necessary to achieve their strategies. Although this procedure provides the resources to achieve the strategies across the organization, it is seen many times by department managers, supervisors, and staff as management by directive. Since the operating personnel have no input into the planning process, the resulting plans are seen as top management's, and there is little motivation for the operating people to achieve success - in fact, there may even be a subtle (or not-so-subtle) sabotaging of efforts. In a bottom-up system, the planning process starts at the lowest levels at which the organization operates. The theory is that operating people are closer, more responsive, and more knowledgeable about the immediate needs and are thus in a better position to develop plans. Since they are totally involved in the planning process, they will be more committed and motivated to make the plans succeed. The potential flaw here, however, is that top management commitment is also necessary to make the plans work.

B. SPREADSHEET-DRIVEN PROCESS

With the advent of the microcomputer and spreadsheet software, the planning process has become, for many organizations, a spreadsheet proliferation of income statements and balance sheets for years into the future. Focus tends to be more on projecting past financial data into the future than planning for the future. Elegant accounting methods, complex spreadsheets, and reams of data that are easy to generate but nearly impossible to analyze and understand take the place of considering and evaluating alternatives and making intelligent estimates of what is likely to really happen.

C. FINANCIAL OBJECTIVES ORIENTATION

In many instances, organizations will set their goals and objectives relative to short-term financial measures such as sales, profits, return on investment measures, market share, and so on. With these factors dominating, other goals and objectives often become vaguely stated or relatively insignificant in the planning process. Frequently, however, this zeal to improve short-term financial performance can be detrimental to production, marketing, product development and other functions vital to the long-range future success of the enterprise.

Exhibit 3.5   Some Pitfalls of a Planning System

D. PLANNING RIGIDITY

Organizational plans that are too rigidly followed may result in inhibiting actions that are necessary for the organization. What results is a defensive mind-set on the part of many managers that manifests itself in an "it's not in the budget" attitude, which tends to eliminate or sharply reduce proposals for change.

E. LACK OF COMMITMENT

Often, an organization is very adept at producing excellent plans but falls short in the implementation process. The result is a sophisticated set of plans sitting on the shelf unused. There may also be lack of commitment to making the plans work at the top or throughout the organization. The plans are not sufficiently integrated with detail operating plans, and there is not an effective control and monitoring system to make it successful. Another situation that may occur is that top management is not willing to enforce the process with requisite discipline. Whatever the cause, the result is a lot of wasted resources expended with no benefit to the organization.

Exhibit 3.5   Some Pitfalls of a Planning System (continued)

SHORT-TERM PLANNING

> *MANAGEMENT GOALS MUST BE TRANSLATED INTO SPECIFIC OBJECTIVES.*

One of the most important benefits of an organizational planning system is that it forces managers, supervisors, and others in the organization to take the time to consider strategic questions and alternatives for achieving the most effective results. Without this focus, day-to-day operations (and related crises) would normally consume all the available time. An organizational planning system enables management to respond to both the external and internal environments and allows managers to run a complex organization with the aim of achieving an integrated and coordinated result—despite ceaseless changes, nerve-wracking uncertainty, and all-too limited resources.

Organizational planning is the term used to describe planning for the organization as a whole, and encompasses decision making at all levels of the organization. Within this framework, we have earlier discussed strategic planning, which provides the basic direction and focus of the organization—the big picture. Strategic planning is concerned with top-management decisions relative to the future direction of the organization in terms of such things as business focus, resources, products/services, and markets. Long-range planning, which is often thought of as synonymous with strategic planning, more typically provides a time frame for the strategic plan, typically three to five years (but possibly much longer, depending on the nature of the business).

The organizational long-range goals established by top management have to be translated into more specific departmental/segment goals and objectives. The following example demonstrates the relationship between long-term goals and short-term goals and objectives. The long-term goal of an organization is "To become the industry sales leader for product line YY." The related short-term goal is "To increase sales in units of product line YY." The specific objective for this planning cycle is "To increase sales in units of product number 3 of product line YY by at least 10 percent over last year." This specific objective can then be translated into specific detail plans (i.e., how to go about achieving the specific objective) and related performance expectations for the sales department, the manufacturing department, the finance department, and other affected areas of the organization.

These short-term performance objectives can then be translated into levels of production, inventory to be carried, labor requirements, manufacturing capacity, and other short-term decisions. In effect, these short-term objectives and related detail plans become the starting point for the budget process. The beginning budget will then reflect what is necessary (in terms of labor, materials, facilities, equipment, and other costs) to meet agreed-upon short-term objectives. When top management approves each budget, it will reflect the authorized level of expenditures needed to fulfill the objectives by following through on agreed-upon plans. At this point, each manager/supervisor has theoretically been delegated the authority to incur the expenditures to make each detail plan workable. Finally, each manager/supervisor can be evaluated based on his or her ability to effectively work his or her plan to achieve the short-term objectives.

Short-term planning, or operational planning, provides the framework for implementing the strategic and long-term plans into a short-term time frame, usually a one-year operating period. It should be a direct derivation from the strategic plan and is the logical next step in converting top management's strategic decisions into short-term operating actions. The operating plan works with present resources and the current situation to create a detailed blueprint for achieving agreed-upon goals and objectives for the various segments of the organization.

SHORT-TERM PLANNING DRIVES OPERATIONAL ACTIVITY.

Presumably, as the organization grows in size and complexity, management will realize that crisis management and purely intuitive planning and control are no longer sufficient. More structured planning concepts and techniques may then find their rightful place in the organization's recurring business development activities. A schematic of the planning cycle is shown in Exhibit 3.6. This schemat-

TOP MANAGEMENT   I   SEGMENT MANAGEMENT

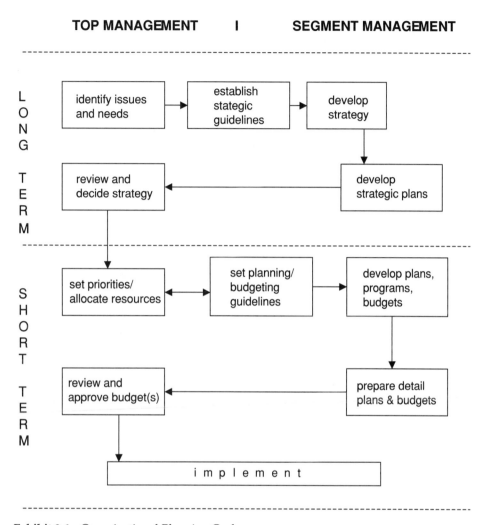

Exhibit 3.6   Organizational Planning Cycle

ic graphically depicts the relationship between strategic planning and the short-term planning process. It also shows the interactive relationship between top and segment management that is required to make the entire planning process fully effective.

Underlying Theory Behind Short-Term Planning

The short-term planning life cycle is shown in Exhibit 3.7. As shown, the starting point is the strategic or long-range plan as approved by top management. The next step is to develop corporate and segment goals and objectives that support the strategic plans. These are normally formulated by top management with built-in feedback to allow lower levels of management to review the goals and objec-

TOP MANAGEMENT | COMBINED | SEGMENT MANAGEMENT

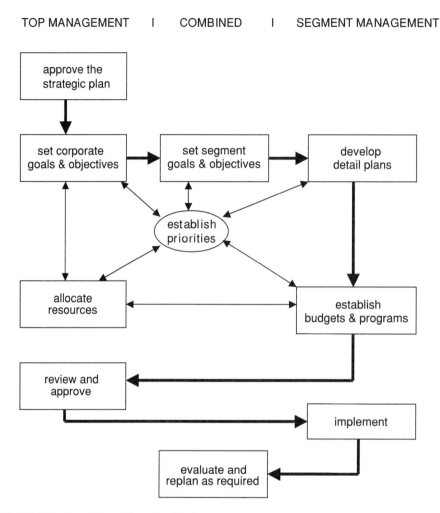

Exhibit 3.7 Short-Term Planning Cycle

tives and assure that they are consistent with operational needs—and that no constraints exist that could prevent successful attainment. Once these plans are in place, priorities must be established so that senior and segment management know the extent of resources that need to be allocated to allow the goals, objectives, and detail plans to be attained.

The short-term planning system at the segment level is a process in which lower levels of management develop detail plans in accordance with their own understanding of what top management requires of them. Upper management then exercises top-down direction to support the broad framework of total organizational objectives. In this two-way flow of ideas and purposes, a deeper understanding is achieved as to the nature of the organization and how each organizational unit plays a supportive role in accomplishing what the organization wants to achieve.

Segment mission determines segment functions, and from these plans, budgets and programs are derived. This in turn leads to implementation, review, and replanning. The combination of bottom-up development and top-down direction and review is the foundation for the effectiveness of short-term planning procedures. It brings about the maximum involvement of managers, supervisors, and operational personnel in the development of operating goals, objectives, and detail plans; while at the same time ensures that these plans will be compatible with overall organization mission and strategic plans as well as shorter-term goals and objectives.

Effective short-term planning necessitates participative management. This does not necessarily mean a complete change in the management system, but it does place more emphasis on certain management techniques such as getting things done through other people. Managers must delegate in order to derive the greatest benefit from the planning system. They must give their employees freedom to devise their own methods for attaining their goals and objectives. This carries with it, of course, the freedom to fail—frightening to some, but a major learning process for subordinates.

> ### *SHORT-TERM PLANNING PROVIDES THE FRAMEWORK FOR IMPLEMENTING THE LONG-TERM PLAN.*

Short-Term Operating Plan

Short-term planning is the process whereby top management, operating management, and others in the organization jointly identify common goals and objectives, define each individual's major areas of responsibility in terms of results expected, and use these measures as guides to operating each organizational unit and assessing the contribution of each staff member. Short-term planning also permits management at all levels of the organization to concentrate on those matters requiring attention and to devote only minimal effort to those activities that are running smoothly. This concept is known popularly as management by exception.

The process for developing, approving, and implementing short-term planning activities is depicted in Exhibit 3.8. Shown on this graphic are the roles of the CEO, functional managers, and administrative (financial) personnel in the process. Note that the process is based on a cooperative relationship between top and functional management, ensuring an integrated plan for all levels of the organization. As a result, all members of the organization are working toward the same targets.

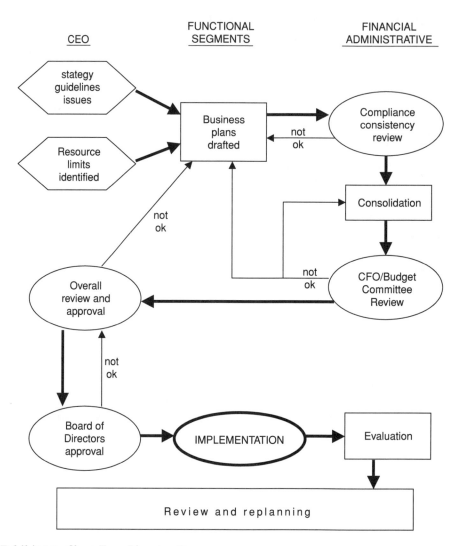

Exhibit 3.8   Short-Term Planning Process

The general steps normally required in the short-term planning process are shown in Exhibit 3.9, and can be discussed more fully as follows:

1. *Planning.* Based on corporate goals and objectives, each segment will state its mission (its reason for existence) and its major functions; will analyze its strengths, weaknesses, opportunities, and threats (SWOT analysis); and will develop its goals and objectives (specific goals to be attained).

2. *Detail plans and programming.* Once management agrees upon the segment goals and objectives, segment staff will develop alternatives as to how they will accomplish their objectives. Through a priority-setting process,

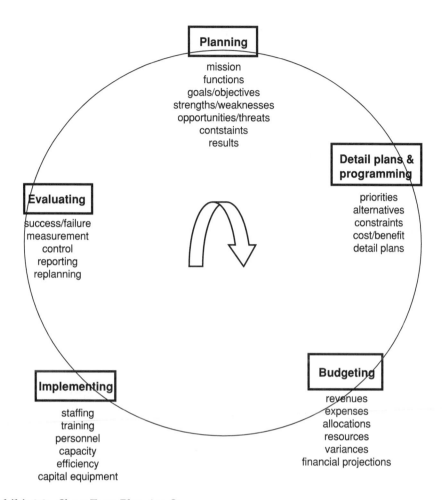

Planning
mission
functions
goals/objectives
strengths/weaknesses
opportunities/threats
contstaints
results

**Detail plans &
programming**
priorities
alternatives
constraints
cost/benefit
detail plans

Evaluating
success/failure
measurement
control
reporting
replanning

Implementing
staffing
training
personnel
capacity
efficiency
capital equipment

Budgeting
revenues
expenses
allocations
resources
variances
financial projections

Exhibit 3.9   Short-Term Planning Steps

they should consider existing constraints (obstacles to success) and prepare cost-benefit analyses to determine the optimum detail plan or set of
activities that will accomplish the objectives.

3. *Budgeting.* After the detail plans have been agreed to, resources need to be
allocated to each activity. During the budget process, revenues are projected, priorities are set (how much can we do with limited resources?),
resources are allocated to relevant activities (expense budgeting), and
additional sources of funding are identified, if required. Established budgets should represent the delegation of authority from top management to
segment management to carry out their agreed-upon plans. This integrates the planning and budgeting phases of the entire process.

4. *Implementing.* Following agreement and approval of the detail plans and
related budgets, the segment becomes responsible for implementing the
plan. Since the steps and activities of the detail plan have been agreed to

as the optimum way for the organization to achieve desired objectives, segment personnel must be held accountable for making the plans work as effectively as possible.

5. *Evaluating.* The evaluation process in a short-term planning cycle consists of establishing effective reporting systems that will inform if objectives are, in fact, being met. Based on these evaluations, management can determine if the plan should be continued, changed, or dropped entirely. This is the replanning process, which is the start of a new planning cycle.

Implementing the Short-Term Planning System

There are four major steps in implementing short-term planning systems at the segment level in the organization:

1. Stating the mission and functions
2. Developing segment goals and objectives
3. Converting objectives into detail operating plans
4. Measuring progress toward achievement of objectives

Stating the Mission and Functions
Short-term planning implementation begins with a statement of mission and functions for each operating unit of the organization. The mission can be defined as a statement of purpose and responsibility of the segment. The functions are all the major responsibilities of the units that are required to carry out the mission. Many times, this becomes one of the most beneficial exercises in the total planning process, as it requires each manager and staff member to analyze the role of the unit in relation to the overall mission of the organization.

Developing Segment Goals and Objectives
The next step is the development of goals and objectives, which is usually done one year at a time and involves either improvement to an existing situation or correction of an activity that is below acceptable standards. Objectives are specific in that they focus very closely on the actual effort required to carry out the responsibilities of the segment.

Development of objectives (and related detail plans) should go hand in hand with the development of the budget. Hence, every objective must be supported by the resources allocated to the segment. If a change in the resource allocation is required to support the achievement of objectives, allocation revisions must be approved concurrently with the approval of the objectives.

Regular goals and objectives are those that relate to the segment's routine functions. They should not be in conflict with regular duties and responsibilities; rather, they should be an integral part of these activities. After these regular goals and objectives have been defined, it may be desirable to establish one or more special objectives for the period. Special objectives generally involve one-time projects of particular importance to the organization. Therefore, they should be limited in number. Development of a new reporting system is an example of a special objective. Wherever possible, objectives should be quantified so that performance can be measured. For example, four objectives may be needed to carry out the function of a particular department:

1. Reduce the number of people-days lost from 150 to 75.
2. Increase the number of actual production hours available from 50 to 55.
3. Control operating expenses—do not exceed $180,000 compared with the existing level of $200,000.
4. Implement a quality control system that will enable rejected customer deliveries to be less than 1 percent of total shipments.

> ## *THE MORE SPECIFIC THE OBJECTIVE, THE MORE LIKELY IT WILL BE ATTAINED.*

Establishing explicit objectives in terms of dollars, hours, or pieces will generate greater likelihood of achievement than will generalized statements of desired objectives expressed in percentages or nonquantitative terms. With such careful quantification of objectives, it is easier to follow progress towards achievement throughout the planning and implementation period.

After establishing objectives, recognize that they may have different degrees of importance within the organization, so it may be necessary to determine their relative values. This should be a joint process between the staff member and the manager.

Objectives to encourage higher performance and/or to force corrective action should receive relatively high weights. Nominal weights are given to significant but lower-priority activities in which average performance is acceptable or to areas not requiring special attention at this time.

Some objectives are, by their nature, not quantifiable. An objective calling for the development of a quality control system is an example. Progress toward the achievement of such an objective can be followed by monitoring a schedule of events. If, for example, the development of a reporting system is subdivided into five steps, completion of each step could constitute 20 percent of the target.

For example:

Objective: Develop a quality control system by 12/1/xx.

Step	Event	Target
1	Establish requirements and specifications by 3/1/xx.	20%
2	Investigate other control systems by 5/15/xx.	40%
3	Design system by 9/1/xx .	60%
4	Test system by 11/1/xx.	80%
5	Obtain necessary approvals from Engineering, Manufacturing, and Sales Engineering by 11/15/xx.	100%

By definition, achievement of a nonquantifiable objective is limited to 100 percent, which on the surface eliminates the possibility of overachievement. However, a completed objective can also be eligible for a quality rating if the work contribution toward the achievement is considered outstanding enough to merit it.

Converting Objectives into Detail Operating Plans
Development of objectives will not produce significant results unless the objectives are turned into a detail operating plan and implemented. In setting up a detail plan, the department manager and staff must determine what general approach should be taken to attain the objectives. They usually deal with ways to raise performance, improve quality or scope of services, or reduce operating costs. An example of an operating plan is depicted in Exhibit 3.10 for one objective.

The first step is to identify events that must be completed to achieve the objective. An estimate of time requirements for completing each event follows and deadlines are established for each event. The same process is repeated in establishing detail operating plans for each objective. Normally, a number of alternative detail plans are developed, (usually two or three), so that department management and top management can arrive at the best priorities and allocation of resources.

Measuring Progress toward Achievement of Objectives
The final step, after implementing the detail plans, in setting up the short-term planning system is to develop an effective follow-up system. Continual evaluation of progress toward achievement of objectives is essential for effective use of a short-term planning system. Since managerial evaluation should be based on

OBJECTIVE:	To reduce days lost from an average per employee of eight per year to five per year for the fiscal year beginning July 1, 20×1	
OPERATING PLAN DETAILS:		Completion Deadline
1. Research absenteeism history		$1/31/\times 1$
2. Research attendance incentive systems		$2/28/\times 1$
3. Develop an appropriate attendance incentive system		$3/30/\times 1$
4. Obtain management approval for the proposed incentive system		$4/30/\times 1$
5. Develop orientation program for employees		$5/30/\times 1$
6. Conduct orientation program		$6/05\text{-}6/15/\times 1$
7. Implement system		$7/01/\times 1$
8. Provide follow-up programfrom		$7/01/\times 1$
9. Monitor and control absenteeism from		$7/01/\times 1$
10. Provide counselling services for abusers from		$7/01/\times 1$

Exhibit 3.10   Operating Plan Details

achievements in relation to agreed-upon goals, objectives, and detail plans, periodic performance evaluation is crucial.

Progress reports should be prepared periodically, but not less than once a month. These reports should indicate to what extent agreed-upon objectives have been attained to that time.

In very large and complex organizations where the kinds of functional activities of each unit vary across a wide spectrum, it is virtually impossible to apply a single rule to every situation. Rather, the judgment and discretion of the reviewing personnel need to be fully exercised in dealing with extreme cases of over- and underachievement. The important point that the unit manager and staff need to understand is that top management requires a balanced effort on their part in relation to all important elements and functions of their units. An erratic pattern of performance often reflects the manager's personal likes and dislikes but does not adequately serve the purposes of the unit.

One of the major benefits of a systematic follow-up program for the short-term planning system is that it creates the vehicle for necessary dialogue between the employee, segment management, and top management. In this context, management can most effectively play its role in motivating staff and exploring ways of removing obstacles to higher achievement. Also, in these review procedures, objectives can be reexamined to test whether they are realistic and feasible in light of any changed conditions. If the short-term planning system is to remain valuable, the segment manager and staff should be prepared to revise detail plans and objectives. The implementation of an effective monitoring system that allows changes to be made can avoid fostering the fatalistic attitude that departments must live out the rest of the year repeatedly explaining variances that have resulted from inappropriate detail plans and related budgets or changes in environmental conditions.

The steps involved in implementing departmental short-term operating plans are summarized in Exhibit 3.11.

Key Results Areas

> ### *IDENTIFYING KEY RESULTS WILL HELP FOCUS PEOPLE'S WORK.*

One of the most important steps in developing objectives is the identification of key results areas, which are those highly selective areas of a department's operations in which a strong level of performance must be achieved to optimize results. The most valuable purpose these key results areas serve is to help work unit personnel direct their limited resources to the most important matters where the return will be the greatest relative to the efforts expended. In this way, they help

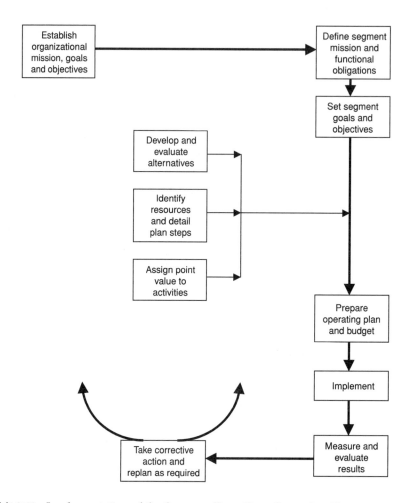

Exhibit 3.11   Implementation of the Segment Short-Term Operating Plan

prevent personnel from falling into the activity or "busy-ness" trap—getting busy and staying busy without first determining what to be busy about.

It is normally easier to identify and select key results areas using a two step approach: (1) list major job responsibilities or job functions; and (2) examine each job function to determine the key results areas. This process is demonstrated below for a financial manager:

Major Functions	*Key Results Areas*
Accounting	Accurate, timely measurement and reporting of performance
Treasury	Cost of capital; availability of capital; return on investable funds

| Credit/Collections | Aging of accounts; bad debt level |
| Data Processing | Machine utilization; personnel utilization; cost–benefit level |

Key results areas normally fall into the following categories:

Quantity	Revenue and production levels
Quality	Customer satisfaction, product quality
Timeliness	Schedule misses (or hits), customer demands
Cost	Cost of services, manufacturing costs

Measurement Techniques: Examples

Some measurement techniques to determine whether results are being achieved include:

- *Profit contribution and cost reduction*
  - Production/Quantity
    - Processing time
    - Machine/employee downtime
    - Actual versus optimal staff size
    - Productivity (output per unit of input)
  - Production/Quality
    - Error rates/rejects
    - Losses (dollars, lost sales, etc.) resulting from errors
    - Number of occurrences of errors
    - Adherence to quality assurance procedures
  - Costs
    - Adherence to budget (on flexible budgeting basis)
    - Overtime costs
    - Materials and supplies costs
    - Labor costs
    - Overhead (manufacturing, selling, and administrative) costs
- *Accounting controls*
  - Adherence to audit schedules
  - Number of exceptions
  - Response time to correct exceptions
  - Timeliness and accuracy of reports
- *Management controls*
  - Systems and methods improvements
  - Personnel turnover rate
  - Absentee rate
  - Individual task performance

- Training programs
- Management and staff development
- *Coordination*
  - Understanding of operations
  - Problems solved
  - Sales forecast versus production schedule
  - Customer relations; employee relations; bank relations
  - Inquiry delays
  - Number of praises or complaints

CONCLUSION

It would be nice to think that every organization has an effective planning system as described above. However, management may find that very few organizations come close to planning and budgeting in this manner. In cases in which such planning systems do not exist or are found to be deficient, management must superimpose such concepts on the organization or area under study to establish desired results prior to commencing the cash management study. The company must also keep in mind that their task is not merely to determine the existence of such planning systems, but the effectiveness of these planning systems in moving the organization in the right direction toward more positive cash flow. To be most effective, the planning system must be continually attended to and the related budget flexible so that it supports the plan rather than making it more difficult to achieve results.

> ## THE MORE THE INPUT, THE BETTER THE PLAN.

CHAPTER 4

Analyzing the Sales Function

> **COMPANY PLANS DIRECT THE SALES FUNCTION; THE SALES FUNCTION DOES NOT DIRECT THE COMPANY.**

Cash flow management is often perceived as a strictly financial function that needs to be handled by the accounting and/or treasury staff of the company. While certain aspects of cash management do fall within the purview of the financial or accounting section (e.g., borrowing, investing, allocating capital, handling cash transactions, banking and custodial arrangements), principal cash flow—in or out—results from the basic operations of the company. Incoming cash is generated from payments by customers for goods or services provided. Outgoing cash is used for purchased parts and material, payroll, manufacturing or service provision expenses, sales and marketing, research and development, capital purchases, and a slew of other costs particular to the specific business under review. These cash inflows and outflows are not produced by the finance or accounting personnel. They result from activities carried out by the operating personnel within the company—the manufacturing, service, engineering, marketing, sales, purchasing, maintenance, and other employees.

For a cash management process to work effectively within the company so as to ensure sufficient cash to continue to run the operations, it is essential that the operating activities be run not only to satisfy customers and make profits, but also to conserve and generate cash. That means that the operating personnel cannot leave cash responsibility solely to the accountants. They must be aware of cash flow and its impact on the company as a whole. And most importantly they must carry out their responsibilities in a cash-aware manner. To that end, in this and the following two chapters, we will be discussing some of the major aspects of company operations with the idea that these operational activities, though not specifically cash focused, will ultimately determine the cash flow of the organization.

CASH MANAGEMENT STUDY

The company's cash management study starts at the top of the organization. That is, top management should define and communicate its strategic plans for the company, including ideas about expansion, retrenchment, and status quo. At the same time, management members should identify the businesses they want to be in, the businesses they do not want to be in, their basic business principles and belief systems, and their expectations for each function within the organization.

For instance, top management may define an expectation for the sales function, which may have historically sold whatever it could to customers: to become more integrated with the planning process and other functions such as manufacturing and engineering. In defining their wishes, members of management may identify attributes such as:

- Sales forecasts more realistically related to actual customers and products to be sold
- A larger percentage of the sales forecast (at least 80 percent) matched by real customer orders
- Sales efforts driven by management's identification in the planning process of what to sell, to whom, and at what quantity
- A sales forecast with a high percentage of real customer orders that allows the company's production to be based on customer orders and expected delivery times, at a specified quality level
- A sales function that is geared more toward providing customer service than toward making sales that maximize sales personnel's compensation
- A sales activity that measures cash flow contribution to the company as well as profitability
- A sales function that works within the company's plans together with the other functions of the company, such as manufacturing, engineering, purchasing, accounting, and marketing

The sales function should be established to work as an integrated function that supports the business, not as an independent function set up for its own existence and survival. The sales function supports the business and not vice versa.

PURPOSE OF THE SALES FUNCTION

> *MANAGEMENT EXPECTATIONS DICTATE SALES*
> *EXPECTATIONS.*

The starting point for any organization is to decide why it is in business. As noted in the introduction, all businesses exist to make money and to survive—in the right way—through quality customer service and expeditious cash conversion. If a company desires to stay in business for the long term (i.e., to survive), it must expand its long-term thinking and recognize its customers (and noncustomers) as an integral part of its life cycle. It can no longer use its customers as a dumping ground for excess inventory, a source of quick orders, a place for salespeople to visit, and so on. Customer requirements and the company's ability to please those customers keep it in business. The sales function is the conduit between the company and its customers. True customer service is heavily driven by the sales function.

Top management may define its expectations for the sales function regarding customer services and making the right sales to the right customers as follows:

- Make sales to customers that can be collected profitably.
- Develop realistic sales forecasts that result in a present or future real customer order.
- Sell those products as determined by management to the right customers, at the right time, in the right quantities.
- Sell products that add cash flow to the company along with profits.
- Correlate actual customer sales directly with management's long- and short-term plans.
- Ensure that sales efforts, and corresponding compensation systems, reinforce the goals of the company.
- Integrate customer sales with other functions of the company, such as manufacturing, engineering, accounting, purchasing, and so on.

Also mentioned previously is that a company should not be in the following businesses:

- Sales business
- Customer order backlog business
- Accounts receivable business
- Inventory business
- Property, plant and equipment business
- Employment business
- Management and administration business

In many organizations, the sales function is treated differently from other functions of the company. For instance, it may have a different compensation program (salary plus commissions), various incentives (trips, cars, meals, vacations, exotic locations for conferences), flexible hours (both in and out of the office), more liberal expense accounts (customer meals, sporting events, company car), and so forth. In these circumstances, the sales employees may see themselves as being in business for themselves. That is, their business is to generate sales, and the company's business is to provide the goods or services and the other necessary support (including the cash to carry out their activities).

There may be limited coordination between the sales function and the company, and often the sales function and the company end up working at cross-purposes to each other. The results are unacceptable customer order backlogs, products that cannot be shipped (and billed) on time, accounts receivable that are collectible too slowly or not at all, inventory on hand that is not being sold, facilities and personnel that are not being used efficiently and effectively, and ineffective management. The sales function ends up being in businesses it should not be in—and customer service, cash conversion, and making money suffer.

In effect, although sales (and possibly net income) may be up, the company cannot pay its bills. The sales function must then be brought back onto the same path the company is taking (assuming the company knows where it is going). The beginning point is always, "What goods or services we should provide, and to whom (i.e., what its markets should be)?". The sales function should provide significant input to this process, as they are the ones who most typically deal directly with the customers.

The purpose of the sales function is to service, not just to sell, the customer—that is, to keep the customer in business so that the company stays in business. The goal should be to provide the highest quality goods and services to customers at the lowest possible price, while still achieving an adequate return and cash flow for the company. If this can be done successfully, both the company and its customers will grow and prosper. If the sales function can also become an integral and unique part of its customers' businesses, it will enlarge its sales to these customers as well as minimize the effect of competitors. The sales function, then, is the communication link between the company and its customer base.

SERVICE, DON'T JUST SELL THE CUSTOMER.

The purpose of the sales function, therefore, is not just to make sales (and increase the numbers month after month), but to make the right sales to the right customers at the right time. To do this, the sales function staff must be more fully integrated into the overall company planning system. They need to know the direction the company wishes to follow and then direct their sales efforts along the same path.

Organizational Planning Systems

Earlier, we suggested that organizational planning systems be developed as a collaborative effort between top management and all the operating functions of the organization. This was an attempt to get all the various functions of the company working toward the same goals and objectives. The initial concern was to develop more sophisticated procedures to plan and control the company's direction, both in the long- and the short-term. The major goals of an integrated sales planning system are shown in Exhibit 4.1.

1. Deliver High Quality Products
   - Exceed customer expectations = customer satisfaction
   - Bring quality product to market faster
   - Improve quality on an ongoing basis
   - Program of continuous improvement
     - Quality improves
     - Costs go down
     - Profits go up
     - Products reach market more quickly

2. Reduce Costs
   - Direct (material and labor) and indirect
   - Inventory and carrying/time costs
   - Improve cash flow
   - Reduce defects/rework/scrap
   - Reduce quality control
   - Reduce wasted time (meetings, phone, etc.)
   - Reduce materials costs
     - Better prices
     - Less costly alternatives
     - Less rework/scrap
     - Less material issued
   - Reduce labor costs
     - Setups: fewer and more efficient
     - Improved productivity
     - Flexible us of personnel
     - Motivate self-disciplined behavior

3. Bring Products to Market Faster
   - Recoup investment in shorter period
   - Product life decreasing
   - Profitable sooner: to fund next new product
   - Time to produce/sell volume to achieve break-even revenue

4. Make Changes Faster and More Manageably
   - Competitive edge = best at managing change
   - Customers = faster turnaround time
   - How fast is change to meet customers' needs
   - Change cannot be controlled but can be managed

Exhibit 4.1 Major Goals of an Integrated Sales Planning System

As planning needs were defined, it became apparent that all functions had to work together, including the sales function. To develop an effective organizational plan, various factors must be considered, such as:

- The organizational business plan and related budget, the starting point for organizational planning
- The nature of the business, type of manufacturing/service provided, relations with vendors and customers, operating processes, products or services to be produced, and so on
- What businesses the company should be in, what products or services it should be selling, to whom, and to what extent
- What businesses the company should not be in and a full understanding of why these businesses should be avoided
- The control and feedback features required to manage and control operations (including sales) so as to meet commitments
- Reporting requirements that enable the organization to operate in the most economical, efficient, and effective manner

Planning and Budget System

The master planning and budget steps for an organization are shown in Exhibit 4.2.

As can be seen, the starting point in the process is the sales and market forecast (both short-term and long-term forecasts). This is the definition of what goods and services the company expects to sell and to whom. However, because the effectiveness of the organizational plan is dependent on the accuracy of such a market or sales forecast, many companies experience planning problems before going any further, a result of their having sales forecasts that are more fiction than reality. So for most companies the first step in effective planning is to work toward more accurate sales forecasts on which to base their plans. A good rule of thumb is that an effective sales forecast should consist of at least 80 percent real customer orders. This means that the sales function may have to do what they may not have done in years—communicate with and service the customer.

> ## THE SALES FORECAST DRIVES
> ## THE PROFIT AND CASH BUDGETS.

The organization, together with the sales function, must determine what products or services (or product lines) it wishes to sell in the coming period. This decision is made by analyzing past sales, customer (and noncustomer) needs and desires, inventory levels, production/service delivery capabilities, futuristic considerations, competitive factors, and so on.

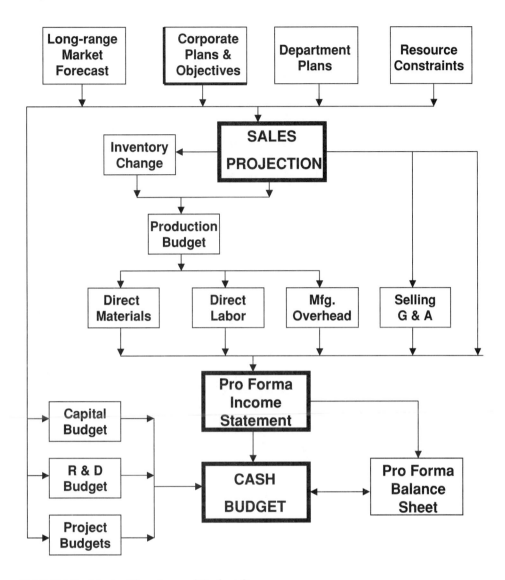

Exhibit 4.2   Master Planning and Budget Steps

An example of such a product analysis is shown below in Exhibit 4.3. Based on the analysis of these three products (or product lines), the company has to determine what it wants to do with these products in the future.

For instance, product A is a low cost/low selling price item with low profit margins. The company may question whether it wants to stay in this business for competitive reasons—in other words, making a low-cost alternative available for those customers for whom price is a strong consideration—or to get out of this part of the business. It is not only realizing an unacceptable level of return, but is also tying up resources (facilities and personnel, including sales, and cash) that could

Product	Selling Price	Cost	Gross Profit	% G.P. of Sales	Unit Sales Forecast	Actual Unit Sales	Actual Sales $$	% of Total Sales $$	Total Gross Profit	G.P. % of Total G.P.
A	$18.00	$15.00	$3.00	16.70%	800	540	$ 9,720	2.20%	$ 1,620	0.92%
B	$32.00	$20.00	$12.00	37.50%	12,000	9,800	$313,600	70.20%	$117,600	66.66%
C	$56.00	$30.00	$26.00	46.40%	3,600	2,200	$123,200	27.60%	$ 57,200	32.42%
TOTALS					16,400	12,540	$446,520	100.00%	$176,420	100.00%

Exhibit 4.3 Product Analysis

be used more effectively with other products. And while the specific information is not included in the exhibit, it is likely that any cash flow generation is small.

Product B is the company's bread and butter; it sells these items repetitively at a more than acceptable profit level (37.5 percent) with a high probability that cash flow is favorable. Product B might well be a cash cow, since sales of these items account for more than 70 percent of its total business and 67 percent of its gross profits. These are the items the business is geared for and for which the sales function can easily obtain customer commitments. This is the part of the company's sales forecast that must be accurate. With modest effort by sales personnel this can be achieved, if only they talk to the customers.

Product C is the high-price, top-of-the-line model for those customers who are willing to pay more for a luxurious look or additional options—often a status, rather than price, consideration. Although the company sells fewer items of product C than product B, its profits (and usually sales commissions) are greater. Accordingly, there is likely a tendency for sales personnel to spend more time selling Cs than Bs, which may be counter to the company's plans to sell more Bs. Typically, the company does not know what the real costs (and added costs) are for such top-of-the-line items, and what internal strife this causes in producing and delivering its standard B items. Sales needs to consider the company's plans for Product C—increase this business, deemphasize the business, or maintain it approximately where it is at present.

Whatever they decide, company management must direct the sales function so that its efforts are expended where desired. The cash flow generated (or lost) by each of the products should be included as part of the decision making.

Sales Forecasts

> ## THE SALES FORECAST SHOULD REPRESENT REAL CUSTOMER ORDERS.

The sales forecast is one of the primary inputs into the company planning process. Not only is it necessary to know what was sold in the past and to whom and at what price, profit margin, and cash contribution, but also to know what the company is going to sell in the future. It is this future sales forecast that the company will use to develop its profit plan, as depicted in the "Master Planning and Budget Steps" (Exhibit 4.2). This becomes the sales budget on which it plans its production budget of goods and services (taking into account what already exists in inventory) and with accurate and realistic costs, its profit plan and cash budget. The greater the number of real customer orders in the sales budget, the more accurate the profit plan will be. With inaccuracies and guesstimates based on prior year's inaccurate sales forecasts in the current sales forecast, the company will produce more for inventory than for customers, which will in turn result in failure to meet

Product	Units Forecast	Actual Unit Sales	Difference	% of Forecast
A	800	540	260	32.5%
B	12,000	9,800	2,200	18.3%
C	3,600	2,200	1,400	38.8%

Exhibit 4.4   Sales Forecast to Actual Sales

its profit plan and in an unfavorable cash position. Sales unit forecast figures compared to actual unit sales for products A, B, and C are shown in Exhibit 4.4.

Analysis of this exhibit shows that the sales forecast is way out of line for all three products, but is closest for Product B. With such a forecast discrepancy, it is difficult for the company to plan effectively. It is apparent that the company must have more realistic sales forecasts in order to plan their operations and expected results. This usually means that the sales staff must get closer to their customers. The company must be able to establish realistic sales goals for each product (or product line) in order to direct the sales function and plan their internal operations. In addition, although maintaining sales statistics by product and customer is important, the company must learn how to analyze and interpret what these numbers really mean. For instance, it must identify the customers to whom it is selling products A, B, and C, and determine how these customers are purchasing—that is, strictly by ordering on their own, through the company's direct sales effort, from its catalog or other means. In effect, the company must define the relationship of past sales to future forecasts: Will they increase, stay about the same, or decrease, and to what extent? It is only through the sales function that the company can determine this needed information.

As previously mentioned, organizations need to move toward more realistic sales forecasts in which the largest proportion possible (i.e., 80 percent or more) is made up of real customer orders. In this manner, realistic sales, production, cost, pricing, profit, and cash flow plans can be developed. It is the sales function that a company depends on to make the plan happen.

Summary of Management and Sales Responsibilities

In developing an accurate sales plan/forecast for a company, one must be aware of the responsibilities of both management and the sales function. Generally, top management is responsible for defining the direction for the company—what businesses it is in, what products to sell, whom to sell to, and so on. The sales function is then responsible for putting top management's plan into action by developing realistic sales forecasts and producing desired results. The main responsibilities for management and the sales function are:

- *Management*
  - Top-level commitment: the plan is sacrosanct

- Delegation of authority and responsibility over the sales function: provide the direction, then move out of the way
- Effective and realistic business and sales planning, including cash flow considerations
- Decision making: what to sell, to whom, and how much

- *Sales*
  - Realistic sales forecasting (related to real customer orders)
  - Customer service orientation
  - Customer involvement and problem solving
  - Sales efforts consistent with business plan
  - Effective customer and sales analysis and follow-up

> ## *MAKE THE RIGHT SALE TO THE RIGHT CUSTOMER AT THE RIGHT TIME.*

Pricing Strategies

What to sell, how much, and to whom are important planning decisions. Equally (if not more) important is the pricing strategy or decision—that is, what price is to be asked for each item and what pricing flexibility can be tolerated to still cover costs and contribute to profits and cash flow. Effective pricing strategies, working in conjunction with the sales function, should enable a company to meet its sales and profit plans. There are various methods or strategies for developing a pricing structure, which include the following:

- *Percentage markup.* Using a desired percentage of costs (e.g., 40 percent), usually thought of as a gross profit markup to calculate the selling price. For instance, an item with a calculated cost of $100, and a 40 percent markup, would have a selling price of $140. Although this method is a quick way to calculate selling prices and maintain consistent profit margins, it has the built-in disadvantage of penalizing customers for the company's cost inefficiencies. For example, if the cost of the same $100 item increased to $150, the new selling price would be $210 (a markup of $60— 40 percent × $150). The customer is now expected to reimburse the company for its cost inefficiencies and pay an additional 40 percent markup on those additional costs. In many cases, such pricing policies can put the company in a difficult competitive position, require the sales function to work harder for each sale, and possibly result in lost customers.
- *Dollars per item.* Using a consistent dollar markup per item over costs. In the above example, if the company desires to earn $30 per item, the selling price at $100 cost would be $130; and at $150 cost, it would be $180;

and at $80 cost, a $110 selling price. This process tends to stabilize profit margins, rewards customers for the company's cost efficiencies (without penalizing them extra for the cost inefficiencies), and clearly identifies the dollar amount of gross profit per item. However, if costs increase legitimately, and the markup is not adjusted, the company's profit margins and cash flow will deteriorate.

- *Market pricing.* Using the marketplace as the starting point for setting prices. For example, if the standard price for the company's goods or services is $200 in the marketplace, this becomes its basis for pricing. Theoretically, if a company lowers its prices from the market price, its sales should increase; and raising prices should decrease sales. This approach typically stresses sales and may tend to disregard setting selling prices to recover costs and contribute to profits and cash flow.

- *Competitive pricing.* Setting prices to beat competitors, regardless of whether the additional business is profitable or desirable. Companies, sometimes get caught up in the "beat the competition" game, losing sight of some of their real reasons for being in business (making money and surviving). If a company finds itself in a competitive selling position—either in total or in part of its business—many times the best approach is to provide the highest quality product at the least possible cost. This should allow the company to stay competitive, serve its customers, make money, and generate the cash required to continue to grow and prosper.

- *Unique niche.* Having a product or service that is unique or different from others being offered by your competitors—for example, a unique process (automatic camera), unique features (higher speeds), specialized uses (fax and copier), and so on. If a company can develop such a unique niche, it usually provides a marketing and sales advantage, particularly where there is a high customer demand. A company can decide to take full advantage of its advantages by setting higher selling prices and possibly maximizing its return in the short term. However, such a policy (with high profit margins and cash flow) usually results in other competitors entering the field and possibly driving prices below acceptable levels (or the company out of the business—e.g., the microcomputer business). A better approach may be to increase the barriers to entry by continually controlling costs and keeping prices as low as possible and quality as high as possible. This approach may not maximize short-term profits, but it should maximize returns in the longer term and tend to discourage competitors from entering the field (e.g., Wal-Mart).

- *Quality strategy.* Establishing an image in the marketplace for quality of product and/or service (e.g., Ritz-Carlton, Hertz, Toyota, Maytag, etc.). Typically, customers will be willing to pay more for such perceived quality, and this can provide a competitive advantage. However, it may cost the company considerably to establish and maintain the quality image— and it must continuously deliver such quality. If quality suffers appreciably, the downward sales cycle may develop faster than the original upward sales flow.

- *Price-sensitive strategy.* Competing based on being able to sell at the lowest price (e.g., Dollar Stores, Bic pens, Hyundai, Amazon.com, etc.). Using this approach to set selling prices requires a company to be closely in touch with its costs, profit margins, and break-even points as well as its cash flow. Should it have to raise prices (and customer service, or the lack thereof, remains at the same low level), the resultant loss of sales may grossly exceed the safety level of the company's existing volumes.

There may be pricing strategies other than those described that a company wishes to use. The important factor to consider is that the pricing strategy fits into the company's business and sales plan and allows it the flexibility to ensure success. Typically, this means using a combination of the aforementioned techniques, either in total or by individual product line or item. What is most important is that the company develop effective pricing strategies that enable the sales function to service its customers and maximize the amount of profitable sales. While considering customer and market concerns, do not lose sight of cash flow issues. These often tend to be overlooked in the quest for profitability, market share, and competitive advantage. Without full consideration of the cash flow prospects, the other successes may become Pyrrhic victories.

> ### *PRICING STRATEGIES SHOULD SERVICE CUSTOMERS AND MAXIMIZE CASH FLOW.*

Product Analysis

The company should be analyzing its product items (or services) and related product lines on a periodic basis to determine such things as:

- Relationship to sales forecast and company plans
- Products/product lines doing better or worse than expected
- Product contribution to profits
- Product contribution to cash flow
- Customer sales statistics
- Unforeseen occurrences: lost sales, unexpected sales, returns, inability to deliver, large backlogs, and so on
- Effects of competition
- Necessary or requested product changes
- Relationships to inventory levels

There should be an expectation that such product analysis exists. However, should very little or no such analysis exist, not only would this be a cash management deficiency, but also such sales statistics would have to be developed in order to evaluate sales function performance. Typically, the 80/20 rule (Pareto's Law) applies; that is, 80 percent (or more) of the company's sales come from 20 percent (or less) of its customers; and 80 percent of its profits come from 20 percent of its products. These customers and products should be identified and evaluated with regard to their effect on sales and company operations.

Based on this analysis, the company might ask:

- On which customers and products does the sales force spend most of its time?
- Is adequate consideration being given to whether the prime customers pay their bills on time?
- Is sufficient emphasis being placed on selling those products that contribute adequately to company cash flow?
- What is the sales emphasis, on the top 20 percent or on the other 80 percent?
- Is the focus on existing top customers, other customers, or potential new customers?
- Is there any emphasis on finding new uses for the top 20 percent of customers and products?
- Are sales personnel aware of customer and product statistics, and do they actively alter their sales plans based on such statistics?
- Is sales emphasis on dollar sales resulting in sales commissions rather than on company goals and profitability?
- Does sales staff communicate problems with products regardless of the products' salability (high sellers as well as low sellers)?
- What is being done about the 80 percent or so of customers and products that produce only 20 percent of sales and profits? Are there any sales efforts to increase sales of those products and to those customers?
- Are there new products that need increased sales efforts or older products in decline that should be considered for elimination or phasing out?
- Does sales staff provide adequate customer service to all customers—top, middle, bottom, and potential? What is the extent of customer service for the top 20 percent, others, and new customers?
- Are opportunities such as product enhancement, new products, changes in use, decline in demand, and so on recognized?

Methods of Sales

There are a number of different ways of selling products and providing related customer service, among which are:

- Direct sales to the ultimate customer
- Selling to original equipment manufacturers (OEMs)

- Selling to distributors
- Industrial sales for additional manufacturing
- Wholesale sales
- Retail sales
- Broker sales
- Manufacturing sales representatives
- Point-of-sale selling
- Goodwill sales
- Combination of these approaches

The company must understand the different types of sales and desirable practices for each. The company may question whether it is using the right sales technique for each product or product line and the related effectiveness.

Methods of Compensation

> ### SALES COMPENSATION SYSTEMS SHOULD PRODUCE SALES THE COMPANY WANTS.

The sales staff tends to be compensated differently from the rest of the company – typically, to some extent with commissions based on sales made. This often places the sales staff emphasis on selling those products that maximize their commissions rather than on those products and customers that maximize the company's goals. Sales compensation policies must coordinate with the agreed-on direction of the company. Sales commissions must also relate to profitability and collectibility. Many companies have instituted commission payments based on profitability and delay commission payment until the cash has been received. This can have a significant impact on company cash flow. If the sales staff gets their commissions only when the invoices have been collected, it creates a strong incentive for the salespersons affected to be sure that (1) the invoices are paid on a timely basis, and (2) the sales are made to customers who are likely to pay. Having the sales force as an entire additional collection department is likely to improve cash flow significantly.

The method of compensation must also encourage the proper level of customer service, necessary to increase sales from existing major and minor customers, potential new customers, and noncustomers. In addition, the sales force must be available to service the customer after the sale—and after the sales commission has been earned. Many times, a salesperson will do what has to be done to make the sale and earn a commission but considers other areas of customer service nonproductive. Many sales personnel have burned out to some extent and would rather wait for the sales orders to come in and earn the easy commissions than do the full customer service and sales job they were hired to do. The company must provide proper supervision and direction and institute accountability (and related reporting systems) to ensure that the sales function is performing effectively in accordance with company direction so that sales performance coordinates with:

- *Company plans.* By customer and product line
- *Sales forecasts.* With a high percentage of real customer orders (80 percent or higher)
- *Customer service requirements.* Before and after the sale
- *Cash conversion requirements.* Selling to customers with timely payment records
- *Other functions.* For example, manufacturing, engineering, shipping, customer relations, accounting, product service, and so on
- *Product profitability.* Selling the right product for the company, not to maximize commissions
- *Product cash flow.* Selling products that generate positive cash flow for the company on sales made
- *Customer satisfaction.* Selling what the customer needs
- *Sales timing.* Selling for the long term, not for short-term sales commissions or sales incentives
- *Internal ability to produce, deliver on time, and service the customer.* During and after the sale
- *Inventory levels.* Items to be sold from inventory, items to be made upon receipt of the order, items to be discouraged

There are numerous methods for compensating sales personnel other than on a strict commission basis. The company must evaluate the method of sales compensation on the basis of whether it results in moving the company toward its goals or tends simply to enrich the sales staff (often to the detriment of the company).

The method of compensation must motivate the sales force to effectively sell so that the company's, the customers', and the sales personnel's needs are all met. It must support the coordination of all of these factors and encourage the salespeople to work together with the organization and its plans.

Other compensation methods include:

- Salary plus commission (over a specified level)
- Salary based on results (sales level plus customer service)
- Customer calls or contacts
- Variable commission (based on customers and/or products sold)
- Collections (payment based on sales collected)
- Profitability (payment based on sales profit)
- Customer base or territory
- Group compensation based on defined results
- Salary plus profit sharing
- Salary only

Sales Information and Reporting Systems

SALES MUST INTEGRATE WITH OPERATIONS.

The company must understand what the elements of a desirable sales information and reporting system should include. An effective sales information system must provide for integration with the operating components of the company such as manufacturing and production control, engineering, accounting, inventory control, quality control, shipping, credit and collections, and so on. The information system must provide sales personnel with the information they need to properly service the customer and work cooperatively with the other operating areas of the company. In essence, a well-designed information system allows the sales function to provide an effective communications link between the customer and the company. A desirable sales information and reporting system should include the following elements:

- Realistic sales forecasts that integrate with organizational business and sales plans
- Reporting of sales forecast versus actual sales by product line or item and by customer, with a mechanism for revisions to the sales forecast
- Sales statistics showing items ordered, sold, delivered, and collected
- Customer statistics showing items ordered, comparison to prior sales, amount of sales, new items, and so on
- Profitability analysis by product and by customer, indicating plus and minus variances
- Cash flow analysis by product and by customer showing cash contribution by product and by customer
- Sales staff statistics showing sales by individual, profitability by product and customer, customer sales and projections, orders in process, and so on
- Relationship of sales to other company factors such as backlog, inventory levels, production availability, engineering requirements, other customer requirements, and so forth
- Product line analysis that relates sales to company goals and direction, cost–volume–profit (C-V-P) and breakeven analysis, expected profit goals, cash contribution, comparison and trend analysis, and so on

Performing the Sales Function Analysis

A number of initial questions must be answered prior to the start of an analysis of the sales function. These include:

- *Type of business.* Manufacturing, service, distributor, wholesaler, retailer, and so on.

- *Type of process.* Make to order, sell from inventory, direct sales, broker sales, and so on
- *Type of sales.* Direct sales, OEM sales, engineering sales, point of sales, goodwill sales, and the like
- *Type of sales organization.* Company sales force, broker, distributive, manufacturers' representatives, combination, and so on
- *Sales office locations.* Headquarters, remote sales offices, selling from home, individual offices, and so on
- *Organizational hierarchy.* Sales manager, sales supervisors, number of sales personnel and support staff, and so on
- *Information systems.* Sales forecasts, planning systems, sales and customer statistics, product line and item profitability, and the like
- *Method of compensation.* Commission, salary and commission, salary only, salary and bonuses, team compensation (based on sales made or invoices collected), and the like
- *Systems and procedures.* How the sales function operates and how it is integrated with the rest of the company
- *Purpose of the sales function.* Sell what they can, customer service orientation, communication link between the company and the customer, goodwill representation, and so on

In effect, it is incumbent on the analysis team to find out as much as possible about the sales function to be analyzed. If appropriate, the analysis team should consider an analysis of the company's planning procedures. This enables the team to gain a complete understanding of the company's sales function as well as determine the most critical areas affecting contributions to positive cash flow. A list of sales function desirable operating practices and efficiencies is shown in Exhibit 4.5.

A sample initial survey form for the sales function is shown in Exhibit 4.6. This type of survey form is a good tool to use to provide a quick synopsis of the sales function in the determination of the critical areas affecting positive cash flow. The completion of the initial survey form can be done exclusively by sales management and personnel, by the analysis team, or in combination. It is often a good practice to have the operations personnel themselves provide such data, as this gives the analysis team direct feedback on their perceptions about how things work, as well as identifying patterns among such perceptions. The analysis team can, if appropriate, test selected (or all) user-provided responses to ascertain the validity of the answers provided.

Should the analysis team desire to perform further analysis work as to sales department functions and how they affect company goals and positive cash flow, they may wish to use an analysis work program. A sample sales function analysis work program is shown in Exhibit 4.7. Note that the analysis work program is developed for those critical areas identified in the initial analysis. In this example, based on mutual agreement with company and sales function

1. A sophisticated sales forecast system that correlates closely with actual customer orders
2. Sales forecast procedures that allow for integration with production scheduling techniques
3. Sales forecasts and plans that are directed toward selling the desired product lines and that allow for monitoring actual versus planned results
4. Sales statistics and reporting systems that accurately detail what has happened so that remedial action can be taken
5. Effective sales management that properly directs and controls the sales force
6. Sales compensation and commission policies that integrate with sales planning and assist in achieving the desired results
7. Sales systems that accurately compute sales commissions and ensure that sales personnel are paid at the right time
8. Sales statistics by product line, individual product, and customer that enable sales management to make the correct decisions and take appropriate actions
9. Sales management procedures that provide for direct supervision of sales staff, including proper training, orientation and review
10. Customer relations policies that are exemplified by direct customer orders, nondependence on specific sales personnel, product loyalty, and customer satisfaction
11. An ongoing customer base that consistently purchases an expected level of product and can be counted on
12. Information system that provides the ability to relate sales efforts and related costs to sales levels achieved
13. Maintenance of selling costs as an expected percentage of total sales.
14. Selling and promotional techniques that can be directly related to the success of the sales effort
15. Customer information system that provides data relative to the sales effort, product quality, timeliness of deliveries, product changes, desired services, after-sales service, and so on

Exhibit 4.5   The Sales Function: Desirable Operating Practices and Efficiencies

management, it was decided to further analyze the following sales function responsibilities:

- Sales function authority
- Sales forecast and planning systems
- Sales function operations
- Sales information systems

Planning:
1. Is there an organizational planning document? If so, obtain copy.
2. Does the planning document include
    –Mission/vision statement?
    –Organizational goals and objectives?
    –Departmental goals and objectives?
    –Departmental detail plans?
    –Budgets relating to plans?
3. Does the sales function planning include
    –Goals and objectives?
    –Detailed plans?
    –Budgets relating to plans?
    –Sales forecasts?
4. Does the sales forecast include
    –Comparison to prior years?
    –Customer sales statistics and trends?
    –Real customer orders? To what extent?
    –Product line analysis?
    –Coordination with organizational plans?
    –Detailed backup to all numbers and calculations?
5. Does the sales function have a system for monitoring its performance against the plan? Describe. Obtain a copy of monitoring documents.
6. Are the sales function's goals and objectives consistent with the organization's goals and objectives? Was the sales function part of the planning process?

Information Systems:
1. Is the sales function (management and staff) provided sufficient information to adequately operate and control their areas? Describe and obtain copies of information system elements.
2. Do members of the sales function believe they need information in addition to what they now receive to be more effective? Describe and document.
3. Is the information being provided accurate, relevant, up-to-date, and usable? Document exceptions.
4. Do sales function personnel receive (or have access to) departmental and organizational financial information necessary to effectively service their customers? Describe and document.
5. Has the sales function identified the information they believe they need to effectively operate their function? Document. Is there any of this information that is not being provided?
6. Is information being received in a timely manner so that sales personnel can take corrective action, particularly as it related to customer requirements?
7. Are there adequate sales and customer statistics reporting to enable the sales function to focus on and target individual product items and cus-

Exhibit 4.6   Sales Function: Initial Survey Form

tomers as part of the overall company sales plan? Obtain copies of reports.

7. Are there any elements of an adequate sales reporting system that are not present, such as product and customer profitability, product line analysis, operating data and ratios, and so on? Document pieces of the reporting that appear to be missing.

Organizational Issues:

1. Does the sales function have documented policies and procedures? Are they current, accurate and being used? Obtain copies.
2. Is authority and responsibility delegated to the levels of responsibility within the sales function (for example, customer relations and service)? Describe the process.
3. Is there a system of working together rather than counter competition (cooperation versus competition) so that the entire sales function is moving in the same direction? Describe.
4. Is there a coordinated system of prioritization? Does it coordinate with the company's goals? Describe.
5. Is there a system for identifying opportunities and threats? Is it related to setting priorities and determining the degree of criticality? Describe.
6. Are objective data provided from an adequate information system that are used to make decisions? Describe.

Organization and Personnel:

1. Does an organizational chart for the sales function exist? Obtain or prepare copy.
2. Does the organization chart show
   −Clear lines of authority and responsibility?
   −Balance between sales management and staff?
   −Functional job responsibilities?
   −Clear reporting relationships: functional, customers, and products?
3. Is there an open atmosphere within the department where staff are free to have open and frank discussions? Describe.
4. Are there effective systems for
   −Hiring?
   −Training?
   −Evaluations?
   −Promotions?
   −Firings?
5. Describe and obtain any documentation.
6. Does sales management appear to be concerned about developing sales staff employees. Describe.
7. Are sales employees being cross-trained, particularly for critical functions and/or customers? Describe.
8. Is there a method of ongoing evaluation and effective action for good and bad performance? Describe.
9. Is there a fair compensation plan? Describe.

Exhibit 4.6 Sales Function: Initial Survey Form (continued)

10. Is there a system that stimulates individual and group innovations? Describe.
11. Is the sales function understaffed or overstaffed? Explain and document.

Internal Operations:
1. Are internal operations evaluated on a cost versus benefit basis? Describe the system of evaluation.
2. Do key sales personnel understand the direction the company and the sales department are heading? Describe the direction and how the sales department is integrated.
3. Does the sales department understand their role in the organization? Describe their role as they see it.
4. Does the sales department understand how their results relate to the goals of the company? Describe their understanding.
5. Is the sales department accomplishing expected results? Describe the responding system. If not, explain why not.
6. Does the sales department have the authority to independently operate its function? Document those areas where authority seems to be inadequate?
7. Is there a periodic review of operations directed toward a program of positive change? Describe.
8. Is the assignment of sales territories or customers effective in meeting goals of sales and customer service? Describe and document sales assignments and indicate effectiveness or not.
9. Are sales assignments adequately balanced so as to foster cooperative efforts from the sales force? Describe.
10. Are sales office(s) efficiently operated to enhance the sales function and promote customer service? Obtain a list of sales office locations and describe general procedures.

Sales Analysis:
1. Does the method of compensation support progress toward company and sales function goals? Describe the method of sales compensation and comment as to its effectiveness.
2. Is a product line (or product item) analysis performed so that the company can make effective decisions as to sales, pricing, inventory levels, customers, collections, and so on? Describe and comment on the system's effectiveness.
3. Are the sales promotion, customer service, advertising, and marketing efforts integrated with company plans? Describe.
4. What are the criteria for adding a product, changing a product's sales efforts, or dropping a product? Describe.
5. Is there a periodic review of all products and product lines as to future direction? Describe the system.
6. Is the sales function organized to stay current as to new developments related to such things as competitors, customers, processes, product changes, problem areas, etc.? If so, what were the conclusions? Describe.

Exhibit 4.6   Sales Function: Initial Survey Form (continued)

1. SALES FUNCTION AUTHORITY
   A. Organizational Status of Sales Function
      1. Secure or prepare an organizational chart of the sales department with descriptions of each work unit's and/or sales person's specific functions.
      2. Determine to whom the head (i.e. Vice President of Sales or Sales Manager) of the sales function reports. Analyze the situation and determine whether such reporting is proper or whether it results in operational concerns and problems. The sales function should operate independently but be integrated and coordinated with other company functions. Analyze each work unit's and individual's functions to determine whether they are appropriate and necessary sales department functions.
      3. Document the duties and responsibilities of each sales department employee. Obtain copies of existing job descriptions and validate through interviewing each employee and related supervisor.
      4. Observe actual work being performed for each employee. If a large number of personnel, select a reasonable number. For all employees., have each one maintain a time ladder (in 15-minute increments) showing how they spend their time for a two-week period. Determine the necessity of each activity performed based on observations and review of time ladders.
   B. Sales Function Responsibility
      1. Obtain or prepare company policy and procedures on sales functions and activities. Determine that the responsibilities of the sales function are clearly defined and understood by sales department personnel and other within the organization.
      2. Ascertain through interviews whether the sales staff has knowledge of conflicting sales responsibilities assumed by top management or others.
      3. Document any conflicting responsibilities or sales function performed by others that should be sales department responsibilities.
      4. Obtain or prepare policy relative to other departments' or individuals' relations with customers as to contacts, discussions, and/or correspondence.
      5. Review above activities of others to determine the extent of such customer relations. Select a number of "major" customers to survey (telephone, written response, and field visit) as to their relations with these other areas. Determine whether any conflicts exist.
   C. Sales Authorization
      1. Obtain copy or document policies as to
         • Management approval of sales forecast/plans.
         • Approval of customer sales.

Exhibit 4.7   Sample Sales Function Analysis Work Program

- Approval limits as to amount, what items, and how much to sell to each customer.
- Sales personnel itineraries.
- Sales department and location budgets.
2. Analyze procedures through the review of selected sales transactions looking for incidents of
  - Improper or unapproved sales.
  - Sales to customers exceeding their credit limits.
  - Sales of items not in the sales forecast or company planning system.
  - Sales to new customers.
  - Sales to existing customers greatly exceeding past purchases.
  - Sales placed in backlog, shipped directly from inventory, or made to order.
3. Observe, review, and analyze sales function operations at a selected number of sales office locations, including sales personnel working in the field on their own. Determine whether there are any redundant, duplicate, inappropriate, or inconsistent (with company and sales plans) activities being performed and document same.

2. SALES FORECAST AND PLANNING SYSTEMS
  A. Sales Forecast Procedures
    1. Document the manner in which the sales forecast is developed. Determine whether the following practices are followed:
      - Sales forecast is developed in conjunction with other functions such as top management, manufacturing, engineering, accounting, and so on.
      - Sales forecast is prepared based on company plans as to items to be sold, how much, and to whom.
      - Sales forecast is based on sound principles of Cost-Volume-Price (C-V-P) and break-even analysis.
      - Sales forecast is prepared with direct customer input and concerns.
      - Sales forecast contains a large percentage of real customer orders (i.e. 80% or greater).
      - Sales forecast is realistic in relation to past sales by product item and customer.
      - Sales forecast process includes plans for making present non-customers into customers.
      - Sales forecast is supported by realistic detailed plans as to how the forecast is to be met.
      - A mechanism exists for review and replanning.
      - The sales forecast is developed jointly within the company and is not prepared and approved solely by the sales function.
    2. Is there a system in place for ongoing review of actual sales to forecast and related replanning procedures? Obtain copies of any

Exhibit 4.7   Sample Sales Function Analysis Work Program (continued)

related reports and document such procedures. Determine the effectiveness of such procedures and any recommendations for improvement.
- B. Sales Planning
  1. Document the organization's planning system and the integration of the sales forecast. Obtain copies of the most recent plan.
  2. Obtain copies of any reports that show sales plans versus actual results. Determine their accuracy and use for replanning. Analyze their effectiveness and whether anything is missing that should be present.
  3. Review sales department operations and determine whether sales planning is used on an ongoing basis or is strictly a periodic (usually once a year) planning exercise that goes unused at times throughout the year.
  4. Determine whether all members of the sales staff are part of the planning process, and whether the process itself includes effective customer input.

3. SALES FUNCTION OPERATIONS
- A. Sales Department Procedures
  1. Obtain or prepare a copy of the sales department operating procedures.
  2. Prepare flowcharts of the major sales department operations, such as customer requests, customer orders, processing of sales orders, customer coordination relative to open sales orders, after sales service, and so on.
  3. Review procedures relating to responding to customer for bids – successful responses, unsuccessful responses, and non-responses.
- B. Sales Department Forms
  1. Obtain a copy of each specialized form used by the sales department. Review and analyze each form so that the purpose and usage is thoroughly understood.
  2. Obtain a copy of all internally produced reporting forms such as customer contacts, requests, and complaints. Determine their use and effectiveness.
  3. Determine whether there is too much form preparation and reporting and whether any additional forms or information should be present.
- C. Sales Locations
  1. Obtain a list of all sales office locations and/or sales personnel working on their own.
  2. Visit a selected number of sales locations and document the methods of operations – particularly with regard to their consistency with company and sales department goals.
  3. Prepare a layout flow diagram of selected sales locations show-

Exhibit 4.7 Sample Sales Function Analysis Work Program (continued)

ing their layout, work flow, facilities, and equipment, with particular attention to
- Work flow efficiencies and inefficiencies.
- Arrangements for customer visits.
- Degree of privacy (i.e. for talking to customers).
- Office layout for effective/ineffective operations.

 D. Customer Contacts

  1. Document the system for ongoing customer contacts in general and by each sales person. Determine the basis for when to contact a customer.

  2. Obtain copies of customer reporting that is used as a basis for customer contact (for example, not ordering, order in process, late delivery, customer complaint, item analysis (past sales), new customer contact, and so on).

  3. Observe a selected number of telephone conversations by sales personnel with present and potential customers and document script of conversation.

  4. Accompany sales personnel on a selected number of customer calls – with different sales personnel and different types of customers – and document the various methods of operations (both for successful and unsuccessful customer orders).

  5. Document incidents of customer service both related to specific customer orders and in general.

4. SALES INFORMATION SYSTEMS

 A. Elements of the Information System

  1. Obtain copies of all reports pertaining to the sales function within the company.

  2. Review and analyze the above reports and determine that the elements of a desirable sales information and reporting system are present, such as
- Realistic sales forecasts that integrate with organizational business and sales plans.
- Sales forecast versus actual sales reporting by product line or item and by customer, with a mechanism for revisions to the sales forecast.
- Sales statistics showing items ordered, sold, delivered, and collected.
- Customer statistics showing items ordered, comparison to prior sales, amount of sales, new items, and so on.
- Profitability analysis by product item and by customer indicating plus and minus variances.
- Sales staff statistics showing sales by individual, profitability by product and customer, customer sales and projections, orders in process, and so on.

Exhibit 4.7 Sample Sales Function Analysis Work Program (continued)

- Relationship of sales to other company factors such as backlog, inventory levels, production availability, engineering requirements, other customer requirements, etc.
- Product line analysis that relates sales to company goals and direction, C-V-P and break-even analysis, expected profit goals, comparison and trend analysis, and so on.

3. Based on desirable reporting elements, determine whether there are any reports or information that should be present but are not. Note: The examination and evaluation of records, reports, and sales information has two objectives:

   a. Verification of the accuracy of the information that is maintained or reported. This should be done on a test basis. For example, if a sales order is shown in backlog, its actual existence should be verified.

   b. Evaluation of the value to the sales department or individual sales person using or receiving the information. In this evaluation, the auditor should ascertain the answers to such questions as

      - Is information and/or report really used?
      - Does each report or data element serve a useful purpose?
      - Does each report give a complete and accurate picture?
      - Are reports incomplete, so that important factors are not brought to sales management and personnel attention?
      - Is there any additional information required that is not present?

B. Use of Reports

   1. Review the use of sales reports with selected sales personnel and determine whether they are used for the purpose for which they are intended. Document incidents of reports or information not used, information added to reports by hand, related information spread over two or more reports, information not present, and so on.

   2. Review the use of reports with sales management. Is information being provided of a summary nature that allows these individuals to manage effectively?

   3. Determine whether sales personnel reports and information are sufficient for adequate appraisal of sales personnel performance.

Exhibit 4.7   Sample Sales Function Analysis Work Program (continued)

CONCLUSION

The sales function must be considered as an integral part of the company's planning process. Top management must define for the company the businesses it is in, its basic business principles, and the products/services to be sold to what customers at what times. It is within this overall planning framework that the sales function develops its plans (or sales forecast) to integrate with top management's expectations. Such sales plans must incorporate the maximum level of real customer orders (e.g., 80 percent of total forecast), so that the company can exert its efforts on servicing these customers and turning the sales orders into deliveries and cash collections in the shortest time possible.

In addition, each customer and sales order must be looked at as a profit and cash flow center. That is, the total sales amount must be profitable, but also provide a contribution to positive cash flow. To accomplish this, the company must exercise adequate control over product, functional, and customer costs. Not only does each dollar of cost savings produce an additional dollar to the bottom line, but it also allows company management greater freedom in making pricing decisions. While the emphasis in most companies is on controlling product costs, functional costs (e.g., sales order processing, accounts receivable, and collections) and customer costs (e.g. customer service, installation, and after sale support) must also be considered in evaluating the efforts of the sales function. These cost considerations will be more fully covered in the next chapter.

Although in many situations sales prices may have to be set based on outside influences such as market pressures, competition, and customer acceptance, the company must strive for the greatest flexibility in price setting based on maximizing the differential between real assigned costs to selling price. Accordingly, the sales function must be analyzed as an integrated part of company operations. No longer can the sales function operate on its own (as if it were in business for itself) without clear direction from top management and integration with the other operating areas of the company. It is within this context that the sales function must be analyzed as part of customer service and cash conversion, and as an effective contributor to positive cash flow. It is no longer acceptable to make sales that cannot be produced, delivered, and/or collected in a timely fashion, that is, sales that may produce a sales commission but do not produce desired cash flow.

> *SALES ARE PLANNED, NOT FOUND.*

CHAPTER 5

Cost Reduction Analysis Procedures

As making sales to the right customers, of the right products, at the right price, at the right time—which can be collected timely—can be a major contributor to positive cash flow, effective cost reduction can be an even greater contributor. While increased sales may add net profit margin contributions to positive cash flow, cost reductions add dollar-for-dollar contributions to positive cash flow. Hence, there is more to be contributed to positive cash flow by reducing and eliminating unnecessary costs, and the company has greater control over making this happen.

While sometimes all that is needed to reduce company costs is good common business sense, there are other management and operational techniques that have been used effectively in the past or are currently in vogue, such as:

- Total quality management (TQM)
- Participative management
- Benchmarking strategies
- Restructuring, reengineering, and reinventing
- Principle centered leadership
- Learning organizations
- Revision of mental models (and shifting of paradigms)
- Spirituality in the workplace
- Activity-based costing/management (ABC/ABM)
- Strategic, long-term, short-term, and detail planning
- Flexible budgeting
- Systems theory
- Complexity theory (complex adaptive systems)

Two techniques—benchmarking and activity-based costing—are presented as examples to illustrate how specific cost analysis and reduction methods can be effectively used to contain costs and thereby improve company cash flow. As we have indicated, any process that helps reduce costs will result in an improvement in cash flow as long as it does not impair sales activity or customer relations or otherwise jeopardize the survival of the organization. Benchmarking and activity-based costing are well-accepted techniques to accomplish improved operations and reduced costs as well as to improve bases for pricing of products and services.

BENCHMARKING STRATEGIES

Benchmarking identifies, implements, and maintains objective internal appraisal and external comparison and analysis. It is becoming the tool of choice for gathering data related to cost-reduction analysis, programs of continuous improvement, and to gain competitive advantage.

Benchmarking can be defined as a process for analyzing internal operations and activities to identify areas for cost reduction and process improvement in a program of continuous improvement. The process begins with an analysis of existing operations and activities, identifies areas for cost reduction and improvement, and then establishes a performance standard against which the activity can be measured. The goal is to improve each identified activity so that it can be the best possible—economically, efficiently, and effectively—and stay that way. The best practice is not always measured in terms of lowest costs, but may rather reflect what stakeholders value and expected levels of performance.

> *BENCHMARKING PROVIDES TARGETS TO ATTAIN.*

The Concept of Stakeholders

Benchmarking processes are directed toward the continuous pursuit of cost reduction and operational improvements, excellence in all activities, and the effective use of best practices. The focal point in achieving these goals is the customers—both internal and external—who establish performance expectations and are the ultimate judges of resultant quality. A company stakeholder is defined as anyone who has a stake or interest in the ongoing operations of the organization, or anyone who is affected by its results (type, quality, and timeliness). Stakeholders include all those who are dependent on the survival of the organization, such as:

- Customers/end users
- Owners/shareholders
- Suppliers/vendors/lenders
- Management/supervision
- Employees/subcontractors
- Special-interest groups (environmental, diversity, union, etc.)
- Government agencies, legislation, etc.

BENCHMARK AGAINST STAKEHOLDER EXPECTATIONS.

Strategic Concepts

Benchmarking results provide the company—owners, management, and employees—with data necessary for effective resource allocation and the strategic focus for the organization. The benchmarking process provides for those objective measures to determine the success of the company's internal goals, objectives, and detail plans, as well as external and competitive performance measures. Benchmarking the company's performance against stakeholder expectations enables the company to pursue its program of continuous improvement and the road to excellence. Effective benchmarking encompasses both internal and external needs. Some examples of internal and external benchmarks for the organization include the following:

- Increased sales: in total, by product line, and by product
- Earnings per share
- Total assets
- Return on investment
- Return on assets
- Gross profits
- Net profits
- Debt/equity ratio
- Stock price
- Dividends
- Cash flow changes
- Survival and growth
- Internal excellence (positive changes)
- Competitive excellence: quality, timely, cost, responsive
- Supplier excellence: preferred vendors
- Employer excellence: employee participation, empowerment, and so on

Whereas owners may be most concerned with short-term benchmarking criteria such as stock market price and earnings per share, other stakeholders may be more concerned with longer-term criteria such as real earnings growth, customer satisfaction, and ongoing positive cash flow. There should be a meaningful balance between such short-term and long-term goals of diverse stakeholders for the benchmarking process to be most successful. Benchmarks for organizational growth include the following:

- Cost reductions: short-term pain for long-term gain
- Price increases: may create more competition

- Sales volume increases: present and potential customers
- New market expansion: local, national, international
- New distribution channels: OEM, wholesale, retail, mail order, Internet, customer calls
- Market share increase in existing markets
- Sale or closing of a losing operation/location
- Acquisition of another company, division, operation, product
- New product/service development
- Efficiency/productivity improvements: achieve more with less
- Elimination of non-value-added activities

> ## COMPARE WHAT IS WITH WHAT SHOULD BE.

Types of Benchmarking

Internal Benchmarking
Internal benchmarking includes analysis of existing practices within various operating areas of the company—to identify activities and drivers and best performance. Drivers are the causes of work or triggers (for example, a customer order) that set in motion a series of activities. Internal benchmarking focuses on looking internally before looking externally. Significant improvements can be made as the company asks questions such as:

- Is that activity needed?
- Why do we do that?
- Is that position/material really needed?
- Can the activity be done better in another manner?
- Is that step necessary? Does it provide added value?

Internal benchmarking is the technique used to identify and implement operational cost reductions because it provides the framework to compare internal practices within the company as well as to external best practice benchmark data.

External Benchmarking
External benchmarking is used to compare the company's operations with those of other organizations, particularly in developing cost reduction and positive cash flow recommendations, and includes the following types of benchmarking:

- *Competitive benchmarking.* Looks to the outside to identify how other direct competitors are performing. Competitive benchmarking identifies the strengths and weaknesses of the company's competitors and is helpful in determining its own successful competitive strategy. It can also help to prioritize specific areas for improvement such as customer service, operating efficiencies, cost data, performance results, and so on.

- *Industry benchmarking.* Extending beyond the typical one-to-one comparison of competitive benchmarking, industry benchmarking attempts to identify trends, innovations, and new ideas within the entire industry. Such identification can help to establish better performance criteria, but may not lead to competitive breakthroughs, since others in the industry may be going through the same benchmarking process.

- *Best-in-class benchmarking.* Looks across multiple industries to identify new, innovative practices, regardless of their source. This search for best practices should be the ultimate goal of the benchmarking process. It supports continuous improvement, increased performance levels, and movement toward best practices, and identifies opportunities for improvements in all areas of company operations.

> ## *FIND AND EMULATE*
> ## *THE PREMIER PRACTITIONER.*

Internal Benchmarking Comparisons

In performing an internal benchmarking study as part of a cash management cost-reduction analysis, there are a number of bases on which to compare to present practices, such as:

- Comparisons between individuals performing similar functions within the same work unit
- Comparative analysis between different work units within the company that perform similar functions
- Comparisons to industry standards
- Comparisons to published benchmark standards
- Comparisons to tests of reasonableness

In analyzing present conditions, the company must be aware of what conditions are expected to meet organizational goals and objectives. In determining the proper benchmark for comparison to a specific activity, the company can review such areas as relevant legislation and laws, existing contracts, policy statements, systems and procedures, internal and external regulations, responsibility and authority relationships, standards, schedules, plans and budgets, principles of good management and administration, and so on. In determining the correct benchmark for a specific function, the company should answer the following questions concerning the activity:

- What should the function be?
- What is it measured against?
- What is the standard procedure or practice?
- Is it a formal procedure or an informal practice?

This results in comparing what is to what should be—the benchmark. In evaluating operating practices, one should be aware that procedures are formal methods of doing things, usually documented in writing and prescribed by management. Practices are the actual way that work activities are performed and are rarely documented in written form. Questions that should be asked by the analysis team include the following:

- *People*
  - Who is involved? And why?
    - Number of people
    - Number of positions
    - How organized and managed
    - Current personnel resource demands
  - Are all personnel needed?
    - Reasons for involvement
    - What are they doing?
    - Value or non-value added
    - Vital operation or task
    - Special expertise
  - Who has responsibility for outcomes?
    - Hierarchical pyramid: power and control
    - Management oriented: review and redo
    - Employee self-motivated disciplined behavior
      ...Delegation of authority to lowest operational levels
      ...Empire building: work continues but reason no longer valid
- *Procedures*
  - Why task is performed? (e.g., "It's always been done this way")
  - Necessary or unnecessary? (e.g., "That's the way we do it")
  - Adding value to customer? (internal versus external viewpoint)
  - Unnecessary bureaucracy? (e.g., unwieldy hierarchy)
  - Ineffective, inefficient, or redundant procedures?
  - What does each of the people do and why do they do it? (foundation for internal improvements)
  - What are the bundles or groups of value and non-value-added procedures and activities?

The benefits of using internal benchmarking comparisons and identification of best practices include the following:

- Defines existing processes and activities—establishes baseline of acceptable performance (helps to trigger continuous improvement efforts)
- Identifies gaps in performance in similar internal processes (provides a clear picture of the organization's problems)
- Brings all internal operations up to the highest possible level of performance (within existing constraints)
- Recognizes areas of internal operational improvements without going outside the organization
- Establishes standards for common practices and procedures (overcomes the "Not created here" syndrome)
- Opens up communication lines within the organization (focuses resources on problems that affect more than one area).
- Institutes organization-wide commitment to internal benchmarking concepts (recasts the problems facing the company)
- Builds groundwork for external benchmarking (competitive, industry, and best-in-class) efforts (ensures greater results when external benchmarking is done)
- Prioritizes critical areas for benchmarking opportunities
- Identifies and classifies the key performance drivers

Internal Benchmarks

Examples of internal benchmarks that can be used for such comparison purposes include the following:

- *Internal to the organization*
  - Organizational policy statements
  - Legislation, laws, and regulations
  - Contractual arrangements
  - Funding arrangements
  - Organizational and departmental plans: goals and objectives
  - Budgets, schedules, and detail plans

- *Developed by the Internal Benchmarking Team*
  - Internal performance statistics: by individual or work unit
  - Performance of similar organizations
  - Industry or functionally related statistics
  - Past and present performance
  - Engineered standards
  - Special analysis or studies
  - Benchmarking team's judgment

- Sound business practices
- Good common business sense

Examples of internal benchmarking performance measures are shown in Exhibit 5.1; quantitative benchmarks are shown in Exhibit 5.2; qualitative benchmarks are shown in Exhibit 5.3; and sample benchmarking measures by function are shown in Exhibit 5.4.

Organizational Structure and the Role of Management

Theoretically, organizations are put together so that the entity can conduct its business more efficiently, and so that the owners and/or top management can multiply their effectiveness—that is, maximize their desired results. Organizing is intended to be a helping process to enable a company to conduct its business better. However, for many organizations it has become a costly obstructionist process. As part of its cost reduction analysis, the company must ascertain whether it is properly organized or whether improper organization is the cause of its problems and a causal factor in excessive costs.

- Organizational environment
- Company policy
- Management and employee skills and abilities
- Market constraints (e.g., price, quality)
- Product constraints (e.g., labor/material intensive)
- Technology (e.g., high, low, innovative)
- Organizational structure
- Management philosophy
- Organizational culture
- Type of structure
- Single product/diversified
- Locations/number of facilities
- Upward/downward/horizontal communication patterns
- Control elements (e.g., strong central versus delegated)
- Job and behavioral expectations
- Imbedded value system
- Evaluation and reward systems
- Performance related
- Hiring, orientation, training, evaluation, and promotion practices and criteria
- Turnover or lack thereof
- Delegation of authority and responsibilities
- Unwieldy organizational hierarchy
- Overlaps of responsibility and job functions
- Emphasis on economy, efficiency, and effectiveness
- Quality and use of information systems

Exhibit 5.1 Examples of Performance Measures

Productivity:
- Productivity/number of employees
- Cost per good unit produced
- Total productivity/total cost
- Orders processed per hour by employee
- Orders shipped per hour by employee
- Increase/decrease in inventory by item
- Inventory turnover ratios

Quality:
- Number of good pieces/scrap
- Amount and cost of rework
- Amount and cost of quality inspection
- Amount of vendor rejects
- Number of customer returns/complaints
- Warranty claims
- Returns and allowances
- Good units produced/material in
- Parts availability
- On-time deliveries
- Sales forecast accuracy

Timeliness:
- On-time deliveries
- Design time: customer to finished design
- Production lead time
- Purchasing to vendor delivery time
- Shipping time
- Number of late orders
- Number of late deliveries
- Number of back orders
- Set-ups: number and time
- Inspections: number and time
- Non-productive time
- Order processing time

Accounting:
- Number of items: invoices, payments, payroll time cards
- Number bills at time of shipment
- Number of payments within terms
- Accuracy of processing
- Number of accounts payable debits
- Number of accounts receivable credits
- Employee productivity statistics
- Timeliness and accuracy of reporting

Exhibit 5.2   Quantitative Benchmarks

Product/Service:
- Number of products/services
- Number of activities/moves
- Number of total parts/activities
- Number of options
- Number of products/services produced: by unit, equipment, location
- Number of stockouts
- Amount of delays/time promised changes

Facilities/Capacity:
- Number of work units
- Number of personnel
- Number and location of bottlenecks
- Number of changes
- Amount of preventive maintenance
- Number of quality control inspections

Customer Satisfaction:
- Amount of repeat business
- Satisfaction: with what?
- Actual performance vs. promises
- Referrals to others
- Perceptions: quality, price, ease of use, features

Marketing/Sales:
- Number of salespeople
- Amount of marketing effort
- Increases in sales: number, profits, by customer, by salesperson
- Customer support provided
- Amount of flexibility
- Product success rates
- Sales to existing customers
- Number and sales to new customers

Processing:
- Time to process an order
- Number of contacts per order filled
- Number of errors
- Time to get order into production
- Time to process shipping
- Time to process billing
- Collection statistics
- Number of orders in backlog
- Amount of backlog never realized

Exhibit 5.3 Qualitative Benchmarks

Sales Forecasts:
1. Forecast to Actual: Total, by Customer, by Salesperson, by Product
2. Forecast to Real Customer Orders
3. Forecast: This Year to Last Year
4. Forecast to Lost Orders
5. Customer Contacts: Number, Type, Results

Sales Order Backlog:
1. Sales Order to Production Order: Time Processed
2. Average Time in Backlog
3. Reduction in Backlog: Current, Compared to Past
4. Backlog Statistics: Conversion to Real Orders/Lost Orders

Manufacturing Orders:
1. Average Processing Time: Sales Order Receipt to MO
2. Timeliness into Production: Per Schedule, Production Ready
3. Timeliness Of Start: Materials On Time, Production Start
4. Movement through WIP: Timeliness, Queue Time, Move Time
5. Comparison to Standards: Material, Labor, Scrap, Rejects, Rework
6. Quality Control: Number of Inspections, Rejects
7. Receiving: Personnel, Time, Process
8. Shipping: Process, Timeliness, Method, Costs
9. Delivery: On Time, Customer Satisfaction, Returned Items

Inventory:
1. Raw Material: Amount JIT, Amount on Hand, Amount Decreased
2. WIP: Maximize Throughput, Schedule versus Actual, % JIT
3. Finished Goods: Completed On Time, Shipped Directly, Amount
4. Records: Physical to Records, Type of Data/Reporting
5. Statistics: Turnover, Obsolete, Inaccuracies

Purchasing:
1. Process Type: Direct, Purchase Orders, EDT, Blanket
2. Numbers: POs, Personnel, Vendors
3. Timeliness: PR to PO, PO to Vendor
4. Vendor Relations: Number, By Personnel, Negotiations
5. Vendor Statistics: Prices, Quality, Timeliness, Purchase Data
6. Expediting: Open Purchases, Time/Cost, Late Deliveries

Engineering:
1. Bill of Materials: Accuracy, Number of Changes
2. Specifications: Accuracy, Number of Specs
3. Timeliness: New Products, Change Orders
4. Costs: New Design, Change Orders, Maintenance

Exhibit 5.4   Sample Benchmarking Measures by Function

Billing, Accounts Receivable and Collections:
1. Billings: Timeliness, Accuracy, Process, Cost
2. Method of Preparation: Manual, EDP, EDT
3. Billing Cycle Time: Prep/Mail/Receipt by customer
4. Personnel: Number, Time Per Bill, Staff versus Managers
5. Collections: Days Outstanding, Cost Per Dollar Collected
6. Bad Debts: To Sales, Amount
7. Cash Receipts: Process, Time to Deposit, Average Days
8. Credit: Process, Approvals, Over/Under Limits
9. Invoices Returned : Bad Addresses, Inaccuracies

Accounts Payable:
1. Process: Direct Pay, EDT, EDP, Manual
2. Payments: Number, Timeliness, Accuracy/Errors
3. Costs: Per Payment, Personnel, Distribution/Mailing
4. Payment Errors: Number, Costs
5. Discounts: Taken, Lost, Costs

Payroll:
1. Process: Method, Internal/External, Frequency, Distribution
2. Process Errors: Number, Type, Costs, Correction Methods
3. Employee Benefits: Number, Type, Costs
4. Reporting: Frequency, Media, Accuracy, Timeliness
5. Costs: Per Employee, Per Check

Accounting/Financial:
1. Reporting: Late Reports, Errors in Reports, Not Needed
2. Outside Auditors: Cost, Timeliness, Errors Found, Benefits
3. Errors: Process, Personnel, Costs to Correct
4. Data Entry Errors: Number/% By Application
5. Journal Entries: EDP, Manual, Number, Correcting Entries
6. Cost: Per General Ledger/Journal Entry Transaction

Personnel:
1. Organization: Number of Personnel, Functions
2. Costs: Departmental, Per Employee, Per Function
3. Processing: In House/Outside, Level Of Inclusion
4. Result Statistics: Hires, Training, Orientation, Discharges
5. Employee Benefits: Type/Number, Administration

Exhibit 5.4   Sample Benchmarking Measures by Function (continued)

Adequate organizational control requires that all employees know clearly what their roles and functions are in the organization, and exactly what authority and responsibility have been assigned. It also requires proper separation of duties so that the same individuals are not charged with responsibility for performing a task and reporting on how it has been accomplished.

IT'S SOMETIMES EASIER TO SHUFFLE PEOPLE THAN TO DO THE RIGHT THING.

Those who have ever been managers know that it is usually easier to just do a task than spend the time necessary to make sure the person to whom they have assigned the task has done it correctly. The main reason for having people reporting to a manager is to more effectively accomplish the organization's mission, goals, and objectives. In many instances, however, it is the organization itself, not the accomplishment of results, that has become the reason for being. Organizing, reorganizing, and implementing the latest organizational panaceas (such as total quality management and benchmarking) become their goals—as if the structure of the organization were causing the problems. Many times, the type of organization is not the cause of the problem; it is just easier to shuffle people around than to do the right thing.

So why do organizations in the private and public sectors place so much emphasis on the organizational structure of their operations? The answer, often, is that this is how it has always been. The thought is that if people were not required to report to others, they would not know what to do—and how could they be trusted to do their jobs without someone else to watch them? A frequent practice is to departmentalize people without requiring individual responsibility. Many times, the real problem is ineffective top management—and rather than admit to that, management consultants are called in to do what management should have been doing in the first place.

The real answer to why organizations should organize is so that they can accomplish their desired results (be most effective) in the most economical manner (with optimum use of limited resources) using the best available methods of operations (being most efficient). Theoretically, the organizational structure and management's goals should be the same, and each should support the other in the efforts toward making the organization successful. That this has not happened is evident by what is occurring in many organizations, both large and small today: downsizing, reengineering, layoffs, cost cutting, total quality management, and its ilk. Rather than using one of these new management miracles, hoping for quick, short-term fixes that often result in longer-term problems, it may be time to go back to organizational basics whereby all those working for the organization take responsibility for their part of the organization's successes or failures.

The organizational structure is the tool that is supposed to enable the organization to conduct its business in the desired manner. The purpose of both management and the organizational structure is the same, namely, to use the limited resources entrusted to them to accomplish agreed-upon results using the most efficient methods of operation available. If a business used this principle when it put organizations together and made managers and other employees accountable for their results, it would have avoided many of the present pitfalls of unwieldy organizational structures.

> ## ASK HOW THE ORGANIZATION ORGANIZES TO ACHIEVE RESULTS.

Organizational Structure Examples

Exhibit 5.5 depicts a representative top-level organization chart, graphically showing the reporting relationships from the president down through departmental levels. This typical structure would fit many organizations. It is based on a hierarchical pyramid concept in which the ultimate power starts at the top and is delegated down through the pyramid. Its purpose was command and control—maintain control within the organization through a chain of command, demanding obedience from each level of the organization that reported to a higher level.

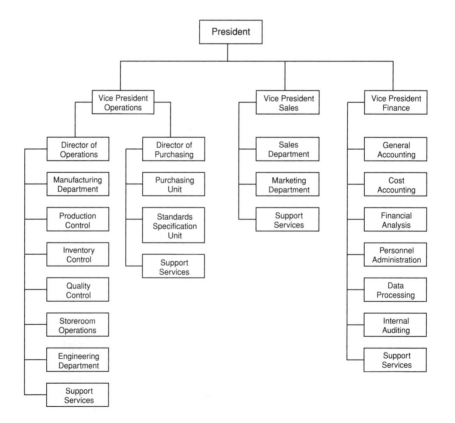

Exhibit 5.5 Top-Level Organization Chart

To this day, many business organizations still function in this manner, with the purpose for the organizational hierarchy being to police and control those reporting to them to make sure they do their jobs.

The structure is also set up with the intrinsic message that those in a higher position on the chart know more. Hence, much of their time is spent on reviewing the work of those under them and then having those under them redo it so it looks more like what the manager would do. If these policing and control, review and redo processes exist, that makes many supervisors and managers superfluous (non-value-added) organizational overhead, and often more hindrance than help. If these non-value-added processes are eliminated, management is strictly limited to necessities, and the organization creates an atmosphere that encourages the motivation of self-disciplined employee behavior. Then many of these layers of unnecessary organization and costs could be eliminated.

A look at Exhibit 5.5 may raise many questions and reveal areas for review related to making this organization more effective and efficient and, as a result, more economical. The following are areas that may be considered:

- The need for vice-presidents and their real functions
- Directors' level and their purposes
- The number of functions reporting to the vice president of operations and the related control structure
- The number of department levels and breakdowns in the manufacturing and finance areas
- Which departments or units are necessary, could be combined, could be eliminated, could be provided more economically in another manner, and so on
- Reporting relationships throughout the organization, such as between the president and vice presidents, the vice presidents and directors/department heads, and so on
- The degree of value-added management/supervision, as opposed to policing and control, review and redo procedures
- The ability of personnel in general to perform their functions in a motivated self-disciplined mode without the need for close supervision or management
- The purpose of support services for each branch and their related functions

Exhibit 5.6 shows a further breakdown of the functional areas reporting to the vice president of operations.

A review of this organizational chart, with particular attention to the purchasing function, reveals some areas for further review, such as:

- Why does the purchasing department report to the vice president of operations?

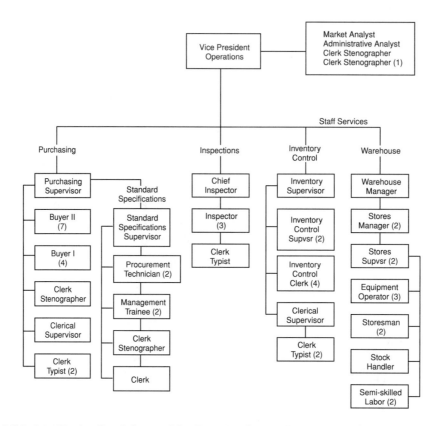

Exhibit 5.6 Further Breakdown of the Functional Areas Reporting to the Vice President of Operations

- What are the functions, responsibilities, and authority of staff functions such as market analyst and administrative analyst?
- Why are two clerk stenographers reporting directly to the vice president of operations? What do they do?
- What is the function and authority of the purchasing supervisor? (Note: This position was listed as Director of Purchasing on the top-level organization chart).
- What are the buyers' functions and how are they used within the purchasing department?
- What is the difference between a Buyer II and a Buyer I?
- Are all the buyers necessary based on division of the workload?
- What is the function of the clerk stenographer and how does it differ from those of the clerical supervisor and clerk typists?
- What does the clerical supervisor do, and is supervision of the two clerk typists necessary?
- What are the functions of the two clerk typists, and is the workload appropriate?

- What is the function of the Standards Specifications Unit? Is it needed to this extent or at all? Can its functions be eliminated or outsourced?
- Is the personnel complement within the Standards Specifications Unit appropriate to the present work required?
- What are the specific functions of the Standards Specifications Unit personnel, and are they necessary?
- Should other units such as Inspections, Inventory Control, and Warehouse be reporting to the same individual, vice president of operations, as the Purchasing function? To what extent are these functions necessary?

Sample Planning Phase Organizational Work Program
The following are work steps that may be considered in a cost reduction analysis with regard to the organizational structure for the organization represented in Exhibit 5.5 and 5.6:

1. Secure or prepare an organization chart with descriptions of each department's and work units' specific functions.
2. Determine formal and informal reporting relationships from top to bottom, bottom to top, and across functional lines.
3. Analyze actual operations to determine whether such reporting is proper in relation to how the organization actually functions and whether it results in operational concerns and problems.
4. Analyze each work unit's functions to determine whether they are appropriate.
5. Document the duties and responsibilities of each employee. Obtain copies of existing job descriptions or prepare them through the use of user provided data such as a Job Responsibility Questionnaire.
6. Interview the president, vice presidents, managers and supervisors, and each employee, to validate their functions.
7. Observe actual work being performed to determine the necessity of all duties and responsibilities.
8. Obtain or prepare company policies and procedures relating to each function under review.
9. Determine that authority and responsibility relationships are clearly defined and understood by all personnel.
10. Ascertain that all employees know their delegated authority and responsibilities; ensure that the responsibilities are proper for the function and do not overlap or duplicate another area.
11. Look for functions and individuals that either are not providing value-added services or are not being cost-effective. Examples may be isolates, dispatchers, controllers, unwieldy hierarchies typified by policing and control, and management/supervision that gets in the way.

12. Review hiring, orientation, training, evaluation, promotion, and lay-off/firing practices.
13. Question inefficient practices such as management policing and controlling, employee redoing, inappropriate following of policies, and so on.
14. Ascertain the level of self-motivated disciplined behavior.

Building Organizations

There seems to be a trend toward empire building and the power and control that come with it. Even with the present movement toward downsizing, restructuring, reengineering, and so on, with emphasis on getting by with fewer people, those in power are trying to hold onto empires consisting of unnecessarily large numbers of people. Although they are quite agreeable about cutting the other guys' empires, there is considerable resistance when it comes to reducing the size of their own houses. In many instances, even with these quick and short-term remedies for staff reductions, there still remain individuals and layers of organizational hierarchy that are unnecessary (in part, or in total). It is really important to learn how to build organizations and maintain them properly at all times, using the correct techniques for the various situations.

Making employees responsible for meeting expectations and results, through motivating self-disciplined behavior and an effective monitoring system, eliminates the need for management and supervisory personnel that exist mainly to police and control individual employees. Use of operating systems that make sense to the employees who use them (who should have had input in developing these systems), within a cooperative atmosphere, will increase productivity to the extent that fewer employees overall are needed. The trick is to avoid adding unnecessary personnel as the organization grows, so that it is never in a position to have to cut back drastically. Often, individuals are penalized, being laid off for something beyond their control.

Many techniques for building an organization structure do not depend on the typical bottom-to-top military model, based on policing and controlling those reporting to each higher level, that is used by most organizations today. These include participative management, shared management, team management, self-motivated disciplined behavior (no manager), coaching and facilitative supports, and so on. There is no right answer for all situations—it is important to learn to use a combination of these techniques as they fit the particular situation. Emphasize controlling costs and results, not people.

Example of Organizational Cost Reductions

CONTAIN COSTS TO IMPROVE CASH FLOW.

The following is an example of how analyzing organization and personnel and related costs can reduce and eliminate unnecessary functions, reduce costs, increase productivity, and contribute to positive cash flow. As part of the company's cost reduction analysis, the analysis team reviewed manufacturing operations and found inefficient manufacturing procedures, with diminished productivity, inventory out of control, production employees getting in each other's way, increased amount of rejected items and rework, more than 20 percent overtime for production workers, and an on-time delivery record of less than 40 percent. In addition, present manufacturing procedures result in excess personnel and inefficient methods, which cost the company more than $1 million annually in unnecessary expenses. The analysis team estimates that the company can conservatively save more than $900,000 in annual personnel costs alone as shown in Exhibit 5.7 by implementing more efficient operating procedures.

Comparisons Among Individuals

> *SET COMPENSATION NOT ON THE TIME PUT IN, BUT WHAT IS PUT INTO THE TIME.*

Comparing individuals performing similar functions (i.e., production workers, engineers, salespeople, accounting personnel, etc.) is not an exact science, as no two individuals' functions are exactly the same. However, the reviewer can identify better practices as to how to use one's expertise and ways of doing the job with others. An automatic transference of how one performs an activity to another is not usually accomplished easily. For instance, review the following case example of an internal benchmarking team working with a small manufacturer of specialty boxes.

At one time, the specialty box business was quite profitable, with gross profit margins of 43 percent. Now, however, competition and new, less costly methods had reduced gross profit margins to under 20 percent and falling. Still not too shabby, but cause for alarm. The owners had asked the team to benchmark their productivity in both manufacturing and the office areas. They had increased sales to a level they believed was practical for their capabilities and had cut costs where they felt they could. Now, they believed they had to increase productivity in all areas to reduce unit costs, negotiate sales prices more competitively, and increase resultant profits.

The team reviewed manufacturing operations and found that all processes had been automated to the extent practical. Those functions still requiring personal intervention were of a mechanical and measurable nature (e.g., storeroom operations, loading automated equipment, movement from one process to another, folding, packing, shipping, etc.). The company had a fairly well designed reporting system for these operations that told plant management productivity by employee and compared the results with those involving similar employees and an expected standard. The foreperson in each area was to analyze the reports the

#	Present Condition Position	$	#	Proposed Condition Position	$	#	Savings $
1	VP-Production	$ 74,000	1	Plant Manager	$ 36,000	0	$ 38,000
6	Forepersons	144,000	0	None	-0-	6	144,000
6	Team Leaders	132,000	3	Trainer/Coach	66,000	3	66,000
36	Production	576,000	28	Production	448,000	8	128,000
5	Repair/Maint.	120,000	1	Repair/Maint.	24,000	4	96,000
4	Packer/Shipper	52,000	4	Packer/Shipper	52,000	0	-0-
3	Receivers	30,000	1	Receiver	10,000	2	20,000
1	Inv. Cont. Mgr	18,000	1	Inv. Cont. Mgr.	18,000	0	-0-
1	QC Manager	26,000	0	None	-0-	1	26,000
6	QC Inspectors	132,000	4	QC Inspectors	88,000	2	44,000
2	QC Clerical	32,000	0	None	-0-	2	32,000
71		1,336,000	43		742,000	28	594,000
	Overtime (Team Leaders & Production) @ 20%	141,600			-0-		141,600
		1,477,600			742,000		735,600
	Fringe Benefits @ 32%	472,832			237,440		235,392
	Totals	$ 1,950,432			$ 979,440		$ 970,992

These estimated savings do not include the additional productivity to be gained through these recommendations, estimated to be at least 25 percent of present production levels.

Exhibit 5.7   Schedule of Present and Proposed Personnel Costs

following morning and to take remedial action. Such action typically consisted of berating those employees who compared poorly with others and/or the standard. The reviewers noted minimal improvement (in fact, just the opposite) from this "management practice." The review team analyzed each employee's performance over a period of time (number of good items produced and number of rejects, rework, and returned items), which resulted in a pattern for each employee—that is, a narrow range of productivity for each employee and all employees working in similar functions. In other words, each employee and function had its own standard or level of production.

Interestingly, as each employee's productivity increased, the number of rejects also increased. The reviewers concluded that each employee had developed a narrow range of productivity within quality expectations, and that present reporting and management practices were not creating any improvements. Payroll analysis disclosed minimal differences among hourly rates. Compensation was based on seniority, regardless of the level of quality productivity. There was no incentive to improve productivity. In fact, the number of good units produced per dollar of payroll cost moved inversely with the number of years employed. In other words, the newer, less costly employees were more productive per dollar of wages than the older employees.

A review of office functions disclosed that there were no productivity expectations, no controls over or reporting of results, and no effective means of evaluation. In analyzing specific areas (e.g., purchasing, customer service, personnel, engineering, accounting, data processing, etc.), the team found them all overstaffed. There was no way to determine results, relative productivity, or what it was costing the company. The analysis also disclosed that the younger and/or newer hires were doing the bulk of the work, while the older, "more experienced" higher-paid employees were doing the least they could get away with. Much of their time was spent talking to each other and watching the newer employees work.

It was apparent that present procedures were not working. There was no real incentive for increasing productivity in either the plant or the office—actually the opposite. Compensation was based more on time put in with the company than on what was put into the time. It was apparent that a system had to be implemented that would better correlate productivity with compensation. The first step was to install procedures to ensure that all employees knew exactly what was expected of them and the results to be achieved. The next step was to determine the present competencies of each employee and the related levels of quality productivity. No one can make a .300 hitter out of a .225 hitter through hope and desire—one has to start with present capabilities and then work on fundamentals.

It was then necessary to develop a method of compensation that rewarded employees based on results achieved, and that would be equitable to all. To make this point, the reviewers selected three employees with differing levels of present productivity and compensation, as follows:

	Productivity	*Rate of Pay*
Employee A	8 units per hour	$ 12/hour
Employee B	10 units per hour	$ 10/hour
Employee C	12 units per hour	$ 8/hour

Members of management were asked to rank these employees based only on levels of productivity, and they, of course, put them in A, B, C order. When they were told that the order, in reality, was just the opposite, they would not believe it until the actual data were disclosed. They all nodded and said in unison "that must be the plant, we know we have trouble there." When they were told that, no, these were not plant personnel but customer service employees, and that the plant numbers were even worse, they became silent. Finally the chief financial officer (CFO) asked what could be done about this. A three-step plan was recommended, which included expectations, competencies, and compensation.

Quality expectations were developed for each function in the company, and related compensation was established, based on the level of productivity achieved (for example, 8 units = $8/hour, 10 units = $10/hour, 12 units = $12/hour, etc.). Each employee was thus compensated based on results achieved, not on seniority. If the owners wanted to give additional compensation for years in, it was suggested that this be done separately from results compensation.

The next step was to look at each employee's competencies and determine how to make them more productive and better compensated. It was agreed that the lowest present level of productivity in each function was acceptable, but only for a commensurate level of compensation. If an employee wanted to earn additional compensation, productivity would have to be increased. It was understood that the employees would not be able to do this on their own or under the present system of control, reporting, and management. Twelve forepersons and supervisors/managers were replaced with four coaches, whose job was to help each employee continually improve. As they improved and productivity increased, the employees would be compensated at the higher level of productivity. As overall profits increased and management calculated the results of increased productivity, additional compensation would be shared with all employees. Under this system, a number of improvements were accomplished:

- Making all employees entrepreneurs (i.e., in business for themselves) responsible for their own level of compensation
- Fostering cooperation (and eliminating competition) among employees, as it now became beneficial for all to increase productivity and resultant profits
- Creating an atmosphere of self-disciplined behavior, characterized by individual responsibility, working together, and self-learning
- Eliminating many so-called foreperson and management personnel with the use of a few coaches to create a program of continuous improvement and productivity rather than stagnation and unnecessary costs
- Removing costly compensation practices with an inverse relationship to results achieved
- Reducing overall personnel, as levels of staff now became related to productivity levels in direct areas as well as management
- Using older, experienced personnel (where productivity levels could no longer be maintained) as coaches/facilitators so that their experience would be effectively used

Alternative Criteria

In many cases, internal benchmarks may not be available, and must be developed. In the absence of existing internal standards or benchmarking criteria with which to evaluate performance, three alternative approaches are available to the reviewer:

1. Comparative analysis
2. Use of borrowed statistics
3. Test of reasonableness

Comparative Analysis

> ## PICK THE BEST PERFORMANCE
> ## AND MAKE IT THE STANDARD.

Comparative analysis is a technique that can be used, where specific internal standards do not exist for comparison, to compare the reviewed activities to similar situations within the company. This analysis can be accomplished in two ways:

1. Current performance can be compared to past performance.
2. Performance can be compared with that of another similar work unit within the organization.

Comparing current with past periods has the advantage of possibly disclosing trends in performance. For example, if the cost for an employee procedures manual rises from year to year, one may question whether (1) costs have risen, (2) inefficiencies in manual preparation have increased, (3) employees are being given larger quantities, or (4) a better and more expensive quality of material is being used. The situation can then be analyzed further to determine exactly why the cost per manual has increased.

In this example, the criteria by which actual performance is evaluated are not part of a predetermined plan or a formal set of performance standards, but are simply those practices that were followed in prior years. Using such comparisons does not provide sufficient data to tell whether the rise in procedures manual cost per employee is good or bad, or whether costs are too high. This method does, however, identify the causes so that management can judge performance as it occurred. Although trends are possible to note and examine by this method, meaningful comparisons of alternative methods or procedures cannot usually be accomplished.

The comparison of two separate but similar work units normally provides the opportunity to evaluate different approaches to operations management. By determining the results of different operational approaches, the reviewer can make some helpful recommendations for improving efficiency and effectiveness.

There are, however, some disadvantages in comparing two separate but similar work units. The major disadvantage is the failure to recognize factors that justify differences between the two units. For example, it is difficult to compare manufacturing locations, as no two facilities will have exactly the same type of manufacturing systems, hire the same type of employees, use the same type of equipment, or have the same proximity to materials and other essentials. The two manufacturing locations would, however, have many of the same types of problems regardless of their differences. The similarity of problems enables the reviewer to analyze how each location's management group handles these common problems. The reviewer can then analyze such alternatives for improving the efficiency and effectiveness of operations, and resultant recommendations can reflect the review team's judgment based on the results produced by each alternative.

Use of Borrowed Statistics
Many groups and organizations throughout the country, such as manufacturers, hospitals, and banking associations, provide uniform and comparable industry and benchmark standards for evaluating performance. In addition, many professional associations and journals publish benchmarking results and standards on an ongoing or periodic basis. These borrowed standards can then be used to compare performance of organizations in similar endeavors. Although such comparisons make performance evaluation quicker and easier, there are some disadvantages to this procedure as well.

One disadvantage is that national averages and broad-based statistics hardly ever relate to specific situations. Although such statistics provide some indications of an organization's performance, they cannot be used for precise measurement or evaluation. Another disadvantage is that very few national averages or uniform statistics actually exist. In those cases where such statistics do exist, such as by standard industry code, for hospitals, banks, service industries, schools, libraries, and so forth, they either relate to only a small portion of the areas subject to review or are limited to very restricted areas, and are of limited use.

The Test of Reasonableness

REASONABLENESS CAN BE A LEGITIMATE STANDARD.

When there are no internal standards and comparisons with other organizations are impossible, or borrowed benchmarks are unavailable, the reviewer can still test organizational performance by a benchmark based on the test of reasonableness. Through experience, members of the review team may have become familiar with how things are done economically, efficiently, and effectively in other organizations. The review team should then be able to relate these experiences to the current functions included in the operational review and internal benchmarking study.

Accordingly, the operational review team can often spot operational irregularities and weaknesses that may escape the notice of others without such a background. In an operational review internal benchmarking study, perceptions of a situation are based on the cumulative experience of the internal review team. In addition, there exist what may be termed "general standards of society" that apply to good management in any field, public or private. For example, reviewers can often spot work being done in a loose, unsatisfactory, and inefficient manner, even without specific standards or benchmarks. Many times, this work has been considered acceptable—"That's the way we've always done it."

Obsolete inventory, excessive supplies, personnel who are continually absent from work, abuse in the use of resources such as automobiles and expense accounts, or negligence in processing documents or handling cash funds are examples of items that can be evaluated through the test of reasonableness. The reasonableness test is also an appropriate tool for quickly reviewing operating areas not subjected to detailed analysis. Even where the operational review team has analyzed in detail, the reviewers should still examine their conclusions for reasonableness. This ensures that the team has not become so engrossed in statistics that they have overlooked important items or placed too much weight on minor ones. The test of reasonableness can also be viewed as application of good common sense or prudent business practice to the situation. Some indicators of internal benchmarking deficiencies are shown below.

- *Management and organization*
  - Poor planning and decision making
  - Too broad a span of control
  - Badly designed systems and procedures
  - Excessive crisis management
  - Poor channels of communication
  - Inadequate delegation of authority
  - Excessive organizational changes

- *Personnel relations*
  - Inadequate hiring, orientation, training, evaluation, and promotion procedures
  - Lack of clearly communicated job expectations
  - Idle, excessive, or not enough personnel
  - Poor employee morale
  - Excessive overtime and/or absenteeism
  - Unclear responsibility/authority relationships

- *Manufacturing and operations*
  - Poor manufacturing methods
  - Inefficient plant layout
  - Excessive rework, scrap, or salvage

- Idle equipment and/or operations personnel
- Insufficient or excessive equipment
- Excessive production or operating costs
- Lack of effective production scheduling procedures
- Poor housekeeping
- Excessive, slow-moving, or obsolete inventory

- *Purchasing*
  - Not achieving best prices, timeliness, and quality
  - Favoritism to certain vendors
  - Lack of effective competitive bidding procedures
  - Not using most effective systems such as blanket purchase orders, traveling requisitions, telephone ordering, and so on
  - Excessive emergency purchases
  - Lack of a value analysis program
  - Purchasing unnecessarily expensive items
  - Unmet procurement schedules
  - Excessive returns to vendors

- *Financial indicators*
  - Poor profit/loss ratios
  - Poor return on investment
  - Unfavorable cost ratios
  - Unfavorable or unexplained cost/budget variances

- *Complaints*
  - Customers: bad products or poor service
  - Employees: grievances, gripes, or exit interview comments
  - Vendors: poor quality or untimely deliveries
  - Production: schedules not met, material not available, deliveries not on time, poor quality, and so on

Internal Benchmarking Case Study

A company being reviewed decided to earmark specific customers and related sales forecasts for its product line, XXX business, by salesperson. For the first quarter of such directed sales planning, the results for the three salespersons were as follows:

	Sales		Difference	
Salesperson	Forecast	Actual	$	%
Brown	2,500	4,000	1,500	160%
Gray	3,500	3,200	(300)	91%
White	4,000	3,600	(400)	90%
TOTALS	10,000	10,800	800	108%

Salesperson	Number of Customers	Personal Contacts	Phone Calls	Memos Sent
Brown	18	84	146	63
Gray	26	38	73	28
White	44	26	48	12

Suppose that a reviewer is conducting an internal benchmarking review of the sales function and is comparing sales results to efforts:

- What additional data would the reviewer gather?
- What factors would the reviewer consider for internal benchmarking?
- Are there any conclusions/inferences the reviewer can draw from the information available?

Additional Data to Gather

Sales data:

- Seniority of salespeople
  - Years with company: White 12 years, Gray 8 years, Brown 1 year
  - Age: White 54, Gray 46, Brown 27
  - Annual pay: White $124,000, Gray $88,000, Brown $37,000

- List of customers and customer statistics/history
  - How long a customer
  - Sales history by product with trends
  - Salesperson assigned
  - New customer/lost customer history

- Salespeople history
  - Sales by customer history and trends
  - Sales efforts versus results
  - Forecast to actual sales history
  - New customer history
  - Lost customer history

- Sales forecast data
  - Sales forecast by customer/products versus actual
  - New customers not in forecast
  - Lost customers or sales in forecast
  - Amount of sales not materializing
  - Amount of sales not on forecast

Contacts data:

- Customer survey
  - Satisfaction with company, products, salespeople

- Relationship with assigned salesperson
- If sales have decreased, why, and are customers buying elsewhere?
- What would help them to buy more?
- Positive and negative experiences
- What the company does right—and wrong
- Competitor relationships and their advantages

- Type of contacts
  - *Effectiveness.* Personal contact, phone call, memos
  - *Relationship.* Contacts to salespeople (present and future)
  - Quality of contacts by salesperson
  - Contact procedures by each salesperson

Factors for Benchmarking

- *Process.* Sales contact procedures and follow-up
- *Timeliness.* How responsive is sales function to customer?
- *Quality.* Relationship with customer, products, sales follow-up
- *Cycle.* How often is customer contacted - pre sale, during sale, and after sale?

- Numbers
  - Contacts/sale
  - Sales forecast/actual sales
  - Sales/sales efforts
  - Sales cost/gross sale/net profit on sale

Conclusions/Inferences

- The greater the sales contacts/customer service, the greater possibility of increased sales.
- Sales forecasts have little basis in reality and are not related to real sales efforts or plans.
- The greater the seniority of the salesperson, the less sales efforts and fewer customer contacts.
- Sales compensation is based more on seniority than on efforts and results.
- Sales forecasts are based on historical sales and cannot be counted on to plan production based on real customer orders.
- There is little incentive for older sales personnel to fully service present customers and bring in new customers.

External Benchmarking Targets

As a result of the internal benchmarking work steps, the review team should identify other areas for external benchmarking including the identification of activity drivers and performance measures, such as those listed here:

- Purchase requisitions
  - *Process.* Manual, computer, automatic by plan
  - *Control.* Work unit, department, automatic, computer
  - *Account coding.* Manual, employee, management, computer
  - *Number.* Company, department, unit, employee, type
  - *Budget check.* Automatic, computer, manual, preapproved
  - *Policy.* Purchasing, petty cash, direct cash system
  - *Practices.* Traveling requisitions, inventory automatic, direct purchase

- Purchase orders
  - *Process.* Manual, computer, automatic, electronic data transfer
  - *Number.* Location, department, unit, employee, vendor, type
  - *Open order control.* Employees, number, vendor, computer
  - *Approval.* Management, computer, automatic by plan
  - *Copies.* Number, manual, computer, electronic data media
  - *Value analysis.* Prices, quantities, needed or not, alternatives, vendors
  - *Form and distribution.* Number of copies, who to, filing, electronic media
  - *Costs.* To process, personnel, forms, expediting
  - *Vendor negotiations.* Blanket purchases, competitive analysis, vendor analysis

- Receiving procedures
  - *Number.* Receipts, partial receipts, employees
  - *Process.* Manual, computer, bar coding, automated update, direct
  - *Receiving inspection.* Process, rejects by vendor/number
  - *Delivery data.* On time by vendor, partial receipts
  - *Cost.* Employees, process, forms, per receipt

- Inventory update
  - *Process.* Manual, bar coding automatic, computer terminals
  - *Routing.* Direct production, inventory, holding area
  - *Integration.* With production, inventory/accounting records
  - *Levels.* Reorder Points/Economic Order Quantities (RP/EOQ), zero inventory, just-in-time (JIT) raw materials and finished goods
  - *Work-in-process.* JIT, process times, schedule integrity

- Accounts payable
  - *Process.* Vendor invoices, pay on receipt, electronic data transfer
  - *Invoice receipt.* Mail, direct, computer, electronic data transfer
  - *Number.* Employees, open vouchers, payments, checks
  - *Payments.* Total, by vendor, by type of item
  - *Returns.* By vendor/number, process
  - *Discount policy.* Take all, ignore, negotiate in price
  - *Timeliness.* In/out discount terms, processing
  - *Practices.* Electronic data transfer, integrated receipt/payment, prepays

ACTIVITY BASED COSTING PRINCIPLES

> ## *ACTIVITY BASED COSTING IDENTIFIES*
> ## *OPPORTUNITIES FOR IMPROVED RESULTS.*

Activity based costing (ABC) is a cost accounting methodology for assigning costs of resources to cost objects based on operational activities. In an operational cash management study, such costing can then be used to make comparisons, identify critical areas for review, and develop recommendations for cost reductions and elimination so as to improve both profitability and cash flow. Using ABC methods, it is the activities, not the products or services (as in traditional cost accounting systems), that cause the costs. The ABC approach to cost accounting recognizes the causal relationship between cost drivers, resources, and activities. ABC defines a process, which could occur in the providing of a product or service or in production or the office, in terms of the activities performed, and then develops costs for these activities. ABC does not, contrary to traditional cost accounting techniques, develop costs by organizational cost centers but in terms of the activities performed. In addition, ABC assigns overhead based on the activities (cost drivers) that cause the overhead to occur, rather than allocating overhead via some arbitrary allocation base such as direct labor hours or dollars. As costs are developed, each activity is appraised as to its necessity and its extent. As activities are reduced or eliminated, their attendant costs are also reduced or eliminated driving these cost savings directly to the bottom line and to positive cash flow.

Many organizations are struggling with better methods for product/service costing and resultant pricing strategies, together with overall cost management, performance measurement, return on investment, and so on. In this context, ABC is only one of the tools for effective survival, competitiveness, and growth and prosperity that challenge organizations today in an ever-changing business environment. ABC methodologies, if implemented correctly, can be the central core that provides the elements of an effective organization-wide cost and cash management system that enables the company to identify opportunities for improvement and make recommendations to enhance positive cash flow.

A summary of Activity Based Costing objectives is shown in Exhibit 5.8, a summary of cost accounting decisions affecting positive cash flow is shown in Exhibit 5.9, a list of cost reduction targets is shown in Exhibit 5.10, and a list of areas for improving activities and cash flow is shown in Exhibit 5.11.

Organizational Concerns

ABC concepts have evolved greatly in a relatively short period of time. Originally conceived as a methodology for product cost improvement and accuracy, ABC is

ABC Objective	Potential Impact on Cash Flow
Lower inventories (raw material, work-in-process, finished goods)	Conserve cash
Lower product costs (material, labor, and overhead)	Increase cash
Smaller manufacturing lots (just in time manufacturing)	No spending until needed
Build quality into the process rather than add it onto the process	Decrease quality control costs
Decreased lead times (on-time deliveries)	Compress cash conversion period
Increased productivity	Produce more at less cost
Improved customer satisfaction	Increase customer service business and additional quality sales
Identification of value-added cost elements	Reduction and elimination of non-value-added cost elements
Control costs of nonproduction related activities	Reduce or eliminate these

> ### *EVERY DOLLAR SAVED IS A DOLLAR OF POSITIVE CASH FLOW.*

Exhibit 5.8 ABC Cost System Objectives

- Manufacture versus purchase (make versus buy)
- Vendor selection (price, quality, timeliness)
- Single versus multiple sourcing
- Manufacturing in-house versus outsourcing
- Manufacture versus assembly
- Cost elements and product item costing
- Pricing strategies
- Capital expenditures (effective use of facilities)
- Production processes and use of personnel
- Product line analysis (what products to sell)
- Inventory levels (in-house versus vendors/distributors)
- Lot sizing (how much to produce)
- What businesses to be in (expand, status quo, curtail, or disband)

Exhibit 5.9 Cost Accounting Decisions Affecting Positive Cash Flow

1. Labor—direct and indirect
2. Materials—direct and supplies
3. Processing time
4. Lead time
5. Paperwork
6. Set-up time—manufacturing and administration
7. Parts and supplies
8. Vendors
9. Queue time
10. Move time
11. Wait time
12. Cycle time—manufacturing and administration
13. Overuse and underuse of scarce resources
14. Scrap and obsolescence
15. Stockouts—manufacturing and administration
16. Customer complaints: quality, quantity, timeliness
17. Uneven production and delivery (i.e., 60 percent of orders shipped during the last week of the month)
18. Unplanned downtime
19. Excesses (i.e., raw material and finished goods inventory, work in process, supplies, equipment)
20. Not shipping or providing services
21. Employee surveys (i.e., anger and frustration)
22. Personnel levels (and related costs)
23. Processes/activities (value and non-value-added)
24. Duplications/nonintegration of functions
25. Unnecessary activities

A DOLLAR OF COST SAVINGS IS A DOLLAR DIRECT TO THE BOTTOM LINE.

Exhibit 5.10   Cost Reduction Targets

now considered a comprehensive organization-wide performance measurement system supporting a wide range of purposes such as:

- *Strategic priorities.* Identifying, setting, and implementing; as well as developing of organizational, departmental, and detail plans, together with flexible budgeting procedures
- *Cost performance measurement.* Identifying cost-reduction opportunities, quality improvements, product/service design, process improvements, and so on

- Eliminate function/work step
- Eliminate duplication
- Combine functions/work steps
- Balance workloads
- Reduce/eliminate bottlenecks
- Improve process flow
- Improve work layout and flow
- Improve scheduling: work and personnel
- Eliminate causes of rejects and rework
- Strengthen education and training
- Increase use of coaching and facilitation
- Simplify work steps and processes
- Improve automation efforts and results
- Increase standardization—decrease customization
- Maintain schedules
- Practice good housekeeping
- Continuously improve
- Meet realistic targets
- Implement effective planning and budgeting systems
- Achieve flexibility: do the right thing
- Exercise performance measurement and continual review and analysis
- Take an operational perspective
- Implement the concept of economy, efficiency, and effectiveness

> *ECONOMY, EFFICIENCY, AND EFFECTIVENESS (AND MAKING MONEY) IS EVERYONE'S BUSINESS.*

Exhibit 5.11   Areas for Improving Activities and Cash Flow

- *Analyzing cost performance.* Identifying such things as material and labor (and other normal overhead type costs) economy and efficiency improvements
- *Continuous improvements.* Operating methods, use of facilities and equipment, productivity, use of personnel, vendor and customer relations, inefficiencies, waste elimination, and so on
- *Capital investment.* Using scarce resources in the most economical, efficient, and effective manner
- *Organizational management.* allowing management to operate and control the organization in the optimum cost-versus-benefit manner.

- *Cash management.* Identifying areas for cash conservation, reduction and elimination of unnecessary costs, development of pricing strategies that maximize bottom line contributions, and implementation of operational economies and efficiencies that result in effective use of resources

Activity Based Management (ABM) uses ABC system provided information to improve the management and operation of ongoing activities. The goal of ABM and ABC should be to increase the value of the products/services provided to customers and to increase company profits by providing higher quality/added value to customers at the lowest possible costs. ABM/ABC works toward improving critical organizational decisions in such areas as:

- Product design and mix (what to sell and provide)
- Pricing considerations (what to charge)
- Customer mix (whom to sell)
- Sourcing (vendors, in house/outsource, markets)
- Improvement priorities (on what areas to concentrate)
- Cash management (where to allocate scarce resources)

In this endeavor to improve the organization, customer service, and compress the cash conversion period through the implementation of best practices in a program of continuous improvement, ABM/ABC looks at the following areas:

- *Products/services.* What to offer, continue or discontinue, expand or contract, as well as cost-volume-profit (CVP) considerations, product/service break-even analysis, and product line analysis
- *Customers.* To whom and how to sell (present and potential), customer service considerations, profitability, customer statistics (sales, costs, and profits), and sales forecasts
- *Activities.* Those that bring value to the product/service, such as material, labor, and product related and those that offer support to the organization at additional cost but provide no value to the product/service (non-value-added), such as administration, support functions, and top management
- *Indicators of poor performance.* Operational measures that provide an indication that there is an area for improvement, such as scrap, vendor returns, customer returns, rework, and rejects

ABM and ABC concepts provide the methodology for measuring the success or failure of the company's cash management endeavors as well as other performance improvement programs such as Total Quality Management (TQM); Just In Time (JIT) concepts for purchasing, manufacturing, and customer deliveries; benchmarking; program of continuous improvements; and so on. These concepts also provide for more effective management and operational decision making. In conducting the cash management study, the company should consider the use of

---

- Customer complaints (returns, rejects, complaints)
- Idle inventory (raw material, work in process, finished goods)
- Late deliveries (vendors, customers)
- Change orders (purchasing, manufacturing, shipping)
- Processing (manufacturing, purchase, and sales orders)
- Recording (purchase requisitions, time cards, move tickets, etc.)
- Quality control (receiving, in process, final)
- Equipment (idle time, setups, maintenance, downtime)
- Production schedule changes (moves, wait time, lost time)
- Customer service (late, inadequate, nonresponsive)

> **COST IS NOT ALWAYS MEASURED IN DOLLARS.**

Exhibit 5.12   Nonfinancial Cost Measures

any or all of these concepts as appropriate. The more concepts such as ABM and ABC that study team members are aware of as they analyze operations and related costs, the greater the results to be achieved. Since one of the major goals of the cash management study is to bring the company up to the optimum level of best practices in a program of continuous improvements, such knowledge of other concepts helps to ensure this will happen.

> **THE ABM GOAL IS TO INCREASE VALUE TO CUSTOMERS AND PROFITS TO THE COMPANY.**

In conducting the cash management study, the company should be aware of the yardsticks, criteria, or benchmarks for best practices and improvements. A list of nonfinancial cost measures to consider in looking at ABM/ABC principles is shown in Exhibit 5.12. In addition, the company should be aware of the costs associated with not doing what is expected. A summary of the cost of such non-compliance elements associated with not doing what is expected is shown in Exhibit 5.13.

Traditional versus ABC Cost Concepts

> **TRADITIONAL COST ACCOUNTING MAY CREATE MORE PROBLEMS THAN SOLUTIONS.**

The cost of noncompliance measures the dollars associated with not doing what is expected.

Failure to Meet Established Standards
- Time (setups, processing, turnaround)
- Cost (i.e., per purchase order, data entry, raw materials)

Time Delays
- Vendor deliveries
- Customer deliveries
- Work-in-process moves (to production schedule)

Production/Service Delivery Deficiencies
- Time commitments
- Quality
- Quantity

Administrative Performance Shortcomings
- Goals, objectives, and detail plans
- Sales forecasts/real customer orders
- Budget versus actual versus what it should be

Schedule Misses
- Selling requirements (when to sell)
- Development (i.e., product engineering)
- Production schedule
- Production control
- Shipping/delivery schedules
- Billing schedules

Exhibit 5.13   Cost of Noncompliance Elements

Traditional cost accounting practices have resulted in confusing decision making and difficulty in identifying true cost elements. With their emphasis on financial measurement, traditional cost techniques have resulted in:

- Short-term thinking
- Ineffective problem identification and improvement
- Deemphasis on effective cost reduction
- Organization-wide versus product/service cost concepts
- Emphasis on external versus internal results
- Bottom line versus operational thinking
- Lack of identification of areas for improvement
- Quick fixes for cost cutting (labor and material)
- Ignoring internal areas of waste

ABC systems, on the other hand, provide for the following features:

- A total cost system
- A program of continuous improvements
- Areas to eliminate waste and reduce costs
- Assignment to each product/service of its true share of activity costs (rather than using an overhead allocation formula)
- Focus on internal operations and results
- Areas for profit improvement
- Elimination of non-value-added activities or improvement of value-added activities
- Reduction or elimination of waste associated with a measured activity

Examples of factors that should be considered in defining the company's cost structure are shown in Exhibit 5.14.

Traditional Cost Elements

The traditional cost accounting system looks at the following cost elements in determining product costs:

- Direct material
- Direct labor
- Overhead—allocation formula (e.g., 140 percent of direct labor)

Problems associated with using these traditional cost elements include:

- Product costs not reflecting actual costs
- Passing costs (excess costs and inefficiencies) onto the customer through selling price calculations (e.g., a percentage markup based on costs)
- Emphasis on external financials, not on internal costs (and operations) and ways of cost reduction
- Job of accounting: information for external financial reports versus information to improve and control internal operations
- Switch in cost structures: less labor, greater material, and more overhead to be allocated
- Excessive emphasis on direct labor
- Short-term results emphasized versus long-term profitability
- Cost and operating systems (i.e., manufacturing, sales, engineering) not integrated
- Lack of coordination between functions (e.g., sales, manufacturing, engineering, accounting)

Products
- Individual item
- Product group
- Product line

Functions (distinct areas within an organization structure)
- Departments
- Cost centers
- Responsibility centers
- Profit centers

Activities (within functions)
- Manufacturing (i.e., product assembly)
- Forms preparation and handling
- Data entry
- Maintenance

Elements (types of costs generated by activities)
- Direct labor
- Direct material
- Repairs and maintenance
- Support work

Exhibit 5.14   Defining cost structures—representative factors

The traditional cost accounting system encompassing the cost elements of labor, material, and allocated overhead has remained constant in many organizations, whereas the makeup of these elements of product/service costs may have changed, as follows:

	Past	*Present*
Material	25–50%	30–60%
Labor	25–50%	5–20%
Overhead	25–50%	30–65%

Trends in most organizations show direct labor costs decreasing, direct material costs increasing, and overhead (indirect) costs, while not always fully known, increasing even more rapidly as a result of more control systems (quality control, inventory control, production control), scheduling (production scheduling, process scheduling), compliance (safety, affirmative action, environmental) and related advancements in manufacturing and service processes.

Using these cost elements (material, labor, and overhead), the reviewer might calculate product costs as follows:

Product A—50 items

	Cost	%
Direct material @ $5 per item	$ 250	36.7%
Direct labor: 15 hours @ $12	180	26.4%
Overhead: 140% x direct labor cost	252	36.9%
Total Product Costs	$ 682	100.0%
Cost per Item	$ 13.64	

Product B—10 items

	Cost	%
Direct material @ $53.80 per item	$ 538	78.9%
Direct labor: 5 hours @ $12	60	8.8%
Overhead: 140% x direct labor cost	84	12.3%
Total Product Costs	$ 682	100.0%
Cost per Item	$ 68.20	

Questions that may arise using traditional cost accounting techniques include:

- *Direct material.* Are these at the lowest possible costs, looking at activities such as purchasing, stocking, use, scrap, rework and rejects, and so on?
- *Direct labor.* Is it at the lowest possible level, looking at activities such as set-ups, processing times, productivity, use of engineering standards, and so on?
- *Overhead.* Is it accurate and at its lowest level, looking at activities and questions such as:
  - Amount of overhead being the same for both products (140 percent of direct labor)
  - Differences in number of items produced
  - Indirect costs associated with each product (e.g., purchasing, receiving, storing, issuing) not properly accounted for
  - What costs are lumped into overhead (value-added versus non-value-added)?
  - What is the cause and effect between cost and activities?
  - How are cost drivers identified and what is their impact on total product cost?
  - Why the emphasis on direct material and labor, with all other costs accounted for by an overhead allocation?
  - How can value-added cost elements be identified back to the product/service item?

Cost and Process Views

ABC has two main views—cost assignment and process. The cost assignment view reflects the organization's need to trace or allocate resources to activities or cost objects (products as well as customers) to analyze critical decisions such as pricing, product mix, priority setting, and so on. The process view reflects the organization's need for information about events that influence the performance of activities—that is, what causes the work and how well is it done. Such performance feedback information is then used to improve operations and results.

Cost Assignment View

Resources (the sources of costs) are economic elements that are applied to the performance of activities; which could include:

- Direct labor and material
- Support staff (e.g., salaries and fringe benefits)
- Indirect costs (e.g., facilities, heat, light, phone, electric)
- Administrative costs (e.g., computer operations, advertising, public relations)
- Selling and marketing costs

Resources flow to activities, which are processes or procedures that cause work to be performed. In a purchasing department, activities can include requisition processing, vendor negotiations, purchase order processing, open order control, expediting, and so on. Such related activities are typically considered to constitute an activity center (purchasing activities). Factors that are known as resource drivers are used to assign resource costs (for example, salaries) to activities (for example, purchase order processing). Each type of resource becomes a cost element (for example, amount of resource used by an activity) as part of an activity pool (total cost of an activity).

Each activity cost pool is traced to the cost objects by means of an activity driver, which is the measure of the use of the activity by the cost objects. The activity driver is used to assign resources from the activity to the cost system. Processing of purchase orders, for example, is traced to products based on the number of times the item is purchased.

The cost object, the final point to which cost is traced, is any activity, organizational unit, contract, or other work unit for which a separate measurement of cost is desired; it is the reason that work is performed and may be either a product/service or a customer. The cost traced to each product or customer reflects the cost of the activities used by that cost object. The company may use the same cost to record and report against a product, service, activity, function, level, customer, or some other basis as is appropriate in the situation—the user designs the system.

Process View

The process view (cost drivers, activities, and performance measures) provides information about the work accomplished in an activity and its relationship to other activities. A process can be viewed as a series of activities that work together to achieve a specific purpose (e.g., various manufacturing functions working together to produce a finished product). Internal activities can be considered as links to another activity—all working together to produce a result.

The process view of ABC provides information relative to cost drivers and performance measures for each activity in the network, which are primarily non-financial, that can be used to analyze and improve the performance of an activity and the entire process or function. Cost drivers are those events that cause a change in the total cost of an activity. Cost drivers determine the workload and effort required to perform an activity. They tell why (e.g., processing a manufacturing order in response to a prior event such as a customer order), and how much effort is required (e.g., 24 minutes) to perform the task.

> ### COST DRIVERS—EVENTS THAT CAUSE A CHANGE IN THE COST OF AN ACTIVITY.

Performance measures are indicators—financial and non-financial—of the work performed and the results achieved in an activity. They tell how well the activity was performed and whether it is meeting the needs of its purpose. They can include measures of the efficiency of the activity, time to perform the activity, quality of the results, and so on.

ABC Activities

ABC systems focus on the activities to be performed to produce products/services. Activity costs are assigned to products/services based on each item's use of those activities. For instance, in a typical organization, there may be the following levels of activities:

- *Unit level.* Performed each time a unit is produced (e.g., manufacturing operations, quality control)
- *Batch level.* Performed each time a batch of items is produced (e.g., set-ups, material handling)
- *Product level.* Performed to support the providing of each different type of product/service (e.g., product specifications, order handling)
- *Facility level.* Performed to support the facility's general purposes (e.g., utilities, security, cleaning, and maintenance). These costs are typically allocated to products/services based on someone's judgment.

Typically, ABC systems report costs per individual unit (e.g., full absorption product/service costs). Such unit costs are obtained by:

- Calculating unit-level costs
- Batch-level costs divided by number of units in each batch
- Product-level costs divided by the number of product items produced in all batches
- Facility-level costs divided by the number of total product items produced in the period
- Adding the results of the preceding items

It should be noted that the product ABC costs as calculated here will not equal product costs produced by traditional cost accounting systems. However, the ABC system costs will produce more accurate product/service costs because they more accurately identify what causes the cost to be incurred.

An example showing the calculation of total cost, unit cost, and selling price by product using traditional and ABC cost systems is shown in Exhibit 5.15.

Note that as unit costs are calculated differently (but more accurately) using ABC concepts, the calculations also affect the selling price. Accordingly, ABC cost systems can turn a loser into a winner and vice versa. For example, product A with a present unit cost of $10.50 and a selling price of $15.00 when recalculated using ABC concepts shows a unit cost of $30.65. Using this more accurate unit cost, it is evident that the company cannot sell this product for $15.00 and make money. Management, confronted with the ABC data, must now decide what to do about this product—stop selling it, greatly reduce costs, raise the price, continue to sell it at a loss, or some other action.

Under ABC system concepts, where overhead activities and their related costs are assigned to the product based on usage of the activity, true product costs are calculated more accurately. A sample bill of activities used to assign such overhead activity costs to product A is shown in Exhibit 5.16. Note that when using such data in the cash management study, the study team also focuses on these activities as to whether each one is needed or can be eliminated, reduced, or made more efficient. For example, if the company can eliminate the necessity for the preparation of purchase orders, it also eliminates the total cost of $320, which goes directly to the bottom line. In addition, the study team would analyze the remaining allocated cost activities (usually non-value-added activities such as management and administration) for elimination, reduction, combination, or efficiency.

Overhead Considerations

Overhead is typically defined as all manufacturing/service costs other than direct materials and labor. Traditionally, those costs that cannot be directly associated with direct product or service costs are classified as overhead and allocated on

Traditional Cost System:

Product	Units Made	Material Costs	Direct Labor Hours	Direct Labor $10/hr	Overhead $20/DL Hr	Total Cost	Unit Cost	Selling Price
A	20	$ 60	5	$ 50	$ 100	$ 210	$10.50	$15.00
B	60	180	25	250	500	930	15.50	22.00
C	140	420	65	650	1300	2370	16.93	24.00
D	300	900	180	1800	3600	6300	21.00	30.00

Note: Selling price = 140% X unit cost (rounded to higher dollar)

Activity-Based Cost (ABC) System:

Product	Units Made	Material Costs	Labor Costs	Unit Activity	Batch Activity	Product Activity	Total Cost	Unit Cost	Selling Price
A	20	60	50	170	33	300	613	30.65	None
B	60	180	250	140	38	500	1108	18.47	22.00
C	140	420	650	240	96	700	2106	15.04	22.00
D	300	900	1800	210	110	1000	4020	13.40	20.00

Notes:

Unit-level activities: Procuring materials ($50 per item), Manufacturing supervision ($20 per hour)

Batch-level activities: Set-ups (number X direct labor cost of $10). Material handling (hours X $6)

Product-level activities: Order handling ($200 per customer order, $100 per manufacturing order)

Selling price based on competitive market conditions.

Exhibit 5.15 Traditional Cost System versus Activity Based Costing System

Traditional Costs:				
Material				$ 350.00
Labor				400.00
Overhead (200% of direct labor dollars)				800.00
Total Cost				$1,550.00
Item Cost				$ 155.00

ABC Bill of Activity Costs: (with efficiencies)

Direct Costs				ABC Cost
Material				$ 230.00
Labor				280.00
Activities	Output Measure	Use per Unit	OM Cost	
Bill of material	Hours	1.5	$20.00	30.00
Routing/process	Hours	2.2	34.00	74.80
Purchasing	Pos	4	80.00	320.00
WIP moves	Number	6	8.00	48.00
Inspections	Number	3	25.00	75.00
Packaging	Unit	1	18.00	18.00
Shipping	Unit	1	13.00	13.00
Total Activities				578.80
Allocated Costs				180.00
Subtotal				758.80
Total Cost				$1,268.80
Item Cost				$ 126.88

Exhibit 5.16   Sample Bill of Activities: Product A—100 items

some basis. Although many of the components of overhead may be necessary, a great number may not be. Often, the organization has hidden such unnecessary or wasteful costs as overhead so as not to attract attention to them. Overhead costs must be analyzed to determine those that are unnecessary and wasteful.

> ## OVERHEAD COSTS ARE REAL COSTS
> ## —AND THEY NEED TO BE CONTROLLED.

Overhead in many organizations has become the biggest depository of costs. Overhead affects product costs, profit margins, resultant profits, and cash flow just as direct costs do. Those overhead costs that add value should be directly charged to the activity; those that do not should be eliminated.

The company should review and analyze each function (e.g., sales, engineering, manufacturing, accounting, etc.) and determine which activities are direct product or service cost. Those activity costs that are direct should be assigned back to the products/services that use such activities. To accomplish such a functional analysis, each activity has to be fully analyzed to determine which ones are direct product costs (and the method of allocation or assignment) and which ones are not (to be eliminated).

For example, consider some typical activities in an administrative-type department (such as sales, purchasing, accounting, customer service, etc.):

- Telephone calls—incoming and outgoing
- Computer use—data processing, e-mail, Internet, and so on
- Receiving, reviewing, and filing paper
- Memo preparation and mailing
- Expediting/checking/reviewing activities
- Database maintenance
- Meetings—within and outside the department
- Breaks and lunches
- Surveys and audits
- Travel— internal and external
- Processing activities

In analyzing the function and its related activities, the company must look at the total cost of operating the function, department, or cost center. Some elements can be captured directly as product/service costs, while others may have to be allocated based on some formula. Other costs that are not relevant to product/service costs should be eliminated. Note that not all expenses can (or should) be allocated or assigned directly to the product/service level. However, the company should make every effort to assign as many of these expenses as is logical and practical.

Functional Cost Controls

Another important aspect of an ABC system is to analyze and control each function of the organization, such as sales, manufacturing/service delivery, engineering/service design, computer processing, accounting, and so on. The starting point is to review and analyze the function as it is presently being performed so as to identify areas for improvement together with recommendations for such improvements. Typically, an individual or a study team is assigned responsibility for each major function. The goal of this analysis is to begin the ABC functional control system with the most economical and efficient systems and procedures as possible – and at the least cost. From that point, it becomes easier to maintain a program of continuous improvements.

Some tools for analyzing functions and their related costs are presented in Exhibits 5.17 to 5.21.

1. Purchase Requisition by User
   - Preparation
   - Review
   - Authorization
   - Submission to Purchasing Department

2. Purchasing Department
   - Review of Purchase Requisition
   - Vendor review and selection
   - Existing vendor
   - New vendor
   - Competitive bidding
   - Contracting
   - Data entry
   - Purchase Requisition
   - Purchase Order
   - Purchase Order processing
   - Printing
   - Forms separation, distribution, and filing
   - Purchase Order submission to vendor
   - Mailing process
   - Electronic ordering
   - Purchase Order filing

3. Matching Process—By User
   - Open Purchase Requisition file
   - Receiving Purchase Order copy
   - Match Purchase Order to Requisition
   - File open Purchase Order

4. Accounts Payable
   - Receive open Purchase Order copies
   - File in open Purchase Order files: by vendor, by PO number

Exhibit 5.17   Identifying Activities for the Purchasing Function

ABC Case Study

ABC COST SYSTEMS CAN TURN LOSERS INTO WINNERS AND VICE VERSA.

A company, ACE Inc., manufactures a commercial product that is highly competitive. The company was the original inventor of the product and at one time had 74 percent of the market. However, with strong competition (particularly from the

Cost Data:

- Average cost of PO process activities = $130 (labor and materials)
- POs processed in period: 240 X $130 = $31,200 total cost
- By product item: Item #123 = 82 PO's X $130 = $10,660

Costing by Product: Purchase Order Processing

Product	# of POs	%
1	183	6.6%
2	346	12.5%
3	639	23.1%
4	621	22.4%
5	468	16.9%
6	512	18.5%
TOTAL	2,769	100.0%

Total cost for Purchasing Department for period = $ 88,766.

Assigning functional costs to products:

Product	%	Cost
1	6.6%	$ 5,859
2	12.5%	11,096
3	23.1%	20,505
4	22.4%	19,883
5	16.9%	15,001
6	18.5%	16,422
TOTAL	100.0%	$88,766

Exhibit 5.18   Using Functional Costs to Assign Costs to Products

overseas market), market share has dropped to 32 percent over the past few years. Although its product is still perceived to be the best quality in the market place, ACE's four competitors have been able to basically copy the product and sell it from 10 to 30 percent less than ACE, as shown below:

Company	Selling Price	% of ACE S.P.	Market Share
ACE, Inc.	$129	100%	32%
1	$ 89	69%	36%
2	$ 98	76%	17%
3	$109	84%	8%
4	$116	90%	7%

As can be seen, this has become a price-sensitive product, with the greatest sales going to the lowest-price seller. Some customers of ACE are still willing to

1.	Inventory Carrying Cost (ICC) of items on hand waiting for delivery of stockout inventory =	$ .02
	ICC × Inventory Value × # of Days =	
	.02 × $ 8,200 × 6 days =	$ 984
2.	Expediting costs	
	Personnel: $15/hour × 22 hours =	330
	Computer: $20/hour × 2 hours =	40
3.	Shipping charges (priority)	124
4.	Production time lost: 4 hours × $350 =	1,400
	Total cost of a stockout	$ 2,878
	Number of stockouts: 26	
Total cost of stockouts for the period: 26 × $2,878=		$74,828

Exhibit 5.19   Cost of an Inventory Stockout—Representative Example

Labor hour cost: $12 per hour

Activity	Time	Cost
1. Receive PO copy from Purchasing and file in open PO file	10 min	$ 2.00
2. Receive delivery and verify that delivery is ours: check bill of lading, packing slip, and sign	20 min	4.00
3. Compare delivery to open PO and record receipt on PO	15 min	3.00
4. Count parts—record on open PO reconcile to PO amount ordered	15 min	3.00
5. Produce receiving report using open PO copy — Partial: PO back to open file — Final: PO to accounts payable — Receiving report to accounts payable	30 min	6.00
6. Wait for quality control inspection	4 hrs	-0-
7. Move: storeroom, shop floor, or internal department	30 min	6.00
Total Cost of Receiving		$24.00

Exhibit 5.20   Receiving Costs

pay more for what they perceive to be better quality, and there is an indication of some customer loyalty. ACE is implementing ABC cost principles in an attempt to better control its costs, achieve flexibility in pricing, and get back its previous market share. The company believes that the public will buy its product instead of the competitors' if it sells the same high quality at lower prices.

The following cost workups show the differences between product costs and selling prices under different cost concepts.

Traditional Cost Data

Material Costs:

Lot size of 100, item cost of $34.68, 120 items into production.

Labor Costs:

Labor rates:	Direct = $12/hour	Indirect = $16/hour
Storeroom issues/returns =		2 hours
Staging/get ready =		1 hour
Number of set-ups =		4 @ 6 hours each
Moves = 4 @ 1/2 hour each =		2 hours
Processing Time =		126.4 hours/lot
Quality Control =		8 hours/lot
Packing/shipping =		4 hours
Supervision =		6 hours/lot
Supplies =		$4.80 unit
Other Costs (allocated) =		$8.40 unit

Overhead Costs:

Overhead rate = 140% of direct labor costs (set-up and processing)

Selling Price Markup: 150% of total costs

Calculate the traditional cost and selling price per item:

	Total Cost	Unit Cost
Materials	$4,161.60	$41.62
Direct Labor		
Setups	288.00	2.88
Processing	1,516.80	15.17
Total Labor	1,804.80	18.05
Overhead	2,526.72	25.27
Total Cost	$8,493.12	$84.94

Selling Price: 150%	Markup $127.41	Rounded to $129

Labor hour cost: $16 per hour

Activity	Cost Element	Time	Cost
1. Receive PO from purchasing and file in open PO file	Labor	15 min	$ 4.00
2. Receive "receiving report" from receiving, pull open PO from file and compare hold in open receipts file	Labor	20 min	5.33
3. Receive invoice from vendor and match to open receipts or pull open po and compare and hold as open invoice	Labor	30 min	8.00
4. Invoice/receiving errors	Labor	0	0.00
5. Computer data entry	Labor	10 min	2.67
6. Computer check prep	Labor Checks	10 min	2.67 0.15
7. Mail checks	Labor Envel., postage	10 min	2.67 0.50
8. File paid payable	Labor	15 min	4.00
9. Meetings, phone, fax	Labor, phone	0	0.00
Total Cost			$29.99

Exhibit 5.21   Accounts Payable Costs

ABC Costs Using Traditional Cost Data

Calculate ABC costs from the information provided:

	Total Cost	*Unit Cost*
Materials	$4,161.60	$41.62
Direct labor	1,804.80	18.05
ABC costs:		
Storeroom	32.00	0.32
Staging	16.00	0.16
Moves	32.00	0.32
Quality control	128.00	1.28
Packing/shipping	64.00	0.64
Supplies	480.00	4.80
Supervision	96.00	0.96
Other costs	840.00	8.40
Total ABC Costs	1,688.00	16.88
Total Cost	$7,654.40	$76.55

What selling price should be recommended?

ABC Costs Integrated with Operating Efficiencies and Cost Reductions

Through analysis of operations and processes, the following activities could be eliminated:

- Storeroom
- Staging
- Moves

In addition, through effective repurchase negotiations material costs could be reduced to $26.00 per unit and 100 pieces placed into production to produce 100 items.

Direct labor times could also be reduced as follows:

- Setups: 3 @ 4 hours each
- Processing time: 108.8 hours per lot
- Quality control: 2 hours per lot
- Supervision: 1 hour per lot

Task: Recalculate ABC costs based on the preceding data.

	Total Cost	Unit Cost
Materials	$2,600.00	$ 26.00
Direct labor		
Setups	144.00	1.44
Processing	1,305.60	13.06
Total	1,449.60	14.50
ABC costs:		
Quality control	32.00	0.32
Packing/shipping	64.00	0.64
Supplies	480.00	4.80
Supervision	16.00	0.16
Other costs	840.00	8.40
Total ABC Costs	1,432.00	14.32
Total Cost	$ 5,481.60	$ 54.82

What selling price should be recommended at this cost?

ABC Costs with Identification of Specific Elements of Other Activity Costs

Further analysis identified specific elements of other activity costs of $840.00 to be as follows:

	Output Measure	Per Unit	OM Cost	Total Cost	Unit Cost
Bill of material	Hours	2.0	$30.00	$ 60.00	$0.60
Routing/Process	Hours	1.5	20.00	30.00	0.30
Purchasing	POs	4	75.00	300.00	3.00
Receiving	Number	4	12.00	48.00	0.48
Storeroom moves	Number	2	18.00	36.00	0.36
Work–in-process moves	Number	6	12.00	72.00	0.72
Inspections	Number	3	25.00	75.00	0.75
Packaging	Unit	1	18.00	18.00	0.18
Shipping	Unit	1	13.00	13.00	0.13
Accounts payable	Number	4	32.00	128.00	1.28
Total Activity Costs				$780.00	$7.80
Allocated Costs				60.00	0.60
Total Cost				$840.00	$8.40

What activities should be considered for further analysis leading toward further cost reductions? Remember that a dollar of savings from any source produces a dollar of profit to the bottom line and to positive cash flow. Accordingly, any of these activities that can be eliminated or reduced will result in direct increases to the bottom line and positive cash flow.

CONCLUSION

The production/service costs the company incurs represent the most significant cause of company cash outflows. In order to improve cash flow, therefore, it is essential for the organization to control those costs effectively. While cost control is a well-accepted way for a company to improve its profitability, its relevance to cash flow is often not understood, not recognized, or (in the worst case) deliberately ignored.

Benchmarking and ABC are two formalized methods that can be used to institute better cost control within the company. Benchmarking allows the company to compare its processes and related costs to objective outside standards—methods developed by others and proven to be best practices. ABC is a method of analyzing company costs to determine just what drives those costs and assigning the costs to particular products or services based on how many of those drivers are actually used by the particular products or services. In this chapter we have attempted to provide some illustrations of how these techniques might be applied. While the examples are necessarily illustrative rather than definitive, an understanding of the principles underlying the techniques should allow them to be adapted and applied to virtually any company situation.

> *THE GREATEST CAUSE OF CASH OUTFLOWS*
> *IS OPERATING COSTS.*
> *THE GREATEST OPPORTUNITY TO IMPROVE*
> *CASH FLOW IS TO CONTROL OPERATING COSTS.*

CHAPTER 6

Analyzing Non-Value-Added Functions

CONVERT NON-VALUE-ADDED ACTIVITIES TO VALUE-ADDED.

The cash management study starts at the top of the organization. That is, top management should define and communicate its strategic plans for the company, including areas of expansion, retrenchment, and status quo. At the same time, management should identify the businesses they want to be in, the businesses they do not want to be in, their basic business principles and belief systems, and their expectations for each function within the organization.

With the clear identification and communication of management's expectations, each function will have a clear idea of where it is heading and the basis for its evaluation. The purpose of the cash management study then becomes one of a helping agent, assisting each function to achieve its stated goals and objectives as related to management's expectations. The performance of the cash management study is thus less a critical evaluation of what a particular function is doing and more an appraisal of what needs to be done to help the function achieve its goals and become the best it can be at the least possible cost.

As the study team works with each function within the organization, it helps that function to understand what it needs to do to become what it should be. As best practices and improvements are recommended and implemented, each function moves toward its proper place within the organization—and the company becomes a learning organization by function and overall. The company achieves its goals and objectives at the least cost possible and maximizes the resultant positive cash flow.

In today's organizational atmosphere of cost cutting, downsizing, and reengineering, cash management must be sensitive in its approach so as to maintain needed services in the most economical, efficient, and effective manner. Whereas management may be focusing on reducing costs, operations may be focusing on providing an increase in quality services. The company must be careful to maintain a proper perspective so that it directs its efforts toward overall organizational goals as well as the individual requirements of each function.

A cash management study is an effective process to use in looking at a company's operations to measure current economies, efficiencies, and effectiveness of results. In addition, the study process assists in the identification of performance gaps—the difference between present and desired operating results as compared with internal goals and external competitors. A thorough understanding of such performance gaps enables company and departmental management to seize these opportunities for improvement. There has always been a demand, and perhaps more so today, to decrease costs, increase positive cash flow, and improve product/service/customer quality—all directed toward increasing profits.

As a way of illustrating how to deal with non-value-added functions, we will use accounting as an example. This is not to say that accounting is inevitably a non-value-added activity. Properly organized and led, accounting can certainly add value to the organization. But it is a function that is often, and sometimes accurately, perceived as not adding significant value. As such it is an appropriate representative part of the organization to use as an example. The approach illustrated can be adapted to other perceived non-value-added activities within the organization as necessary.

LOOKING AT THE ACCOUNTING FUNCTION

In the current business environment, the accounting function in many organizations is perceived as a prime candidate for cost reduction and, in extreme situations, for elimination. Many of its functions (e.g., preparing customer invoices, collecting payments, processing vendor payments, preparing payrolls) are viewed by company management as necessary but not adding significant value. In other words, these things may have to be done, but can the company accomplish them with as little cost as possible (none, it hopes)? It is within such a framework that the cash management study may have to work. Rather than analyze how present functions can be performed in a better manner, the company may be asked to look at how such functions can be severely reduced or eliminated.

With the nature of most businesses changing from a predominantly mechanical operation to a more customer service oriented approach, the company must also appraise the accounting function from this perspective. That is, the company must not only review and appraise the accounting function's present activities, but must also be aware of the services the accounting function should be providing to its company in-house customers.

Accordingly, the study team must work with each function within the organization to assist in redefining its role as expected by top management and the most effective way to get there. The company must also consider the impact of each function on others within the company and how best for all functions to work together in an integrated fashion. The study team must possess the knowledge of the overall direction of the company, management's desires for the function under review, and the manner in which the two can be coordinated.

The cash management study process can assist in reducing accounting function costs through the use of more efficient systems and procedures, along with a clear identification of desired results. At the same time, the quality of the accounting/financial value-added services provided can be greatly enhanced. In effect, the accounting function can be an active value-added function that contributes effectively to the company's profit and positive cash flow.

INCREASE POSITIVE CASH FLOW: DECREASE NON-VALUE-ADDED ACTIVITIES.

A cash management study of the accounting functions begins with the analysis of existing practices within the various accounting areas of the company to identify activities and performance drivers, and functions that can be improved as to best practices. Performance drivers are the causes of work (e.g., all vendor invoices must be verified by recalculation) or triggers (e.g., a customer order) that set in motion a series of activities. The cash management study process focuses on questioning such performance drivers and triggers as to their elimination and to the ultimate elimination of the corresponding activities. Significant improvements can be made as study team members ask questions such as:

- Is this activity needed?
- Why is this activity performed?
- Is this position/material really needed?
- Can the activity be done better and less expensively in another manner?
- Is this step necessary? Does it provide added value?

The study process can also include the comparison of similar operations, functions, or activities within an organization to identify opportunities for improvement and best practices within a common environment. For an organization to maximize the benefits to be derived, it is best for it to fully understand and document its existing systems and procedures.

The various analysis steps help to identify critical areas of the company's activities, related performance drivers, and opportunities for improvements. This may arise as one part of the company, division, or work unit learns from another. In this manner, overall communication processes improve, areas of excellence are identified, and operating procedures are changed to reflect best practices.

Once the critical areas within the accounting function are identified, an initial analysis is performed to obtain data on activities such as:

- Who is involved and how they relate to the activity, its desired results, and each other. Document such things as the number of individuals, relative positions, and method of organization and management.
- Why each individual is involved and his or her value or non-value-added activities. Does each one perform necessary operations, have special

expertise, or have specific responsibility? Or is he or she just excess structure?

- What activities are being done and whether each one has to be done, can be done more efficiently, or is being done well (a best practice)?
- Why each activity is being done. Does each of the activities relate to desired goals and objectives, and is each one being performed most effectively?
- What resources are assigned to each activity. Is the assignment most economical, and are resources excessive, deficient, or proper to achieve desired results?

When the study team members have a clear understanding of how the area operates, including such things as performance drivers, organizational, departmental, and work unit belief systems, and basic business principles for conducting activities within the area, they can begin to identify the following:

- Key aspects of the function's activities and performance results
- Inherent, structural, and performance drivers
- Critical operational areas and opportunities for improvement (one part learning from another)
- Channels of communication within the company
- Pockets of good, desirable practices (best practices, and areas of excellence)
- Standards for good practices so as to reflect the adoption of best practices

Defining the elements of each activity, and determining whether it is a value-added or non-value-added activity, and what each individual does in the process, as well as why he or she does it, is the basis for analysis as to improvements. A list of questions to be addressed is shown in Exhibit 6.1. Some benefits to be derived from the cash management study are shown in Exhibit 6.2.

CHOOSING WHAT TO ANALYZE

The cash management study team, in consultation with management, decides which accounting functional areas it will include in the study and which areas are to be addressed by management and operations personnel. For instance, the analysis of the accounting and financial functions can be looked at in a number of ways, such as:

- *Functional.* Accounting, information processing, treasury, reporting, and so on
- *Process.* Accounts payable, accounts receivable, payroll, general ledger, budget, cash management

---

PEOPLE
1. Who is involved? And why?
   • Number of people
   • Number of positions
   • How organized and managed
   • Current personnel resource demands

2. Are all personnel needed?
   • Reasons for involvement
   • What they are doing
   • Value-added or non-value-added
   • Vital operation or task
   • Special expertise

3. Who has responsibility for outcomes?
   • Hierarchical pyramid: power and control
   • Management oriented: review and redo
   • Employee self-motivated, disciplined behavior
   • Delegation of authority to lowest operational levels
   • Empire building: work continues – reason no longer valid

PROCEDURES
1. Why is the task performed? (e.g., It has always been done this way)
2. Is it necessary or unnecessary? (e.g., That is the way we do it)
3. Does it add value to customer? (internal versus external viewpoint)
4. Is there unnecessary bureaucracy? (e.g., unwieldy hierarchy)
5. Are there ineffective, inefficient, or redundant procedures?
6. What do people do, and why do they do it? (foundation for internal improvements)
7. What are the bundles or groups of value-added and non-value-added procedures and activities?

Exhibit 6.1 Cash Management Study Questions

- *Industry.* Specific manufacturing, retailing, banking, and so on
- *Business cycle.* Based on the concept of closed loop activities such as:
  - *Sales cycle.* Sales order—shipping—invoicing—accounts receivable—collections
  - *Purchase cycle.* Purchase requisition—purchasing—receiving—vendor invoicing—accounts payable—cash disbursements
  - *Payroll/Labor distribution cycle.* Time and job verification—data entry—payroll/labor distribution processing—pay distribution—record keeping
  - *General ledger/financial statement cycle.* Subsystem data collection—journal entries—general ledger posting—financial reporting

1. Defines existing processes and activities; establishes baseline of acceptable performance (helps to trigger continuous improvement efforts)
2. Identifies gaps in performance in similar internal processes (provides a clear picture of the organization's problems)
3. Brings all internal operations up to the highest possible level of performance (within existing constraints)
4. Identifies areas of internal operational improvements without going outside the organization (keeps the information inside the company)
5. Establishes standards for common practices and procedures (overcomes the "not created here" syndrome)
6. Opens communication lines within the organization (focuses resources on problems that affect more than one area)
7. Establishes organization-wide commitment to cash management improvements (recasts the problems facing the company)
8. Establishes groundwork for internal operations efforts (ensures greater results when operations personnel do it themselves)
9. Prioritizes critical areas for cash management improvement opportunities
10. Identifies and classifies the key performance drivers (e.g., organization atmosphere, rigid policies, strict procedures, unwieldy hierarchy, and so on).

Exhibit 6.2 Cash Management Study Benefits

- *Cost accounting cycle.* Material/labor/overhead data collection—computer processing—operating reports—off line action—reporting by task, job, and period

ACCOUNTING CANNOT WORK IN ISOLATION.

The accounting functions (e.g., accounts payable, accounts receivable, payroll, and general ledger) cannot be isolated from those other functions that are supported by and integrated with the specific accounting activity (e.g., accounts payable with the purchasing, receiving, and manufacturing functions). It is thinking that accounting functions such as accounts payable can be isolated that has allowed them to be drastically cut back in many organizations to the detriment of purchasing, receiving, and manufacturing. In reality, each component of the specific business cycle is equally as important as the others. Therefore, to most effectively analyze one of the accounting functions, it is best to look at it as part of its business cycle. For the purpose of an analysis of the accounting activity, each of these accounting functions must be considered as a part of its corresponding business cycle.

IDENTIFYING GOALS AND BASIC BUSINESS PRINCIPLES

Prior to the start of the analysis of the accounting functions, the study team should be clear as to management's goals and expectations for each of these functions. For the management team to identify such goals and expectations, they have to be clear as to the purpose of each of the functions and the results that will be most beneficial to the overall operations of the company. There must be more than just a desire to eliminate unnecessary costs and increase cash flow; there must also be a full understanding of why each of these functions should exist. For example, management may identify goals and desires for each of the major accounting functions as follows:

- *Accounts payable*
  - The elimination of the function, to the extent possible, where the cost of processing vendor payments exceeds the value to the company in delaying such payments
  - The elimination of the processing of vendor payments where the cost of processing exceeds the amount of the payment
  - The least costly most efficient methods of processing remaining vendor payments
  - The ability to computer integrate accounts payable data with other subsystems such as cost accounting, vendor statistics, manufacturing controls, inventory controls, production controls, and cash management
  - An economic balance between necessary controls and the cost of implementing such controls

- *Accounts receivable*
  - The elimination of the function, to the extent possible, where the cost of billing, collecting, and processing of customer payments exceeds the value to the company of extending credit to such customers
  - The elimination of the processing of customer billings and collections where the cost of processing exceeds the amount of the billing
  - The least costly, most efficient methods of processing remaining customer bills
  - The ability to computer integrate accounts receivable data with other subsystems such as credit controls, sales forecasts, customer and sales statistics, collection controls, and cash management

- *Payroll processing*
  - The least costly, most efficient methods for processing payroll and the maintenance of necessary records
  - The ability to integrate payroll data with other subsystems such as cost accounting, personnel records, planning and budget systems

- The ability of a computerized payroll system to automatically process labor distribution or labor costs to production jobs (e.g., production employees time processing at their pay rates to job costs), maintain personnel records (e.g., vacation, leave absenteeism records), and post to the budget system as it processes payroll transactions

- *General ledger*
  - Full computer integration with all other subsystems so that the general ledger is automatically updated on a real-time basis
  - Automatic generation of all repetitive journal entries, allowing for minimal manual journal entries
  - Ability to produce financial statements – balance sheet, income statement, and statement of cash flows – on demand

- *Accounting and financial reporting*
  - Automatic generation of all accounting and financial reports, showing exceptions to key operating indicators
  - Integration of accounting and financial reporting with operating statistics
  - Ability to analyze and interpret all such reports so that each report is most useful for both management and operational purposes
  - Use of real time reporting via computer screens, and the requirement for positive action to be taken in all areas

> **EACH FUNCTION'S REASON FOR EXISTENCE MUST BE UNDERSTOOD.**

In addition, management must clearly state its basic business principles, such as the following five points:

1. Produce the best quality product at the lowest possible cost.
2. Set selling prices realistically, so as to sell all the product the company can produce within the limits of production capabilities.
3. Build trusting relationships with critical vendors—keeping them in business keeps the company in business.
4. Recognize that the company is in the customer service and cash conversion businesses.
5. Focus on the survival of the company, which allows it to serve its customers, take care of its employees, and achieve its goals.

Members of top management should also define their agreed-upon basic business principles as related to the accounting functions. Examples of such basic business principles are:

- The cost of processing should always be less than the amount of the item—the price at which it is sold or the amount of the vendor payment.
- All unnecessary or non-value-added accounting functions should be eliminated.
- All redundant or duplicate activities should be eliminated.
- All necessary accounting functions should be accomplished in the least costly and most efficient manner.
- All accounting processing and data should be fully integrated with all other applicable subsystems.
- Accounting and financial reporting should be fully integrated with operational reporting so that management and operations personnel can make the best decisions.
- The accounting functions—accounts payable, accounts receivable, payroll, and general ledger—should be fully integrated into the operations of the company.
- The accounting functions should be value-added providers of financial and operational data so that the value provided exceeds the cost of their operations.
- Accounting personnel must be able to design, develop, and implement effective reporting systems that assist the company in reaching its operational and profit goals.
- Accounting personnel must become analyzers and interpreters of data for management decisions, rather than mere processors of data and transactions.

PRIORITIZING ACTIVITIES

One of the first steps in the cash management study is to identify and prioritize those activities related to the selected accounting functions to include in the study. The areas selected should be the most critical to the company as related to positive cash flow and operating results as well as feedback from management and operations personnel via such tools as surveys, interviews, and group brainstorming sessions. For purposes of the analysis, six areas are identified:

1. Organizational issues
   - Authority, responsibility, management
   - Personnel functions: who does what and why
   - Operating policies, belief systems, and performance drivers
   - Budget and actual costs

2. Accounts payable and cash disbursements functions
   - Accounts payable processing
   - Open payables control
   - Vendor payment processing
   - Cash disbursement processing
   - Record keeping and analysis

3. Accounts receivable processing
   - Credit policies: establishment and maintenance
   - Sales order processing
   - Billing procedures
   - Open receivables control
   - Collection procedures
   - Customer statistics
   - Record keeping and analysis

4. Payroll processing
   - Processing procedures
   - Payroll statistics: types, frequency, number of personnel, cost, dollar amount
   - Reports produced
   - Personnel statistics
   - Record keeping and analysis

5. General ledger
   - Chart of accounts
   - Processing procedures
   - Journal entry processing
   - Reports produced
   - Record keeping and analysis

6. Accounting, financial, and operational reporting
   - Reports produced
   - Information lacking
   - Use of reports
   - Analysis and interpretation

FINANCIAL REPORTING

INTERNAL FINANCIAL STATEMENTS MUST CLEARLY COMMUNICATE OPERATING RESULTS.

Often, the only financial reporting within the company consists of a monthly balance sheet and income statement generated by the general ledger function. These statements, once the controller is sure of their accuracy, may be distributed to all management personnel—as strictly confidential—more than 10 days after the end of the month. Most management personnel merely file these financial statements; some look at them, but very few understand them. The statements have no effect on their operations.

An example of these statements is shown in Exhibit 6.3. These statements may be distributed as shown, with no additional comments or explanation. Many times, other departments maintain their own internal reporting systems, as they cannot rely on the general ledger section to provide the information they need on a timely basis.

Quarterly, an outside accounting firm may come in to perform a "review" and prepare resulting financial statements for the company's lenders. These statements are often considered irrelevant and ignored internally.

The general ledger section provides no explanations with its submission of these financial statements. Operations management wants to know how these numbers reflect what their areas are accomplishing. They need to know the differences between financial and accounting data and operational data that they can use to improve their operations. Specifically, they need to understand the following differences between accrual- and cash-based accounting:

- Sales are recorded when made (when the goods are shipped to the customer) and set-up as accounts receivable, with cash payment for a sale received at time of customer payment (typically 30 days or later).
- Expenses are incurred on a different timing schedule from cash receipts. For example, payroll, material, supplies, and other expenses are paid when due, but the payback from the customer sale will be some time (if at all) in the future (reflecting the time to complete delivery to the customer plus the collection period).
- Profits shown on the income statement are based on accrual accounting
- An increase in inventory is a cash outlay, but not an expense; an inventory reduction is an expense, but not a cash outlay. This means that an inventory reduction program will have a positive effect on cash flow but a negative impact on profits.
- Some expenses, such as depreciation and amortization, are recorded via accounting entries and do not represent cash outflows; similarly, prepaid items are expensed currently, but represent prior disbursements of cash.
- Expenditures for fixed assets (e.g., property, plant and equipment) are paid for currently, but do not immediately appear on the income statement as expenses.
- Financial statements do not provide all of the necessary data needed to manage and operate effectively. For instance, operations management should know operating facts such as the real costs and profits generated

ASSETS	
Cash	$ 60
Accounts receivable	3,720
Inventory	5,360
Current Assets	9,140
Property, plant and equipment	7,580
Accumulated depreciation	(2,160)
Net property, plant and equipment	5,420
Other assets	840
TOTAL ASSETS	$15,400

LIABILITIES AND STOCKHOLDERS' EQUITY	
Accounts payable	$ 1,960
Notes payable	200
Current maturities of long-term debt	840
Other current liabilities	560
Current liabilities	3,560
Long-term debt	7,680
Total Liabilities	11,240
Common stock	200
Additional paid-in-capital	200
Retained earnings	3,760
Stockholders' equity	4,160
TOTAL LIABILITIES AND EQUITY	$15,400

Exhibit 6.3a Balance Sheet
as of December 31
($$ in 000s)

Net Sales	$12,500
Cost of Goods Sold:	
Material	2,260
Labor	3,260
Manufacturing Expenses	2,080
Total Cost of Goods Sold	7,600
Gross Profit	4,900
Selling expenses	1,120
General and administrative expenses	1,480
Total Operating Expenses	2,600
Net Profit	2,300
Provision for income taxes	640
NET INCOME	$ 1,660

Exhibit 6.3b Income Statement
for Year Ending December 31
($$ in 000s)

by each customer and manufacturing order, the number of on-time quality deliveries, the amount of returned customer merchandise, and the amount and cost of scrap, rework, and rejects.

> ## *ACCRUAL ACCOUNTING DOES NOT REFLECT THE REALITIES OF CASH FLOW.*

DEVELOPING THE CASH MANAGEMENT ANALYSIS SURVEY FORM

One of the most important elements of the cash management study is the survey form. The main purpose of a survey form is to reduce large amounts of data into categories or classifications that can be more easily compared. The questions on the survey form are developed by members of management and the study team and are directed toward those areas that have been defined as most critical. An initial survey can be used to gather general data and look for patterns in identifying critical areas.

The survey questions should be designed to elicit information that is significant. Each question should focus on one factor of an area to be analyzed. The questions should be designed to generate objective answers and data relative to the performance criteria in question, and to identify unique methods and best practices. Each question is probed as to its objectivity, purpose, data to be provided, and close-endedness. Typically, a survey form is designed specifically for the company and its functions. A sample survey form related to the accounts payable function is shown in Exhibit 6.4. A similar survey form would be developed for each of the other accounting functions—accounts receivable, payroll, and general ledger—as well as for any other activities in the organization that may not add value.

COMPILING THE DATA

When the survey forms have been returned by all employees—management and operations—each one needs to be reviewed and analyzed for inappropriate, misleading, or inadequate responses. This usually requires going back to the respondent for clarification, either by phone or in a personal visit. If possible, it is good practice to have one or more individuals assigned to each respondent. By effectively working together they will be able to finalize all responses for each participant.

Once the study team is satisfied with the legitimacy of each of the participants' survey responses, the next step is to summarize these responses in one document for analysis purposes. This analysis is to help identify areas of operational deficiencies, gaps from desired performance results and basic business principles,

1. Organizational Issues
   a. How is this function organized? Hierarchical, Vertical, Integrated, etc. Provide an organization chart showing positions and personnel.
   b. To whom does each activity within the function report to? Title and name.
   c. Who manages each activity? Title and name.
   d. How many employees are included in each activity?
   e. What are the major accounts payable policies? (e.g., dollar limit for accounts payable). Provide documented policies and procedures.
   f. What are the total budget and actual allocations for this function?
   g. Do you have a functional job description for each position? Provide a copy of each one.

2. Accounts Payable Processing
   a. On what basis and what percentage of total payments do you pay vendors?
      • Pre-pay at time of order
      • Payment upon receipt
      • Payment with invoice/receipt within discount terms
      • Payment with invoice/receipt within 30 days
      • Do not take discount
      • Take discount anyway (beyond discount period, e.g., 10 days)
   b. How often do you process payables for payment?
   c. Do you make any exceptions between payment periods?
   d. Do you provide for offline manual vendor payments?
   e. On average, what is the amount of new payables at any time? Number of payments? Total dollars?
   f. Is accounts payable processing part of an integrated computer system?
   g. What is the amount of annual payments? Number of payments? Total dollars?

3. Open Payables Control
   a. Are open payables part of an integrated computer system?
   b. How often do you process payments?
   c. Is there a policy to take vendor discounts? Within/at the discount period? Regardless of the discount period?
   d. On average, what is the amount of open payables? Number of vendor invoices? Total dollars?
   e. Are open payables accessible on an on-line basis? Only accessible by accounts payable personnel? By others? (describe)

Exhibit 6.4 Sample Cash Management Analysis Survey Form—the Accounts Payable Function

4. Vendor Payment Processing
   a. Do you provide a prepayment listing of due bills prior to processing?
      - On screen
      - Listing only
      - Both options
   b. Can an authorized individual select bills for payment?
      - Manually
      - Online
      - Additions
      - Deletions
      - Changes
   c. Can an authorized individual determine the dollar amount for total payment? What is the basis for selection?
   d. How often do you process checks for payment? Do you hold to that schedule? How many times did you go off that schedule last year?
   e. Do you automatically combine vendor invoices into one payment?
   f. Do you provide detail as to what invoices are being paid?
   g. Do you reconcile vendor statements to individual invoices?
   h. Do you ignore vendor statements and pay only by invoice?
   i. Do you automatically net vendor debits against payments?
   j. On average, what is the amount of vendor debits?
      Number of debits _____ Total Amount _____
   k. Once selected for payments, are checks with payment detail automatically processed? Provide sample of check and detail memo.
   l. What is your cost per payment?
   m. What is your cost per processing cycle?
   n. On average, how many payments do you process at one time?
      - Per process run
      - Per month
      - Annually

5. Cash Disbursement Processing
   a. Are payments as processed automatically sent to the vendor? Electronic data transfer? Mail?
   b. How often do you process cash disbursements?
   c. On average, what are the number of checks written?
      By process _____ Monthly _____ Annually _____
   d. Do you combine payments by vendor? On what basis?
   e. On what basis do you process payment? Receipt of items? Invoice? Both? Other?
   f. Do you use a remote bank location?
   g. Do you use any methods to slow the receipt of the payment to the vendor? Describe.

Exhibit 6.4 Sample Cash Management Analysis Survey Form—the Accounts Payable Function (continued)

    h. What is your cost per check disbursement? What is your cost per disbursement cycle?

    i. How many times have checks been processed late? In the last year? Sent out late?

    j. What percentage of checks has been reported as having errors upon receipt? How many hours and cost are spent in correcting errors, and at what cost?

    k. Do you provide electronic data transfer (EDT) for vendor payments?

    l. Is timeliness of payment (e.g., EDT) considered a factor in vendor price negotiations?

6. Record Keeping and Analysis
   a. What records do you keep for each payment?
      - Purchase requisition   - Purchase order
      - Receiver/bill of lading - Vendor invoice
      - Payment voucher   - Check copy
      - Other   - All computer maintained
   b. What type of analysis do you do relative to payments?
      - Payments by vendor: numbers and dollars
      - Returns by vendor
      - Billing errors
      - Processing errors
      - Other
   c. Are there other records/analysis that you keep/do? Describe.
   d. What report options do you provide?
      - Standard in software
      - Custom defined
      - User
   e. What software do you use for these functions?
      What computer hardware configuration do you use? Provide details.

7. Vendor Relations, Negotiations, Analysis
   a. What is the total number of vendors in your system?
   b. Are your vendors coded by commodity class?
   c. Can you provide a summary of vendors by commodity class?
      Commodity Class: _____ Number of Vendors _____
   d. How often do you negotiate with vendors? Each purchase, monthly, annually, other.
   e. How many vendors make up approximately 80 percent of your total purchases? Can you provide this information by commodity class?
   f. Do you use long-term contracts or blanket purchase orders to lock in price, quality, and on-time deliveries?
   g. Do you integrate purchases of raw materials into your production schedule?

Exhibit 6.4 Sample Cash Management Analysis Survey Form—the Accounts Payable Function (continued)

---

h. Do you maintain vendor analysis statistics? Do they include the following?
   - Total sales volume
   - Total sales volume by item
   - Quality data
   - Merchandise return data
   - On-time delivery data
   - Other
   Provide a sample report(s) of such statistics?
i. Are company individuals assigned contact responsibility for major vendors?
j. How often are long-term purchase contracts renegotiated?
k. Do you have an ongoing process for identification of potential vendors? Describe.
l. How many vendors have you added during the past year?
m. How many vendors have you deleted during the past year?

Exhibit 6.4   Sample Cash Management Analysis Survey Form—the Accounts Payable Function (continued)

and best practices among survey respondents in total and by individual area. Summarization can be done easily by recording each participant's responses directly on the survey document itself.

The study team should then individually and collectively (normally in a brainstorming session) identify areas for improvement, and summarize process deficiencies for those areas determined to be most critical, for presentation to management. They may decide to spend additional analysis time with specific functions and activities to ascertain the accuracy of survey responses. They may also decide to visit other companies (e.g., competitors or others in similar industries) to evaluate what others are doing and whether their operational practices and related costs are more economical and effective.

A form summarizing the survey and possible process deficiencies, identified with an *, for the accounts payable function under review is shown in Exhibit 6.5.

> ## *QUESTION EACH ACTIVITY*
> ## *—ITS PURPOSE AND ITS COST.*

ANALYZING THE DATA

Data collected with the use of such survey forms is known as user-provided data. The study team uses these forms as a quick means of accumulating information

1. Organizational Issues
   a. How is this function organized? Hierarchical, Vertical, Integrated, etc. Provide an organization chart showing positions and personnel.
   Response: Hierarchical*
   The organization chart for all accounting functions, including accounts payable, is shown in Exhibit 6.6.
   b. Who does each activity within the function report to? Title and name.
   Response: Accounts Payable Manager (Ray Simms) reports to the Controller (Dave Behal). Accounts Payable Supervisor (Betty Grimes) reports to Ray Simms. All others (five accounts payable processors and two clerical personnel) report to Betty Grimes.
   c. Who manages each activity? Title and name.
   Response: Accounts Payable function; Ray Simms, Accounts Payable Manager. Accounts Payable processing activities; Betty Grimes, Accounts Payable Supervisor.
   d. How many employees in each activity?
   Response: Manager - 1, Supervisor - 1, Processing - 5, Clerical - 2
   e. What are the major accounts payable policies? (e.g., dollar limit for accounts payable)
   Response: All vendor purchases for $50 or more are processed through the purchasing department. The accounts payable department is responsible for processing all vendor invoices for these purchases. * There are no documented policies and procedures.
   f. What is the total budget and actual allocations for this function?
   Response: Budget: $346,000 Actual: $385,000 *
   g. Do you have functional job descriptions for each position? Provide copies of each one.
   Response: No

2. Accounts Payable Processing
   a. On what basis and percents of total payments do you pay vendors?
   – Pre-pay at time of order Response: None
   – Payment upon receipt Response: None
   – Payment with invoice/receipt within discount terms. Response: 30%
   – Payment with invoice/receipt within 30 days. Response: 70% take discount
   – Don't take discount
   – Take discount anyway
   b. How often do you process payables for payment?
   Response: Twice a week *
   c. Do you make any exceptions between payment periods?
   Response: Yes – 10 to 20% of all transactions *
   d. Do you provide for offline manual vendor payments?
   Response: Yes – about 3 to 5% of all transactions *

Exhibit 6.5 Sample Cash Management Analysis Survey Form—the Accounts Payable Function—Summary of Responses

    e. On average, what is the amount of new payables at any time? Number of payments? Total dollars?
       Response: 800, $460,000 *
    f. Is accounts payable processing part of an integrated computer system?
       Response: No *
    g. What is the amount of annual payments? Number of payments? Total dollars?
       Response: 26,000, $14,800,000 *

3. Open Payables Control

    a. Are open payables part of an integrated computer system?
       Response: No
    b. How often do you process payments?
       Response: Twice a week
    c. Is there a policy to take vendor discounts? Within/at the discount period? Regardless of the discount period?
       Response: Yes
    d. On average, what is the amount of open payables? Number of vendor invoices? Total dollars?
       Response: 1,400, $1,620,000 *
    e. Are open payables accessible on an on-line basis? Only accounts payable personnel? Others? (describe)
       Response: No

4. Vendor Payment Processing

    a. Do you provide a prepayment listing of due bills prior to processing?
       – On screen
       – Listing only
       – Both options
       Response: No *
    b. Can an authorized individual select bills for payment?
       – Manual
       – Online
       – Additions
       – Deletions
       – Changes
       Response: Manual only *
    c. Can an authorized individual determine the dollar amount for total payment? What is basis for selection?
       Response: Yes/ dollars available for payment
    d. How often do you process checks for payment? Do you hold to that schedule? How many times did you go off that schedule last year?
       Response: Twice a week/yes/never

Exhibit 6.5   Sample Cash Management Analysis Survey Form—the Accounts Payable Function—Summary of Responses (continued)

e. Do you automatically combine vendor invoices into one payment?
Response: No *

f. Do you provide detail as to what invoices are being paid?
Response: No *

g. Do you reconcile vendor statements to individual invoices?
Response: Yes *

h. Do you ignore vendor statements and pay only by invoice?
Response: No *

i. Do you automatically net vendor debits against payments?
Response: No *

j. On average, what is the amount of vendor debits?
Number of debits _____ Total amount _____
Response: 140/ $28,000+ *

k. Once selected, are checks with payment detail automatically processed?
Response: No

l. What is your cost per payment?
Response: $48 *

m. What is your cost per processing cycle?
Response: $1,800+ twice a week *

n. On average, how many payments do you process at one time?
– Per process run
– Per month
– Annually
Response: 350/2,800/34,000 *

5. Cash Disbursement Processing

a. Are payments as processed automatically sent to the vendor? Electronic Data Transfer? Mail?
Response: mail only *

b. How often do you process cash disbursements?
Response: twice a week

c. On average, what are the number of checks written?
By process ____ Monthly _____ Annual _____
Response: 350/2,800/34,000 *

d. Do you combine payments by vendor? On what basis?
Response: No *

e. On what basis do you process payment? Receipt of items? Invoice? Both? Other?
Response: Both

f. Do you use a remote bank location?
Response: No

Exhibit 6.5 Sample Cash Management Analysis Survey Form—the Accounts Payable Function—Summary of Responses (continued)

g. Do you use any methods to slow the receipt of the payment to the vendor? Describe.
Response: No

h. What is your cost per check disbursement? What is your cost per disbursement cycle?
Response: $1.12/$392 *

i. How many times have checks been processed late? In the last year? Sent out late?
Response: 12/12 *

j. What percent of checks have reported errors upon receipt? How many hours and cost are spent in correcting errors?
Response: 12%/180 hours/ $3,600 *

k. Do you provide Electronic Data Transfer (EDT) for vendor payments?
Response: No *

l. Is timeliness of payment (i.e. EDT) considered as a factor in vendor price negotiations?
Response: No *

6. Record Keeping and Analysis

a. What records do you keep for each payment?
   – Purchase requisition   – Purchase order
   – Receiver/bill of lading   – Vendor invoice
   – Payment voucher   – Check copy
   – Other   – All computer maintained
   Response: All *

b. What type of analysis do you do relative to payments?
   – Payments by vendor: numbers and dollars
   – Returns by vendor   – Billing errors
   – Processing errors   – Other
   Response: None *

c. Are there other records/analysis that you do? Describe.
   Response: None *

d. What report options do you provide? – Standard in software – Custom defined – User
   Response: Standard only *

e. What software do you use for these functions?
   Response: low end *

f. What computer hardware configuration do you use? Provide details.
   Response: PC network with 3 stations

7. Vendor Relations, Negotiations, Analysis

a. What is the total number of vendors in your system?
   Response: 587 *

b. Are your vendors coded by type of commodity class?
   Response: Yes

Exhibit 6.5   Sample Cash Management Analysis Survey Form—the Accounts Payable Function—Summary of Responses (continued)

---

   c. Can you provide a summary of vendors by commodity class?
      Response: Yes
   d. How often do you negotiate with vendors? Each purchase, monthly, annually, other.
      Response: By exception *
   e. How many vendors make up approximately 80% of your total purchases?
      Response: 128 *
   f. Do you use long term contracts or blanket purchase orders to lock in price, quality, and on-time deliveries?
      Response: Rarely *
   g. Do you integrate purchases for production raw materials into your production schedule?
      Response: No *
   h. Do you maintain vendor analysis statistics? Do they include?
      – Total sales volume
      – Total sales volume by item
      – Quality data
      – Merchandise return data
      – On-time delivery data
      – Other
      Provide a sample report(s) of such statistics?
      Response: No *
   i. Are company individuals assigned contact responsibility for major vendors?
      Response: No *
   j. How often are long-term purchase contracts re-negotiated?
      Response: Rarely *
   k. Do you have an ongoing process for identification of potential vendors? Describe.
      Response: No *
   l. How many vendors have you added during the past year?
      Response: 57 *
   m. How many vendors have you deleted during the past year?
      Response: 68*

Exhibit 6.5   Sample Cash Management Analysis Survey Form—the Accounts Payable Function—Summary of Responses (continued)

about the function under review. The study team summarizes the data to identify patterns of bad practices, operational deficiencies, cash management concerns, and areas for further review. The accumulation and analysis of such user provided data often becomes the starting point for further analysis. Thus, the analysis form is a good tool to bring immediate focus to those areas to be considered in cash management improvements.

Data reported via such a survey may be unclear and misleading as the result of any number of factors:

- Methods of data gathering
- Misunderstanding of terminology
- Attitude of person providing the data
- Incompleteness and inaccuracy of database
- Misunderstanding of data requested

> ## *WATCH OUT FOR MISLEADING, INACCURATE, OR INCOMPLETE DATA.*

Because of the possibility of data inaccuracy, the study team will usually analyze thoroughly the data provided prior to identifying operational and cash management deficiencies for further review. As study team members may rely on the data provided by management and operations personnel in determining their conclusions about areas for further review, they must determine whether any data elements require further backup from the respondent as to methods of estimation, formulas used, and calculation routines. Normally, a range of results emerges, so that if one respondent's replies are unreasonable, it becomes readily apparent. This allows the study team to easily identify those items out of the range and to contact that respondent for further review and resubmission.

Based on an analysis of survey form results, the study team develops its work program to include those critical areas. Typically, the survey form procedure is supported by interviews with appropriate management and operations personnel, physical review and observations of actual operations, and review of documentation such as policies and procedures, organization charts and job descriptions, and workload statistics.

ORGANIZATIONAL ISSUES

As identified in the survey form for the accounts payable function, the accounting function appears to be overstaffed. A review of all other functions within the accounting area supports this conclusion.

A full organization chart is shown in Exhibit 6.6.

Among the concerns the study team could raise, based on an analysis of this exhibit are:

- The need for 38 people to provide accounting functions of primarily a non-value-added character

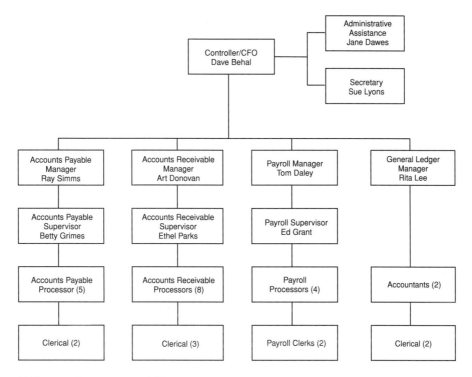

Exhibit 6.6   Organizational Chart: the Accounting Function

- The purpose of having a controller/chief financial officer (CFO), together with an administrative assistant and a secretary, to oversee basically repetitive accounting functions
- The necessity for a manager for each of the accounting functions: accounts payable, accounts receivable, payroll, and general ledger
- The need for supervisors, in addition to managers, for the accounts payable, accounts receivable, and payroll functions
- The use of the present number of operations personnel in each function:
  - Five accounts payable processors
  - Eight accounts receivable processors
  - Four payroll processors
  - Two general ledger accountants
- The need for nine clerical personnel assigned to these functions:
  - Accounts payable (two)
  - Accounts receivable (three)
  - Payroll (two)
  - General ledger (two)

The company must look for ways to reduce costs in these areas, perform these accounting activities more efficiently, and produce results that enable the company to manage better and make more profitable decisions.

> ## *USE THE ORGANIZATION CHART TO IDENTIFY INEFFICIENT USE OF PERSONNEL.*

BUDGET ANALYSIS

A list of personnel with corresponding budget and actual costs for each of the accounting functions is shown in Exhibit 6.7. As shown in this list, it is costing the company about $860,000 in actual dollars to provide accounting services of a non-value-added nature. This appears to be too costly for a company with $12.5 million in sales.

The accounting function costs total about 7 percent of sales—far too much for a company of this size. A quick benchmarking review of five other similar companies this size resulted in a range of accounting function costs of two to three percent of sales, which may also be too high.

An analysis of the accounting function budget breakdown, as shown in Exhibit 6.7, presents the company with nine particular concerns:

1. The cost for a controller/CFO, budgeted at $82,000 with actual cost of $86,400. It appears that this person's function is merely supervising mechanical accounting functions. What additional expertise and advice that might be provided by this individual could be provided more adequately at less cost?

2. Total controller functional costs of $173,600. It would be quite surprising if the company is realizing sufficient value for these costs.

3. Controller function costs budgeted at $160,000 with actual costs of $173,600—an 8.5 percent increase over budget. It is possible that the controller is building an empire and/or using company funds indiscriminately.

4. Managers for each function at a total cost of $142,000 budgeted dollars ($136,800 in actual costs). This appears to be a superfluous cost, particularly when added to supervisors and processing personnel.

5. Supervisors for accounts payable, accounts receivable, and payroll at a budget cost of $86,000 (actual cost of $71,400). Again, do these individuals provide value?

6. Processors and accountants for each of the functions. Are they merely mechanically processing accounting transactions, or are there any value-added activities?

7. Clerical support costs for each function. How many support personnel are really necessary, and what do they actually contribute? Are they really doing the mechanical work, or do they merely duplicate the work that higher paid personnel should be doing? Could their functions be handled by computer, necessitating fewer personnel?

	Budget	Actual
Controller/CFO	$ 82,000	$ 86,400
Administrative Assistant	26,000	28,200
Secretary	18,000	22,700
Total Personnel Costs	126,000	137,300
Other Costs	34,000	36,300
Total Controller Costs	160,000	173,600
Accounts Payable Manager	38,000	36,700
Accounts Payable Supervisor	28,000	24,300
Accounts Payable Processors (5 @ $18,000)	90,000	72,400
Clerical support (2 @ $14,000)	28,000	22,600
Total Personnel Costs	184,000	156,000
Other Costs	12,000	8,400
Total Accounts Payable Costs	196,000	164,400
Accounts Receivable Manager	44,000	39,300
Accounts Receivable Supervisor	36,000	28,500
Accounts Receivable Processors (8 @ $22,000)	176,000	144,800
Clerical support (3 @ $16,000)	48,000	41,200
Total Personnel Costs	304,000	253,800
Other Costs	18,000	10,300
Total Accounts Receivable Costs	322,000	264,100
Payroll Manager	34,000	32,400
Payroll Supervisor	22,000	18,600
Payroll Processors (4 @ $16,000)	64,000	56,700
Payroll Clerks (2 @ $12,000)	24,000	20,800
Total Personnel Costs	144,000	128,500
Other Costs	10,800	8,200
Total Payroll Costs	154,800	136,700
General Ledger Manager	26,000	28,400
Accountants (2 @ $22,000)	44,000	46,800
Clerical support (2 @ $16,000)	32,000	36,300
Total Personnel Costs	102,000	111,500
Other Costs	6,000	8,400
Total General Ledger Costs	108,000	119,900
Summary of Costs		
Personnel Costs	$860,000	$787,100
Other Costs	80,800	71,600
Total Accounting Function Cost	$940,800	$858,700

Exhibit 6.7 Accounting Function Costs—Budget versus Actual

8. Other costs of $80,800 budgeted, $71,600 actual. What are these costs? Are they necessary or just an invitation to spend money?
9. The aspect of accounts payable, accounts receivable, and payroll actual costs being less than budgeted dollars. Are the budgets set unrealistically high? Is the controller keeping costs down to look good (possibly holding off budget cuts), or are these the realistic costs? What should these costs be?

ANALYSIS OF FUNCTIONAL COSTS

Another important aspect of the analysis of the accounting functions is to analyze each activity of the function and determine its cost. The starting point is to review and analyze the function as it is presently being performed in order to identify those activities that result in added on costs. This can be done through observation, interviews, workload statistics, and the development and analysis of systems flowcharts. This process will not only allow the study team to fully understand how the function operates, but will also identify areas for improvement and generate recommendations for such improvements. The goal of this analysis is to begin the development of best practice recommendations so that each function operates with the most economical and efficient systems as possible.

> *GOOD COST MANAGEMENT LEADS TO IMPROVED CASH FLOW AND COMPANY SUCCESS.*

For example, the study team may identify and develop costs for those activities that make up the accounts payable and accounts receivable functions as follows:

- Accounts payable
- Receive open Purchase Order (PO) copies from purchasing department
- File in open files: by vendor, by PO number
- Obtain "receiving report" from receiving department
- Pull open purchase order from file and compare to receiving report
- If no invoice, hold in open receipts/no invoice file
- If invoice exists, pull from invoice/no receipt file
- Receive invoice from vendor
- Match invoice to open receipts
  - If match, process for payment
  - If no match, hold in invoice/no receipt file
- Process any invoice or receiving errors
- Enter payment data into computer system

- At time of payment, set up computer system for check preparation
- Mail checks to vendors
- File paid accounts payable voucher
- Handle vendor inquiries

- Accounts receivable
- Receive billing information from shipping department: bill of lading, sales order, and so on
- Match to sales order copy in open sales file
- Prepare bill on computer system
- Verify accuracy of bill
- Mail bill to customer
- Receive payments from customers: usually checks in the mail
- Match payment to amounts due in computer system
- Code bill as to allocation to open customer invoices
- Process payment into computer system
- Follow-up on any discrepancies (e.g., wrong amount, improper discount taken)
- Expedite open customer invoices not paid within time terms (e.g., net/30 days)
- Initiate collection procedures for overdue accounts
- File payment data by customer (e.g., check stub, copy of bill, sales order, etc.)
- Prepare cash receipts for bank deposit
  - Prepare daily cash receipts report
  - Prepare bank deposit
- Handle customer inquiries

As study team members identify each activity in the preceding list and determine its cost, they question whether the entire function is necessary (e.g., does it have to be purchased and paid for in this manner?), or whether each activity is necessary (e.g., is it necessary to have customer bills or can electronic data transfer be used?). The total costs for each activity—accounts payable and accounts receivable processing—are based on the methods presently used to process these transactions. There may be other processes that should be performed that are not being done because of the constraints of time, volume, or limited personnel. In addition, the cost to process an individual transaction may be undercalculated owing to the time pressures to complete each transaction (e.g., in a hurried, incomplete manner). Moreover, if the volume is somewhat reduced, the cost per transaction will probably increase if the corresponding costs of processing are not reduced.

An example of such activity costs for the accounts payable function and its related activities is shown in Exhibit 6.8, and for the accounts receivable function and its related activities in Exhibit 6.9.

Labor hour cost: $16 per hour

Activity	Cost Element	Time	Cost
1. Receive PO from Purchasing and file in open PO file	Labor	2 min.	$0.50
2. Receive "receiving report" from receiving, pull open PO from file and compare hold in open receipts file	Labor	4 min.	1.00
3. Receive invoice from vendor and match to open receipts or pull open po and compare and hold as open invoice	Labor	6 min.	1.60
4. Invoice/receiving errors	Labor	—	—
5. Computer data entry	Labor	3 min	0.80
6. Computer check prep checks	Labor, computer	2 min.	0.50
7. Mail checks	Labor, envel., postage	2 min.	0.50
8. File paid payable	Labor	2 min	0.50
9. Meetings, phone, fax	Labor, phone	4 min	1.00
Total cost			$6.40

Number of payments processed per year: 26,000
Cost of processing annual payments: 26,000 × $6.40 = $166,400
 (actual costs = $164,400)

Exhibit 6.8   Accounts Payable Activities and Costs

Although the activities and costs shown in Exhibits 6.8 and 6.9 are rough estimates of the processing of accounts payable and accounts receivable, they represent the expenditure of resources allocated to these two activities. Theoretically, it could be assumed that each vendor payment or customer bill that could be eliminated from processing would result in a $6.40 or a $9.00 savings to the company.

In reality it does not work that way. A significant number of vendor payments or customer bills must be eliminated to provide a noticeable reduction in work effort resulting in substantial cost savings. However, the costs of processing a vendor payment and the cost of processing a customer bill can be used in the company's internal cost system in convincing management that its costs are too high. These figures can also be used to calculate cost savings and increases in positive cash flow.

Labor Hour Cost: $20 Per Hour

Activity	Cost Element	Time	Cost
1. Receive billing information from shipping department	Labor	2 min.	$ 0.67
2. Match to sales order copy in open sales file	Labor	2 min.	0.67
3. Prepare bill on computer system	Labor	5 min.	1.67
4. Verify accuracy of bill	Labor	3 min.	1.00
5. Mail bill to customer	Labor, bill, env., postage	2 min.	0.67
6. Receive payments from customers	Labor	—	—
7. Match payment to amounts due in computer system	Labor	3 min.	1.00
8. Code bill as to allocation to open customer invoices	Labor	3 min.	1.00
9. Process payment into computer system	Labor	3 min.	1.00
10. Follow-up on any discrepancies	Labor	—	—
11. Expedite open customer invoices	Labor, phone	1 min	0.33
12. Initiate collection procedures	Labor	1 min.	0.33
13. File payment data by customer	Labor	1 min.	0.33
14. Prepare cash receipts for bank deposit	Labor	1 min.	0.33
15. Handle customer inquiries	Labor, phone	—	—
Total Cost			$9.00

Number of customer bills processed per year: 30,000 +
Cost of processing annual customer bills: 30,000 x $9.00 = $270,000
    actual costs = $264,100)

Exhibit 6.9   Accounts Receivable Activities and Costs

The study team compares such costs and number of transactions to those of three comparable companies with the following results:

- *Accounts payable*

    - Number of payments processed annually:
      Us = 26,000; #1 = 16,000; #2 = 18,000; #3 = 12,000

    - Amount of annual payments:
      Us = $4,800,000; #1 = $2,200,000; #2 = $3,300,000; #3= $2,800,000

- Cost of accounts payable function:
  Us = $164,400; #1 = $128,000; #2 = $111,000; #3 = $84,000

- *Accounts receivable*

  - Number of customer bills processed annually:
    Us = 30,000; #1 = 14,000; #2 = 16,000; #3 = 8,600

  - Amount of annual customer bills:
    Us = $12,500,000; #1 = $15,600,000; #2 = $18,800,000; #3 = $22,500,000

  - Cost of accounts receivable function:
    Us = $264,100; #1 = $187,000; #2 = $156,000; #3 = $68,000

It can be seen from the foregoing that the company handles the largest volume of accounts payable and receivable transactions at the greatest cost of all four competitors. As part of the cash management study, the study team should visit each of these other companies to determine their best practices in an effort to develop the best practice for the company.

> ## *SEARCHING FOR BEST PRACTICES IS A CONTINUAL PROCESS.*

ANALYSIS OF ACCOUNTING OPERATIONS

In an effort to determine the cost of operations and which functions can be reduced or eliminated (thus increasing positive cash flow) each accounting function is analyzed.

Accounts Payable

The accounts payable manager, Ray Simms, is responsible for making sure that the required work gets done and vendor payments are made properly—no overpayments individually or in total. The accounts payable supervisor, Betty Grimes, is responsible for ensuring that each day's detail work gets accomplished. She is quite proud that the day's work is always completed before the staff leaves for the day—even if it means that nobody leaves until all the work is done. Three of the five accounts payable processors are responsible for processing vendor receipts and payments for payment. Before a vendor invoice can be paid, each item on the invoice must be checked for proper budget approval, for proper accuracy of the receipt, and for correct billing by the vendor. All of these operations are duplications of computer processing.

The other two accounts payable processors spend the bulk of their time dealing with vendors—primarily adjusting debits to the vendor's bills for defective and returned merchandise. The two clerical personnel spend most of their time filing and refiling accounts payable data—open purchase orders, vendor receiving data, vendor invoices, paid vouchers, and so on. The result of all of these operations is the payment of vendor invoices, with few value-added functions.

An analysis of accounts payable transactions using the present computer system for the current year disclosed the following:

Overall data

Total number of payments	26,000
Total amount of dollars	$ 4,800,000
Cost to process a payment	$ 6.40
Total cost of accounts payable	$ 164,400
Average time to pay invoice	22 days

Payment Statistics

Payment Amount	Number	Percent	Amount	Percent
Under $20	5,760	22.2%	$ 72,000	1.5%
Between $20 and $50	8,440	32.4%	306,000	6.4%
Between $50 and $100	6,680	25.7%	561,200	11.7%
Between $100 and $1,000	1,640	6.3%	1,033,200	21.5%
Over $1,000	3,480	13.4%	2,827,600	58.9%
Totals	26,000	100.0%	$4,800,000	100.0%

A further analysis of vendors and related payments disclosed the following:

Vendor Name	Number	Percent	$ Amount	Percent
Peterboro, Inc.	4,628	17.8%	$ 816,000	17.0%
Roadway Company	4,030	15.5%	782,400	16.3%
Dellilah Manufacturing	3,848	14.8%	753,600	15.7%
Delta Controls	3,614	13.9%	724,800	15.1%
Eager Specialties	3,432	13.2%	561,600	11.7%
North Facing	2,808	10.8%	412,800	8.6%
Subtotals	22,360	86.0%	$4,051,200	84.4%
Other Vendors	3,640	14.0%	748,800	15.6%
Total—All Vendors	26,000	100.0%	$4,800,000	100.0%

Accounts Receivable

The accounts receivable manager, Art Donovan, is responsible for making sure that all accounts receivable activities are done properly—customer billing, collection efforts, posting to accounts receivable record, and cash deposits. The accounts receivable supervisor, Ethel Parks, is responsible for ensuring that all customer bills are sent out on time (within three days of shipment), receipts are posted in a timely fashion (within two days of receipt), and that unpaid bills are followed up (after 60 days from the date of the invoice). Five of the eight accounts receivable processors are responsible for computer processing customer bills, setting up and maintaining the computer accounts receivable files, processing customer cash receipts, and submitting nonpayments (after sixty days) to the collections unit in the sales department.

The other three processors spend most of their time working with the credit unit in the sales department, dealing with customers as to returned merchandise and obtaining the proper credits, and processing billing adjustments. Customer credit limits are established by the credit unit of the sales department and monitored by the accounts receivable section. When customers place orders that exceed the credit limit—outstanding bills plus current order—the accounts receivable unit notifies the credit unit for disposition. The normal recourse is that the credit unit increases the credit limit, making the credit policies almost meaningless. This has resulted in extending the collection period from an average of 28 days to over 48 days with a corresponding increase in uncollectible receivables. As the amount of returned merchandise has increased, so have the amount of bills paid late and uncollectibles. Three clerical personnel are responsible for correspondence and filling/refiling activities.

An analysis of customer sales statistics and accounts receivable data disclosed the following:

- Number of customer bills processed annually: 30,000
- Cost of accounts receivable function: $264,1000
- Total sales for the year: $12,500,000
- Accounts receivable at the end of year: $ 3,270,000
- Average collection period: 48 days
- Billing terms: 1 percent 10 days/net 30 days

Billing Statistics

Billing Amount	Number	Percent	Amount	Percent
Under $100	14,220	47.4%	$ 898,560	7.2%
Between $100 and $500	11,810	39.3%	2,869,830	22.9%
Between $500 and $1,000	2,300	7.7%	1,453,600	11.6%
Between $1,000 and $5,000	1,280	4.3%	3,143,680	25.1%
Between $5,000 and $10,000	180	0.6%	1,138,320	9.2%
Over $10,000	210	0.7%	2,996,010	24.0%
Totals	30,000	100.0%	$ 12,500,000	100.0%

Sales Statistics

Customer name	Number	Percent	Amount	Percent
Paul Brothers Company	5,460	18.2%	$ 2,412,500	19.3%
Apex Industries	4,890	16.3%	2,325,000	18.6%
Kontrol Manufacturing	4,410	14.7%	1,562,500	12.5%
Sandstone, Inc.	3,930	13.1%	1,075,000	8.6%
Textite Industries	2,880	9.6%	962,500	7.7%
Ace, Inc.	2,520	8.4%	1,300,000	10.4%
Subtotals	24,090	80.3%	9,638,303	77.1%
Other Customers	5,910	19.7%	2,861,697	22.9%
Total—All Customers	30,000	100.0%	$12,500,000	100.0%

Payroll

The payroll unit is responsible for processing biweekly payrolls for the following:

- Manufacturing operations—102 employees on an hourly basis
- Manufacturing supervision—26 employees on salary basis
- Office operations—72 employees on salary basis
- Sales personnel—12 employees on salary plus commission basis (paid at time of sale, regardless of when customer pays)
- Management payroll—8 employees on salary plus quarterly bonus

The payroll manager, Tom Daley, is responsible for making sure that all payrolls are accurately processed. He reviews and approves all payroll changes and payroll registers prior to payroll check processing. He is also responsible for the maintenance and processing of the management payroll. The payroll supervisor, Ed Grant, is responsible for ensuring that all daily operations are performed correctly due to the sensitivity of payroll. The four payroll processors are responsible for the following functions:

- Maintenance of computerized payroll and personnel records—including all additions, changes, and deletions (Ed Grant reviews and approves all daily changes.)
- Maintenance of offline controls by type of payroll to ensure the integrity of each computerized payroll file
- Review and reconciliation of manufacturing operations personnel labor distribution charges to manufacturing orders and nonchargeable time (This is done on a daily basis to ensure that these costs are recorded accurately on an ongoing basis.)
- Reconciliation of all payrolls to offline controls and review of computer processing as to its accuracy

- Distribution of payroll checks on an individual basis (All employees are paid at the end of the same biweekly period.)
- Maintenance of records and preparation of federal, state, and local payroll tax and related reporting—monthly, quarterly, semiannual, and annual
- Maintenance of personnel records such as sick leave, vacation time, status and pay changes, location changes, and so on

The two payroll clerks are responsible for clerical duties such as correspondence, filing and refiling of payroll details and computer reports, and control of various forms.

An analysis of payroll processing disclosed the following data:

Payroll Type	Number of Employees	Annual Dollars	Average Pay
Manufacturing:			
Manufacturing operations	102	$ 2,284,800	$ 22,400
Manufacturing supervision	26	975,200	37,500
Total Manufacturing	128	$ 3,260,000	
General and administrative:			
Accounting functions	38	$787,100	$ 20,700
All others	34	692,900	20,380
Total General and Administrative	72	$ 1,480,000	
Sales department—salespeople	12	$ 620,000	$ 51,700
Management	8	$ 512,000	$ 64,000
Total—All Payrolls	220	$ 5,872,000	$ 23,488

General Ledger

The integrity of the general ledger, which includes a record for each account in the company's chart of accounts, is the responsibility of the general ledger manager, Rita Lee. She is also responsible for establishing and maintaining the company's budget system for both manufacturing operations and line item budgets for each of the nonmanufacturing support functions. The two accountants are responsible for doing whatever is requested of them by Rita. The two clerical personnel do whatever else needs to be done. There are no standard assignments.

The company has an integrated computerized accounting system where each of the subsystems such as accounts payable, accounts receivable, and payroll automatically update the general ledger. However, general ledger personnel also trace each entry into the computerized general ledger to ensure its accuracy. Rita Lee oversees the posting of all journal entries to the general ledger—manually preparing the journal entry and then tracing it into the general ledger after computer processing. She does not trust the computer producing automatic journal entries—even for standard entries such as depreciation and allocation of prepaid expenses.

This unit is responsible for developing the annual budget and entering it into the computer system. They are also responsible for ensuring that no expenses are incurred that would put any line item in an overbudget position. They do this by reviewing every purchase request against the budget prior to allowing the purchasing department to prepare a purchase order. If a line item total expense does exceed the budgeted line item, the general ledger unit will analyze the cause for such an excess and move the overage to a line item which still has money left in it. They do this laboriously for each line item in the budget at the end of each month. If a department or unit needs additional budgeted dollars subsequent to the beginning of the year, they need to request a budget change from the general ledger unit. It is rarely approved regardless of the need.

An example of the static budget system monthly report for the company's two manufacturing divisions is shown in Exhibit 6.10.

ACTIVITY BASED COSTING APPLICATIONS

In Chapter 5, we discussed Activity Based Costing (ABC) at some length and provided examples of how this process could be used to:

- Develop more accurate costs for products or services by the company
- Help identify costs that provide no value added and could therefore be considered for elimination

These same principles can be applied to the accounting function and any non-value-added activities that occur within the organization.

	Division A			Division B		
	Budget	Actual	Variance	Budget	Actual	Variance
Units produced	20,000	18,000	(2,000)	20,000	24,000	4,000
Sales	$ 1,000	$ 940	($60)	$ 1,000	$1,152	$ 152
Costs:						
Material	200	190	10	200	225	(25)
Direct labor	140	130	10	140	160	(20)
Variable overhead	135	125	10	135	158	(23)
Fixed overhead	175	170	5	175	173	2
Total Costs	650	615	35	650	716	(66)
Gross Profit	$ 350	$ 325	($25)	$ 350	$ 436	$ 86

Exhibit 6.10 Manufacturing Budget Report
($$ in 000s)

Effective cash flow management maximizes cash generation for the company. This means the generation of positive cash flow by applying effective techniques for conserving cash (e.g., keeping expenses and costs to a minimum) and for collecting cash due (e.g., customer sales) as soon as possible. For the company to survive, it must have cash when it is needed. At present, this company has no way of knowing its cash situation. Its expenses are exaggerated, its accounts receivables are excessive, and its ability to pay vendors on a timely basis is questionable. Sufficient cash availability (cash in and cash out) is necessary for the company to grow and survive.

The company uses a basic cost accounting system that accumulates direct labor from employee time sheets, direct material from purchases and inventory issues, and an allocation of overhead based on a percentage of direct labor hours and costs. There are many inaccuracies in labor reporting (e.g., reporting as much time as possible to customer orders and the least to nonchargeable time) and material reporting (e.g., charging scrap, rework, and rejects back to the customer). Any such labor and material cost inefficiencies are merely passed on to the customer together with overhead allocation errors. This has resulted in the company's arriving at greatly overstated costs and correspondingly high prices, which has made it difficult for them to maintain their existing customer base. They have become the high cost last alternative for many of their customers. Rather than building their business from a sound base of existing customers, the company's sales staff is continually searching for new (many times undesirable) customers. The company needs to adopt a sound cost and pricing system to remain competitive—and to survive. It should consider Activity Based Costing principles.

The costs that are accumulated to develop product costs do not all behave in the same manner. Some costs may vary in proportion to changes in volumes or activity (variable costs—e.g., labor or machine hours), other costs may not change regardless of the volume (fixed costs—e.g., rent or maintenance), and still others vary with changes in volume but not proportionately (semivariable costs—e.g., repairs or use of overtime). An effective analysis of such cost behavior should be used by the company for:

- Cost–volume–profit break-even analysis to determine the impact on profits of such factors as product prices, product mix, activity volume, variable costs of products, and the fixed costs of the business (which should be continuously analyzed for reduction)
- Variance analysis and cost control so that the company can address the cause of variances and take corrective action so that each operation can be made the best it can and be kept that way
- Short-term decision making such as make or buy decisions or the acceptance or rejection of a large special order
- Appraisal and evaluation of managerial and operational performance so that corrective action can be taken to avoid the same mistakes from happening over and over again

- Use of associated systems such as flexible budgeting, Activity Based Costing, responsibility reporting, profitability reporting by production order, process, and customer

As defined previously, Activity Based Costing (ABC) is a cost accounting methodology for assigning costs of resources to cost objects based on operational activities. Using ABC methods, it is the activities not the products or services (as in traditional cost accounting systems) that create the costs. The ABC approach to cost accounting recognizes the causal relationship between cost drivers, resources, and activities. ABC defines processes, which could occur in the providing of a product or service or in production or the office, in terms of the activities performed, and then develops costs for these activities.

EVALUATE COSTS IN TERMS OF ACTIVITIES PERFORMED RATHER THAN BY COST CENTERS.

ABC does not, contrary to traditional cost accounting techniques, develop costs by organizational cost centers but in terms of the activities performed. In addition, ABC assigns overhead based on the activities (cost drivers) that cause the overhead to occur—rather than allocating overhead based on some method such as direct labor hours or dollars. The more activities that can be assigned, rather than arbitrarily allocated, to product costs, the greater the level of the accuracy of the costs used to develop competitive product pricing.

Many organizations are struggling with better methods for product costing and resultant pricing strategies, together with overall cost management, performance measurement, return on investment, and so on. In this context, ABC is only one of the tools for effective survival, competitiveness, growth, and prosperity that face organizations today in an ever-changing business environment. ABC methodologies, if implemented correctly, can be the central core that provides the elements of an effective company-wide cost management system.

The greater the knowledge of management systems like ABC, the greater the opportunity for the company to develop the best practices. It is not an exercise in merely taking such systems and recommending them for implementation, but the skill in determining how such systems and concepts can be most beneficial for the company.

DEVELOPING RECOMMENDATIONS

The successful completion of the cash management analysis study is the development of recommendations on the action that should be taken to correct any undesirable conditions. These recommendations should logically follow an explanation of why the present conditions are happening, the underlying causes, and how to prevent them from recurring. Recommendations should be practical and reasonable so that management easily sees the merits in adopting them.

In developing recommendations, try to answer these questions:

1. What is recommended to correct the situation?
2. Is the recommendation based on a logical connection to the present practice?
3. Is the recommendation practical and reasonable for implementation?

Many times, a workable recommendation seems to suggest itself, but in other cases the study team may need some ingenuity to come up with a recommendation that is sensible and has a reasonable chance of being adopted. Recommendations should be as specific and helpful as possible, not simply that operations have to be improved, controls must be strengthened, or planning systems must be implemented. Team members should do their best to make certain that their recommendations are practical and acceptable to those responsible for taking action.

> ### *RECOMMENDATIONS SHOULD BE LOGICAL, PRACTICAL, REASONABLE, SPECIFIC, AND HELPFUL.*

The study team should strive for a cooperative atmosphere with management and operating personnel, whereby the team's role becomes one of a helping and a change agent. In such a working relationship, there is a much greater likelihood that management will accept the recommendations.

SPECIFIC RECOMMENDATIONS

The cash management study team performs the following work steps:

1. Observation of all accounting function activities
2. Development, analysis, and summary of survey forms for each accounting function
3. Interviews of all accounting management and operations personnel
4. Development and analysis of systems flowcharts for all accounting functions and activities
5. Development and analysis of data as shown above for each area of the accounting function
6. Contact with and visits to three representative competitors to determine similarities and differences and to identify best practices

7. Periodic meetings with accounting personnel to review findings and conclusions to determine their appropriateness

Based on the preceding work steps, the following recommendations are
developed by functional accounting area:

Accounts Payable

The following five recommendations were made for accounts payable:

1. Reduce the number of accounts payable payments through consideration
   of the following recommendations:
   • Eliminate all payments for $100 or less by establishing a direct payment
   system such as department credit cards, immediate cash payments, or
   telephone orders as a release from a total dollar commitment.
   • Reduce the number of payments for larger items by negotiating with the
   major vendors as to paying at the time of merchandise receipt with the
   guarantee of on-time quality deliveries. Items to consider in such negotiations include long-term commitments with shorter term releases, the
   ability to deliver on time at close to 100 percent quality (no returned
   items), the loss of a discount (at present mostly 1 percent for 10 days or an
   annual rate of 18.4 percent), and savings in accounts payable processing
   • Solicit other vendors to become part of a similar payment system. The
   study team talked to the six major vendors, and they are all interested in
   developing such a pay-on-receipt system. Two of the company's competitors have already installed such systems. It is estimated that the company
   can reduce the number of accounts payable payments to be processed
   from the present level of 26,000 annually to fewer than 6,000.
2. Work with major (and other) vendors to educate them on how the company operates so that they can be directly plugged into the company's
   production control system, allowing for 100 percent on-time deliveries
   and quality of product.
3. Integrate the receipt of merchandise with the approval of the payment
   that will eliminate the need for accounts payable personnel to review the
   same documentation. In effect, the receipt of the merchandise should trigger the processing of the payment.
4. Reduce the number of personnel assigned to the accounts payable function, once the above recommendations are in place, from the present level
   of nine people to no more than two. There is no need for a manager and a
   supervisor or accounts payable processors. The remaining processing can
   be accomplished through the use of two data base analyzers. This should
   result in an annual savings of over $115,000 based on last year's actual
   costs of $164,400.

5. Integrate the above cost savings into product cost structures so that the company can effectively reduce its product costs and related pricing to become more competitive.

Accounts Receivable

Six recommendations were developed for accounts receivable:

1. Integrate the sales forecast system into the overall company plan so that manufacturing can produce to a higher level of real customer orders assuring a greater degree of quality on-time deliveries. This will allow the company to better negotiate with their major customers as to long-term commitments and increased overall sales.
2. Establish long-term contracts with each of the company's major customers including the ability to receive payment via electronic data transfer at the time of shipping merchandise. This will require the company to guarantee 100 percent quality and on-time deliveries. If this can be accomplished, the company can negotiate such long-term contracts locking in price, production and delivery schedules, and future payments for cash flow purposes. This will enable the company to prepare better profit and cash flow projections.
3. Reduce the number of customer billings through the implementation of the following recommendations:
- Establish a direct cash payment system for items less than $500, using credit cards, direct cash payments, and similar vehicles.
- Implement a policy of payment upon shipment or receipt of merchandise for major customers, considering such factors as ability to make on-time quality deliveries, negotiated long-term contracts with adequate notice as to delivery schedules so as to incorporate such deliveries into the production schedule, the loss of a 1 percent 10 day discount for the customer, and the ability of the customer to pay on this basis.
- Encourage other customers to accept either the direct cash or pay on receipt system. With better control over costs and pricing, the company should be able to lower prices overall to make these systems attractive to their customers. Three competitors are already implementing such systems into their operations. It is estimated that the company can reduce the number of customer bills from the present level of 30,000 annually to less than 4,000.
4. Establish effective credit policies so that customers are sold only the amount of merchandise they can pay for. Such credit policies must be flexible so that each customer's sales can be maximized without sacrificing the risk of long or no payment.
5. Once the above recommendations are in place, reduce the number of personnel assigned to the accounts receivable function from the present level of 13 personnel to no more than 4 individuals. There is no need for a man-

ager and a supervisor or accounts receivable processors. The remaining processing can be accomplished through the use of two database analyzers, one customer service contact, and one credit and collections coordinator. This should result in annual savings of over $150,000 based on last year's actual costs of $264,100.

6. Integrate billing, accounts receivable, and collections into the overall company computer system so that minimal offline processing is necessary. This will result in the use of two database analyzers rather than accounts receivable processors.

Payroll

The biweekly payrolls being processed by the company do not incorporate any features that would be unexpected in standard payroll processing. It is presently costing the company over $136,000 annually to process these payrolls. It is recommended that the company consider one of three proposals for an outside payroll service providers to take over these functions at an annual savings of at least $100,000. We have talked to the following payroll vendors and their annual costs to support the company's 250-person payroll would be as follows:

ABC Payroll	$35,000
The Payroll Company	$28,000
Your Payroll Inc.	$32,000

All of these vendors are reputable in the field, and all offer the features necessary for the company:

- Uploading of payroll data from the company's computer systems
- Integration of payroll processing with manufacturing labor distribution and the company's budget system
- Processing of all salary payrolls on an exception basis; that is no input required unless there has been a change
- Processing and control of all payroll changes, with feedback and approval by the company, prior to payroll processing
- Full maintenance of personnel related data fields such as vacation time accrued and taken, sick time, personal leave, nonchargeable time, and so on
- Confidentiality in processing all payrolls including the management payroll
- Downloading of data files and reports from their computer system to the company's as a standard or a request basis, or in combination
- Preparation and submission of all payroll reports to regulatory and taxing authorities
- Preparation of W-2's for each individual at the end of the year

All five of the company's competitors that were visited presently handle their payrolls in this manner.

General Ledger

The company has an integrated computerized accounting system in which each of the subsystems automatically updates the general ledger. It also allows for automatic posting of standard journal entries. There is little else that needs to be entered into the general ledger. The company should allow the system to work as intended. Through the use of one data base analyzer the company should be able to presume that the general ledger is accurate. With such up-to-date processing accuracy, the company should be able to prepare financial statements (via screen display or hard-copy report) whenever it desires.

Within the company, functional disciplines (e.g., sales, manufacturing, marketing, purchasing, accounting, and computer processing) are interdependent. All of these functions must work together to successfully achieve organizational goals and objectives. The overall plans of the organization must be clearly communicated so that each functional area is aware of what needs to be done to ensure smooth integration with other areas and the entire company. Effective profit planning and budgeting are among the tools used to coordinate the organizational plans and the detailed activities of each of the disciplines. The budget then is a detailed plan depicting the manner in which monetary resources will be acquired and used over a period of time. The budget is the quantitative manifestation of the current year of the company's strategic plan. It is an integral part of the company's short-term operating plan.

The company's budget system, within the preceding definitions, can be initiated and maintained through the computer system. Revenue transactions can be automatically posted through the recording of sales transactions. These sales data can be compared to sales forecasts (by sales person, customer, product, customer, and so on). Expense transactions can be automatically posted against the budget system with suspect items flagged and automatic budget adjustments processed. The budget should be considered as part of the company planning process and as a continual process (not once a year) with flexible budgeting concepts considered. In this manner, the company plan can be continuously reviewed and updated along with the corresponding budget.

> *FLEXIBLE BUDGETING MEANS A CHANGE IN THE REPORTING OF THE BUDGET—NOT A CHANGE TO THE BUDGET ITSELF.*

A manufacturing budget report was shown in Exhibit 6.10. An example of a flexible budget, using the same data, is shown in Exhibit 6.11. The adjusted budget figures in Exhibit 6.11 reflect what the budget would have been at the actual level of units produced.

The preparation of a flexible budget requires the company to know its fixed and its variable costs, so that the budget numbers can be adjusted appropriately. Flexible budgeting does not mean a change in the budget—only a change in the reporting of the budget figures to reflect the company's actual activity level (Units Produced in this example). This process allows the company to compare actual costs incurred to what those costs should have been at the experienced level of activity, and thereby allows more realistic and effective cost control to be established.

With the implementation of the preceding recommendations, the company will be able to eliminate the entire general ledger function, with annual savings of $120,000. One of the previously mentioned database analyzers would also be responsible for the general ledger data files.

Internal Statements for Profit Improvement

The reporting process in the company is typically given little attention unless it is unsatisfactory to the recipient. Effective reporting is the means by which the accounting function communicates with the rest of the company. Good reporting can do wondrous things in communicating effectively within the company, while poor reporting can be doubly negative in its impact: first, because poor reporting may have unusable, incorrect, or untimely information and thereby lead to improper understanding and decisions; and second, because poor reports, even if accurate, can cause the reader to turn away in frustration if the information desired is buried deep within a morass of irrelevant (to the reader) or confusing

	Division A			Division B		
	Adj. Budget	Actual	Variance	Adj. Budget	Actual	Variance
Units produced	20,000	18,000	(2,000)	20,000	24,000	4,000
Sales	$ 900	$ 940	$ 40	$ 1,200	$ 1,152	($48)
Costs:						
Material	180	190	(10)	240	225	15
Direct labor	126	130	(4)	168	160	8
Var. overhead	122	125	(3)	162	158	4
Fixed overhead	175	170	5	175	173	2
Total costs	603	615	(12)	745	716	29
Gross Profit	$ 297	$ 325	$28	$ 455	$ 436	($19)

Exhibit 6.11   Manufacturing Budget Report—Flexible ($$ in 000s)

facts and figures. Good reporting should encompass effective concepts and features, such as:

- *Exception reporting.* Highlighting only those areas requiring attention
- *Flexible budget reporting.* Directed toward a range rather than a single level of activity and that can be adjusted to reflect changes resulting from variations in activity
- *Summarized reporting.* Providing appropriate information for each level within the organization so that these activities can be operated effectively
- *Comparative reporting.* Comparing operating results with realistic standards such as:
  - Actual versus budget (or what it should be)
  - Current year or period versus previous year or period
  - Standard costs and/or revenues
  - Company goals, objectives, and detail plans
  - External benchmarks, such as competitors' results or industry standards

> ## *GOOD REPORTING IS ACCOUNTING'S OPPORTUNITY TO COMMUNICATE EFFECTIVELY WITH OPERATING FUNCTIONS.*

The company's typical financial statements, consisting of a balance sheet, income statement, and statement of cash flow are primarily directed toward the reporting of historical results to management and a host of outsiders such as lenders and creditors, shareholders and investors, and regulatory agencies. It often takes at least 10 days to complete these financial statements after the end of a month. Although this information may be useful to those to whom the reports are directed, it has more limited operational value to those responsible for running major areas of the company and generating results. The primary reason for this reduced value is that the financial reports are geared toward the expectations and needs of the external users, and these expectations are different from the needs of internal users who require data to tell them what is happening operationally at present that will assist them in future decision making.

In order to develop meaningful internal statements and reports, an analysis of operations is performed to determine what useful information is needed to properly conduct operations in the most economical, efficient, and effective manner. To this end, the company has to recognize both the internal and external environments in which it operates. Among the internal and external issues that have to be considered are:

- Market and customers
- Production or service provision processes

- Growth opportunities and/or requirements
- Systems: computer, control, personnel, inventory
- Workforce needs
- Human resource philosophies
- Strategic directions

TRADITIONAL FINANCIAL STATEMENTS DON'T MEET OPERATIONAL NEEDS.

To effectively analyze financial data and related statements and determine how the organization is doing, and to zero in on critical areas needing attention and assistance, the company can use certain analytical tools:

- *Comparisons.* Financial statements are historical documents that are basically static—showing data related only to a specific period of time. However, business owners and managers (and other financial statement users) are concerned not only with the period being reported, but also with the trend of events over longer periods of time. Accordingly, financial statement analysis for just one period of time is of limited value.

  However, when financial statement data are compared with one or more of the following, the company can gain a better understanding of trends and make proper decisions about their significance. Although none of us can change the past (or predict the future), the company can use past performance as a yardstick or benchmark of present position for making more accurate decisions for the future. Possible comparisons include:
  - Historical performance of the business itself (results of prior periods)
  - Competitors' performance (other similar businesses)
  - General industry performance (other businesses within the same industry)
  - Organizational goals, objectives, and detail plans

- *Trend percentages.* Financial statement analysis can also be accomplished through the use of trend percentages, which are used to state a number of years' financial data in terms of a base year. The rule in using trend percentages is that at least three data points must be examined before a trend can be identified.
- *Common-size statements.* A common-size financial statement shows the line items as in percentages as well as in absolute dollars. Each line item on the financial statements is shown as a percentage of a total, either total assets or sales. The presentation of common-size statements is known as vertical analysis—revealing changes in the relative amount of each line item.

- *Financial and operational ratios.* Proper financial analysis of the company's results provides for the measurement and evaluation of progress towards accomplishing both financial and operational goals and objectives (i.e., earning an adequate return on investment or maintenance of a satisfactory market position). The company's financial position usually involves two fundamental considerations:

  1. Potential for survival: Measured by liquidity (ability to meet short-term financial obligations), solvency (ability to meet long-term financial obligations), and leverage (ratio of external to internal funds used to make up the capital structure of the company)
  2. Performance: Toward meeting financial and operational goals, measured by asset management and profitability results

Ratios, which represent a mathematical relationship between two quantitative conditions, are the primary method used for such analysis. When measured over a period of time, ratios identify changes or trends in the company's operations. They also provide valuable information in identifying operational trouble spots. Identifying the real operational problems of an organization and the inherent causes (not the symptoms) can be extremely difficult, and sometimes only a creative approach will uncover the real underlying situation.

The company should develop and provide a financial statement and internal operations reporting package that:

- Integrates the company's financial statements with the operating needs of the organization
- Uses financial data in an operating format to identify operational problems and causes within the organization
- Uses financial and operating data for more effective decision making directed toward positive growth

The preparation and analysis of the basic financial statements is only the starting point for developing an encompassing financial and operational reporting package. If financial statement analysis is done properly, it can provide useful information about the company's past financial performance and current status. However, without recognizing the company's internal operations (and external environment) and the manner in which it operates, financial analysis alone cannot tell the entire story. The internal operating and external issues that have to be considered can include the following:

- *Product analysis.* What to sell, to whom, product costs, and what to charge (pricing structures)
- *Customer base.* What markets to be in, who to sell, how much of which products, how to service

- *Sales forecasting.* How much of which products, to whom, and how to sell
- Manufacturing or service providing processes: what to provide, how to provide, and efficiencies to use
- *Integrated systems.* Sales/marketing, manufacturing, engineering, financial, and personnel
- *Planning and budgeting systems.* Strategic, long-term, short-term, and detail plans

> ## WITHOUT UNDERSTANDING THE BUSINESS'S INTERNAL AND EXTERNAL ENVIRONMENT RATIOS TELL ONLY PART OF THE STORY.

Businesses that do not understand these principles and use improper internal operations reporting may engage in many bad practices that sacrifice good customer sales for immediate cash, such as:

- Selling off inventory at less than desirable prices (sometimes at a real loss) to acquire cash. This results in unfavorable sales and jeopardizes more favorable future sales. It also may set a bad precedent and unfair expectations for customers.
- Selling more to existing customers at larger than normal markdowns, which may result in sacrificing future sales and establishing a bad precedent.
- Selling to existing customers greatly in excess of their established credit limits, which may result in the customers' inability to pay and discontinuation of future orders.
- Relaxing payment terms so as to sell off excess goods or services. Although the business may make a sale, it may not be able to collect on it for a long time—or ever.
- Selling to less than desirable customers. Again, the company may make the sale, but never collect on it. It must be kept in mind that the company is not in the sales and accounts receivable business.

A suggested set of financial reports are shown in Exhibits 6.12 through 6.16.

Review of Internal Operations

The information uncovered through the preceding financial reporting and analysis assists management and operations personnel in identifying the impact of financial policies and conditions on the company's cash and profitability positions. However, effective operational analysis should go beyond financial analysis

	Current Year		Previous Year	
	$	%	$	%
ASSETS				
Cash	$ 60	0.4	$ 400	4.1
Accounts receivable	3,720	24.2	2,160	21.9
Inventory	5,360	34.8	2,400	24.3
Current Assets	9,140	59.4	4,960	50.3
Property, plant and equipment	7,580	49.2	5,680	57.6
Accumulated depreciation	(2,160)	(14.0)	(1,540)	(15.6)
Net property, plant and equipment	5,420	35.2	4,140	42.0
Other assets	840	5.4	760	7.7
TOTAL ASSETS	$15,400	100.0	$9,860	100.0
LIABILITIES AND EQUITY				
Liabilities:				
Accounts payable	$ 1,960	12.7	$ 840	8.5
Notes payable	200	1.3	200	2.0
Current maturities long-term debt	840	5.5	680	6.9
Other current liabilities	560	3.6	440	4.5
Current liabilities	3,560	23.1	2,160	21.9
Long-term debt	7,680	49.9	5,200	52.8
Total Liabilities	11,240	73.0	7,360	74.7
Equity:				
Common stock	200	1.3	200	2.0
Additional paid-in-capital	200	1.3	200	2.0
Retained earnings	3,760	24.4	2,100	21.3
Stockholders' equity	4,160	27.0	2,500	25.3
TOTAL LIABILITIES AND EQUITY	$15,400	100.0	$9,860	100.0

Exhibit 6.12a Comparative Balance Sheets and Income Statements
Balance Sheet as of December 31 ($$ in 000s)
Showing % of Total Assets

to include a more in-depth review and analysis of specific areas of the company's operations as well.

Most companies are in more than one business; that is, they offer their customers a number of different product lines. For instance, the company may offer a low-end, a medium-end, and a high-end line; or a basic, standard, and custom or specialty line; or it may provide a basic piece of equipment (e.g., copy machine),

	Current Year		Previous Year	
	$	%	$	%
Net sales	$12,500	100.0	$9,360	100.0
Cost of goods sold:				
Material	2,260	18.1	1,720	18.4
Labor	3,260	26.1	2,340	25.0
Manufacturing expenses	2,080	16.6	1,720	18.4
Total Cost of Goods Sold	7,600	60.8	5,780	61.8
Gross Profit	4,900	39.2	3,580	38.2
Selling expenses	1,120	9.0	840	9.0
General and administrative				
expenses	1,480	11.8	1,040	11.1
Total Operating Expenses	2,600	20.8	1,880	20.1
Net Profit before Taxes	2,300	18.4	1,700	18.1
Provision for Income Taxes	640	5.1	480	5.1
NET INCOME	$ 1,660	13.3	$1,220	13.0

Exhibit 6.12b   Income Statement for Year Ending December 31 ($$ in 000s) Showing % of Sales

USES OF FUNDS

	$ Change	% Change
Accounts receivable	$1,560	72.2%
Inventory	2,960	123.3%
Net property, plant and equipment	1,280	30.9%
Other assets	80	10.5%
Total	$5,880	62.2%

SOURCES OF FUNDS

	$ Change	% Change
Retained earnings	$1,660	79.1%
Long-term debt	2,640	44.9%
Accounts payable	1,120	133.3%
Cash reduction	340	85.0%
Other liabilities	120	27.3%
Total	$5,880	53.8%

Exhibit 6.13   Uses and Sources of Funds from Previous Year to Current Year ($$ in 000s)

	$ Change	% Change
SALES	$3,140	33.5%
Cost of goods sold:		
Material	540	31.4%
Labor	920	39.3%
Manufacturing expenses	360	20.9%
Total Cost of Goods	1,820	31.5%
Gross Profit	1,320	36.9%
Selling expenses	280	33.3%
General and administrative expenses	440	42.3%
Total Operating Expenses	720	38.3%
Net Profit	600	35.3%
Provision For Income Taxes	160	33.3%
NET INCOME	$ 440	36.1%

Exhibit 6.14   Income Statement Change from Previous Year to Current Year ($$ in 000s)

replacement parts, and supplies. An analysis of the company's records can be used to develop individual income statements for each of its product lines.

In many cases, such an analysis, employing existing records, may be extremely difficult or costly. Therefore, it is best to establish what information will be needed in setting up the company's reporting system. Data collection and computer processing procedures should be established to automatically provide the operating data and statistics desired for effective management.

Income statements can then be constructed using the following process:

- *Net sales.* Analysis of actual invoices for the year and distribution of sales amounts to respective product lines
- *Cost of goods sold.* Material, labor, and manufacturing expenses assigned to product line, based on totals derived from actual manufacturing orders and production data
- *Operating expenses.* Actual marketing and administrative costs by product line may be difficult to determine. If so, these costs can be prorated based on sales volume of the product line or some other logical basis for allocation

An example of an income statement by product line is shown in Exhibit 6.17. Note that each product line can be considered a separate business or profit center. In addition, the company can consider each product within a product line

	Current Year Dollars	Trend Index	Previous Year Dollars
Net Sales	$12,500	1.34	$9,360
Cost of goods sold:			
Material	2,260	1.31	1,720
Labor	3,260	1.39	2,340
Manufacturing expenses	2,080	1.21	1,720
Total Cost of Goods Sold	7,600	1.31	5,780
Gross Profit	4,900	1.37	3,580
Selling expenses	1,120	1.33	840
General and administrative expenses	1,480	1.42	1,040
Total Operating Expenses	2,600	1.38	1,880
Net Profit	2,300	1.35	1,700
Provision for income taxes	640	1.33	480
NET INCOME	$1,660	1.36	$1,220

Exhibit 6.15 Income Statement Trend Percentages from Previous Year to Current Year
Previous Year = Base Year @ 1.00 ($$ in 000s)

	Current Year	Previous Year
1. Survival Ratios		
a. Liquidity ratios		
• Current ratio	2.57 : 1	2.30 : 1
• Quick ratio	1.06 : 1	1.19 : 1
b. Leverage/solvency ratios		
• Debt to equity	2.70 : 1	2.94 : 1
• Debt to assets	0.73 : 1	0.75 : 1
2. Performance Ratios		
a. Accounts receivable		
• Turnover	3.36 ×	4.33 ×
• Collection period	108.6 days	84.2 days
b. Inventory		
• Turnover	1.96 ×	2.89 ×
• Age	186.2 days	126.3 days
c. Accounts payable		
• Days	70.1 days	40.0 days
• To Accounts Receivable	1.90 ×	2.57 ×

Exhibit 6.16 Financial and Operational Ratio Analysis: Current and Previous Year

	Total	Products A	B	C
Net Sales	$12,500	$5,900	$4,300	$2,300
Cost of goods sold:				
Material	2,260	760	740	760
Labor	3,260	1,600	1,300	360
Manufacturing Expenses	2,080	1,040	720	320
Total Cost of Goods Sold	7,600	3,400	2,760	1,440
Gross Profit	4,900	2,500	1,540	860
Selling expenses	1,120	348	586	186
General/administrative expenses	1,480	816	246	418
Total Operating Expenses	2,600	1,164	832	604
NET PROFIT	$ 2,300	$1,336	$ 708	$ 256
Sales—% of total	100.0%	58.1%	30.8%	11.1%
Gross Profit—% of sales	39.2%	42.3%	35.8%	37.4%
Net Profit—% of sales	18.4%	22.6%	16.5%	11.1%

Exhibit 6.17   Income Statement by Product Line ($$ in 000s)

as a separate profit center, as well as each production job, customer order, or each individual customer. Each of these analyses helps to determine exactly what is happening currently, trends in previous periods, and what remedial action may be necessary.

Product-line reporting should be integrated with the original sales forecast and modifications, which should be part of the company's planning process. This reporting allows company management to determine whether they are progressing toward the right goals and whether any action must be taken. Such action could result in product modifications, sales and marketing changes, or changes in customer philosophy, work plan, or sales methodologies. It is the ability to determine specifically what information is significant to report that makes the reporting most valuable to the individual users and to company management.

IDENTIFY THE COMPANY'S KEY OPERATING INDICATORS.

In addition to financial data, ratios, and trends, the company should look at other key operating indicators such as backlog, real customer sales, accounts receivable and collections, inventory changes, personnel levels and use, and so on.

Based on the operational analysis, it is apparent that sales, accounts payable, accounts receivable, and the number of employees have all increased. Is this the sign of a healthy, growing company? Growing, yes; healthy, not necessarily. Such increases can be interpreted completely differently. For example:

- Increased sales may be the result of sales to existing customers exceeding safe credit limits or to less desirable customers, creating possible collectibility or non-payment problems.
- Increased accounts payable and accounts receivable may mean increases in returned merchandise to vendors and to the company by its customers, indicating unacceptable vendors and dissatisfied customers.
- Increased accounts receivable may mean recorded sales without corresponding collected accounts.
- Increased number of employees may mean more management and increased expenses, without corresponding increases in value-added productivity.
- Increased work volumes may be more a function of building personnel empires and keeping those employees busy than of real volume increases.

The correct interpretation of what is really happening in a company could well be distinguishing between the healthy company with best practices from the sick organization with many operating deficiencies. It is best to identify such

	Products		
	A	B	C
1. Sales prices and units sold			
Total sales in $	$5,900	$4,300	$2,300
Units sold in 000s	62.0	55.4	65.6
Average unit price	$95.16	$77.62	$35.06
2. Backlog statistics			
Total backlog in $	$1,980	$1,360	$1,060
Percent of sales	33.6%	31.6%	46.1%
3. Accounts Receivable			
Total accounts receivable in $	$1,680	$1,240	$ 800
Collection days	103.	106.1	127.0
Turnover times	3.5	3.4	2.9
4. Inventory			
Total inventory in $	$2,400	$1,760	$1,200
Turnover times	1.4	1.6	1.2
Average inventory age in days	258	230	304

Exhibit 6.18 Operating Information by Product Line ($$ in 000s)

	Current Year		Previous Year	
	Number Employees	Annual Dollars	Number Employees	Annual Dollars
Type of Payroll				
Manufacturing:				
Manufacturing operations	102	$2,285	90	$1,624
Manufacturing supervision	26	975	17	841
General and administrative:				
Accounting functions	38	787	31	634
All others	34	693	26	522
Sales department:				
Sales staff	12	620	10	465
Sales management	8	512	6	348
Total—All Payrolls	250	$5,872	180	$4,434

	Current Year		Previous Year	
	Sales per Employee	Payroll % of Sales	Sales per Employee	Payroll % of Sales
Payroll Costs to Sales				
Manufacturing operations	$ 122,549	18.3%	$ 104,000	17.4%
Manufacturing supervision	480,769	7.8%	550,588	8.9%
Accounting functions	328,947	6.3%	301,935	6.8%
Other general & administrative	367,647	5.5%	360,000	5.6%
Sales staff	1,041,667	5.0%	936,000	5.0%
Sales management	1,562,500	4.1%	1,560,000	3.7%
Total employees	50,000	47.0%	52,000	47.4%

	Current Year	Previous Year
Average Cost Per Employee		
Manufacturing operations	$22,400	$18,044
Manufacturing supervision	37,500	49,470
Accounting functions	20,700	20,452
Other general & administrative	20,380	20,077
Sales staff	51,700	46,500
Sales management	64,000	58,000
Total	23,488	24,633

Exhibit 6.19   Payroll and Employee Analysis ($$ in 000s)

Customer Name	Current Year		Previous Year	
	Sales $	Percent	Sales $	Percent
Product A				
Paul Brothers Company	$1,978	33.5%	$1,440	29.4%
Apex Industries	1,706	28.9%	1,230	25.1%
Kontrol Manufacturing	566	9.6%	453	9.2%
Sandstone, Inc.	346	5.9%	578	11.8%
Textite Industries	270	4.6%	434	8.9%
Ace, Inc	442	7.5%	259	5.3%
Subtotal	5,308	90.0%	4,394	89.7%
Other customers	592	10.0%	501	10.3%
Total—All Customers	$5,900	100.0%	$4,895	100.0%
Product B				
Paul Brothers Company	$ 335	7.8%	$ 460	15.0%
Apex Industries	475	11.0%	640	20.8%
Kontrol Manufacturing	678	15.7%	368	12.0%
Sandstone, Inc.	252	5.9%	84	2.7%
Textite Industries	173	4.0%	36	1.2%
Ace, Inc	858	20.0%	637	20.7%
Subtotal	2,771	64.4%	2,225	72.4%
Other customers	1,529	35.6%	845	27.6%
Total—All Customers	$4,300	100.0%	$3,070	100.0%
Product C				
Paul Brothers Company	$ 100	4.3%	$ 220	15.8%
Apex Industries	144	6.3%	212	15.2%
Kontrol Manufacturing	319	13.9%	69	4.9%
Sandstone, Inc.	477	20.7%	187	13.4%
Textite Industries	520	22.6%	368	26.4%
Ace, Inc.	0	0.0%	142	10.2%
Subtotal	1,560	67.8%	1,198	85.9%
Other customers	740	32.2%	197	14.1%
Total—All Customers	$2,300	100.0%	$1,395	100.0%

Exhibit 6.20 Customers by Product Line ($$ in 000s)

problem areas before and as they happen—and take quick remedial action—rather than wait until it is too late. The practice of preparing effective operating reports that provide such information to management and operations personnel needs to be instituted at the company.

Examples of such operating reports are shown in Exhibits 6.18 through 6.20.

Responsibility Accounting

> # *HOLD PERSONNEL ACCOUNTABLE FOR ONLY WHAT THEY CAN CONTROL.*

Responsibility accounting and reporting is a control system in which managers and operating personnel are held accountable for only those activities over which they exercise a significant amount of control. Such a system assists in establishing standards of performance against which to measure. Individual and group results are then evaluated on the basis of performance, and positive remedial action (e.g., coaching or facilitating) is offered to those not performing to expectations. A system of responsibility reporting should be implemented by the company to control and monitor the successful achievement of planned activities and results, as well as the effective use of resources (i.e., maximizing revenues and minimizing expenditures).

Under a responsibility reporting system, individuals are delegated decision making authority and held accountable for those activities occurring in their areas of responsibility. The system operates according to the principle that individuals should be responsible for their own performance (e.g., self-motivated disciplined behavior) and the performance of all activities within their scope of responsibility (e.g., vendors, customers, other employees). Advantages to the company of using responsibility reporting include:

- Facilitates the delegation of authority and decision making
- Enables the company to implement planning and control programs focused on establishing goals and objectives and the subsequent evaluation of progress toward such objectives
- Establishes standards of performance to be used for evaluation purposes
- Provides criteria for performance evaluation
- Allows for identifying areas of concern by focusing on important variances from standards
- Assists in identifying the causes of problems so that the problems can be fixed, rather than blame assessed
- Communicates clearly to each individual in the company those responsibilities for which they will be held accountable, how they will be rewarded, and remedial action to be taken to prevent the recurrence of a negative situation

- Pins responsibility to the individual or work unit where corrective action needs to be taken and ties the concern to other areas of the company that might be affected by the condition and might be involved in the corrective solution

ORGANIZATION RECOMMENDATIONS

The accounting functions are primarily working as if an integrated computerized accounting system does not exist. Each function, although it inputs data into the computer system, works on a stand-alone basis. Many of the activities that characterize a manual accounting system (e.g., matching physical documents, checking for coding errors, verifying math calculations) are still being performed. In addition, for limited control advantages, the company processes almost all vendor payments, customer billings, and collections on a manual basis. The cash management study team's recommendations to reduce the amount of accounts payable and accounts receivable transactions, to outsource the payroll function, and to allow the computer system to predominantly maintain the general ledger should allow the company to realize personnel (and cash) savings of $692,700, as follows:

- Eliminate the internal controller position and its related staff positions. For those functions such as borrowing, investing, capital expenditures, and so forth, the company should engage the services of an external controller. Study team members have talked to three extremely competent individuals and their firms about assuming these duties and reviewing financial and operational activities on an ongoing basis. Each one of them would perform such services for a monthly fee of $3,000.
- Eliminate the manager and supervisor positions in each of the accounting functions. The company should establish a policy of motivated self-discipline for their employees so that such positions are unnecessary for policing the activities of their employees—in effect, all employees are responsible for their own results.
- Use the integrated computer system as it was intended, so that the company does not have to pay processors but can engage database analyzers and coordinators instead.
- Eliminate the clerical positions through the use of computerized routines that are based on electronic data rather than on paper documentation.
- Streamline all remaining systems so that procedures can be accomplished most economically, efficiently, and effectively, using computerized routines to the extent possible and eliminating all non-value-added activities.
- Dovetail all other company operations that would be affected by such changes so that the company achieves overall benefits.
- Identify by-product benefits and best practices that can be implemented within the remaining accounting activities and other related areas.

The effective implementation of the preceding recommendations will result in the following personnel requirements for the accounting functions:

External controller at $3,000 per month	$ 36,000
Outside payroll processor	35,000
Database analyzers: for accounts payable, accounts receivable, general ledger, and reporting systems (two at $30,000 per year)	60,000
Systems coordinator to provide interface with the other internal departments and the outside payroll processor	25,000
Total Proposed Personnel Costs	156,000
Present Personnel Costs	787,100
Proposed Personnel Savings	$631,100

In addition to these proposed personnel savings, the company should not have to spend more than an additional $10,000 per year on other costs to support these activities. This represents an additional annual savings of $61,600, based on the current year's actual costs of $71,600.

In reviewing the organizational concerns within the accounting functions, the study team identified the following concerns to be addressed within the accounting area as well as all other areas of the company:

- The need for a highly paid individual at the vice president level (e.g., controller) for each function within the organization. This practice appears to be justified by the perceived need to police and control those individuals reporting to these persons. There is minimal value added by these individuals. For instance, the team is recommending the replacement of the controller (but not necessary functions) by the use of an external controller service.
- The use of managers for each function who report directly to a person at the vice president level. These individuals are responsible for overseeing the activities performed in their areas, but offer minimal value added efforts. This appears to be an extension of the costly policing and control philosophy.
- Individuals with the title "Supervisor," who appear to be responsible for accomplishing the daily activities but are really chief workers.
- The practice of adding individuals to the workforce rather than simplifying work systems so that fewer personnel are required. For instance, there are eight processors in the accounts receivable section, where no more than two (even with present work volumes) are needed for most of the month.

- The assignment of clerical personnel to each functional activity. Although a certain amount of clerical support is required for each activity, it is rare that such support constitutes a full-time job (once redundancies and unnecessary work steps are eliminated).

OTHER AREAS FOR REVIEW

The scope of this part of the company's cash management study is to review and analyze those functions and activities associated with the accounting division of the company that can be eliminated, reduced, or performed more economically and efficiently. However, the study team finds that many of their observations, conclusions, and recommendations have an impact on other functional areas of the company as well. Accordingly, they must bring these areas to the attention of management so that they can take the appropriate follow-up action as part of a quest for best practices in a program of continuous improvements. Examples of other such areas for review are grouped in four major categories:

1. The recommendation to reduce the number of accounts payable transactions includes the use of a direct cash payment system for small purchases and payment to vendors at the time of receipt for large, long-term contractual type purchases. Such practices will require the company to address related activities in various ways:
   - Responsibility of each department and work unit to control its own budget and related expenditures using a direct cash system.
   - Reduction in the number of purchase requisitions and purchase orders. This will affect all departmental support staff as well as reduce purchasing department efforts.
   - Increased responsibility for purchasing department personnel to effectively negotiate with vendors, especially major vendors.
   - With the present high level of merchandise returned to vendors, the company must work more closely with its vendors to ensure close to 100 percent of on-time, quality deliveries.
   - Manufacturing systems, such as production and inventory control, must be fine-tuned so that they can effectively accommodate just in time practices based on the reliability of vendors rather than on excessive internal quality controls.
   - Increased reliance on computer processing systems rather than elaborate manual control systems.

2. Accounts receivable recommendations that encompass payment upon receipt for small and low ticket sales and payment upon receipt for large sales to major customers will require the company to consider the following areas as well:

- Establishment of procedures and controls to accommodate a cash payment system for low-ticket items.
- Effective negotiations with major customers to develop long-term contracts with guaranteed delivery dates at prices at which the company can improve its profit margins. This will require a full analysis of cost systems so that the company can produce the items at the lowest cost possible. Each customer contract should be considered a profit center.
- Integration of the sales function with company planning. Sales forecasts must be more realistic so that they can be relied on to plan production activities. Product should be produced for real customer orders rather than for inventory. The sales department should be guided by the company plan rather than by the desire to maximize compensation. Such changes may require a full analysis of the sales and manufacturing areas, as well as the company planning processes.
- Customer analysis to determine with which present customers to increase or decrease sales and which customers to terminate. In addition, there should be effective planning on which products to sell, in what quantity, and to whom. Part of such a plan should be the identification of prospective customers and how they can be approached.
- Increased attention to peripheral activities such as credit policies, collection procedures, factoring, electronic data transfer, and so on.
- Increased discipline within the manufacturing area so the company can meet all of its customer commitments on an on-time, quality basis. Production schedule and control procedures must be integrated with customer requirements. The company has to remove itself from the inventory business and move back into the customer service and cash conversion businesses.

3. The change from an internal Payroll Department to an outside payroll processor necessitates that the company look at the following concerns:
   - Accurate data discipline by all operating areas, as there will no longer be personnel in-house to correct payroll input errors, which never should have happened in the first place. Corrections can be made only on an after-the-fact basis.
   - Investigating the effective use of such outsourcing concepts for other areas—for instance, the use of an external controller. Economies and efficiencies can be realized in other areas as well, including manufacturing operations (e.g., grinding and smoothing), sales (e.g., brokers and representatives), and engineering (e.g., per diem personnel as needed).
   - Integration of outsiders into company operations, making them part of the organization even though they are not employees. The company

must change its belief that everything must be controlled internally with its own employees.

- Elimination of in-house activities and controls that will be taken over by the outside servicer, such as data controls, numeric reconciliations, and output verifications.
- The reduction and change in activities and related job positions, which allow greater efficiency at much less cost within the accounting functions, should be considered in an analysis of all other functions of the company.

4. Integration of the general ledger with computerized subsystems and the implementation of responsive financial and operating controls and reporting will have an impact on company operations in the following ways:
   - Real time information will necessitate immediate action to address the cause of a problem rather than the symptoms. This will require self-motivated discipline by all employees and less reliance on managers (and fewer managers) within a working together atmosphere. Such a reporting system will assist the company in becoming a learning organization.
   - The reality of a continuous planning and flexible budget system will require quick responsiveness to changes and more effective management of each employee's responsibilities.
   - Adoption of an effective cost accounting system according to Activity Based Costing principles will aid in reviewing all costs and activities in an effort to bring costs and related prices to the minimum possible. This will allow the company to become more competitive and build business on a core of satisfied customers.
   - Use of effective cash flow management techniques will allow for pushing costs to their minimums (e.g., labor and material), collecting sales proceeds as soon as possible, and making payments as economically as possible.
   - Employees will have the flexibility to go to the work, rather than wait for the work to come to them. Each employee should be evaluated and rewarded based on results accomplished rather than a subjective system such as seniority or personal preference.
   - There will be greater reliance on computer procedures than on manual controls, which should be implemented in all areas of the company.

CONCLUSION

Effective cash management study procedures allow a company to identify its critical problem areas and opportunities for improvement—maximizing positive aspects of existing procedures and focusing the study on the most critical areas.

Through coordinating activities of various areas, the cash management study process achieves positive changes in these areas simultaneously. The process also allows such areas to work together in the analysis of present practices and the implementation of new systems and procedures. In this manner, all areas learn with less reinventing and change within the same time period.

The cash management study can be a stand-alone project to identify critical problem areas and provide standardized improvements. It can also minimize the practice of reinventing good practices that already exist in another part of the organization. The study can also provide a comparison between the ways in which different people perform the same task in the same area, or a comparison of performance across different work units within the company. It can also provide the knowledge of operations and its effect on company cash flow.

In the review of the accounting function, a number of areas of potential improvement are identified to make the company operate more economically, efficiently, and effectively. The implementation of such improvements places the company in a better position for future growth and profitability and will enable the company to compete more effectively in the marketplace. Although there are many other aspects of the company's accounting practices that can be addressed for productivity, cash flow, or profit improvements, these materials contain effective examples of the types of conclusions and recommendations that can result from such a cash management study. Because each company is different and each cash management study is different, the resulting findings, conclusions, and recommendations will also be unique to that study of the particular company.

In the present business atmosphere, with emphasis on customer service, quality, economies and efficiencies, profit maximization, and cash management, the cash management study becomes not a one-time, stand-alone project, but an ongoing process of searching for best practices in a company program of continuous improvements. The application of cash management procedures is everyone's responsibility.

> *CASH MANAGEMENT*
> *IS EVERYONE'S RESPONSIBILITY.*

CHAPTER 7

Investing, Financing, and Borrowing

> ## *IDLE CASH IS A LAZY ASSET.*

O nce the company has put its cash management systems in place, the level of discretionary funds available for investing or shortfalls that have to be covered by borrowing become apparent. One of the key ingredients in a successful cash management system is putting that excess cash to work for the company in the most effective manner. Without following through on this, the entire cash management effort will lose most, if not all, of its benefits. Cash sitting idly in a checking account not earning interest is a lazy asset, and a totally inefficient resource.

Covering cash shortfalls must be planned for in advance as well. Banks do not like lending money to people who have a sudden need for it. They are far more comfortable and flexible with people who plan for their needs in advance and address these needs before they become crises. Acquiring long-term funding requires an even higher degree of advance planning. Choosing among new equity issues, bonds, or long-term financial institution borrowing takes time to conceive and implement. Having plans in place prior to deciding on how funds will be acquired is an integral part of the responsibility of overall cash management.

INVESTING EXCESS CASH

Short-Term Investing Policy Issues

What, then, can be done with that excess cash that has been generated by the company's attention to cash management procedures? Obviously, the answer is to invest the funds safely with maximum earnings. However, before running off and aimlessly investing funds in some rock solid or go-go type instrument, there are company policy issues that should be addressed to help develop a coherent, consistent investment program that meets the needs of the company.

DECIDE POLICY ISSUES BEFORE STARTING THE INVESTMENT PROGRAM.

Among the significant policy issues that should be agreed upon prior to setting up the short-term investment program for the company's excess cash are:

- *What is the company's basic short-term investment goal?* Examples include maintaining safety of principal, maximizing earnings, cash availability (liquidity), minimizing transaction costs, and so on.
- *How much risk is the company willing to assume?* Are aggressive investment strategies appropriate or is a more conservative approach that reduces yields but improves safety and liquidity more acceptable?
- *Are there any investment restrictions, limitations, or preferred concentrations?* Can the company invest in any instrument that meets basic criteria, or are there certain types of investments that should be avoided or emphasized (e.g., no tobacco or liquor company investments, or only investments in U.S. government securities).
- *Who is responsible for investment activities, and what authority should be given to that person or persons?* This is an organizational concern that addresses the issues of authority, responsibility, and control.
- *What kind of approval and reporting steps should be established?* Should a second level of approval be required for transactions? How frequently and in what detail should reports on investment activity be prepared?
- *What degree of concentration or dispersion should the investment program have?* Should the company concentrate investments in similar types of instruments such as bank certificates of deposit (CDs) or Treasury bills, or should it diversify its portfolio by using a variety of available instruments?
- *What type of investment audit programs should be established and who should be responsible for carrying them out?* For a large investment program, formal audit procedures should be developed with steps for following them. For smaller investment programs, management needs to make sure adequate controls exist to ensure that policies are followed.

Investment Opportunities

Once overall investment policy guidelines have been established, the company can begin to evaluate the alternative investment opportunities that are available. There are a number of macroeconomic conditions that have a direct impact on the yield and availability of investment instruments. The level of overall economic activity in the country (and increasingly around the world) certainly has an effect—as economic activity grows, the demand for funds tends to increase, which puts upward pressure on interest rates. If the company is able to generate excess cash during that part of the economic cycle when other businesses are in need of funds, its opportunities for obtaining attractive yields are greatly improved. Conversely, if cash excesses are generated when other businesses also have excess cash, then the interest yields will tend to be lower.

Another factor that will affect the company's investment opportunities is the eagerness on the part of financial institutions to seek out its business. When financial markets are open and highly competitive, banks (and others) aggressively seek new business. This opens up the possibility of attractive investment alternatives that might otherwise not be available. The amount the bank is willing to pay for excess cash is a function of the overall market demand for funds. The greater the demand, the greater the upward pressure on interest rates; or the greater the cost of those funds to the bank and the greater the return to the investing company. The company's investment in a bank instrument is a source of funds to the bank that can be turned into a loan to another customer. But investment yields on bank instruments must be lower than lending rates, since banks make their profits on the spread between what they pay to an investor of excess cash and what they charge a borrower.

A final element in the overall cost of funds is the pressure on the market placed by the biggest borrower of all—the U.S. government. Should the country's deficit grow larger, the government's need for borrowed funds to meet its obligations increases. This places a potentially huge demand on the overall supply of funds and drives up the cost of money in the marketplace, generating improved yields for those with excess cash, but also creating higher costs for those who must borrow. In times of surpluses or declining deficits, the opposite occurs, lowering the cost of borrowing, but also lowering the yields to those with excess cash.

In evaluating alternative investment instruments, there are certain criteria to consider, including:

- *The overall quality of the investment.* The safer (higher quality) the investment, the lower the yield; the riskier (lower quality) the investment, the higher the yield.
- *Price stability and risk.* High risk tends to create a more volatile market price. Conversely, an instrument displaying relatively low price volatility is likely to carry a lesser degree of risk.
- *Marketability and liquidity.* The greater the marketability, the greater the liquidity but the lower the yield. Strong marketability reduces risk and improves liquidity, but at a reduced yield. Higher yields can be attained, but typically at a higher risk associated with reduced liquidity and marketability.
- *Maturity date.* Normally, the farther out the maturity date, the higher the return (to compensate for the higher risk of the longer term exposure). Conversely, shorter maturities usually result in lower yields because of the reduced risk.

- *Return on investment and yield.* Equals the income received divided by the amount invested and factored for the time period covered. Yield includes not only the interest received, but also any capital appreciation (or depreciation).

All of the items listed are yield, return on investment (ROI), or risk issues. The investment strategy objective should be to maximize investment yield consistent with attitude toward risk, liquidity, and overall investment quality.

HIGHER RETURN —HIGHER RISK
LOWER RISK—LOWER RETURN

A summary of some major investment alternatives and significant features is shown in Exhibit 7.1.

Evaluating Longer-Term Investment Opportunities

The company has probably been confronted many times in the past with the decision as to the best allocation of financial resources to various possible capital investment projects. For instance, increased plant capacity, new or rehabilitated equipment, financial investments, refinancing, acquisitions, etc. represent the kinds of decisions that must often be made. All these examples represent capital investment opportunities for which there are established decision-making methods.

Capital investment decisions are critical for most organizations. The organization's future success or failure very often depends on making the correct capital investment decision. The critical nature of these decisions can be recognized by the manner in which they are handled within the organization – such as having approval required by the Chief Financial Officer (CFO), Chief Executive Officer (CEO), and/or the Board of Directors. However, in many organizations, capital investment decision procedures can be quite unsophisticated. For example, management may approve capital investments without considering and evaluating alternative investment opportunities, or they may consider alternatives but not use the available data in an effective manner to reach an optimal decision.

Discounted Cash Flow
Discounted Cash Flow (DCF) is the method used for evaluating future cash flows in terms of what they are worth today. Discounting is the opposite of compounding.

Compounding calculates what the values of a cash amount today will be worth in the future, given an interest rate at which it is expected to grow. For

Instrument	Typical Minimum Investment	Guarantee	Life	Interest Payments
Market rate savings	$2,500	Bank; FDIC up to $100,000	Daily	Usually monthly
Money market funds	Varies— $1,000 to $5,000	Underlying investments of funds	Daily	Daily
Repurchase agreements	Varies—as low as $50,000	Bank underlying security	1 day to several months	Maturity
Certificates of deposit	Best rates at $100,000 and over	Bank; FDIC up to $100,000	7 days to several years	Maturity, monthly, quarterly, etc.
Banker's acceptances	Usually $100,000	Bank	1 day to 1 year	Discount basis
U.S. treasury bills	$10,000	U.S. government	90 days to 1 year	Discount basis
U.S. treasury notes	$1,000 to $5,000	U.S. government	Over 2 years	Semiannual
U.S. government agencies	Usually $10,000	Faith and credit of issuing agency of U.S. Government	Varies—30 days to 30 years	Maturity or annual
Commercial paper	$25,000 to $100,000	Issuing corporation	Overnight to 270 days	Discount basis
Municipal notes and funds	$1,000 and over	Faith and credit of municipality issuer	1 year to 30 years	Usually semi-annual
Financial futures	Varies	Backed by issuing institution	Up to 3 years	Not applicable

Exhibit 7.1 Investment Alternatives

example, $1,000 compounded at 10 percent grows to $1,610.51 in five years as
follows:

Year 1	$1,000.00 × 110% =	$1,100.00
Year 2	$1,100.00 × 110% =	$1,210.00
Year 3	$1,210.00 × 110% =	$1,331.00
Year 4	$1,331.00 × 110% =	$1,464.10
Year 5	$1,464,10 × 110% =	$1,610.51

Compounding, of course, means earning interest on interest, and the difference between the $1,610.51 calculated and $1,500.00 [$1,000 + (10% * 5 years)] is
the effect of the interest earned on prior interest.

Discounting, as stated above, is the reverse process—that is, determining
how much a future amount of cash is worth today at a given discount rate. For
example, $3,300.00 to be received in six years, discounted at 12% is worth
$1,671.88 today, as follows:

Year 6	$3,300.00 / 112% =	$2,946.43
Year 5	$2,946.43 / 112% =	$2,630.74
Year 4	$2,630.74 / 112% =	$2,348.87
Year 3	$2,348.87 / 112% =	$2,097.21
Year 2	$2,097.21 / 112% =	$1,872.51
Year 1	$1,872.51 / 112% =	$1,671.88

Use of computer software or appropriate financial tables makes these calculations much less tedious, especially for longer term evaluations.

Cash Flow Considerations
Capital budgeting/investment decisions are based on the measurement of cash
flows, not on accounting profits and losses. Accordingly, allocations, attributions,
and similar non-cash factors that do not result in changes to the underlying cash
flows should not be included in the DCF calculations. Some cash flow factors to
consider include:

- *Incremental cash flows.* Include only those cash flows that change as a
  result of the capital project activities.
- *Residual values.* Consider the remaining value of the capital item or project at the end of the project life. Frequently, this sale value at the end of the
  project makes the difference between a good and a bad deal. For example,
  computer equipment or automobile leases are very precise about such
  end-of-term sale values and often fly or fall based on such residual values.

- *Depreciation.* Depreciation, a noncash expense, should itself not be considered in the DCF calculations, but the tax savings which result from the depreciation tax shield must be considered as part of the positive cash flow.
- *Tax considerations.* Tax laws applicable to capital investments have a direct impact on the project's cash flows. For instance, investment tax credits (when they are available) on a large investment can be a major factor because they can produce significant cash inflows early in the project's life. Other tax considerations include regular income tax vs. capital gains rates, losses providing carry-back or carry-forward tax benefits, accelerated depreciation, and the like. Property taxes, tangible personal property taxes, and other state or municipal assessments also need to be taken into account because they represent cash flow to the organization.

Time Value of Money

Capital budgeting decisions are generally more critical and risky than short-term operating-type decisions because (1) the organization will usually recoup its investment over a much longer period of time (if at all), and (2) they are much more difficult to reverse. Additionally, funds are tied up over a longer period of time, and this constitutes an opportunity cost of the potential differential earning capacity of these funds had they been invested in another manner.

Time value of money means that money on hand today has greater value than money to be received in the future. Money has time value for the following reasons:

- Cash on hand can be used to earn more money in the form of interest, dividends, or increased value (appreciation).
- Money to be received in the future has an opportunity cost of not being able to be used right away—either for investment or for pleasure as in spending it for something wanted or needed.
- Money to be received in the future will have less value than today because of the ravages of inflation.
- Money to be received in the future carries with it the risk of being lost—partially or entirely.

TIME VALUE OF MONEY—
A DOLLAR IN HAND TODAY
IS WORTH MORE THAN A DOLLAR
IN THE FUTURE.

Capital budgeting/investment decisions relate to the committing of resources (usually of a financial nature) for time periods longer than a year. The company must clearly understand the concept of the time value of money and how to use it effectively to compare various capital investment alternatives so as to arrive at optimum decisions. To evaluate such decisions, the capital investment required must be identified together with its resulting cash flows (both inflows and any additional outflows). Future cash flows may occur due to additional revenues, additional expenses, cost savings, tax benefits, scrap sales, and so on. A critical factor to consider in capital budgeting/investment evaluations is that most, if not all, of the numbers used in the analyses are likely to be estimates. Therefore, a methodology that provides the most accurate inputs to any analyses should be applied. The final result is only as good as the least accurate of the estimates used.

Net Present Value
The net present value (NPV) method of evaluating capital investment opportunities is a DCF technique that takes the time value of money into account. These DCF techniques discount future cash flows to their present value, based on an appropriate interest (discount) rate. The net present value method determines the present value of the cash inflows and compares the result to the present value of the cash outflows at a specified discount rate (may be the company's cost of capital or a desired minimum rate of return, which is referred to as its hurdle rate). The NPV is the difference between the present value of the cash inflows and the present value of the cash outflows. If NPV as calculated is positive, then the capital investment is acceptable quantitatively as it is projected to earn a return higher than the discount rate used in the calculations. If NPV is negative, the capital project is quantitatively unacceptable since it is projected to generate a rate of return less than the targeted return. Exhibit 7.2 shows how an NPV calculation is made.

Since the NPV is positive, the rate of return for this capital project is greater than 16 percent. If the NPV were zero, the actual rate of return for this project would be exactly 16 percent. And if the NPV were negative, the actual rate of return would be less than 16 percent. By comparing the NPVs of a number of capital investment alternatives, management can determine which project is the most desirable from a rate-of-return perspective.

Internal Rate of Return
The internal rate of return (IRR) is a capital investment method that determines the actual rate of return on a proposed capital project considering the time value of money. This technique is sometimes called the time-adjusted rate of return. It is similar to the NPV method, but instead of determining whether the project produces a desired rate of return, the IRR method calculates the actual rate of return being generated by the project. The calculated actual rate of return can then be reviewed to decide if the project return is acceptable. Calculation procedures for IRR depend on whether the capital project has even or uneven cash flows. Using the Exhibit 7.2 example of an $80,000 investment with annual cash inflows of

Cash Outflows = $ 80,000 capital outlay (Project Investment)
Cash Inflows = $ 22,000 operating cost savings per year
Project Life = 8 years
Targeted Rate of Return (hurdle rate) = 16%

This is an annuity calculation because the amounts of return are a series of constant payments for a specified number of time periods.

	Year(s)	Amount	16%PV annuity factor*	Present Value
Cash Outflow	0	$80,000	1.0000	(80,000)
Cash Inflow	1–8	$22,000	4.3436	95,559
Net Present Value (NPV)				$15,559

*These factors come from a "Present Value of an Annuity" table.

Exhibit 7.2 Example of a Net Present Value Calculation

$22,000 for the next 8 years, the IRR that will be earned on this investment can be calculated as follows:

The formula for calculating present value is:

PV = cash flow $\times$ PV factor (from table)

In our example, 80,000 = 22,000 $\times$ PV factor; or

PV factor = 80,000/22,000 = 3.6364

By referring to a "Present Value of An Annuity" table, the corresponding discount rate can be found. In this example the discount rate represented by the cash flows in the example is about 21.8 percent. This is consistent with the NPV calculation above, where NPV at 16 percent equaled a positive $15,559. Obviously, this means that the IRR would be substantially in excess of 16 percent.

Determining IRR with uneven cash flows is more complicated than with level cash flows. It involves a trial-and-error process; and since the cash flows are not the same every year, the present value must be calculated on a year by year basis (rather than on an annuity basis). The first step is to determine a discount rate that may be close to the actual IRR and use this discount rate to calculate the PV of the cash flows for the project. If the PV of the cash inflows exceeds the PV of the investment, the discount rate selected was too low; while if the discounted cash flow is negative, the discount rate selected was too high. Recalculate the PV using a discount rate that is appropriately higher or lower. An attempt should be made to find two discount rates between which the actual rate lies, and then find the actual rate by interpolation. To see how this works, look at the example in Exhibit 7.3.

Comparison of Capital Investment Evaluation Techniques

The following matrix highlights in simple form the two methods under discussion above, and some key attributes of each.

Technique	Description	Purpose	Advantages	Disadvantages
Net Present Value (NPV)	Net value of expected cash flows discounted for the time value of money	To estimate gain or loss in constant time period terms; to compare alternative investments of similar dollar magnitude	Considers time value of money; allows easy comparison of investments of like dollar amounts	Requires estimation of a discount rate; difficult to interpret results; compares only investments of like amounts
Internal Rate of Return (IRR)	Exact discount rate at which the net present value of the investment is zero	To calculate actual return of the investment in percentage terms	Considers time value of money; provides standard method for evaluating investments of any amount	Time consuming and complex; results must be developed iteratively through trial and error

The Element of Risk

The evaluation of the risk or uncertainty of a capital investment project is crucial to the investment decision process. The evaluation of risk is complex, but it needs to be factored into the company's decision-making efforts. Naturally, there should be a higher return for a project with greater risk than for one with less risk.

When dealing with a capital project in which risk or uncertainty can be subjectively evaluated, it may be desirable to establish a range of discount or hurdle (target) rates to reflect the differing levels of risk. For example:

	Required Rate of Return
"No" risk (investment in T-bills)	8%
Minimal risk (replacement machine)	10%
Normal risk (new piece of equipment)	12% *
High risk (new product line)	18%
Extremely high risk (international market penetration)	25%

* company hurdle rate

Investment (Year 0)   = $50,000
Cash flow returns
        Year 1   =   10,000
        Year 2   =   20,000
        Year 3   =   40,000

What is the Internal Rate of Return (IRR) on this project?

| | | | Step 1—Try 15% | Step 2—Try 16% | |
Year	15% Disc. Cash Flow	Discounted Factor	16% Disc. Cash Flow	Factor Factor	Discounted Cash Flow
0	(50,000)	1.0000	(50,000)	1.0000	(50,000)
1	10,000	.8696	8,696	.8621	8,621
2	20,000	.7561	15,122	.7432	14,864
3	40,000	.6575	26,300	.6407	25,628
Net Present Value			+ 118		(887)

The IRR lies between 15% and 16% (because the NPV becomes 0 between these two discount rates).

Step 3—interpolate for a more exact answer.
      NPV at 15%   =   + 118
      NPV at 16%   =   − 887
        Difference   =   1005

Therefore, IRR = 15% + 118/1005 = 15% + .117 = 15.117%

Exhibit 7.3   Example of an Internal Rate of Return (IRR) Calculation

While these rates are shown for illustrative purposes only and do not necessarily reflect rates that would be appropriate for a particular business, the concept of requiring higher rates of return for riskier projects is one that should be incorporated into the company's thinking.

Another element of risk is the fact that results of a future investment cannot be known for certain, and there exists the possibility of numerous possible cash flow outcomes for a given opportunity. Applying a probability to each of the reasonably possible outcomes and weighting these outcomes by their probability of occurrence develops a most-likely-result scenario. For example:

	DCF	Probability	Weighted DCF
Optimistic	$20,000	.25	$5,000
Most probable	15,000	.70	10,500
Pessimistic	(5,000)	.05	(250)
Expected Outcome			$15,250

Some capital investments available to the organization may be more risky than others, thereby introducing the prospect of loss or failure. This leads to measurement of the relative probability of large profits compared with the potential for large losses. Management should consider the possibility of not realizing forecasted results and should factor this possibility into their capital budgeting/investment analyses.

Risk assessment, in most instances, is an intuitive process, and cannot be exactly measured. Examples of higher-risk situations might include investments in the oil and gas industry, gambling casinos, new technology, bioengineering, international ventures, and so on. Some elements that may enter into risk considerations include:

- Economic conditions (inflation/deflation/recession)
- Organizational attitude toward risk (risk averse, risk neutral, risk preferred)
- Individual manager's attitude toward risk
- Business conditions (growth/stability/retrenchment)
- Specific demands for company products or services
- Organization's financial position (ability to absorb losses)
- Magnitude of investment relative to organization's resources (how much can the company afford to invest at risk?)

FINANCING SOURCES FOR THE BUSINESS

A principal responsibility of the company's financial manager is to ensure that sufficient funds are available to meet the company's needs. This concern touches on virtually all aspects of company activities and is often a survival issue for many businesses.

The determination of how much capital is needed is an outgrowth of the planning and budgeting process and develops from the answer to a critical question in this planning and budgeting activity—"Can we afford to carry out this plan?" The development of the cash flow forecast provides the answer. Once it is determined that the company must acquire more funds than will be generated by internal cash flow, the financial manager needs to decide on the source of these funds.

- *Profitability* is the most desirable source of new funds since that is a key reason for being in business. The profitability, however, must be cash flow, not net income, since a company can be extremely profitable on its Income Statement without having enough cash available to meet the next payroll. Also since this means profitability retained in the business, decisions regarding reinvestment of profits and dividend payouts need to be carefully addressed so as to meet the long- and short-term needs and expectations of the company's owners. This is the case regardless of whether there are one, two, or thousands of shareholders.

- *Sale of assets* is a self-limiting source of funds. Unnecessary assets should, of course, be liquidated to free up additional resources whenever possible. But there is only so much self-cannibalization that can take place before the company begins to do itself serious harm.

- *New equity funds* may be a realistic source of funds depending on the company ownership structure. Closely or totally privately held businesses typically cannot easily acquire new equity funds. Issues of control, availability, liquidity, and expense make new equity acquisition difficult. For publicly held companies new equity may be feasible, but even for these companies expense, timing, dilution of ownership, the vagaries of the stock market, and retaining control are complicating factors that can make new equity impossible or undesirable.

- That leaves *borrowing*, aside from profitability, the most commonly used source of new capital for the small business. For a well-managed, profitable, and capital-balanced company, borrowing will typically be the least expensive, easiest-to-handle source of new funds other than reinvested profits. Interest is tax deductible, banks and other financial institutions are in the business of lending money to reliable customers; and borrowing is a respectable, flexible, and generally available source of financing. There are multiple sources of borrowing potentially available even for the smaller business, and borrowing can be obtained on a short- or longer-term basis.

> ## *PROFITS ARE THE BEST SOURCE OF ADDITIONAL FUNDS.*

BORROWING FOR CASH SHORTFALLS

It is unrealistic to assume that the company will always be in a position to invest excess cash. For many companies, the opposite is true—there is an ongoing need to borrow short-term (or working capital) funds to maintain the business's operating cash flow. As in the case of investing excess cash, company policies need to be established relative to a short-term borrowing program. These policies should include:

- An overall borrowing strategy
- Authority and responsibility issues
- Limitations and restrictions as to types or sources of borrowing
- Approval and reporting requirements

- Concentration or dispersion of borrowing sources
- Cost-risk decisions with particular attention to the issue of cost versus loyalty to a particular financial institution
- Flexibility and safety—future availability of funds
- Audit programs and controls

Borrowing Sources

There are numerous opportunities and alternatives for the company to consider in making borrowing decisions, including:

- *The company's bank.* Most borrowers tend to consider their own commercial bank first when looking for alternative sources of borrowing. The bank should be familiar with the company's business and is likely to be best informed regarding the suitability of the loan. It should be willing to commit to the company for short-term loans such as open lines of credit, term notes, demand loans, or automatic cash overdrafts. Common collateral, if required, for short-term loans is accounts receivable (typically to 70 percent or 80 percent of face value) or inventory (30 percent to 70 percent of face value depending on stage of completion and marketability).
- *Life insurance policies.* The cash surrender value of any life insurance policies the company carries for key man, estate planning, buy-sell agreements, or other purposes can be used as a readily available source of relatively inexpensive short-term borrowing. The amount available, however, is typically limited.
- *Life insurance companies.* Loans from life insurance companies are normally long term and for larger amounts than the borrowings we are considering here. This is generally not a good source for short-term borrowing.
- *Investment brokers.* If the company (or its principals) has an account with an investment broker, the securities held may be usable as collateral for short-term borrowings.
- *Accounts receivable financing.* Accounts receivable can be used as collateral for a short-term bank loan or sold outright to a factor.
- *Inventory financing.* Company inventory can be used as collateral for short-term bank loans, though the percentage of the inventory value received is likely to be lower than for accounts receivable.
- *Customers and vendors.* It is sometimes possible to obtain financing from customers via advances against orders or early payment of accounts receivable. This is particularly appropriate if there is a lengthy production or service provision process involved or if there is an expensive specialized order. Vendor financing can be easier, since the vendor is usually very interested in making the sale, and financing may be considered part of the pricing package. In the event of a large-dollar-volume purchase order, it

might be possible to arrange financing through extended payment terms, an installment sale, or a leasing contract.

- *Pension plans.* If there is a company pension plan with a large amount of cash available, a company loan may seem feasible. According to Employee Retirement Income Security Act (ERISA) rules, a company may not borrow from its own pension fund, but a financial manager might consider borrowing from another company's or lending pension funds to another company. This is a very sensitive area, however, since fiduciary and stewardship responsibility issues cannot be ignored without peril. Any activity regarding pension funds needs to be reviewed by competent advisors to avoid the appearance or the reality of impropriety and the adverse effects thereof.
- *Stockholders.* Stockholder loans to privately held companies continue to be a significant source of additional money for organizations. However, it would be wise to check on the latest regulations and restrictions before proceeding on this course to ensure that proper procedures have been followed. IRS activity in this area is vigorous and frequent because of the potential for mischief and abuse. If the IRS determines that what the company says is a stockholder loan is actually a capital contribution, deductible interest becomes a nondeductible dividend and loan principal repayments become returns of capital. The tax consequences of such a determination can be devastating.

Borrowing for Short-Term Needs

Short-term borrowing, which will have to be paid off within a one-year time period, can take on many forms. For the borrower, this type of financing, with exceptions, tends to be riskier, slightly less expensive (although this will depend on the interest rate situation at the time of the borrowing), more flexible because of the greater variety of borrowing possibilities, and more readily available because of the greater willingness of lenders to lend on a short-term basis than longer-term financing.

The most common and most desirable (for the borrower) source of short-term funding is simple trade credit. While virtually all businesses use trade credit at least to some degree, many financial managers do not recognize that this is a manageable resource. If a supplier provides 30-day terms for payment, there is very little to be gained by paying off the bill earlier. The supplier expects to be paid in 30 days and earlier payment (assuming no available cash discounts) will not be an advantage to the customer. In the event of a cash shortage, companies often take advantage of suppliers by stretching their payments, which is where the management process can really have an effect. Suppliers understand that companies have periods when cash is short and money may not be immediately available to pay bills. It has probably happened to them on occasion. A call to the supplier explaining the situation, setting up a schedule for getting back to normal, and a simple request for cooperation may be all that is necessary to maintain a healthy relationship with that supplier without any reduction in credit standing.

> ### *TRADE CREDIT IS FREE MONEY BUT SHOULD NOT BE ABUSED.*

However, unilateral stretching of payment without explanation may not create overt reactions on the part of suppliers, but many will notice—and remember. The retention of the customer may be more important than financial considerations at the time, but at some future time conditions may change and that supplier may drop the company for one with whom they have had a better payment experience. This situation may arise without notice and be a complete surprise—and if it is an important supplier, this could have devastating results. While a somewhat extreme occurrence, it does happen. An open, well-managed, communicative relationship, in which the supplier is informed of what you are doing and why, is likely to preclude this kind of disaster. That is how a company can manage its trade credit resource.

A major concern in deciding on short-term borrowing strategies is the need for flexibility. Every dollar borrowed for even one day costs the company interest. As a result, sufficient flexibility must be built into the borrowing structure to provide for relieving this interest burden as quickly and easily as can be arranged. However, the lender's objectives may run counter to the company's, so each one must understand the other. The management team must understand these relationships as well as the guidelines and best practices for short-term borrowing.

The ultimate in flexibility for short-term borrowing is the open line of credit, which allows the company to borrow as it needs funds in the amount required up to a prearranged limit. The company can also repay the money in whatever amount it has available whenever it wishes. This allows the company to use only the amount actually required, thus keeping its borrowing at a minimum level throughout the term of the loan.

> ### *OPEN LINE OF CREDIT PROVIDES MAXIMUM FLEXIBILITY.*

In exchange for the flexibility of the credit line, the lender may charge, in addition to the interest on the amount borrowed, a commitment fee on the amount of funds that have been promised for the line of credit but not yet borrowed. This commitment fee is usually a nominal amount but does add to the cost of the loan. The bank may also charge a slightly higher interest rate than might be the case for a fixed term loan. An additional consideration is that there may be a requirement that the amount borrowed be reduced to a zero balance sometime during the year. Since the loan is short term and is intended for short-term uses, this condition makes sense; but if the company is unable to meet this requirement, there could be serious consequences for its ongoing operations. Finally, the borrower must realize that a line of credit is not a permanent arrangement. It typically has to be renegotiated each year, which means that properly handling the line of credit during the year is a necessary prerequisite for getting it renewed the following year.

Alternatives to a line of credit include *short-term notes* and *demand notes*. Both have predetermined (fixed or variable) interest rates, but short-term notes have specific maturity dates at which time they must be repaid or rolled over. Demand notes do not have maturity dates, but are subject to repayment "on demand" by the lender. This protects the lender, who can act quickly to call the loan in the case of an undesirable turn of events for the borrower, but also gives the borrower a possible "permanent" loan. If the borrower maintains a strong financial position in the eyes of the lender, the borrower would continue to pay interest, but the demand note principal would theoretically never have to be repaid.

Short-term borrowing may be done on an *unsecured* basis (based on the full faith and credit of the borrower) or it may be *secured* by some of the specific assets of the business. Secured short-term borrowings typically use accounts receivable and/or inventory as the collateral. Accounts receivable, because of their greater liquidity are the preferred collateral for most lenders. Inventory's attractiveness as collateral will be largely dependent on the nature, reliability, and liquidity of the inventory. A hardware store's inventory is readily resalable elsewhere and therefore will be worth more as collateral than will the inventory of a specialized electronics manufacturer with a great deal of partially complete printed circuit boards that are valueless unless used for their specific intended purpose.

Accounts receivable–based borrowings can ordinarily generate up to 80 percent of the face value of the receivable for a borrower if the receivables are from reliable customers and, in fact, are legitimate receivables as perceived by the customers. Different types of arrangements can be established with lenders ranging from a simple overall collateralization of the receivables to specific arrangements whereby the borrower sends copies of the day's invoices and remits all checks to the lender. The lender then forwards a designated percentage of the invoice amounts and returns a designated portion of the remittances based on the percentage of receivables that is being loaned and the amount of receivables outstanding.

A more direct form of receivables financing is *factoring* whereby a financial institution, known as a factor, actually purchases the receivables at a significant discount and pays cash to the borrower based on a prearranged agreement as to percentage and quality of the receivables. The factor may assume responsibility for collecting them. This is factoring with notification (i.e., the customers are notified that their payments are to be remitted directly to the factor). Factoring without notification means the company retains collection responsibility and remits the proceeds of collection directly to the factor on receipt, and customers need not be informed that their accounts have been factored. Factoring can also be arranged with or without recourse. With recourse means that the factor does not assume responsibility for uncollectible accounts, while without recourse means the opposite. The latter, of course, will be more expensive to the company selling its receivables because of the greater risk assumed by the factor. Factoring of receivables, except in some industries where it is common business practice, is typically more expensive than other types of financing and is often considered a last-ditch source of borrowing. For some companies, the stigma associated with factoring, whether or not justified, makes this an undesirable means of financing.

Inventory-based financing can sometimes be arranged with financial institutions from as little as 20 percent to as much as 75 percent or 80 percent of the inventory cost. The types of specific arrangements also vary greatly depending on the quality and nature of the inventory as discussed earlier. Additionally, the closer the inventory is to being immediately salable, the greater the amount that can be financed. Work-in-process inventory will have less financing potential than will finished goods that can be easily sold. The inventory financing process will depend on the requirements of the lender and can range from inventory as general collateral on up to specific bonded warehousing arrangements. Typically inventory financing is more difficult, more expensive, and less available than receivables financing because of greater risk to the lender.

Other forms of short-term borrowing are less often used and are less likely to be available to smaller businesses. Included are *bankers' acceptances* (used for financing the shipment of the borrower's products both domestically and internationally); *commercial paper* (available only to companies with extremely high credit ratings and not feasible for the smaller business); *security-based financing* (if there is a portfolio of marketable securities to use as collateral); loans based on the *cash surrender value of life insurance policies*; loans based on *specific contracts* with customers; loans based on *guaranties* by customers, loans or financing arrangements from suppliers, and so on.

Medium- and Long-Term Borrowing

Longer-term financing has lower risk for the borrowing company because of the longer time in which to plan for and cover the obligations. The typical longer-term financing package has smaller repayment obligations stretched out over a longer time period, which makes it somewhat easier for the borrowing company to handle. As a result the company is not faced with recurring and short-term requirements for repayment and/or refinancing of relatively large amounts of money. Therefore, they can concentrate more of their efforts on using the available funds to generate profits that can be used in the future to repay loans.

However, because of the greater risk exposure to the lending institution, long-term funds can be more difficult to obtain for the smaller business and will generally command a higher interest rate. Evaluating the repayment ability of a smaller organization in the shorter term is easier to do because it principally requires examination of the company's current assets and current liabilities. Long-term loan repayments must come out of earnings generated by the business, and the evaluation of longer-term earnings potential is more difficult for the lender, especially for a smaller business that may not have a long track record of success.

Long-term borrowing, as short-term, can be done on a secured or an unsecured basis. Unsecured longer-term funds are available only to those companies with a strong record of success in which the lending institutions have faith about continuing success. More typically, the banks will require personal guarantees or other collateralization to secure their long-term commitments. They may also require certain restrictions, or covenants, on the financial performance of the company with regard to dividend payments, changes in ownership, financial ratio requirements, and the like to preserve the company's financial status and thereby to protect the lender's interests. Perhaps the bank will require both collateralization and restrictive covenants. These issues may make the issuance of long-term borrowing more complicated to arrange and more difficult for the typical smaller company to accept.

Bonds and *debentures*, forms of long-term financing, are devices available to publicly held companies and rarely are viable options for a smaller company to consider. Long-term borrowings in the form of *mortgages* or *loans* secured by real estate or equipment are more likely to be available to smaller companies. These loans will have maturity dates and required repayment dates that could be monthly, quarterly, semiannually, or annually and with or without balloon payments at the end. Interest rates may be fixed or variable usually calculated as a factor above the prime interest rate charged by the bank. In the event of default by the borrower, the bank can assume title to the item collateralized by the loan and receive its money by converting that asset into cash. This is a last-resort situation for banks. They are not interested in or in the business of taking over collateralized assets—they would rather have their customers be successful and pay off the loans as agreed.

Equipment financing can be arranged with a financial institution or sometimes with the manufacturer of the equipment itself. An advance against the cost of the equipment is paid to the borrower to finance the cost of the equipment. The more marketable and generally usable the equipment is, the more that can be advanced against the cost. For example, a general-purpose lathe will allow a greater percentage loan than will a piece of equipment specially designed for a cow-milking machine that has no use elsewhere. The document used to secure the loan is referred to as a chattel mortgage. Alternatively, a conditional sales contract may be arranged whereby the borrower has the use but not title to the equipment. Title passes only after the financial terms have been satisfied. This preserves the seller's position by allowing the seller to repossess the equipment at any time the buyer fails to meet the terms of the contract.

Leasing is an additional way of securing longer-term funding. An *operating lease* is one that permits the lessee to use the equipment or real property as long as the periodic lease payments are made. At the end of the lease term, the lessee may or may not have the right to acquire ownership of the property for a reasonable market value or to continue with the leasing arrangements. A *capital* or *finance lease*, however, leaves the lessee with ownership to the property at the end of the lease period with the payment of a nominal sum or perhaps none at all. As a practical matter, a capital lease is a financing scheme while an operating lease is, in essence, a rental agreement with a possible option to buy. Leases can be arranged either with the seller of the equipment or property or through a leasing institution.

A major advantage of leasing is that it reduces or eliminates the amount of cash needed for the down payment, which is ordinarily required under the other types of financing discussed. Leasing arrangements do not impose the kinds of financial restrictions that may be required by other lenders. And in the event that land is involved in the lease, depreciation for that land may effectively be available by virtue of the lease payment. However, leasing does not give the lessee the full rights of ownership that come with purchase and financing through other forms of debt (e.g., improvements to the leased items may be restricted, the leased items may not be freely sold, and ownership decisions may have to be made at the end of the lease period when the value of the equipment or property may be seriously diminished).

Managing the Bank Financing Activity

The company's bank is likely to be the principal source of new money for the business along with the cash flow it generates. Cultivation of the bank and its lending officer(s) is a critically important part of the financial officer's job. A good banker will work with the company through its troubles if they are adequately explained and do not come as last minute surprises. Maintaining strong, open lines of communication with the bank and letting it know what is going on in the business—both good news and bad—will typically provide both parties with the foundation for a strong long-term relationship and will help create a symbiotic rather than an adversarial relationship. This should be a high priority goal of the company.

The principal focus in borrowing decisions is usually on the cost, manifested by the interest rate. But in comparing lenders' rates, the company may get an inaccurate picture if it is not careful. For example, interest collected at the beginning of a loan has a higher cost than if paid off during the term of the loan; and interest calculated quarterly costs more than if charged on the monthly outstanding balance. There are other factors to consider such as compensating balance requirements, commitment fees, prepayment penalties, working capital minimums, dividend payment restrictions, alternative borrowing constraints, maximum debt to equity requirements, equipment acquisition limitations, or other operational constraints. These are known as buried costs that can easily offset a lower nominal interest rate. Analyze the entire loan package, not just the interest rate, before deciding on what is best in the specific situation being reviewed.

INTEREST IS ONLY ONE OF THE LOAN COSTS TO CONSIDER.

The company's overall banking relationships should also be considered. It may look attractive to get a cheap loan from a new financial institution, but what if the company has an emergency? Will the new and "cheaper" lender stand behind the company when needed? Consider whether it might be worth paying a little more to maintain a solid, ongoing relationship with the company's lead bank, particularly if that bank has stood behind the company in past times of difficulty.

An additional consideration is what should be financed by short- rather than longer-term debt. The preferred capital structure of a business is one in which short-term needs are financed by short-term debt and its long-term or "permanent" needs are financed by long-term sources—long-term debt or equity. Certain short-term assets (e.g., permanent working capital needs) can legitimately be financed with long-term funds since they represent permanent requirements of the growing business. Seasonal financing should not be financed by use of long-term moneys—seasonal borrowing should be cleaned up seasonally to be sure that the business is being properly managed from a financial perspective. However, it would be better to finance a piece of equipment or a project having multiple-year lives with long-term money than with a short-term loan, since the funds to repay the loan will presumably come from the profits generated by the equipment or project.

The company must recognize that many, particularly smaller, businesses are able to obtain only short-term loans because banks are unwilling to commit to longer term financing. If this is the case, the company must do whatever it must to keep operations going, and theoretical models of how a business capital structure should be built are necessarily tossed aside. As a practical matter, this means that many long-term projects can only be financed by short-term financing. This raises the financial risk of the project to the company, since the loan may have to be repaid or renegotiated before the project generates enough cash to pay it off. If money is not available to roll over the loan or if interest rates rise sharply, it could cause serious financial problems for the company. Nevertheless, the goal of balancing long-term needs with long-term financing and short-term needs with short-term financing should be retained for future application whenever it becomes possible to do so.

Leverage

A major financial advantage of borrowing is the leverage that can be generated as a result of using borrowed funds. Leverage is essentially the economic advantage gained from using someone else's money. A simplified example of the effect or benefits of leverage on the return on investment for the investor is shown in Exhibit 7.4.

As can be seen, the more of someone else's money used to finance a particular project investment, the greater the return to the investor, even though the total dollar return on the project reduces as the company borrows more because of the interest that must be paid. There is a caveat, however. The leverage process works in the company's favor only if the earnings on the investment project are greater than the borrowing cost. If the cost of borrowing exceeds the earnings on the investment, leverage works in reverse—to the detriment of the investor. This is illustrated by the example shown in Exhibit 7.5.

A. INVESTING 100% OF YOUR OWN FUNDS		
Project Investment	$100,000	
Earnings on the project @ 20%	20,000	
Taxes @ 35%	(7,000)	
Net return		$ 13,000
Return on Investment (13,000/100,000)		13.00%
B. INVESTING 50%; BORROWING 50% AT 11% INTEREST		
Invested funds	$ 50,000	
Borrowed funds	50,000	
Total Project Investment		$100,000
Earnings on the project @ 20%	20,000	
Interest – 11% x 50,000	5,500	
Return before taxes	14,500	
Taxes @ 35%	5,075	
Net return		$9,425
Return on investment (9,425/50,000)		18.85%
C. INVESTING 10%; BORROWING 90% AT 12% INTEREST		
Invested funds	$ 10,000	
Borrowed funds	90,000	
Total Project Investment		$100,000
Earnings on the project @ 20%	20,000	
Interest – 12% x 90,000	10,800	
Return before taxes	9,200	
Taxes @ 35%	3,220	
Net return		$ 5,980
Return on investment (5,980/10,000)		59.80%

Exhibit 7.4 Leverage—Benefits

```
A   INVESTING 100% OF YOUR OWN FUNDS
    Project Investment                          $100,000
    Earnings on the project @ 10%                 10,000
    Taxes @ 35%                                   (3,500)
        Net return                                           $   6,500
        Return on Investment (6,500/100,000)                     6.50%


B   INVESTING 50%; BORROWING 50% AT 11% INTEREST
    Invested funds                               $50,000
    Borrowed funds                                50,000
        Total Project Investment                             $100,000
    Earnings on the project @ 10%                 10,000
    Interest – 11% x 50,000                        5,500
        Return before taxes                        4,500
        Taxes @ 35%                                1,575
        Net return                                           $   2,925
        Return on investment (2,925/50,000)                      5.85%


C   INVESTING 10%; BORROWING 90% AT 12% INTEREST
    Invested funds                               $10,000
    Borrowed funds                                90,000
        Total Project Investment                             $100,000
    Earnings on the project @ 10%                 10,000
    Interest – 12% x 90,000                       10,800
        Return before taxes                         (800)
        Tax benefit @ 35%                            280
        Net loss                                             $    (520)
        Return on investment [(520)/10,000]                    (5.20)%
```

Exhibit 7.5 Leverage—Detriments

Here we can see that as more borrowing takes place, the interest cost increasingly exceeds the return on the investment. Since the lender gets a fixed return, all the loss devolves onto the investor with excruciating consequences.

As a rule more borrowing means greater financial risk to the company since it now has both interest and principal repayment obligations to meet. However, if the project is a good one with a return above the cost of borrowing, the return to the investor multiplies as the amount of borrowing increases, thus providing compensation for the extra risk.

While "neither a borrower nor a lender be" may be good advice at a personal level, it does not translate into good advice for a business entity. The absence of borrowing clearly reduces company risk, but it also precludes the company from gaining the advantages of leverage. As in so many other situations, balancing the risk and the return is part of the job of investment management generally and cash management specifically. Using or not using borrowed funds is a choice that the company must make based on its attitude toward the risk as well as the availability of borrowed funds. Company management must review and analyze this process to determine the adequacy of the company's borrowing procedures and whether the company is using borrowing and the concept of leverage effectively.

> *LEVERAGE — USING OTHER PEOPLE'S MONEY*
> *TO MAKE MONEY.*

CONCLUSION

The company that never has a cash excess or shortfall is rare indeed. Because cash flows erratically within the typical organization, it is necessary to plan for both excesses and shortfalls. The latter, to be sure, are more hazardous and such situations need to be dealt with more urgently than the case of excess cash. But an inadequately handled excess of cash means the organization is not properly utilizing all its resources to the benefit of its owners. That represents ineffective financial management and should not be tolerated.

The company has numerous choices as to how to handle both shortfalls and excesses of cash. Identifying the alternatives and deciding which are the appropriate ones for the company to use are as important to the cash management process as any of the others discussed in this book. If the company is well managed and plans its cash flow properly, it normally will not have problems finding resources to use to cover any cash requirements. And setting up policies in advance as to what should be done with any cash excesses will allow the company to handle that situation easily and effectively.

> *NEITHER BORROWING NOR LENDING DO*
> *UNLESS IT MAKES GOOD SENSE TO YOU.*

CHAPTER 8

Planning Cash Flow

> **MANAGING CASH FLOW IS A CONTINUAL PROCESS.**

If companies do any cash planning at all, they typically focus on day-to-day cash balances. While this concentration addresses the issue of daily survival, it does not consider the fundamental need to maintain the proper balance among the sources and uses of cash funds on a longer term basis.

The company's sources (increases) of cash come from:

- Decreasing assets (other than cash), for example, collecting accounts receivable, converting inventory to cash, selling off excess property, plant and equipment
- Increasing liabilities, for example, adding to accounts payable (less cash needed until the additional bills are actually paid), short-term financing, long-term borrowing
- Increasing stockholders' equity, for example, securing additional equity investment, reinvesting profits

The company's uses (decreases) of cash result from:

- Increasing assets (other than cash), for example, purchasing inventory, property, plant and equipment; adding to accounts receivable (less cash coming in until the customers pay their bills)
- Decreasing liabilities, for example, paying off accounts payable, borrowings, other liabilities (pension payments, withholding taxes, other taxes)
- Decreasing stockholders' equity, for example, paying dividends, repurchasing equity, or incurring losses

CASH FLOW PLANNING

> **PLANNING CASH FLOW PLANS SURVIVAL.**

263

Cash flow planning focuses on having future expected sources exceed uses of cash and what needs to be done to maintain that positive flow of cash. Comparing actual results to the cash plan provides a basis for analysis and appropriate decision making. The tools to be considered in the cash flow planning process include:

- Preparation
- Cash forecasting
- Cash planning
- Cash budgeting

Preparation

In order to establish an effective (i.e., usable and reasonably accurate) process for projecting cash flow, it is helpful to examine the company's actual cash flow history. A tedious, but systematic, method is to review in detail 12 months of actual cash flow for the company. For each month all sources of cash receipts and all cash disbursements should be listed by account. This will generate a growing list of receipts and disbursements, some of which will be quite small. But it will be easier to combine items at the end of the process than to have to open a line item into greater detail after all data have been accumulated.

The actual cash flow should be reconciled to the cash balance at the end of each month to ensure that all receipts and disbursements have been recorded. After 12 months of data have been accumulated, the categories can be cross-footed to get totals for each line item. At this time the smaller items can be combined into one or more "other" categories while the larger items ensure that all major classifications of receipts and disbursements have been identified. There is now a basis for establishing a cash flow projection with appropriate detail line items.

Cash Forecasting

In addition to having the necessary internal systems in place to manage and control its cash balances and transactions, the company must also know in advance what kinds of cash flows to expect. In that way, the company can deal with those cash flows on a prospective rather than totally reactive basis. As in every other business discipline, planning is the difference between careful, considered decisions and potential chaos. The advantage of cash forecasting is that it gives the company advance information about cash shortfalls and cash excesses, which allows planning for borrowing and/or investment strategies.

There is a difference between forecasting and planning in cash management as well as in managing profitability. The American Institute of Certified Public Accountants' (AICPA) concept of forecasting is the estimate of the most probable financial position, results of operations, and changes in financial position for one or more future periods. Most probable is the operative phrase, and it presumes no specific action taken by the forecasting organization. A plan, however, involves more than just figuring the most probable results—it is a predetermined course of action. A plan looks at the future, considers alternatives, includes action, and establishes time frames for that action. The plan uses the forecast, but adapts it to help make desirable results happen for the planning organization. The company must focus more on the planning than the forecasting of cash.

Cash Planning

Plans are prepared for short- or long-term periods of time, but these designations are more specific in definition than they are in actual usage. As a general rule of thumb, short-term plans will cover one business operating cycle or up to one year. Long-term planning, depending on the nature of the business, can be six months, two years, or even as long as 50 years. (For some people, long-term planning is deciding at 10 o'clock where to have lunch that day). Plans that cover the intermediate time frame can be short, long, or medium term depending on the designation the planner wants to give. When related to cash flow planning, anything beyond one year will be most effective if done on the basis of total working capital or funds availability rather than simply cash balances.

A further planning refinement is to prepare best, worst, and most likely case projections. These will help to evaluate a range of reasonable possibilities and make plans that will allow the company to react accordingly. Keep in mind that plans are always subject to adjustment based on changes in circumstances or actual results.

> ## PLAN THE SHORT RUN IN DETAIL
> ## AND THE LONG RUN IN GENERAL.

Conventional wisdom suggests that cash plans be done in considerable detail for a relatively short period of time and in more general terms for longer periods, with updates prepared on a rolling basis. The specifics of what kinds of time periods to use will depend on the particular business and its needs. As an example, the company could prepare plans for three months in detail and four additional quarters in more general terms. The three-month plan would be used for specifically managing the cash availability for that period, while the balance of the plan would provide a view of potential trouble spots or opportunities in the more distant future for which appropriate actions can be prepared. Such a planning process would be updated each quarter, thereby always providing a detailed look at the cash situation in the near future. Avoiding surprises should be a major goal in cash planning just as it is in any other form of business planning, and this type of rolling planning approach helps to achieve that result.

In addition to this month-by-month look at the next year and a quarter, it will normally be necessary to take a more immediate look at exactly what bills must be paid within the next week or two and how much cash will be available to meet those obligations. That will require the company to have information about what can be expected in cash receipts for the one- or two-week period and what expenditures need to be made in that same period. Widely accepted accounting software packages provide detailed information about cash requirements with time period breakdowns relevant to the business. This kind of information, together with anticipated receipts from accounts receivable or other sources, provides all that is needed to evaluate cash availability for the immediate future.

Cash planning is a necessary exercise, but will prove to be an act of futility if the results are not put to use in some relevant and appropriate way. The objectives of any cash flow plans should be to:

- *Attempt to smooth out cash flow.* Cash flow typically fluctuates significantly from period to period. Looking into the future to see where problems are coming up also provides the opportunity to take action to do something about those potential problems. Receipts can perhaps be accelerated or selected disbursements deferred in order to smooth out shortfalls and avoid borrowing money or delaying payments to important vendors or suppliers. Knowing about prospective cash excesses will allow the company to use them effectively—either for investment or as a reserve for future requirements.
- *Make investments as early as possible.* Idle cash is a lazy asset, and the opportunity to put cash to work for the company in an interest-bearing account will help to improve overall return to the company. The look into the future provided by a solid cash planning system may alert the company to opportunities to make investments earlier than would otherwise be the case. Larger dollar investments can generate more earnings than equivalent amounts in smaller pieces, and knowing that cash will continue to be generated in increasing amounts in the future may allow investment of more dollars earlier. This kind of anticipatory action is not feasible without good cash planning in place.
- *Delay borrowing as long as possible.* The cash flow plan will show prospective shortfalls for which borrowing may have to be incurred. However, the plan may also show ways to cover the shortfalls by means other than borrowing, or may enable the company to defer borrowing until a later time. This means savings in interest expense, the benefit of which is obvious to everyone—except, perhaps, the company's banker.
- *Get early information.* The advantage of having early information so as to preclude the chaos of dealing with unexpected cash excesses or shortfalls should be obvious to any businessperson who has had to put out a fire or otherwise deal with an emergency. A problem anticipated is a problem at least half solved, and planning is anticipating.

Cash Budgeting

> ## *CASH BUDGETING IS A GOOD IDEA EVEN IF PROFIT BUDGETS ARE NOT PREPARED.*

Cash flow budgeting is an activity that focuses specifically on the company's cash position. A good cash budgeting process is essential for the business to manage its cash flow. Even if the organization does not see fit to do formalized profit and loss budgeting, it should consider cash budgeting. There are many reasons why typical operational profit and loss budgeting may not be desirable:

- Its benefits do not outweigh the costs involved.
- It is too time consuming.
- It requires too much education of operating managers to enable them to participate in the process.
- It does not add anything of value to either planning or control because other systems in place handle these processes effectively.
- It is too expensive.
- No one in the company knows how to do it.
- Operating managers are too busy with their principal responsibilities to get involved in a budgeting process.

Some of these arguments are fundamentally invalid, but they are still used as excuses to avoid budgeting. Without extensively evaluating these excuses, operating budgets, in fact, are often not prepared. Even if they are not, a cash budget should be prepared. It can be done by a financial professional, either from within the company or by use of an outsider. The cash budgeting process does not require that operating managers get involved in the process other than to provide appropriate input regarding anticipated revenues or expenditures. Since cash budgeting can be handled essentially within the financial manager's office, most of the excuses for not preparing an operating budget do not apply. And the critical nature of cash availability dictates that some form of cash plan or budget be prepared.

The typical business does not usually generate a sale in direct exchange for cash—the sale is made in return for the customer's promise to pay within agreed-upon selling terms (thereby creating an account receivable). The business purchases its needed materials (e.g. inventory) and operating expenses on the same basis—with a promise to pay at some agreed-upon time in the future (thereby creating accounts payable or accrued expenses). These economic transactions do not immediately affect the business's cash flow. The cash flow occurs at the time of payment—either when cash is received or disbursed. Effective cash flow control must clearly identify and manage the timing differences between the economic and the cash transactions. The goal of cash conversion is to convert business activities to cash as quickly as feasible. Do whatever possible to maximize cash sales, reduce the collection period, eliminate non-value-added costs, and eliminate transactions where the processing cost exceeds the amount of the transaction.

The cash flow budget projects the cash receipts and disbursements expected in the normal course of business, taking into account the actual time that cash flows in and out. This budgeting process can be divided into the following components:

- Forecasting sales
- Projecting cash receipts
- Projecting cash disbursements
- Projecting cash balances
- Managing cash shortfalls and excesses

Forecasting Sales

The sales plan or forecast is the foundation of the cash flow budget. The more accurate the sales forecast, the more accurate will be the cash flow budget. The sales forecast is the vehicle that determines the expected amount of sales by period and, ultimately, the expected amount of cash receipts in the succeeding time periods. The expected level of sales by period also provides the basis for projected cash disbursements. As is the case in income statement budgeting, the sales forecast is essential to the preparation of the cash flow budget and is a difficult, but vital, determinant of overall accuracy of the projections. The more accurate the sales forecast, and the higher the percentage of *real* customer orders, the more accurate will be the cash budget.

Projecting Cash Receipts

The primary source of cash flow into the business does not come directly from sales (except for cash sales), but from the collection of accounts receivable. If sales and average collection period remain constant from month to month, cash inflow will match sales volume. However, most businesses have a more erratic pattern of sales and collections.

An effective and accurate projection of cash receipts requires a careful analysis of accounts receivable collection patterns to determine as precisely as possible how long after the sale the cash will actually be received. For example, in Exhibit 8.1, the company has determined that 10 percent of any month's sales will be received in that month, 60 percent in the next month, 15 percent in the third month and 10 percent in the fourth month. Five percent cash sales, of course, also represent cash received in the month of sale. The company's actual collection pattern can be determined by reviewing historical receipts relative to

	ACTUAL			PROJECTED					
	OCT	NOV	DEC	JAN	FEB	MAR	APR	MAY	JUN
Sales (actual for first three months; then forecasted)	196	207	203	200	250	400	500	300	200
Collections:									
Cash sales—5%	Actual	Actual	Actual	10	12	20	25	15	10
Current month at 10%	Actual	Actual	Actual	20	25	40	50	30	20
Prior month at 60%	Actual	Actual	Actual	122	120	150	240	300	180
Second prior month at 15%	Actual	Actual	Actual	31	30	30	37	60	75
Third prior month at 10%	Actual	Actual	Actual	20	21	20	20	25	40
Total Cash Inflow from Collections	Actual	Actual	Actual	203	208	260	372	430	325
Other cash receipts	Actual	Actual	Actual	11	2	4	8	10	5
Total Cash Inflow—Month	Actual	Actual	Actual	214	210	264	380	440	330
Total Cash Inflow—Cum.				214	424	688	1,068	1,508	1,838

Exhibit 8.1 Projected Cash Receipts ($$ in 000s)

sales, and the collection pattern determines the model to use in its own cash receipts projections.

For simplicity of presentation the following exhibits use a six-month fore-casting period rather than a more typical 12-month period. Furthermore, the individual schedules are shown separately for ease of understanding. In reality, the entire cash budget will likely be a single document that encompasses all of the elements shown in these exhibits.

Knowing its historical collection patterns, in total and by individual customer, also enables the company to make decisions about differential pricing. Better pricing for timely paying customers rewards them for their good efforts and brings cash into the company more quickly. Higher prices for slow paying customers creates an incentive for them to pay more quickly and helps the company to recover its costs for not having the cash. This allows the company to effectively negotiate prices with its customers based on its internal cost structure and cash availability (i.e. no paper invoices, accounts receivable, or need for collecting reduces the company's costs). These savings work to the advantage of the company (lower costs of processing) and the customers (lower prices).

> ### MORE CASH SALES—MORE CASH IN MORE QUICKLY AND LESS CASH OUT.

An alternative to the specific analysis approach is to estimate the company's collection period in days, using a days' sales outstanding (DSO) calculation. Applying the DSO to projected sales allows an estimate of accounts receivable at the end of each month of the budget period. Then by taking beginning accounts receivable, adding projected sales and subtracting ending accounts receivable, the amount of collections for the period can be determined. Adjustments, if required, can be made for any potential uncollectible accounts. While somewhat less precise, this method may be easier to implement if a consistent pattern of collection is not discernable.

The development of a cash receipts schedule should also motivate company management to question their sales and collection projections as follows:

- Are we making the right sales to the right customers?
- Are our payment terms too lenient or too stringent?
- Are our collection practices adequate to ensure maximum cash flow?
- Are our billing, accounts receivable, and collection procedures too costly and inefficient?
- Is the amount of quick collections (at time of shipment or delivery, or within the same month) too low?
- Is the amount of accounts receivable collections that extend beyond company terms (e.g., net 30 days) too high?

Projecting Cash Disbursements
Cash disbursements generally fall into three major categories:

1. Payment for purchases (including inventory and fixed assets)
2. Payment for operating expenses (including manufacturing/service expenses, payroll, and marketing/administrative expenses)
3. Payment for debt service (loan amortization and interest) and dividends

Normally, the business can project future expenditures with fairly reasonable accuracy. Using the sales forecast as its starting point, the business makes purchase and operating expense commitments to support the expected sales level by period. The repayment of any debt is usually a known amount by period. An

	ACTUAL			PROJECTED					
	OCT	NOV	DEC	JAN	FEB	MAR	APR	MAY	JUN
Sales (actual for first three months; then forecasted)	196	207	203	200	250	400	500	300	200
Cash Expenditures:									
Material purchases	Actual	Actual	Actual	48	60	96	120	72	48
Payroll	Actual	Actual	Actual	37	40	49	55	43	37
Payroll taxes and fringe benefits	Actual	Actual	Actual	2	3	4	5	4	2
Other manufacturing expenses	Actual	Actual	Actual	33	47	91	120	61	33
Commissions	Actual	Actual	Actual	10	12	20	25	15	10
Other SG&A expenses	Actual	Actual	Actual	50	63	100	125	75	50
Capital equipment	Actual	Actual	Actual	0	0	20	0	0	30
Debt service	Actual	Actual	Actual	10	10	10	10	10	10
Other expenditures	Actual	Actual	Actual	5	0	5	5	5	5
Total Cash Payments— Month	Actual	Actual	Actual	195	235	395	465	285	225
Total Cash Payments— Cum.				195	430	825	1,290	1,575	1,800

Exhibit 8.2   Projected Cash Disbursements ($$ in 000s)

example of projected cash expenditures based on a sales forecast is shown in Exhibit 8.2, again using a six-month projection period.

In this example material purchases are at 24 percent of sales; payroll is at six percent of sales plus $25,000 and commissions at five percent of sales; and the company has an ongoing monthly debt service payment of $10,000. Other expenditures are based on the financial manager's knowledge of additional cash requirements that will arise for the business. An analysis of the company's business history can easily and accurately provide the company with the equivalent data that will allow it to prepare this same kind of forecast.

DON'T JUST PLAN, BUDGET, OR PROJECT —EVALUATE AS WELL.

Such a projection of cash disbursements also provides a tool to question each of these planned disbursements. For example, the following might be questioned:

- *Material purchases.* What should they be? Is 24 percent of sales too high or too low?
- *Payroll.* What should it be? Which positions provide value-added results versus those that are considered non-value-added? How much can be reduced or eliminated?
- *Sales commissions.* Is five percent of sales the best method of compensation? Does this system provide for adequate customer service and ensure making the right sales to the right customers?
- *Debt service.* What were the proceeds used for? Was it a proper and necessary use?
- *Other manufacturing expenses.* What are these? Which ones are really necessary? Which could be reduced or eliminated?
- *Other sales, general and administrative expenses.* Which ones are necessary? Which could be reduced or eliminated?

When reviewing and analyzing cash disbursements, the company should remember the principle that a dollar not spent is a dollar that flows directly to the bottom line—and a dollar directed toward positive cash flow. Accordingly, the development of such projected cash disbursements should encourage company management to question each and every element of such cash disbursements.

Projecting Cash Balances

The next step in the cash budgeting process is to interrelate the cash flows—receipts and disbursements—to determine the net effect on the business's cash resources. Exhibit 8.3 shows this interrelationship and the net increase or decrease in cash expected for each period. It is usually wise to show the net cash flow both for the period and cumulatively, and to indicate the projected cash balance at the end of each time period. This provides a clear picture not only of the company's actual cash flows for a period or periods, but also just when the company may be faced with a critical cash shortfall—either a lower-than-required cash balance or even a negative cash position that will require additional action.

Managing Cash Shortfalls and Excesses

At any time, the company will have a measurable amount of cash reserves (positive, if all goes well). The last step in the cash budgeting process is to tie in the existing cash position with the periodic net inflow or outflow of cash. As long as any net cash outflow does not take the cash reserves below some precarious min-

	ACTUAL			PROJECTED					
	OCT	NOV	DEC	JAN	FEB	MAR	APR	MAY	JUN
Sales (actual for first three months; then forecasted)	196	207	203	200	250	400	500	300	200
Projected Cash Inflow	Actual	Actual	Actual	214	210	264	380	440	330
Projected Cash Payments	Actual	Actual	Actual	195	235	395	465	285	225
NET CASH FLOW—Month	Actual	Actual	Actual	19	(25)	(131)	(85)	155	105
NET CASH FLOW— Cumulative	Actual	Actual	Actual	19	(6)	(137)	(222)	(67)	38
Beginning Cash Balance	Actual	Actual	Actual	$100	$119	$ 94	$ (37)	$(122)	$ 33
ENDING CASH BALANCE	Actual	Actual	100	$119	$ 94	$(37)	$(122)	$ 33	$138

Exhibit 8.3 Projected Cash Balances ($$ in 000s)

imum balance, there is little cause for further action. However, if a period's cash outflow brings cash reserves below this minimum, the company must find some form of external financial assistance to fill the gap; or management must avoid the gap by taking some form of operating action such as accelerating receivables collection (reducing accounts receivable), reducing inventory balances by slowing down purchases, or delaying payments to vendors (increasing accounts payable). The use of borrowing to maintain the necessary cash balances as budgeted is shown in Exhibit 8.4. In this example, the company begins the period with a $100,000 cash reserve, has a $300,000 revolving line of credit, and has determined that it requires $100,000 minimum cash reserves at the beginning of any subsequent period. In such a case, the expected cash flow position may also be a signal to exercise other operating options as discussed above (i.e., reducing receivables, reducing inventory purchases, reducing expenses, increasing accounts payable, or even lowering sales volume).

> *REDUCING SALES VOLUME*
> *MAY IMPROVE CASH FLOW.*

	ACTUAL			PROJECTED					
	OCT	NOV	DEC	JAN	FEB	MAR	APR	MAY	JUN
Sales (actual for first three months; then forecasted)	196	207	203	200	250	400	500	300	200
Beginning Cash without Borrowing	Actual	Actual	Actual	$100	$119	$ 94	$ (37)	$(122)	$ 33
NET CASH FLOW— Month	Actual	Actual	Actual	19	(25)	(131)	(85)	155	105
Ending Cash without Borrowing	Actual	Actual	100	119	94	(37)	(122)	33	138
Borrowing required	Actual	Actual	Actual	0	6	137	222	67	0
ENDING CASH BALANCE	Actual	Actual	Actual	$119	$100	$100	$100	$100	$138

Exhibit 8.4   Managing Cash Shortfalls ($$ in 000s)

Lowering sales volume may seem contraindicated in the instance of a cash short-fall. However, cash flow typically improves, temporarily, during times of business slowdowns touched off by recession or other causes. The reason is that during a slowdown the business continues to collect receivables on the basis of prior high-er levels of activity but disburses cash on the basis of anticipated lower levels of future activity (assuming it maintains good control over its expenditures). This creates positive cash flow. Conversely, during growth periods the opposite hap-pens—the company collects on the basis of prior, lower levels of activity, and spends money based on anticipated higher levels of future activity, thereby creat-ing a potential cash shortfall.

This apparent enigma can totally befuddle managers who do not under-stand the differences between cash flow and profitability. All too many managers believe that the solution to all the company's cash flow and profitability prob-lems is more sales, while the truth is that growth is an expensive, cash resource–intensive condition that requires careful management and detailed planning to ensure ongoing viability of the business. The economic landscape is littered with the corpses of fast-growing, profitable companies that have inade-quately managed their cash balances and have run out of money to pay their bills. It is the lack of cash to pay bills that is the immediate and direct cause of business failure, not lack of profits (even though lack of profits may be the root cause of the lack of cash).

> ## THE MORE VOLATILE OR UNPREDICTABLE THE BUSINESS, THE MORE NECESSARY IT IS TO PLAN CASH FLOW.

Cash flow planning is even more critical in a high growth or volatile company than in a stable business, even though forecasting in an unstable environment is far more difficult. Fast-growing hi-tech companies, construction, road building, and other hard-to-predict businesses have great difficulty projecting their cash balances because of their volatility or unpredictability. In those kinds of situations it may seem appropriate not to do cash projection because of the inevitable inaccuracies. In fact, it is even more necessary for them to make projections. Over time, the projections will become less uncertain as the company becomes more experienced in looking into its future. But even with the unavoidable significant errors, having some kind of plan in place that looks at the company's best guess of what will happen will help to manage the cash situation more effectively. The more volatile or unpredictable the business, the *more* necessary it is to make cash flow projections.

There is a further advantage of having a good cash flow projection as shown in the previous exhibits. If the company is seeking a line of credit, the bank is very likely to want a cash flow projection to support the request for the loan. The projection not only indicates to the prospective lender that the company is attempting to manage its cash flow effectively, but also establishes the basis for the amount of the line of credit. In our example in Exhibit 8.4, there is a borrowing requirement showing in April of $222,000. If that is the maximum figure in the entire 12-month projection, the company could logically request a $250,000 line of credit—enough to cover that maximum shortfall plus a small cushion in case of an error. Assuming the company has credibility with its banker and adequate collateral for the loan, it seems quite likely that a $250,000 line of credit would be approved.

Benefits of Cash Planning

As has been discussed, cash resources must be available to support the business's ongoing operations and plans—in the necessary amounts, at the right time, and at the right cost. Successful businesses have learned how to operate within the limits of their available cash resources, and the cash budget is the tool that enables them to accomplish this. Some of the benefits of a cash budget include:

- Identifying peaks and valleys of cash requirements
- Assisting in the identification of related operational needs such as increases/decreases in assets (accounts receivable, inventory, property, plant and equipment) and liabilities (accounts payable, debt, accrued expenses)

- Pinpointing the need for and timing of important cash payments such as payroll, suppliers, debt service, taxes, dividends, and so on
- Showing in advance the need for outside funding, thus providing the opportunity for more effective negotiations
- Recognizing when and how much excess cash will be available to allow for more effective short-term investing
- Identifying the need for additional long-term funding (e.g., for capital improvements) and ability to repay
- Providing definitive information as to the amount of cash needed, when needed, why needed, and for how long
- Indicating when operations can be expanded or should be contracted based on the availability of cash resources or lack thereof

AVOID SURPRISES—PLAN CASH FLOW.

MANAGING CASH BALANCES

Even when all the planning, forecasting, budgeting, and related activities have been accomplished, there is another element of the puzzle which has to be handled—determining how much cash on hand is enough. The company will require some minimum balance of cash on hand at all times just to be able to get through the next batch of bills to be paid—whether they be payroll, vendor payments, taxes, borrowing obligations, or all the above. The person responsible for cash management must also be ready to deal with the existence of an excess amount of cash or a cash shortfall. How can company management make these determinations?

Determining Minimum Levels of Cash Reserves

Just how much cash is enough? This is an important factor to consider in cash planning since the amount of cash required to be left in the coffers to handle working needs must be decided. Keeping too much cash around wastes a valuable resource and reduces the amount of return that can be generated on corporate assets. Too little cash means that certain bills will not be paid on time, and the implication of this can range from annoying through irritating all the way to devastating, depending on exactly what or who does not get paid. How much cash then should be kept on hand?

Basically, the company's cash reserves must be sufficient to meet daily cash expenditure needs. To that minimum level of cash, the company should add a safety cushion to allow for any unforeseen needs or opportunities that may from time to time arise. The company should calculate its average daily (or weekly) cash expenditures over a number of recent periods (probably a year). Then, based on its unique requirements, the company should estimate its cash reserves as a number of days average cash outflow.

There are several factors that must be taken into consideration in estimating ongoing working cash balance needs. The first, of course, is an estimate of how much is required to pay the bills before cash is replenished by the next payments from customers. This requires an estimate of cash disbursements and cash receipts on a specific timing basis. Payrolls, for example, are disbursed at regular time intervals and the amounts are relatively easy to predict unless there are unusual fluctuations in work schedules. Vendor payments, freight bills, expense reimbursements, and the like, are likely to be more erratic. However, in order to make a determination of just when disbursements will be made and of what magnitude, these estimates will have to be formulated. It is a task unique to each business but usually proves to be a much more difficult task in the thinking about than in the doing.

For instance, if the company's average monthly expenditures are $300,000 and the company works on the basis of a 30-day month, its daily cash expenditures can be calculated at $10,000. If the company feels it needs 10 days in cash reserves, its minimum cash balance is $100,000. If cash falls below that level the company needs to take action to recover, while if the balance rises above the minimum level and there are strong indications it will stay there, the company has the opportunity to invest the excess. Safety is determined by considering such factors as the predictability of future cash inflows (i.e., steady or erratic collection patterns), the flexibility available in cash expenditures (i.e., ability to defer payments temporarily without disrupting supplier relationships), and the availability of external financing (i.e., accessibility to borrowed funds or other external financing).

A second factor to consider is the cash balances required to cover any service charges from the bank. While it is not uncommon or unacceptable to pay these charges as incurred, it may make sense to keep enough in the company's account to offset any direct charges. Conversation with the banking officer should get the company the information required to know just how much of a balance has to be maintained to avoid being charged for services. It is possibly less than or close to the balance the company has to maintain anyway just to keep enough on hand for working needs. In that event, service charges become easy to avoid.

Element number three in determining what cash balances to maintain is any compensating balance requirements that arise as a result of lending arrangements with the bank. Compensating balances are, of course, those minimum balances that must be maintained in the company's account as additional compensation for the loans. If the bank has specifically negotiated these, the company knows exactly how much they are. If not (and assuming there are some loans outstanding), it is most likely that the company's existing balances have been sufficient to cover any compensating balance requirements, and the bank has chosen not to raise the issue. It will be raised if the company lets its balances drop too low, however.

The fourth and final piece of the cash balance requirement puzzle is a very subjective one—that of how much of a "cushion" to maintain. We all have different attitudes toward risk. Some of us like to play right up at the edge of the cliff, while others of us prefer to stay back from the brink. The greater the degree of risk of running out of cash the company is willing to take, the less cushion it needs to keep in its bank balances. The more conservative the company is, the greater the cushion needs to be. Some company executives prefer to maintain fairly large cash reserves in order to provide enough "sleep insurance" to be comfortable. Others prefer the riskier approach of lower reserves in exchange for the greater earnings potential. This is not a judgmental observation about whether high or low risk is better, but merely a statement that the security of low risk may result in lower earnings, while the higher earnings potential of a higher risk approach will entail a downside hazard of running out of cash. The choice is the company's to make, and will depend on its culture as well as the needs of its particular business.

> ## WILLINGNESS TO ASSUME MORE RISK CAN REDUCE THE AMOUNT OF OPERATING CASH BALANCES REQUIRED.

If the company does not have access to short-term cash advances or borrowings from an external financing source on short notice, it must consider larger minimum cash reserves. The overarching objective is to ensure, within reason, that sufficient cash balances are always available to take care of upcoming requirements on an as-needed basis.

Using Excess Cash

In the happy event of a projected cash excess, the company has several options available to it. Broadly, these fall into the categories of expansion, investment, purchases, growth, and the like. These are alternatives which most of us like to be able to evaluate since they are opportunistic, expansionary, and progressive in nature. However, as pleasant as they may be, they cannot be done effectively without careful planning and foresight. Any kind of expansionary activity has a risk element attached. Even something as simple as a temporary investment of short-term excess cash carries with it the risk of tying up cash otherwise available for different needs. The risk expands substantially as the length and dollar value of the commitment increases. This means the risk should not be taken without reasonable assurance that it makes economic sense for the organization. Economic sense includes the idea of having enough funds to be able to carry on other routine business operations as well as the cash needs of the new activities. The cash forecasting activity thus becomes vital as part of the process of providing assurance that the project, however, big or small, is doable.

Dealing with Cash Shortfalls

We are all faced, at least occasionally, with the prospect of not having enough cash to accomplish what has to be done or should be done. This is the less happy event of a cash shortfall, which means contraction, curtailment, cutbacks, or consolidation. Cash shortfalls are generally not looked upon with delight, but they are an integral part of growth, which is an expensive process because of the need to finance receivables, inventory, facilities, and staff prior to recouping these investments from sales to customers.

> ## BANKS MAY NOT BE WILLING TO LEND
> ## TO THOSE WHO HAVE AN IMMEDIATE NEED.

The problem associated with a cash shortfall is not so much the shortfall itself as the need to plan for how to handle it. Banks have a reputation of being willing to lend money only to those who do not need it. While this may be an exaggerated and satirical evaluation of bankers, there is a substantial grain of reality in the characterization that is worth noting. Lending officers and their banks do not want to be saddled with problem loans, and loans to companies that do not plan adequately are potential problems. Caution on the part of bankers in their lending procedures is understandable, logical, and prudent. However, the banks make their money by lending funds at rates higher than they have to pay to depositors for the use of those funds. Without lending, banks cannot survive.

To the prospective borrower this means that borrowing is neither an unavailable nor an assured option. Borrowing requirements must be planned as carefully as every other business activity. A company that is able to foresee the need for borrowed funds can go to its bank, present its case for future needs, and satisfy the banker's desire to loan only to those who do not (immediately) need the funds. At the time of the request the need does not presently exist, but when the actual need for funds arises at a later time, arrangements have already been made. The borrower has planned cash flow to identify the need for borrowing, the banker sees a customer who understands and adequately plans for company needs, and both parties get what they desire. This is the kind of mutually beneficial and economically sensible solution both parties should be trying to attain.

CASH PLANNING APPROACHES

There are two primary methods for preparing the cash budget:

1. *Direct method.* Estimate of cash receipts and disbursements
2. *Indirect method.* Adjusted net income form

The Direct Method: Estimate of Cash Receipts and Disbursements

Using this method, the company estimates the gross cash receipts and disbursements by major categories (i.e., accounts receivable collections, new borrowing, payroll, inventory purchases, etc.) for the planning period. For example, major categories might include:

- *Cash receipts*
  - Cash sales
  - Accounts receivable collections
  - Sales of assets
  - Interest and dividends received
  - Proceeds from borrowing
  - Proceeds from new equity
  - Other cash receipts

- *Cash disbursements*
  - Accounts payable
  - Payroll costs (net)
  - Payroll taxes
  - Fringe benefits payments
  - Manufacturing/service expenses
  - Marketing/administrative expenses
  - Interest expense
  - Dividend payments
  - Debt amortization
  - Capital expenditures
  - Rents, royalties, etc.
  - Income taxes
  - Property taxes
  - Insurance premiums
  - Other cash disbursements

Under the terms of Statement of Financial Accounting Standards Board No. 95 (FASB 95) – Statement of Cash Flows, company receipts and disbursements are required to be categorized by cash flows from (for) operating activities, investing activities, and financing activities. For internal reporting and planning purposes, however, these distinctions may be useful but are not mandatory.

The cash budget resulting from using this method is a projection of the cash requirements to operate the business during the ensuing planning period. It enables management to plan cash needs for the period and match those needs with operating funds generated to determine the need for any outside funding. An example of a cash flow statement prepared by the direct method is shown in Exhibit 8.5.

Cash flows from operating activities		
Cash received from customers	$ 13,850	
Cash paid to suppliers and employees	(12,000)	
Dividend received from affiliate	20	
Interest received	55	
Interest paid (net of amount capitalized)	(220)	
Income taxes paid	(325)	
Insurance proceeds received	15	
Cash paid to settle lawsuit for patent infringement	(30)	
Net cash provided by operating activities		$1,365
Cash flows from investing activities		
Proceeds from sale of facility	600	
Payment received on note for sale of plant	150	
Capital expenditures	(1,000)	
Payment for purchase of Company S, net of cash acquired	(925)	
Net cash used in investing activities		(1,175)
Cash flows from financing activities		
Net borrowings under line-of-credit agreement	300	
Principal payments under capital lease obligation	(125)	
Proceeds from issuance of long-term debt	400	
Proceeds from issuance of common stock	500	
Dividends paid	(200)	
Net cash provided by financing activities		875
Net increase in cash and cash equivalents		1,065
Cash and cash equivalents at beginning of year		600
Cash and cash equivalents at end of year		$1,665

Reconciliation of net income to net cash provided by operating activities can be most effectively presented using the same format as cash flow from operating activities under the Adjusted Net Income Cash Flow Reporting Method (Exhibit 8.6).

Exhibit 8.5   Receipts and Disbursements Cash Flow Reporting Method for the Year Ended December 31, 20xx

THE DIRECT METHOD IS GENERALLY MORE ADVANTAGEOUS FOR INTERNAL PURPOSES.

The direct method normally is most useful for short-term (up to one year) cash planning. Anticipated receipts and disbursements are recorded without regard to whether they represent an expense or a balance sheet transaction. This method looks strictly at cash activity, and is therefore most useful for tracking cash availability. For internal cash planning this is generally a preferred way to prepare the projection because it focuses on cash flow. The manager responsible for preparing the projection is forced to think in terms of cash flow, which is likely to result in a more accurate projection. Even more significantly, however, it is much easier to explain to operating managers not trained in finance that the company is spending money on inventory, payroll, equipment, insurance, taxes, dividends, loan repayments, and the like than to have them comprehend the finagling involved in the indirect method. Attempting to explain to an operating manager that cash flow is made up of net income to which depreciation, amortization, and other non-cash expenses are added back and then has to be adjusted for changes in inventory, accounts receivable, and accounts payable often results in confusion, frustration, and disbelief. Using the direct method can ease this problem.

The Indirect Method: Adjusted Net Income Form

The starting point for this method is planned net income which is then adjusted for non-cash transactions (i.e., depreciation, amortization, deferred taxes, etc.) and changes in working capital, resulting in cash generated from operations. Changes caused by financing and investing activities are then calculated to determine the estimated cash balance. An example of a cash flow format using the indirect method is shown in Exhibit 8.6. Note that cash flows to/from investing activities and financing activities are the same under both methods. Only operating cash flows are presented differently.

The adjusted net income method, which is most commonly used in company annual reports and generally preferred by financial institutions, has the advantage of reconciling the income statement forecast to the cash flow forecast. Although it does not show the full picture of cash activity, the final result shows the actual cash balance. This method is normally more useful for longer term funds flow forecasting purposes, but less useful for short-term cash forecasting. And, as explained above, it is much more difficult for operating managers without financial training to comprehend.

CONCLUSION

Cash flow planning, whether referred to as forecasting, planning, budgeting, or projecting, is an indispensable part of managing the company's cash flow.

Cash flows from operating activities		
Net income		$ 760
Adjustments to reconcile net income		
to net cash provided by operating activities:		
Depreciation and amortization	$ 445	
Provision for losses on accounts receivable	200	
Gain on sale of facility	(80)	
Undistributed earnings of affiliate	(25)	
Payment received on installment note		
receivable for sale of inventory	100	
Change in assets and liabilities net of effects		
from purchase of Company S:		
Increase in accounts receivable	(215)	
Decrease in inventory	205	
Increase in prepaid expenses	(25)	
Decrease in accounts payable and accrued expenses	(250)	
Increase in interest and income taxes payable	50	
Increase in deferred taxes	150	
Increase in other liabilities	50	
Total adjustments		605
Net cash provided by operating activities		1,365
Cash flow from investing activities		
Proceeds from sale of facility	600	
Payment received on note for sale of plant	150	
Capital expenditures	(1000)	
Payment for purchase of Company S,		
net of cash acquired	(925)	
Net cash used in investing activities		(1,175)
Cash flows from financing activities		
Net borrowings under line-of-credit agreement	300	
Principal payments under capital lease obligation	(125)	
Proceeds from issuance of long-term debt	400	
Proceeds from issuance of common stock	500	
Dividends paid	(200)	
Net cash provided by financing activities		875
Net increase in cash and cash equivalents		1,065
Cash and cash equivalents at beginning of year		600
Cash and cash equivalents at end of year		$1,665

Exhibit 8.6 Adjusted Net Income Cash Flow Reporting Method
for the Year Ended December 31, 20xx

Without adequate planning the company can never sufficiently know what its cash flow position will be at any particular time. With it, surprises will be mitigated and the company will be able to plan how to handle any shortfalls or excesses. The cash budgeting process is similar to any other kind of budgeting, but the timing of the cash flows has to be taken into account. This requires an understanding of the timing of cash receipts relative to sales made and the timing of cash disbursements relative to when the expenses are actually incurred under accrual-based accounting.

Identifying how much cash needs to be kept on hand for normal operating purposes is a part of the process as is development of procedures for managing any shortfalls or excesses of cash that may occur. Handling these only when they occur is feasible, of course, but will not allow the company to maximize the use of the cash resource. Furthermore, if the company waits until it is out of cash to try and come up with ways to cover that shortfall, it may not find the cash soon enough to keep itself out of trouble.

Planning, determining when any shortfalls may occur, and developing ways to cover such shortfalls—with banks or other financial institutions, by securing additional equity capital, by deferring payments or any other means—will enable the company to make appropriate decisions and take suitable action while there is still enough time to keep itself out of harm's way. Similarly, knowing when and how much excess cash will become available allows the company to make intelligent and informed decisions as to how best to utilize this excess cash. Within reason, there cannot be too much time spent on the cash flow planning process.

MORE POSITIVE CASH FLOW
MEANS EVEN MORE HAPPINESS.

CHAPTER 9

Controlling and Analyzing Cash Flow

CONTROL CASH BEFORE IT'S TOO LATE.

C ash flow analysis is less frequently done than profit analysis, cost analysis, budgeting analysis, capital investment analysis, and various other analyses. Among the reasons may be that:

- Cash flow has only relatively recently become accepted as a specific element to be measured and recorded in the financial statements and as a significant criterion of corporate financial success or failure.
- Analytical techniques for cash flow are not yet part of the standardized package of accounting tools.

Cash flow analysis refers to the tools and techniques that assist in understanding the company's present and future cash position. In this chapter, we will first take a brief look at the basic elements of FASB 95, Statement of Cash Flows. Then we will discuss the following cash flow analysis tools:

- Cash flow projections as they relate to FASB 95
- Cash flow reporting and control
- Interpretation and analysis of cash flow

BRIEF LOOK AT FASB 95

FASB 95 ESTABLISHES THE FORMAT FOR EXTERNAL DOCUMENTS; THE COMPANY NEEDS TO ESTABLISH THE FORMAT FOR INTERNAL DOCUMENTS.

Statement of Financial Accounting Standards No. 95, Statement of Cash Flows (more commonly referred to as SFAS 95 or FASB 95) was released in November 1987 to be effective for fiscal years ending after July 15, 1988. It requires the presentation of a statement of cash flows instead of the previously used statement of changes in financial position that focused on funds flows rather than on cash flows. While not one of the more complex pronouncements, FASB 95 contains a number of specific technical requirements regarding cash flow presentation that need to be understood by any company preparing a package of generally accepted financial statements. Some highlights of FASB 95 include the following, which includes a summary of the three classifications of cash flow (Operating, Investing, or Financing) that represent the heart of the FASB:

Purpose of a Statement of Cash Flows

- To provide relevant information about cash receipts and payments of an enterprise during a time period
- To help investors, creditors, and others to assess:
  - The enterprise's ability to generate future net cash flows
  - The enterprise's ability to generate positive future net cash flows, meet obligations, and pay dividends
  - The enterprise's needs for external financing
  - The effects on the enterprise's financial position of both cash and non-cash investing and financing transactions.

Focus on Cash and Cash Equivalents

Explain the change during the period in cash and cash equivalents rather than the previously used ambiguous terms such as funds.

Classifications of Cash Flows

1. Cash Flows from (for) Investing Activities
   - Making and collecting loans
   - Acquiring and disposing of debt or equity instruments
   - Acquiring and disposing of property, plant and equipment and other productive assets (excluding inventory)

2. Cash Flows from (for) Financing Activities
   - Obtaining resources from owners and providing them with a return on and of their investments (proceeds from issuing equity instruments, bonds, mortgages, or other borrowing; paying dividends or other distributions to owners)

- Borrowing money and repaying principal amounts borrowed
- Obtaining and paying for other resources obtained from creditors on long-term credit

3. Cash Flows from (for) Operating Activities
   - All transactions not defined as investing or financing activities
   - Generally involving the production and delivery of goods and provision of services
   - Cash effects of transactions and events that enter into the determination of net income (including taxes, interest on borrowing, contributions, refunds, etc.)

Content and Form of the Statement of Cash Flows

The content and form of the statement of cash flows must conform to the following:

- Report must reconcile beginning and ending cash and cash equivalents.
- The direct method shows major classes of gross cash receipts and gross cash payments (i.e., cash collected from customers, paid to employees and other suppliers of goods and services, interest and dividends received, interest paid, taxes paid, etc.).
- If the direct method is used, reconciliation of net income to cash flow from operating activities is to be provided in a separate schedule
- The indirect method adjusts net income to reconcile it to net cash flows from operating activities by removing noncash transactions included in net income (i.e., depreciation, deferred taxes, changes in working capital, etc.)
- Inflows and outflows from investing and financing activities should be reported separately
- Cash flow per share is *not* to be reported in the financial statements.

CASH FLOW PROJECTIONS: METHODOLOGY

> *THE CASH FLOW PROJECTION SHOULD BE AN OPERATIONAL RATHER THAN AN ACCOUNTING DOCUMENT.*

As we have previously noted in Chapter 8, cash flow planning is essentially no different than planning for sales, expenses, profits, capital investments, or any other financial component of the business. It requires a good understanding of the business and detailed knowledge of the timing of events such as:

- Cash sales
- Accounts receivable collections
- Cash disbursements
  - Payment of accounts payable
  - Payment of payroll obligations

Additionally, periodic obligations such as loan repayments, dividend disbursements, tax filings, property tax and insurance due dates, special equipment or building purchases, new product development, or plans for new ventures, have to be considered.

It is also necessary to determine frequency of cash flow forecasts and a cash flow planning method that can be used for replication of future planning statements, for controlling cash flows actually incurred, and for documenting calculations and assumptions used in the preparation of the projections. Frequency of preparation (i.e., quarterly, monthly, weekly) is based on the specific needs of the organization. If the company has steady and reliable cash flows without cash problems, it might prepare forecasts and reports on only a quarterly basis. Most organizations, however, prepare at least monthly projections and reports. The greater the volatility of the cash flow, the more frequent should be the preparation of projections and reports.

It may also be necessary at times to prepare informal projections on a weekly or daily basis, particularly if the company keeps its cash balances at minimum levels or is having cash flow problems. Weekly operating cash planning allows the company to make extra payments (or invest excess cash) if it receives more cash than expected and hold back payments if receipts fall behind or disbursements exceed expectations. Even companies with good overall positive cash flow may wish to plan weekly as a supplement to their longer-term projections in case of short-term cash crunches or windfalls that will occur from time to time.

In developing its cash flow projections, the company should identify and prepare a format for the major cash flow items to be recorded and tracked. The format may follow the basic outline of the cash flow requirements under FASB 95, but can be adapted to individual company requirements as appropriate. A cash flow plan is normally an internal document and therefore does not have to adhere to FASB 95 standards. The primary format to be used internally is the Receipts and Disbursements (Direct) method previously illustrated in Exhibit 8.5 (which uses the example illustrated in FASB 95) or a variation thereof. That method has more of a cash flow focus giving it enhanced operational usefulness. The Adjusted Net Income (Indirect) method shown in Exhibit 8.6 is also acceptable, though harder for nonfinancial managers to understand.

The Adjusted Net Income method generally is used by and satisfies the requirements of financial institutions, and it has the advantage of tying the cash flow directly to the company's financial statements. For historical financial statement presentation purposes, using the Receipts and Disbursements method requires that a reconciliation of the company's net income to its operating cash flow be prepared on a separate schedule. Since this means that using the Direct method necessitates everything already required by the Indirect method as well as additional information, it is usually simpler for the company to use the Indirect method for its financial statement presentations.

> ## THE DIRECT METHOD IS EASIER FOR THE OPERATIONAL MANAGER TO UNDERSTAND.

For internal management purposes, however, the Direct method usually provides a more effective and easily understood format for the company. It focuses on the direct sources and uses of cash and is thereby more generally useful for internal planning, control, and management purposes. For planning the company may want to open up the format to allow presentation of more detailed information. An example of a more detailed format is shown in Exhibit 9.1 for the Receipts and Disbursements (Direct) method. The planning format shows monthly projections with classifications that are likely to be useful for a manufacturing organization's operational planning, controlling, and reporting requirements. A service, financial services, retail, or not-for-profit organization's format will necessarily have to be adapted to meet its particular requirements, but the overall structure will likely be similar. The descriptors will be different.

Despite the need for each company to adopt its own formats, there needs to be an awareness of the reasons for certain line items on the receipts and disbursements forecasting method as shown in Exhibit 9.1. For instance, note that payroll projections for weekly, biweekly, monthly, and special payroll periods are shown separately. This is because accrual accounting procedures can adjust different payroll periods to monthly amounts, but for cash flow purposes it is necessary to know in exactly what time period the cash will be needed to meet the particular payrolls. Months with extra pay periods (a third biweekly or fifth weekly payroll) can cause cash flow difficulties if they are not taken into account. Separating them makes the projections easier and more accurate.

Also note that the "change in accounts payable" figure adjusts for the timing differences resulting from paying suppliers at a later time than the incurrence of the obligations. If the company has a purchase journal which records all the commitments obligated within a month, this is a logical basis for the cash flow requirements for those items despite the fact that they will not be paid until some time later. For planning and control purposes the company wants to know when the

	Month 1	Month 2	...	Month n	TOTAL
CASH FLOW FROM OPERATING ACTIVITIES					
Cash Receipts from Operating Activities					
Cash sales	$ 100	$ 100		e	
Accounts receivable collections	1,200	1,250			
Other operating receipts	5	5			
Total Receipts from Operating Activities	1,305	1,355			
Cash Disbursements from Operating Activities					
Material purchases	450	470			
Weekly payroll	125	155			
Bi-weekly payroll	100	100		t	
Monthly payroll	150	150			
Special payroll—vacation/holiday/bonus	0	0			
Payroll taxes/insurance/benefits	55	60			
Manufacturing expenses	60	65			
Selling expenses	35	50			
Administrative expenses	45	45		c	
Interest obligations	15	15			
Property taxes/insurance	50	0			
Income taxes	0	65			
Change in accounts payable	0	0			
Other operating disbursements	25	25			
Total Disbursements from Operations	1,110	1,200		e	
NET CASH FLOW FROM OPERATING ACTIVITIES	195	155			
CASH FLOW FROM INVESTMENT ACTIVITIES					
Cash Receipts from Investment Activities					
Interest/dividend receipts					
Cash from asset sales	10				

Other receipts from investment activities	10	
Total Receipts from Investing Activities		0
Cash Disbursements from Investment Activities		
Fixed-asset purchases	(150)	(25)
Other investment purchases	(5)	(5)
Total Disbursements from Investing Activities	(155)	(30)
NET CASH FLOW FROM (FOR) INVESTING ACTIVITIES	(145)	(30)
CASH FLOW FROM FINANCING ACTIVITIES		
Cash Receipts from Financing Activities		
Loan receipts		
Other financing activity receipts	0	0
Total Receipts from Financing Activities		
Cash Disbursements from Financing Activities		
Debt repayment	(10)	(10)
Dividend payments	(55)	0
Other financing activity disbursements		(25)
Total Disbursements from Financing Activities	(65)	(35)
NET CASH FLOW FROM (FOR) FINANCING ACTIVITIES	(65)	(35)
NET CASH FLOW—current month	(15)	90
NET CASH FLOW—cumulative	(15)	75
Cash Available—beginning balance	1,665	1,650
	1,650	1,650
ENDING CASH BALANCE	$1,650	$1,740

Exhibit 9.1   The Typical Manufacturing Company: Receipts and Disbursements Cash Flow Forecasting Method

cause of the cash outflow has been incurred. The fact that last month's expenses are paid for this month and this month's expenses paid next month can most easily be dealt with by calculating and recording the amount of the change in accounts payable. For planning purposes, it often makes sense to project a zero change in accounts payable on the assumption that the accounts payable pipeline will be reasonably constant over time, and trying to project its monthly changes becomes pure speculation.

The "other" categories that appear throughout the example shown in Exhibit 9.1 are intended to make the company think about any other significant categories of cash flow receipts or disbursements that may occur. These will vary from company to company, but operations must be reviewed carefully to accurately identify and account for special requirements, or cash projections may be seriously wrong. Additionally it is useful to include a general miscellaneous category to cover all those small items of cash flow that do not justify a separate line on the cash flow report but constitute an amount that in total should be recorded. A review of a year of actual cash flow history is typically all that is needed to determine an appropriate amount for this catch-all item.

Another example of a cash flow projection showing a completed 12 month cash flow forecast is shown in Exhibit 9.2. While this particular format does not meet FASB 95 standards (principally because of no separation of operating, investing, and financing activities), it lists the significant sources of and requirements for funds for this particular organization. It is this kind of adaptation to meet the specific requirements of the company that will make the cash flow projection meaningful and useful to the company.

THE CASH FLOW PROJECTION IS ONLY AS GOOD AS THE UNDERLYING ASSUMPTIONS.

The second part of Exhibit 9.2 is a listing of the assumptions used to develop the line items of the forecast. Wherever there are references to estimates or supporting schedules, these will normally be part of the cash flow forecast package. Recognize also that the assumptions listed in this exhibit are applicable only to this distinct projection. Any assumptions that the company prepares will, of course, have to apply to that specific forecast. The preparation of assumptions is a good idea for every line item in any projection. There are two basic reasons for this:

1. If anyone asks the basis for a number in the projection, the assumptions will readily supply that information.
2. In preparing the next projection, having the basis for the prior calculation makes the preparation of the new projection much simpler. Rather than

having to reinvent the projection methodology, the company has merely to look at the prior method of calculation of any line item, review it to ensure that it still makes sense, and apply the same process to the new forecast. If there is a better way to prepare the calculation, that should be done and an adjustment made to the assumptions for the next round.

CASH FLOW REPORTING AND CONTROLS

Once a relevant and effective system of cash flow planning has been developed, the reporting of the actual cash flows should follow naturally. The actual results come from the accounting system. There is no magic or particular difficulty to this process. It is only a matter of recording actual cash flows, summarizing them in a format consistent with the planning system, and reporting them accordingly. The same format should be used to report actual cash flows as is used for the projections so that appropriate comparisons of actual to projections can be made. These actual reports should be prepared at least as frequently as the projections—in some cases more frequently.

Cash Flow Reporting

While it is not always necessary to formally compare weekly actual figures to plan, monthly reports of actual cash flows are desirable. If projections are made on a quarterly basis, the monthly actual results can be compared to one third of the projections to get an idea of the accuracy of the projections. If projections are made on a monthly basis, the actual cash flows can, of course, be compared directly. Either way, the comparison should include a calculation of the differences between projections and actuals, and significant variances need to be investigated and explained. At this point it will be too late to do anything about the variance already incurred, but understanding why and how it occurred can be useful in improving future projections and bringing unacceptable practices under control.

> ## *CASH FLOW CONTROL:*
> ## *1. SET THE STANDARD.*
> ## *2. MEASURE PERFORMANCE.*
> ## *3. EVALUATE PERFORMANCE.*
> ## *4. REACT APPROPRIATELY.*

	20xx			20xy									Total
	Oct	Nov	Dec	Jan	Feb	Mar	Apr	May	Jun	Jul	Aug	Sep	53
# payroll weeks	5	4	5	4	4	5	4	4	5	4	4	5	
NET SALES													
FORECAST	550	560	560	490	520	550	550	560	570	580	550	590	6,630
Ending A/Rec Balance	915	925	930	875	840	890	915	925	940	955	940	950	950
CASH RECEIPTS													
A/Rec collections	520	550	555	545	555	500	525	550	555	565	565	580	6,565
Other receipts	120	10	10	10	10	10	10	10	10	10	10	10	230
Total Cash Receipts	640	560	565	555	565	510	535	560	565	575	575	590	6,795
CASH DISBURSEMENTS													
Inventory purchases—Subsid. #A	59	60	62	55	58	58	58	58	58	58	58	58	700
Inventory purchases—other	95	95	75	90	95	95	95	100	100	95	105	100	1,140
Factory payroll	218	175	218	175	180	225	180	180	225	180	185	231	2,374
Salary payroll	52	41	52	42	42	53	44	44	55	44	44	55	564
Vacation/bonus payroll				65					110				175
FICA deposits	21	17	21	22	17	21	17	17	30	17	17	22	238
Unempl/workers comp. premiums	15			12			20			15			62

Exhibit 9.2a   The Example Company
Cash Flow Forecast—October 20xx to September 20xy
($$ in 000s)

	20xx			20xy									Total
	Oct	Nov	Dec	Jan	Feb	Mar	Apr	May	Jun	Jul	Aug	Sep	
# payroll weeks	5	4	5	4	4	5	4	4	5	4	4	5	53
Medical/life/disability insur. prem.	9	9	9	10	10	10	10	10	10	10	10	10	117
Factory expenses	35	32	33	33	33	33	33	33	33	33	33	33	397
Administrative expenses	30	28	29	28	28	28	28	28	28	28	28	28	339
Property taxes/ insurance	9		15	9			10		27	10			80
Fixed assets			17		22		5		5		5		54
Income taxes				55			70		50			50	225
Advances— Subsidiary #B	25		25		20		20		15		15		120
Other	5	5	5	5	5	5	5	5	5	5	5	5	60
Total Cash Disbursements	573	461	561	600	510	528	595	475	751	495	505	591	6,645
CASH FLOW FROM OPER'NS	67	99	4	-45	55	-18	-60	85	-186	80	70	-1	150
Borrowing - principal			15			15			15			15	60
- interest			5			5			5			4	19
- total	0	0	20	0	0	20	0	0	20	0	0	19	79
NET CASH FLOW - month	67	99	-16	-45	55	-38	-60	85	-206	80	70	-20	71
- cumulative	67	166	150	105	160	122	62	147	-59	21	91	71	

Exhibit 9.2a   The Example Company Cash Flow Forecast—October 20xx to September 20xy ($$ in 000s) (continued)

	20xx			20xy									Total
	Oct	Nov	Dec	Jan	Feb	Mar	Apr	May	Jun	Jul	Aug	Sep	Total
# payroll weeks	5	4	5	4	4	5	4	4	5	4	4	5	53
CASH AVAILABLE													
-checking - beginning balance	127	144	118	102	107	112	74	114	99	93	98	93	127
- ending balance	144	118	102	107	112	74	114	99	93	98	93	73	73
transfer to (from) cash mgt. account	50	125		-50	50		-100	100	-200	75	75		125
-cash mgt													
- beginning balance	150	200	325	325	275	325	325	225	325	125	200	275	150
- ending balance	200	325	325	275	325	325	225	325	125	200	275	275	275
TOTAL ENDING CASH	344	443	427	382	437	399	339	424	218	298	368	348	348

Exhibit 9.2a   The Example Company
Cash Flow Forecast—October 20xx to September 20xy
($$ in 000s) (continued)

1. SALES—estimates with earlier months based on shipment/backlog schedule

2. A/REC COLLECTIONS—calculated to maintain collection period under 50 days

3. OTHER RECEIPTS—October includes tax refund; other months are nominal receipts

4. PURCHASES—estimates based on historical data

5. FACTORY LABOR—October to January – 5,600 hrs/wk × 7.80/hr × # payroll weeks
   —February to July – 5,600 hrs/wk × 8.05/hr × # payroll weeks
   —August to September – 5,600 hrs/wk × 8.25/hr × # payroll weeks

6. SALARIES—October to December – $10,300/wk × # payroll weeks
   —January to March – $10,500/wk × # payroll weeks
   —April to September – $10,900/wk × # payroll weeks

7. VACATION/BONUS – estimates

8. FICA – 7.65% of payroll

9. UNEMPLOYMENT—October – $15,000; January – $12,000; April – $20,000;
   July – $15,000; – all estimates
   WORKERS COMP. – October to November and February to September
   @ $2,000/month; December @ 0

10. MEDICAL … INSURANCE PREMIUMS—estimates

11. FACTORY EXPENSES—estimates based on historical data

Exhibit 9.2b Cash Flow Forecast Assumptions—
October 20xx to September 20xy

12. ADMINISTRATIVE EXPENSES—estimates based on historical data

13. PROPERTY TAXES/INSURANCE—per schedule of premium and tax due dates

14. FIXED ASSETS—estimates plus known expenditures

15. INCOME TAXES—per separate schedule of tax calculations

16. ADVANCES TO SUBSIDIARY #B—estimates

17. OTHER—contingency

18. BORROWING—per separate repayment schedule

Exhibit 9.2b   Cash Flow Forecast Assumptions—
October 20xx to September 20xy (continued)

Cash Flow Controls

The control process consists of the following basic activities:

- Establishing expectations or standards
- Measuring actual performance
- Evaluating that performance
- Taking necessary corrective or other appropriate action.

These four elements are common to all control activities and can be justifiably applied to profits, production output, quality, rejects, customer service, personnel evaluation, or cash flow. Cash flow expectations or standards of performance derive from the cash flow planning process. As is the case in any budgeting/planning activity, the outcome of the planning effort represents the target against which actual results should be measured.

The measuring of actual performance is handled by the reporting of actual cash flows as discussed earlier. Evaluation presents an opportunity for creativity and flexibility for the financial manager. Measures for evaluating cash flow are not as standardized or as precisely defined as other measures of financial performance. Cost center variance analyses, return on investment benchmarks, and related profitability evaluation measures are highly developed and generally accepted by most financial analysts. Cash flow measures are less so, which leaves fewer road maps to follow, but allows a greater degree of freedom for the analyst to be creative and develop new and directly relevant evaluation techniques.

The ultimate test, however, and the most important aspect of the entire control process is the follow-up action taken by the organization to rectify problems or replicate successes. The actual cash flows provide the basis for decision-making as to what should be done next. Any significant differences from plan, whether over or under, need to be investigated so that the company can learn as accurately as possible just what has caused the discrepancies.

> ## *CONTROLLING CASH FLOW REQUIRES RELENTLESS FOLLOW-UP.*

If cash turns out to be short, it may necessitate instant action to preserve company liquidity. At an extreme, emergency measures such as the immediate discontinuance of discretionary purchases, major delays of payments to vendors, panicky attention to collections, desperation borrowing, or other related action to instantaneously increase the flow and/or supply of cash may be called for. In less dire circumstances when the company has adequate cash reserves to get through a cash shortfall, it may only be necessary to rectify any problems identified so they do not happen again or to learn from the circumstances and do a better planning job for the next cycle. Regardless of the outcome or the cause, a good cash management system requires consistent, persistent, and insistent monitoring and control. Examples of control sheets that can be used or adapted by a company for its own cash flow management are shown in Exhibits 9.3 through 9.10 as follows:

- *Exhibit 9.3.* Daily Activity Summary that shows the pieces that make up the cash and accounts receivable balances. It is useful as a daily control over cash balances and to compare actual activities to plans generated for the month.
- *Exhibit 9.4.* Daily Accounts Receivable Collections that shows receivable collections spread in an aging format so the company can see whether the older balances are being paid off.
- *Exhibit 9.5.* Cash Receipts Detail showing the summary of receipts for the full month. It is useful to help identify the sources of any significant receipts in addition to collections of receivables.
- *Exhibit 9.6.* Daily Cash Disbursements Summary showing disbursements by day and by major categories.
- *Exhibit 9.7.* Cash Disbursements Detail, which summarizes disbursements for the month in total. It is useful for estimating future disbursements requirements.
- *Exhibit 9.8.* Daily Cash Sheet is the source sheet for entering information on cash receipts and disbursements each day.
- *Exhibit 9.9.* Daily Invoicing Summary tracks the invoices issued during the month. It is useful for determining if sales are meeting plan throughout the month. The daily invoice amounts also are used to keep the accounts receivable balance up to date.
- *Exhibit 9.10.* Weekly Cash Planning Sheet shows a simple format that can be used for short-term weekly cash planning. It can be used to show the major anticipated sources of receipts and principal cash requirements for the week. It is best prepared at the beginning of the week when opening cash balances are known. It shows whether sufficient cash will be available to meet the week's obligations. The contingency amount ($25,000 in this example) is intended to allow for payments that may arise unexpectedly. The format allows for actual amounts to be entered as a tool to ensure that the projecting process is reasonably accurate.

INTERPRETATION AND ANALYSIS OF CASH FLOW

CASH FLOW ANALYSIS IS AS NECESSARY AS PROFIT ANALYSIS.

Date	A/Rec Collections	Other Receipts	Total Receipts	Total Disbursed	Cash Balance	Net Invoicing	A/Rec Balance
Opening bal.					146,674.03		855,520.45
9/2/xx	97,388.17	-74.52	97,313.65	0.00	243,987.68	0.00	758,132.28
9/3/xx	24,336.92	-242.71	24,094.21	76,318.26	191,763.63	43,741.69	777,537.05
9/4/xx	1,144.90	0.00	1,144.90	0.00	192,908.53	14,820.56	791,212.71
9/5/xx	0.00	43.64	43.64	46,823.01		22,436.70	
Cumulative	122,869.99	-273.59	122,596.40	123,141.27	146,129.16	80,998.95	813,649.41
9/8/xx	59,227.36	86,020.30	145,247.66	0.00	291,376.82	13,647.39	768,069.44
9/9/xx	9,215.26		9,215.26	30,099.73	270,492.35	22,834.61	781,688.79
9/10/xx	0.00	-39.30	-39.30	62,759.90	207,693.15	10,818.74	792,507.53
9/11/xx	0.00		0.00	3,075.00	204,618.15	13,396.22	805,903.75
9/12/xx	333.69	101,987.02	102,320.71	155,856.16		24,250.46	
Cumulative	191,646.30	187,694.43	379,340.73	374,932.06	151,082.70	165,946.37	829,820.52
9/15/xx	70,096.00	8,605.03	78,701.03	0.00	229,783.73	22,600.43	782,324.95
9/16/xx	3,477.89	-15.00	3,462.89	69,359.94	163,886.68	11,601.53	790,448.59
9/17/xx	0.00	0.00	0.00	67,039.58	96,847.10	118,441.79	908,890.38
9/18/xx	6,583.95	-65.64	6,518.31	50.00	103,315.41	16,954.71	919,261.14
9/19/xx	80,953.64	-51.38	80,902.26	10,505.00		24,876.90	
Cumulative	352,757.78	196,167.44	548,925.22	521,886.58	173,712.67	360,421.73	863,184.40

Exhibit 9.3 The Example Company
Daily Activity Summary—September 20xx

Date	A/Rec Collections	Other Receipts	Total Receipts	Total Disbursed	Cash Balance	Net Invoicing	A/Rec Balance
9/22/xx	80,313.31	9.90	80,323.21	0.00	254,035.88	20,170.12	803,041.21
9/23/xx	15,507.14	-98.70	15,408.44	40,938.34	228,505.98	53,875.67	841,409.74
9/24/xx	22,714.28	-114.40	22,599.88	64,101.92	187,003.94	17,800.22	836,495.68
9/25/xx	0.00	14.78	14.78	17,778.83	169,239.89	28,302.70	864,798.38
9/26/xx	1,420.00		1,420.00	612.24		25,400.00	
Cumulative	472,712.51	195,979.02	668,691.53	645,317.91	170,047.65	505,970.44	888,778.38
9/29/xx	28,214.72	-153.00	28,061.72	14,496.43	183,612.94	15,778.92	876,342.58
9/30/xx	17,892.74	-14.90	17,877.84	50,494.59		26,967.86	
Cumulative	518,819.97	195,811.12	714,631.09	710,308.93	150,996.19	548,717.22	885,417.70
Adjustments							
Sept. 20xx	518,819.97	195,811.12	714,631.09	710,308.93	150,996.19	548,717.22	885,417.70

Exhibit 9.3   The Example Company
Daily Activity Summary—September 20xx (continued)

Date	Total Collections	0-30 days Aug/Sep	30-60 Jul	60-90 Jun	>90 Prior	Discounts Taken
9/2/xx	97,388.17	7,519.80	5,842.52	50,364.15	33,661.70	-74.52
9/3/xx	24,336.92	22,640.62			1,696.30	-242.71
9/4/xx	1,144.90	125.00		1,019.90		
9/5/xx	0.00					
Cumulative	122,869.99	30,285.42	5,842.52	51,384.05	35,358.00	-317.23
9/8/xx	59,227.36	12,421.29	23,626.84	18,408.94	4,770.29	-123.42
9/9/xx	9,215.26	4,776.37		4,438.89		-47.68
9/10/xx	0.00					
9/11/xx	0.00					
9/12/xx	333.69	333.69				
Cumulative	191,646.30	47,816.77	29,469.36	74,231.88	40,128.29	-488.33
9/15/xx	70,096.00	27,737.90	31,272.59	11,085.51		-259.94
9/16/xx	3,477.89	1,727.64	1,500.25		250.00	-15.00
9/17/xx	0.00					
9/18/xx	6,583.95	6,583.95				
9/19/xx	80,953.64	36,739.56	61,719.08	-19,140.00	1,635.00	-51.38
Cumulative	352,757.78	120,605.82	123,961.28	66,177.39	42,013.29	-814.65

Exhibit 9.4   The Example Company
Daily Accounts Receivable Collections—September 20xx

Date	Total Collections	0-30 days Aug/Sep	30-60 Jul	60-90 Jun	>90 Prior	Discounts Taken
9/22/xx	80,313.31	22,907.50	47,893.05	9,512.76		
9/23/xx	15,507.14	11,725.24	3,781.90			-98.70
9/24/xx	22,714.28	19,499.83		3,214.45		-114.40
9/25/xx	0.00					
9/26/xx	1,420.00				1,420.00	
Cumulative	472,712.51	174,738.39	175,636.23	78,904.60	43,433.29	-1,027.75
9/29/xx	28,214.72	21,947.32	2,315.88	3,951.52		-153.00
9/30/xx	17,892.74	1,490.00	16,402.74			-14.90
Cumulative	518,819.97	198,175.71	194,354.85	82,856.12	43,433.29	-1,195.65
Adjustments						
Sept. 20xx	518,819.97	198,175.71	194,354.85	82,856.12	43,433.29	-1,195.65

Exhibit 9.4 The Example Company
Daily Accounts Receivable Collections—September 20xx (continued)

	Receipts	Total
A/Rec. Collections	$518,819.97	$518,819.97
Misc. Other Receipts		
Cash discounts allowed	(1,195.65)	
Interest income	1,658.69	
Rental income	1,685.00	
Other receipts	93,663.08	
Subtotal Other Receipts		95,811.12
Borrowing Proceeds		
Savings/Investments Cashed		100,000.00
TOTAL CASH RECEIPTS		$714,631.09

Exhibit 9.5 The Example Company
Cash Receipts Detail—September 20XX

Interpretation of the Statement of Cash Flows

One of the most important factors to remember when reviewing any financial statements is that one period or one point in time is not sufficient to make an evaluation. This is particularly true when reviewing the Statement of Cash Flows. As mentioned previously, cash flow is an erratic activity. Month-to-month variations are typically quite significant and an expected part of normal operations. A single period can have aberrations or unusual occurrences that are not representative of the business activities as a whole. Therefore, multiple time periods must be reviewed before making any judgments about the cash flow performance of the business.

For example, it is possible that the company had to meet a major balloon payment obligation on a loan during a year, and decided to forego any substantial capital investment to have the funds available for that payment. A look at just that year would indicate low reinvestment and high debt repayment that, over the long run, is not a desirable combination. But if it occurred only in one year, and all other years showed lesser loan activities and more substantial reinvestment, the logical conclusion would have to be that the year under review was an aberration and not an indication of a long-term problem. This type of analysis is possible only if multiple years are reviewed, trends are examined, and conclusions drawn from the entire time span, not just a single period.

Three to five years of history generally provides enough information to allow appropriate conclusions about the financial performance of a business, be it profitability, liquidity, return on investment, or cash flow. Less than three years does not provide enough data to permit a legitimate trend analysis; six to ten

Date	Total Disbursed	Payroll & P/R Taxes	Accounts payable	Discounts	Subsid. #B Advances	Other	Special
9/2/xx	0.00						
9/3/xx	76,318.26	65,671.30		-168.85	10,000.00	646.96	
9/4/xx	0.00						
9/5/xx	46,823.01		34,140.04	-168.85		12,851.82	0.00
Cumulative	123,141.27	65,671.30	34,140.04	-168.85	10,000.00	13,498.78	0.00
9/8/xx	0.00						
9/9/xx	30,099.73		24,693.40	-21.38		5,427.71	
9/10/xx	62,759.90	62,098.40				661.50	
9/11/xx	3,075.00					3,075.00	150,000.00
9/12/xx	155,856.16					5,856.16	150,000.00
Cumulative	374,932.06	127,769.70	58,833.44	-190.23	10,000.00	28,519.15	
9/15/xx	0.00						
9/16/xx	69,359.94		69,452.26	-236.32		144.00	
9/17/xx	67,039.58	63,889.58				3,150.00	
9/18/xx	50.00					50.00	
9/19/xx	10,505.00					10,505.00	
Cumulative	521,886.58	191,659.28	128,285.70	-426.55	10,000.00	42,368.15	150,000.00
9/22/xx	0.00						
9/23/xx	40,938.34		41,066.30	-127.96			
9/24/xx	64,101.92	64,014.30			15,000.00	87.62	
9/25/xx	17,778.83					2,778.83	
9/26/xx	612.24					612.24	
Cumulative	645,317.91	255,673.58	169,352.00	-554.51	25,000.00	45,846.84	150,000.00
9/29/xx	14,496.43		49,849.13			14,496.43	
9/30/xx	50,494.59			-198.40		843.86	
Cumulative	710,308.93	255,673.58	219,201.13	-752.91	25,000.00	61,187.13	150,000.00
Adjustments							
Sept. 20xx	710,308.93	255,673.58	219,201.13	-752.91	25,000.00	61,187.13	150,000.00

Exhibit 9.6   The Example Company
Daily Cash Disbursements Summary—September 20xx

	Purchases	Cash Disb.	Total
Purchases - Subsidiary #A	$61,605.05		$61,605.05
Purchases - other			
Co. X	172.33		
Components	72,220.34	18,002.74	
Metal parts	17,278.30		
Heat treating	892.62		
Tooling	465.00		
Miscellaneous	144.01	$18.41	
Discounts	2.92	(752.91)	
Freight	4,506.68	47.64	
Total Other Purchases	95,682.20	17,315.88	112,998.08
Payroll Costs			
Payroll		230,515.11	
FICA, FIT, State w/h		0.00	
Local tax w/h		2,604.11	
FICA expense		13,470.16	
Unemployment/workers comp.	2,014.00	11,974.42	
Medical/life insurance	11,304.24	(2,890.22)	
Total Payroll Costs	13,318.24	255,673.58	268,991.82
Factory Expenses			
Supplies - cleaning	7,969.87	206.25	
-factory	4,690.59	3,866.31	
-processing	(1,136.28)		
-packing/shipping	1,873.82		
-production	4,065.71		
-machine shop	4,113.65		
Maintenance/repairs	2,043.72	5,143.00	
Utilities - power/heat	5,285.01		
Water/sewer	1,590.28		
Other	1,937.38	103.18	
Total Factory Expenses	32,433.75	9,318.74	41,752.49

Exhibit 9.7a The Example Company
Cash Disbursements Detail—September 20XX

years is acceptable if the company wants to process that additional data; but anything beyond ten years is usually too outdated to be of any real analytical value.

Organization of the Statement of Cash Flows

The Statement of Cash Flows, as discussed earlier, is separated into three distinct segments—operating cash flows, investing cash flows, and financing cash flows. In the analysis of the Statement of Cash Flows, each of the three principal

	Purchases	Cash Disb.	Total
Administrative Expenses			
Advertising	2,420.00		
Automobile	915.19	34.27	
Consulting		2,350.00	
Contributions		41.50	
Data processing		702.90	
Employee relations	360.00	54.85	
Insurance	8,701.00		
Office expenses	566.67	8,310.00	
Professional fees	5,829.97		
Real estate taxes			
Telephone	1,380.02		
Travel/entertainment	6,316.09	720.31	
Other	168.83	486.24	
Total Admin. Expenses	26,657.77	12,700.07	39,357.84
Fixed Assets			
Income taxes - state		865.00	
-federal			
Total Income Taxes		865.00	865.00
Advances - Subsidiary #B		25,000.00	25,000.00
Borrowing - principal		15,000.00	
-interest		5,234.53	
Total Borrowing Expenditures		20,234.53	20,234.53
Savings/Investments		150,000.00	150,000.00
Other			
Accounts Payable	$229,697.01	219,201.13	
Accounts Payable Change			(10,495.88)
TOTAL DISBURSEMENTS		$710,308.93	$710,308.93

Exhibit 9.7b   Cash Disbursements Detail—September 20XX

segments should be reviewed separately since each focuses on a distinct part of business activities.

Cash Flows from (for) Operating Activities
The most significant element to examine is the operating cash flows, since these represent what should be the major source of funds to the business over the long term. Generally speaking, if the business does not receive the bulk of its cash from operational activities, it will not be able to sustain itself. Clearly, the most important source of cash is that gained from the profitability of the company— that is a major reason why the company is in business and it represents essentially "free" money. Lack of profitability will eventually result in the termination

		Date: /30/xx
I. CASH RECEIPTS		
A. Accounts receivable collections		
1. Current	$ 1490.00	
2. 30 - 60 days	16,402.74	
3. 60 - 90 days		
4. Over 90 days		
Total A/Rec Collections		$ 17,892.74
B. Cash discounts		(14.90)
C. Miscellaneous cash receipts		0.00
TOTAL DEPOSITS		$ 17,877.84
II. CASH DISBURSEMENTS		
A. Payroll and payroll taxes		$ 0.00
B. Accounts payable		49,849.13
C. Discounts earned		(198.40)
D. Subsidiary #B advances		0.00
E. Other disbursements		843.86
TOTAL CASH DISBURSEMENTS		$ 50,494.59
III. CASH BALANCE		
A. Checking account		$ 30,996.19
B. Cash management account		120,000.00
TOTAL CASH		$150,996.19

Exhibit 9.8   Daily Cash Sheet

of the business activity except in highly unusual situations. Other sources of cash—borrowing, equity investments, or sales of assets—all should be supplemental to operations. There is nothing wrong with any of these as means of bringing money into the coffers, but they should not be the principal sources of funds over the long term.

Part of the profit from operations is, of course, the noncash adjustments to net income—depreciation, deferred taxes, amortization, changes in working capital, and so on. These must be added back to net income to determine the totality of cash generated from operations. Other adjustments to net income (e.g., undistributed earnings of affiliated companies, casualty gains or losses, special charges or credits, lawsuit settlements, or the like) should be evaluated individually to determine if they are part of cash from ongoing activities or

Date	Invoice # Control	# of Invoices	# of CMs	Gross Product	Shipments Special	Credit Memos	Freight	Net Invoicing
9/2/xx	7510							
9/3/xx	7527	16	1	43,932.05		-339.84	149.48	43,741.69
9/4/xx	7539	12		13,530.40	1,200.00		90.16	14,820.56
9/5/xx	7551	11	1	28,741.45		-6,404.60	99.85	22,436.70
Cumulative		39	2	86,203.90	1,200.00	-6,744.44	339.49	80,998.95
9/8/xx	7561	10		13,574.40			72.99	13,647.39
9/9/xx	7575	14		22,723.30			111.31	22,834.61
9/10/xx	7583	8		10,750.00			68.74	10,818.74
9/11/xx	7590	7		13,311.50			84.72	13,396.22
9/12/xx	7605	15		24,184.00			66.46	24,250.46
Cumulative		93	2	170,747.10	1,200.00	-6,744.44	743.71	165,946.37
9/15/xx	7619	13	1	22,522.50		-18.00	95.93	22,600.43
9/16/xx	7623	4		11,557.50			44.03	11,601.53
9/17/xx	7642	19		17,499.50	100,888.50		53.79	118,441.79
9/18/xx	7654	12		16,889.90			64.81	16,954.71
9/19/xx	7670	15	1	25,928.15		-1,152.00	100.75	24,876.90
Cumulative		156	4	265,144.65	102,088.50	-7,914.44	1,103.02	360,421.73

Exhibit 9.9   The Example Company
Daily Invoicing Summary—September 20xx

Date	Invoice # Control	# of Invoices	# of CMs	Gross Product	Shipments Special	Credit Memos	Freight	Net Invoicing
9/22/xx	7684	11	3	20,927.10		-838.39	81.41	20,170.12
9/23/xx	7692	8		53,842.25			33.42	53,875.67
9/24/xx	7708	15	1	17,966.82		-188.20	21.60	17,800.22
9/25/xx	7732	22	2	29,250.77		-1,047.50	99.43	28,302.70
9/26/xx	7759	27		25,312.88			87.12	25,400.00
Cumulative		239	10	412,444.47	102,088.50	-9,988.53	1,426.00	505,970.44
9/29/xx	7773	10	4	16,264.40		-507.68	22.20	15,778.92
9/30/xx	7791	18		26,850.43			117.43	26,967.86
Cumulative		267	14	455,559.30	102,088.50	-10,496.21	1,565.63	548,717.22
Adjustments								
Sept. 20xx				455,559.30	102,088.50	-10,496.21	1,565.63	548,717.22

Exhibit 9.9 The Example Company
Daily Invoicing Summary—September 20xx (continued)

	Date (week of): 9/22/xx	
	Forecast	Actual
CASH AVAILABLE		
Beg. checking a/c balance at ___9/22/xx___	$30,000	$30,000
Cash mgt. a/c balance	144,000	143,713
Estimated receipts		
-A/Rec. collections	115,000	119,955
-certificate of deposit maturities	0	0
-other cash receipts	0	(188)
TOTAL EST. CASH AVAILABLE	$289,000	$293,480
CASH REQUIREMENTS		
-A/Pay per requirements report	$45,000	$40,938
-additional payables	10,000	3,479
-payroll and payroll taxes	65,000	64,014
-Subsidiary #B advances	15,000	15,000
-other requirements		
-contingency	25,000	0
-certificate of deposit purchases	0	0
-income taxes	0	0
-other special payments	0	0
TOTAL EST. CASH REQUIREMENTS	$160,000	$123,431
CASH BALANCE AT WEEK END		
-checking account	$30,000	$30,000
-cash mgt. account	99,000	140,049
TOTAL ESTIMATED CASH AVAILABLE	$129,000	$170,049

Exhibit 9.10   Weekly Cash Planning Sheet

separate items not to be included in the evaluation of current operations. Each company needs to make this determination and apply it consistently over the years to ensure comparable evaluations and appropriate review conclusions. Changes in the elements of working capital (i.e., current assets and current liabilities), included as part of operating cash flows, tend to move up and down within reasonable ranges and do not generally constitute a major consideration in overall operating cash flows. There are plenty of exceptions to this, however, and it should not just be assumed that working capital elements are under control. They need to be examined and tracked to verify that they are indeed adequately controlled.

> ## *CASH SHOULD COME FROM OPERATIONS AND SHOULD BE USED FOR INVESTING, WITH FINANCING AS THE BALANCING NUMBER.*

Cash Flows from (for) Investing Activities

Investing activities are the next part of the Statement of Cash Flows that needs to be examined. These, in most cases, will represent the major uses of the cash flow of the business. Outlays for property, plant and equipment or new business acquisitions represent the company's investment in its own future, and most of the company's cash outflow over time should be in this area. A rule of thumb for the company to consider is that it should reinvest at least the amount of its real, straight-line depreciation in new property, plant and equipment so as to preserve its investment base. Because of inflationary pressures over time, reinvestment by only the amount of depreciation is unlikely to be sufficient, but it can be considered a minimum. Even higher levels of investment may be necessary for certain types of business and generally will be an indication of growth and improvement, but this also needs to be examined carefully. Reinvestment for the sake of reinvestment is wasted cash. The amount of reinvestment should be logical, planned, and appropriate for the circumstances of the company. Too much reinvestment uses up cash indiscriminately—an unwise action on the part of the company managers.

Cash Flows from (for) Financing Activities

Cash from or for financing activities can be considered as a balancing number, and as such is generally subordinate in operating significance to the other two classifications. This is not to say that the financing section can or should be overlooked. It needs to be reviewed carefully to determine how the company is handling its debt obligations and related financing transactions. Too much borrowing over too long a period of time will eventually cause trouble for the company. Too little borrowing may be an indication of overly cautious management and eliminates the possibility of gaining the benefits of leverage. Changes in the capital structure of the company will, from time to time, have to be made and can significantly affect the overall financial position and cash flow of the company. But these kinds of major changes tend to be relatively infrequent and do not have the more immediate impact of cash flow generated by operating and investing activities.

From an interpretation standpoint, it should be obvious that over time the company's main cash flow should be generated by operations and used for investing activities, with financing cash flows as a fluctuating balancing number between the other two. This should be the basis for initially determining the appropriateness of company cash flow. The logical follow-up questions are "How much from operations?" and "How much for investing?" Unfortunately, there are no readily available sources of information that will answer these questions for the company. It will be necessary for each enterprise to develop its own criteria about how much cash it should be generating from operating cash flows, and how much it should be using for investing cash flows. At present, the best source of such internal information is company history. An examination of the last 5 to 10 years of actual cash flows is likely to generate some standards that can be used to develop future expectations.

Operational Analysis of the Cash Flow Statement

While the cash flow statement is usually considered to be a financial document and is generally used, if at all, as part of the financial review of the organization, it can be used for operational analysis purposes as well. To be most useful operationally, focus should be on a direct method–type presentation, with particular emphasis on key parts of the Cash Flows from Operating Activities and Cash Flows from Investing Activities. See Exhibit 8.5 for the source of the line items we will discuss, but do recognize that this particular format is intended to be illustrative only, and the company form of presentation may be different to suit its particular needs.

Cash Flows from Operating Activities
This is the principal source and use of cash for the organization arising from company operations. These are the proceeds from sales of products and services and the expenditures for the operating needs such as material, labor, salaries, and other expenses necessary to keep the business running. Areas subject to operational review include:

- *Cash received from customers.* This, of course, represents the amounts paid by customers during the period for products or services they received. It is the cash paid by these customers, not the sales to them, that is recorded. Examples of analytical approaches to consider could include:
  - Amount of cash received versus expected (planned) receipts
    - By product or product line
    - By customer or class of customer
    - By type of sale (e.g. <$500, >$50,000 or other appropriate breakdown; sales from stock on hand versus special order; sales from product versus spare parts versus service repair; etc.)
  - Percentage of payments received beyond payment terms (e.g., 30 days) versus payments received within terms
  - Percentage of discounts taken versus discounts offered

- *Cash paid to suppliers and employees.* This represents the principal cash outflows for the organization, including cash paid out for material, purchased parts, payroll, manufacturing or service expenses, and marketing and administrative expenses (for sales activity, marketing, finance, accounting, executive, legal and related administrative support costs). Analytical approaches to consider in this area include:

- Payments made versus planned by category (purchased parts, raw materials, supplies, utilities, insurance, property taxes, etc.)
- Payroll paid versus plan—weekly, biweekly, monthly payrolls, overtime, vacation, payroll taxes
- Vendor analysis—payments versus plan, versus prior year, versus last five years, and so on. This can be done by vendor, by class of vendor, in total or any other way that makes sense for the organization.
- Percentage of payments made within 30 day terms, greater than 90 days, and so on.
- Percentage of discounts taken versus discounts offered by vendors and suppliers.

- *Other cash flows from operating activities.* These are likely to be largely financially oriented and outside the area of operational concerns, but they should at least be reviewed for possible operational impact.

Cash Flows from Investing Activities
The principal uses, over time, of the positive cash flows generated by operating activities. The future growth and viability of the company will be determined in large measure by the amount and the effectiveness of the company's investments in its future. Significant areas for operational review include:

- *Proceeds from sales of property, plant and equipment.* The amount of this cash inflow line item is likely to vary significantly from year to year, but the items sold should be reviewed to justify the validity of the dispositions and to see if they trigger ideas for other items that can legitimately be sold and converted into cash. Some sales of property, plant and equipment are a normal part of a company's ongoing process of replacing obsolete, worn out, or otherwise unusable assets. But a consideration also to be aware of is that an unusual amount of sales of these fixed assets may be an indication of excess capacity that has existed within the company. Looking at whether the items sold were needed in the first place could be a useful exercise to try and avoid repetition in the future.
- *Capital expenditures.* These are usually the largest of the investing cash outflows, and this category is used to record purchases of property, plant and equipment. Here again, the amounts will vary from year to year, but the specific expenditures should be reviewed for appropriateness and effectiveness. They should also be looked at from the point of view of whether the items acquired are really necessary for the business or were just "nice to have." Finally, the total amount expended needs to be reviewed to ensure that the company is not spending itself into a cash crisis.

- *Acquisitions of new businesses.* These are likely to appear sporadically and in widely divergent amounts for most businesses. The same review process should be applied as for capital expenditures.
- *Other investing activities.* These are most likely to be financially oriented transactions, subject more to financial than to operational analysis.

Cash Flows from Financing Activities

This is the balancing number between operating and investing cash flows made up of borrowing repayments, new borrowings, company equity sales and repurchases, dividends, and like financial transactions. As such this area is subject more to a financial than an operating review. However, the operational manager needs to be aware that company borrowing may be caused by operating activities that are executed with insufficient attention to their cash flow impacts. The financial and operating functional managers need to communicate with each other to avoid imbalances in the cash flow of the company. Borrowing is an expensive proposition that, if it can be avoided or delayed, saves cash for the company in the form of interest payments that do not have to be made and principal amounts that do not have to be repaid.

> # CASH FLOW IS DRIVEN BY OPERATIONAL ACTIVITIES AND NEEDS TO BE EVALUATED ACCORDINGLY.

Cash Management Operating Indicators

Each company must determine its own reasons for being in existence, its basic business principles, and its own operating principles. Based on these factors, it develops its strategic long- and short-term plans and budgets. Operating indicators and ratios can then be identified and developed to analyze the progress being made toward realizing these plans. Sometimes, such indicators are related to the total category (e.g., sales or accounts receivable), but sometimes it is also significant to relate them to an individual customer or sales order. Many times, analyzing each customer or sales order as a profit center can be helpful in determining specific corrective action to be taken. It is the use of such operating indicators and ratios that enables the company to identify ongoing areas for improvement, performance gaps between actual results and plans, and benchmarks for best practices. Although each company must develop its own operating indicators and ratios to address its own criteria for successful operations, the following are examples that could be considered.

- *Sales*
  - Types and amount of sale
    - To the right customer
    - Of the right product
    - At the right time
  - Type of customer
    - Major customers (20 percent of customer base producing 80 percent of sales)
    - Repeat customers
    - New customers
    - Cash customers
  - Relationship to sales forecast
    - Real customer orders recorded in original sales forecast
    - Real customer orders forecasted
    - Addition to original sales forecast
    - Sales forecast not realized
  - Type of sale
    - Repetitive
    - One time
    - Special order
    - Original product
    - Replacement parts
    - Product service
  - Sales processing
    - Directly into production
    - Backlogged
    - Shipped from inventory
  - Payment criteria
    - Cash sale (e.g., sale amount less than processing cost and other cash sales)
    - Payment upon delivery
    - Credit terms

- *Accounts receivable*
  - Payment with discount (e.g., 1%/10 days)
    - Considered in pricing?
    - Paid within discount period
    - Discounts taken but paid after discount period
  - Payments relative to terms period (e.g., 30 days of invoice date)
    - Between 10 and 20 days
    - Between 20 and 30 days
    - Beyond 30 days, 60 days, 90 days
    - Collection procedures employed

- Change in accounts receivable
  - Increase or decrease in total
  - Payment practices (i.e., quicker, slower)
  - Cash sales versus accounts receivable sales

- *Costs and pricing*
  - Product costs
    - Direct labor: Change in set up and processing time and dollar costs of rejects and rework
    - Material costs: Changes in quantities, amount put into production, cost of scrap and rework
  - Functional costs
    - Manufacturing related: Changes in quality control, receiving, packing and shipping, supervision, and so on.
    - Support departments: Engineering, purchasing, production scheduling, production control, inventory control, accounting, and so on.
  - Customer costs
    - Sales support prior to and during sale
    - Customer service—type and level
    - Type of distribution (one shipment, drop shipment, numerous locations)
    - After sales support
  - Differential pricing
    - Related to product, functional and customer costs
    - Based on method of payment (e.g., cash on delivery [COD], discounts, terms)
    - Profit center concept (e.g., each sale, total sales)

- *Vendors and accounts payable*
  - Vendor analysis
    - Right price
    - Right time
    - Right quality
  - Vendor negotiations
    - Price
    - Delivery
    - Quality
    - Service
    - Payment terms
  - Accounts payable
    - Cash payment if invoice amount less than processing cost
    - Cash payment as part of vendor price negotiations
    - Changes in accounts payable
    - Payment indicators (e.g., discount taken, payment within terms, payment beyond terms)

- *Inventory*
  - Raw materials
    - Decreases by item and product line
    - Just-in-time deliveries
    - Stockouts
  - Work in process
    - Real orders/total mix
    - On-time moves and completions
    - Under/overcapacity
  - Finished goods
    - Just-in-time deliveries
    - Decrease in inventory
    - Availability

Cash Flow Ratios: Operational and Financial

There are basically five major sources of cash and a corresponding five major uses of cash. These are as follows:

Sources of Cash	*Uses of Cash*
1. Profits from operations	1. Losses from operations
2. Borrowing	2. Repayment of debt
3. Sale of equity	3. Payment of dividends
4. Sale of assets	4. Investments/acquisitions of assets
5. Decrease in working capital (except cash)	5. Increase in working capital (except cash)

We have already discussed that acquiring cash from profits and expending cash for investment and acquisitions are the preferable sources and uses—at least over the long term. Profits represent a major reason why companies are in business—they are a principal goal of many organizations. While borrowing and sale of equity are a necessary part of business financing, they are less desirable sources of cash than profits. New borrowing will have to be repaid—with interest. New equity is expensive—and often unwanted or unavailable, especially to smaller businesses. Sale of assets as a source of funds is obviously self-limiting. And working capital reduction as a source of cash is also generally restricted because of its inherent operational limitations.

On the other side of the ledger, the company certainly hopes to avoid operating losses. Repayment of debt, while legally necessary, does little to directly benefit the organization. Dividend payments benefit stockholders, but do nothing directly to help the company; and an increase in working capital ties up cash, which is something management wants to avoid. Reinvestment in assets, however, indicates a commitment to the future—assuming the investment is done in a manner that is intelligent and consistent with the company's strategic planning. It shows the company's interest in future survival and growth and can be seen as a positive statement about progress and advancement.

CASH FLOW RATIOS—AN OPPORTUNITY FOR CREATIVE THINKING.

With these basics in mind, the company's Statement of Cash Flows can be analyzed with ratios. A generally accepted set of cash flow ratios does not yet exist, so the company must look at its own operational and financial position and needs in devising analytical techniques to evaluate its cash flow. Acceptable and unacceptable results will vary from company to company, but norms will emerge for the organization based on its specific uses of cash over a three to five year period. The ratios illustrated below, or modifications of them, can be used to develop a working cash flow evaluation process for the organization. Most of the ratios focus on the impact of various measures relative to cash flow from operations, which is the most significant cash flow element.

There are any number of additional possibilities that could be considered as well. The major problem is not to come up with additional ratios, but to determine which of the myriad possibilities make sense for the company. The ratios below are intended to be idea generators only and should not be construed as a generally accepted set of ratios. Such a set has yet to be developed.

Ratio	*Method of Calculation*
Cash flow from continuing operations to sales. The amount of operating cash flows generated by sales—a cash efficiency measure.	$\dfrac{\text{Operating cash flows}}{\text{Net sales}}$
Cash to income ratio. Percentage of operating income that has been converted into cash—a measure of cash conversion	$\dfrac{\text{Operating cash flows}}{\text{Operating income}}$
Cash sales to total sales. The amount of sales immediately converted into cash—a cash efficiency measure	$\dfrac{\text{Cash sales}}{\text{Total sales}}$
Reinvestment ratio. The amount of operating cash flows used for capital expenditures—a measure of the degree of capital reinvestment	$\dfrac{\text{Purchase of property, plant \& equipment}}{\text{Operating cash flows}}$

Ratio	Method of Calculation
Reinvestment adequacy. The amount of reinvestment relative to depreciation—a measure of the adequacy of capital reinvestment	$\dfrac{\text{Purchase of assets}}{\text{Depreciation}}$
Operating cash reinvestment ratio. How much of operating cash flows is being reinvested in the business—a measure of the degree of capital reinvestment	$\dfrac{\text{Investing cash flows}}{\text{Operating cash flows}}$
Reinvestment to sales. The percentage of sales reinvested – a capital reinvestment measure	$\dfrac{\text{Investing cash flows}}{\text{Net sales}}$
Financing ratio. The percentage of sales used for financing the business	$\dfrac{\text{Financing cash flows}}{\text{Net sales}}$
Debt payoff. The amount of operating cash flows used to pay off debt	$\dfrac{\text{Debt payments}}{\text{Operating cash flows}}$
Cash return on assets. The amount of cash generated from total asset investment in the business—a cash return on investment (ROI) measure	$\dfrac{\text{Operating cash flows}}{\text{Total assets}}$
Cash return on equity. An ROI measure of cash return on stockholder's equity	$\dfrac{\text{Operating cash flows}}{\text{Stockholders equity}}$
Cash return on capital employed. An ROI measure of cash return on capital employed in the business	$\dfrac{\text{Operating cash flows}}{\text{Capital Employed}}$
Cash flow current ratio. Ability of cash generated from operations to cover currrent liabilities	$\dfrac{\text{Operating cash flows}}{\text{Current liabilities}}$
Cash flow fixed charge coverage. Ability of operating cash flows to meet company fixed charge obligations	$\dfrac{\text{Operating cash flows + fixed charges*}}{\text{Fixed charges}}$ *(interest paid + taxes paid + other fixed charges paid [rent, debt principal, leases, etc.])
Debt repayment from operating cash flows. Number of years of operating cash flows required to cover debt obligations	$\dfrac{\text{Total debt}}{\text{Operating cash flows}}$

To be of maximum value, any ratios used should be measured over a three to five year period so that trends can be evaluated rather than just absolutes. Without a set of norms, absolutes have virtually no significance, and those norms will have to be developed individually for each company. Finally, any evaluation should always revert back to the basics of cash flow discussed earlier—cash over the long run should come primarily from profitability (operating cash flows) and should be used primarily for reinvestment in the business (investing cash flows), with financing cash flows serving as the balancing number between the other two.

It is reasonable to presume that accounting practitioners and analysts will eventually develop a workable set of cash ratios that form the basis of a generally accepted set of cash flow ratios comparable to the financial ratios now being used for income statement and balance sheet analyses. In the meantime, the company will have to identify the information it needs to manage the company's cash. The absence of an acceptable set of already developed ratios does mean more work for the analyst, but it also means fewer restrictions and the chance to be creative and innovative in analyzing the company's results. That is an opportunity not to be wasted.

CONCLUSION

Analyzing the cash management process within an organization is an effective tool for determining the economy, efficiency, and effectiveness of the company's use of its cash flow. It forces management to move away from strictly accounting data and look at operations from a cash flow viewpoint, eliminating the perplexity of financial statements that are produced on the accrual (rather than cash) basis and contain numerous noncash accounting treatments. By taking the cash approach to analyzing operations, the analysis strips the business down to those ongoing operations that either add or deduct cash from the company's activities. This enables management to get to the essence of the company's operations and gain greater insight as to what is actually happening operationally within the organization.

> *CASH FLOW ANALYSIS*
> *IS OPERATIONS ANALYSIS.*

AFTERWORD

The materials in this book are intended to provide the guidelines and directions that will enable the organization to take an operational focus on cash management. As we have attempted to point out, cash flow is not principally a financial activity, but comes about as the result of the operations of the entire company. Cash is generated from the company's sales activities and is used primarily by company operations. Everyone in the company is responsible for the use and conservation of cash. It is not solely management's responsibility to plan and monitor the sources and uses of cash, but each employee's responsibility as well. Management has overall responsibility for policies and direction, but if it can make all employees their own profit centers, then it becomes everyone's individual responsibility to maximize income, minimize expenses, and optimize expected results with efficient use of resources, and ensure a continuing positive flow of cash so the organization can survive and thrive. Accordingly, cash management must be fully understood and practices effectively followed by all company employees.

Before the reader closes these pages and shelves the material, we also want to call attention to the Case Study and the Cash Conservation Checklist following this Afterword. The Case Study – on Jack B. Nimble Company – was briefly referred to in Chapters 1 and 2, but is here presented in its totality. We suggest that the Case Study be reviewed and worked out before turning to the suggested solution. This will provide an opportunity to apply some of the issues we have raised within the pages of this book. The Cash Conservation Checklist that follows the Case Study, is an attempt to show on a few pages some (and only some) of the issues the reader might consider when reviewing his or her own cash flow management issues. The Cash Conservation Checklist, because it is just a checklist, is necessarily limited but might serve as a reminder of some concerns and issues and might even trigger some new thoughts that could be applied to the specific situation under review. It is intended as an aid, not an all-encompassing solution.

We realize that there are many operational areas and concerns that affect cash flow that we may not have discussed in the depth desired – or have omitted entirely. Sale/leaseback arrangements, initial or additional public offerings of company stock, accounts receivable factoring, product licensing, mergers and acquisitions, non-traditional borrowing, and so forth are among the myriad additional areas that should be further investigated as related to a specific company or situation. But we hope to have provided sufficient materials and ideas to encourage the development of a comprehensive cash management program with an operational focus for your organization.

Cash management is a continual process. It is also much more than just a management process – it is also an attitude that must be instilled within the entire organizational culture. Only with proper planning, effective operating practices, and diligent analysis and control can positive cash flow be maximized. Cash management is an exercise not only in controlling the expenditure of funds, but also of generating cash from sales, effectively allocating and expending cash resources, and maximizing cash flow and profits. The company must learn the best way in which it can achieve maximum desired results with the most efficient expenditure of cash resources. This has been the essence and purpose of this book. We hope that we have succeeded.

> *LOVE OF MONEY IS THE ROOT OF ALL EVIL;*
> *ABSENCE OF MONEY IS THE ROUTE TO RUIN.*

APPENDIX A

Case Study: Managing Cash Flow

OBJECTIVE:

Given a cash flow forecast, appropriate historical financial information, and assumptions regarding the future, be able to evaluate an organization's cash position and make recommendations about how it can manage its business more effectively to conserve cash.

JACK B. NIMBLE COMPANY
(formerly ABC Machining, Inc.)

Jack Nimble had been employed by ABC Machining for nearly 20 years, serving in a variety of engineering and manufacturing positions for the company. The company owner decided to put the company up for sale, and Jack was eager to buy it, since he knew he could do a better job of managing and running it than was presently being done. There was potential for additional sales; and cost savings through production efficiencies, superior customer service, and reduced administrative expenses (the owner was quite generous to himself) would be easy to accomplish. Jack had no doubt that he could improve things dramatically within a year, and growth possibilities after the first year were extremely attractive.

Jack did not have strong financial skills, but he knew that he had to put together some kind of projected figures to set goals for the company and to satisfy his financial backers, who were members of his family and also not financially sophisticated. Exhibit A.1 shows the income statement projections that Jack prepared.

Based on this projection, which he felt was realistic, Jack did not do any further financial studies, nor did his financial supporters request any more data. Their feeling was that the combination of the sales growth and the attractive improvement in profitability would be enough to avoid any financial difficulties.

Unfortunately, these projections proved insufficient. Jack did not take into consideration three significant factors: (1) He would have to invest in excess of $2

	ABC Machining 12/31/x1 – actual		Jack B. Nimble Co. 12/31/x2 – projected	
	$	%	$	%
Sales	$12,002.7	100.0%	$18,000	100.0%
Cost of goods sold	8,436.1	70.3	11,900	66.1
Manufacturing Profit	3,566.6	29.7	6,100	33.9
Selling, gen. & admin. expenses	2,474.4	20.6	2,500	13.9
Operating Profit	1,092.2	9.1	3,600	20.0
Taxes	395.1	3.3	1,300	7.2
Net Income	$ 697.1	5.8%	$ 2,300	12.8%

Exhibit A.1   Jack B. Nimble Company: Income Statements for Years Ending December 31, 20x1 and 20x2 ($$ in 000s)

million in plant and equipment to gain all the efficiencies and throughput expansion he required; (2) to gain the new customers required to achieve the sales target, he would have to extend 30-day credit terms to all customers; and (3) it would take time to ramp up to $1.5 million monthly sales necessary to attain the $18 million target figure.

As ABC Machining, the company enjoyed a unique position—demand for its products exceeded ability to supply. The company was able to sell all of its monthly production of about $1 million on a continuing basis. ABC required cash payment at time of delivery to virtually all customers, and was still able to sell 100 percent of its output. Jack, however, wanted to increase sales and net profits and recognized the existence of increased competition and other changes in the marketplace. He not only saw the need to retain present customers but also to acquire new customers. To accomplish his goals, he knew he would have to offer credit terms for payment and would have to absorb the cost of carrying the significant increase in accounts receivable investment.

Jack was fully aware of the plant and equipment investment and the accounts receivable factors, but he did not understand the cash flow ramifications they would have on his fledgling business. He simply assumed the profit generated from the new sales would produce enough cash to cover any requirements he would face. He had not taken the ramping factor into consideration at all. If he had done a balance sheet projection, even without taking the ramping into account, the pro forma balance sheet figures in Exhibit A.2 would have appeared, allowing him to plan for the cash shortage contingency.

From the pro forma balance sheet, it is clear that Jack could have anticipated a significant problem with cash. Without that projection, however, Jack only discovered the problem once in the middle of it. Fortunately, because some of his relatives were willing to guarantee Jack's loan, he was able to get a $1.5 million line

($$ in 000s)	12/31/x2 – pro forma	
	$	%
ASSETS		
Cash	$ (925)	(12.2)
Accounts receivable	1,875	24.8
Inventory	2,400	31.8
Current Assets	3,350	44.4
Other assets	4,200	55.6
TOTAL ASSETS	$7,550	100.0
LIABILITIES		
Accts payable & accrued expenses	$1,250	16.6
Other current liabilities	400	5.3
Current Liabilities	1,650	21.9
Other liabilities	900	11.9
Total Liabilities	2,550	33.8
STOCKHOLDERS' EQUITY		
Total Stockholders' Equity	5,000	66.2
TOTAL LIABILITIES & EQUITY	$7,550	100.0

Exhibit A.2 Jack B. Nimble Company: Pro Forma Balance Sheet Figures for December 31, 20x2

of credit from his bank and to increase his long-term loan by $500,000. To complete the picture of his first year of operation, in Exhibit A.3 Nimble's actual financial results are shown compared to the projected figures and to the prior year numbers. Part of Jack's problem (and the solution to his critical needs) was borrowing. At January 1, 20x2, Jack assumed a loan of just over $1 million with a monthly payment of $16,000 including interest at $8\frac{1}{2}$ percent. He added $500,000 to the loan on April 1, 20x2, which increased the monthly payment to $25,000 but did not change the interest rate. He also negotiated a $1.5 million line of credit at a rate of 9 percent. The actual cash flow, by month, for the year is shown in Exhibit A.4.

From these figures, it is clear that Jack made good progress towards achieving his goals. During the year, however, his cash flow difficulties forced him to defer the purchase of certain equipment that he needed, and the impact on future years may be severe. He did a good job controlling expenses and inventory, but his accounts receivable went through the roof. As a result, he is now dealing with a significant line of credit (and related interest charges). He has financed the rest of his requirements partly from the profits he was able to attain and from the addition to his bank loan, but also by not paying his vendors on time. His accounts payable balance has increased dramatically, and is now about 85 percent higher than it should be. Jack's phone is surely ringing off the hook with angry and frustrated vendors who are looking for payment. Additionally the bank is pressuring

($$ in 000s)	12/31/x2I actual		12/31/x2 projected		ABC Machining, Inc. 12/31/x1 actual	
	$	%	$	%	$	%
Sales	$15,073.4	100.0	$18,000	100.0	$12,002.7	100.0
Cost of goods sold	10,290.4	68.3	11,900	66.1	8,436.1	70.3
Manufacturing Profit	4,783.0	31.7	6,100	33.9	3,566.6	29.7
Selling, g & a expenses	2,317.2	15.4	2,388	13.3	2,369.4	19.7
Interest expense	162.9	1.1	112	0.6	105.0	0.9
Operating Profit	2,302.9	15.2	3,600	20.0	1,092.2	9.1
Taxes	912.0	6.0	1,300	7.2	395.1	3.3
NET INCOME	$ 1,390.9	9.2	$ 2,300	12.8	$ 697.1	5.8

Exhibit A.3   Jack B. Nimble Company (and ABC Machining, Inc.) Income Statements for Years Ending December 31, 20x2 and 20x1

($$ in 000s)	12/31/x2 actual		12/31/x2 pro forma		ABC Machining, Inc. 12/31/x1 actual	
	$	%	$	%	$	%
ASSETS						
Cash	$ 10.0	0.1	$ (925)	(12.2)	$ 207.6	4.3
Accounts receivable	2,029.6	26.0	1,875	24.8	142.1	3.0
Inventory	2,512.7	32.2	2,400	31.8	2,457.6	51.1
Current Assets	4,552.3	58.3	3,350	44.4	2,807.3	58.4
Other assets	3,251.6	41.7	4,200	55.6	2,003.1	41.6
TOTAL ASSETS	$7,803.9	100.0	$7,550	100.0	$4,810.4	100.0
LIABILITIES						
Line of credit	$ 101.7	1.3	$ 0	0	$ 0.0	0.0
Accts pay & accd expenses	1,844.0	23.6	1,250	16.6	793.3	16.5
Other current liabilities	425.6	5.5	400	5.3	314.2	6.5
Current Liabilities	2,371.3	30.4	1,650	21.9	1,107.5	23.0
Long-term borrowing	1,346.1	17.2	900	11.9	1,007.3	21.0
Total Liabilities	3,717.4	47.6	2,550	33.8	2,114.8	44.0
STOCKHOLDERS' EQUITY						
Total Stockholders' Equity	4,086.5	52.4	5,000	66.2	2,695.6	56.0
TOTAL LIABILITIES & EQUITY	$7,803.9	100.0	$7,550	100.0	$4,810.4	100.0

Exhibit A.3 Jack B. Nimble Company (and ABC Machining, Inc.) Balance Sheets at December 31, 20x2 and 20x1 (continued)

	Jan	Feb	Mar	Apr	May	Jun	Jul	Aug	Sep	Oct	Nov	Dec	Total
Projected Income Statement													
Sales	1,001.2	1,045.9	1,095.6	1,142.0	1,177.8	1,235.6	1,288.8	1,304.9	1,355.5	1,425.2	1,490.2	1,510.7	15,073.4
Cost of goods sold - var	447.5	452.2	484.1	487.4	509.1	516.9	534.4	555.5	569.4	577.0	600.2	604.8	6,338.5
Cost of goods sold - fixed	291.1	292.5	293.6	295.7	298.8	299.4	331.2	341.1	347.7	366.1	395.9	398.8	3,951.9
Selling, g & a - var.	119.1	122.8	128.9	132.2	141.8	144.3	152.7	157.2	161.9	166.5	172.5	174.9	1,774.8
Selling, g & a - fixed	39.9	41.1	41.9	42.2	42.5	44.0	45.2	47.7	48.2	49.0	49.9	50.8	542.4
Interest	7.1	12.5	15.3	18.4	14.3	12.7	16.3	14.5	14.2	14.1	12.0	11.4	162.9
Profit before taxes	96.5	124.8	131.8	166.1	171.3	218.3	209.0	188.9	214.1	252.5	259.7	270.0	2,302.9
Income taxes	38.2	49.2	52.1	63.8	68.0	86.8	83.0	74.9	85.1	100.2	103.2	107.5	912.0
Net Income	58.3	75.6	79.7	102.3	103.3	131.5	126.0	114.0	129.0	152.3	156.5	162.5	1,390.9
Net Income - % of sales	5.8%	7.2%	7.3%	9.0%	8.8%	10.6%	9.8%	8.7%	9.5%	10.7%	10.5%	10.8%	9.2%
Loan Amortization													
Principal - beg. bal.	1,007.3	998.4	989.5	1,480.5	1,466.0	1,451.4	1,436.7	1,421.8	1,406.9	1,391.9	1,376.7	1,361.5	
Interest	7.1	7.1	7.0	10.5	10.4	10.3	10.2	10.1	10.0	9.9	9.8	9.6	111.8
Principal payment	8.9	8.9	9.0	14.5	14.6	14.7	14.8	14.9	15.0	15.1	15.2	15.4	161.2
Principal - ending bal.	998.4	989.5	980.5	1,466.0	1,451.4	1,436.7	1,421.8	1,406.9	1,391.9	1,376.7	1,361.5	1,346.1	
Interest on line of credit	0.0	5.4	8.3	7.9	3.9	2.4	6.1	4.5	4.2	4.2	2.2	1.8	51.0

Exhibit A.4 Jack B. Nimble Company
Actual Cash Flow For 20x2

	Jan	Feb	Mar	Apr	May	Jun	Jul	Aug	Sep	Oct	Nov	Dec	Total
Cash Flow													
A/R coll. - current month	100.2	105.2	108.7	110.1	118.8	125.1	126.6	129.4	136.5	140.2	144.5	153.2	1,498.5
A/R coll. - prior month	0.0	551.1	577.9	600.1	625.1	648.2	681.1	706.5	715.5	745.9	784.3	815.1	7,450.8
A/R coll. - 2d prior month	0.0	0.0	342.3	359.1	378.9	398.8	405.0	422.2	446.2	450.0	465.9	492.8	4,161.2
New borrowing				500.0									500.0
Total Receipts	100.2	656.3	1,028.9	1,569.3	1,122.8	1,172.1	1,212.7	1,258.1	1,298.2	1,336.1	1,394.7	1,461.1	13,610.5
Cost of goods sold	651.3	657.0	689.6	694.4	718.3	726.5	766.2	794.3	812.8	833.3	877.3	884.0	9,104.8
Selling, gen. & admin.	154.0	158.9	165.8	169.4	179.3	183.3	192.9	199.9	205.1	210.5	217.4	220.7	2,257.2
Interest	7.1	12.5	15.3	18.4	14.3	12.7	16.3	14.5	14.2	14.1	12.0	11.4	162.9
Taxes	100.0			139.5		131.8		244.7					616.0
Other - capital investment	102.2	198.5	99.7	0.0	0.0	594.1	0.0	205.7	0.0	0.0	210.0	197.5	1,607.7
Debt principal	8.9	8.9	9.0	14.5	14.6	14.7	14.8	14.9	15.0	15.1	15.2	15.4	161.2
Total Disbursements	1,023.5	1,035.8	979.4	1,036.2	926.5	1,663.1	990.3	1,229.3	1,291.8	1,073.0	1,332.0	1,328.9	13,909.8

Exhibit A.4 Jack B. Nimble Company
Actual Cash Flow For 20x2 (continued)

	Jan	Feb	Mar	Apr	May	Jun	Jul	Aug	Sep	Oct	Nov	Dec	Total
Net Cash Flow	-923.3	-379.5	49.5	533.1	196.3	-491.0	222.4	28.8	6.4	263.1	62.7	132.2	-299.3
Beginning cash	207.6	-715.7	-1,095.2	-1,045.7	-512.6	-316.3	-807.3	-584.9	-556.1	-549.7	-286.6	-223.8	207.6
Available cash	-715.7	-1,095.2	-1,045.7	-512.6	-316.3	-807.3	-584.9	-556.1	-549.7	-286.6	-223.8	-91.7	-91.7
Line of credit borrowing	725.7	1,105.2	1,055.7	522.6	326.3	817.3	594.9	566.1	559.7	296.6	233.8	101.7	101.7
Ending Cash	10.0	10.0	10.0	10.0	10.0	10.0	10.0	10.0	10.0	10.0	10.0	10.0	10.0

Exhibit A.4 Jack B. Nimble Company
Actual Cash Flow For 20x2 (continued)

him, insisting that he zero out the line of credit for at least one month before they will consider another year's extension.

Because of his cash flow problems, Jack got smart quickly. He decided he needs a reliable cash flow projection for next year, particularly since he wants to catch up on his fixed asset expenditures as well as make additional investments. The assumptions and estimates that support the forecast in Exhibit A.5 are as reliable as can be expected in the circumstances.

FINANCIAL FORECAST INFORMATION

- Sales—January 20x3—$1,600,000; increasing at the rate of 1% per month each month thereafter
- Cost of goods sold
  - Variable CGS @ 40 percent of sales
  - Fixed CGS @ $425,000/month, increasing at $10,000 per month for each following month
- Selling, general and administrative expenses (including bad debt expense, but excluding interest expense)
  - Variable @ 10 percent of sales
  - Fixed @ $55,000/month for six months, then $65,000/month
  - Taxes—40 percent of profit before taxes

CASH FORECAST INFORMATION

- Accounts receivable collections
  - 10 percent of current month sales
  - 55 percent of prior month sales
  - 34.5 percent of second prior month sales
  - 0.5 percent uncollectible
- Cost of goods sold
  - 100 percent of variable costs are cash
  - 70 percent of fixed costs are cash
  - Current month expenses are used as basis for projecting cash flow, although they are actually paid for at a later date
  - Selling, general and administrative expenses
  - $5,000 of fixed costs are noncash; all others are cash
  - Current month expenses are used as basis for projecting cash flow, although they are actually paid for at a later date
- Operating cash—maintain minimum balance of $10,000
- Line of credit—9 percent interest on the prior month end balance
- Loan payments
  - Interest @ 8.5 percent of outstanding balance

- $25,000/month repayment (interest included)
- Balance outstanding @ January 1, 20x3 = $1,346,100
- Tax payments
  - Payment in January, April, June, and September covering in full all tax obligations calculated for the period covered by the payments
- Other obligations
  - All other obligations are for fixed-asset investments
    - January $125,000
    - February $700,000
    - March $175,000
    - Subsequent months $200,000/month

The preparation of this kind of a forecast is not difficult once the basic assumptions and estimates are developed. The picture such a forecast provides the management of the organization is invaluable. The prospect of an excess amount of cash is an opportunity that should be used to the fullest advantage, while a cash shortfall needs to be recognized early and handled wisely to minimize the cost to the organization and to avoid the disaster of not being able to pay off obligations. Either way, typical income statement projections and pro forma balance sheets are not enough. Cash is the ultimate determinant of survival, success, or failure.

TASK

Review the cash flow projection in conjunction with the financial statements and other data previously presented in this case study. Identify opportunities, both financial and operational, for improved cash management and be prepared to make suggestions to Jack that can help him get through his cash crunch and meet his bank's demands.

JACK B. NIMBLE COMPANY CASE STUDY
SUGGESTED SOLUTION

There are many different cash management and operational areas to discuss related to this case study. The company faces a cash flow crisis that has been caused essentially by four factors:

1. Growth in sales without proper attention having been paid to the fact that growth is an expensive proposition, requiring cash for the increase in accounts receivable, inventory, staff, and possibly equipment and/or plant

Projected Income Statement

	Jan	Feb	Mar	Apr	May	Jun	Jul	Aug	Sep	Oct	Nov	Dec	Total
Sales	1,600.0	1,616.0	1,632.2	1,648.5	1,665.0	1,681.6	1,698.4	1,715.4	1,732.6	1,749.9	1,767.4	1,785.1	20,292.0
Cost of goods sold - var	640.0	646.4	652.9	659.4	666.0	672.6	679.4	686.2	693.0	700.0	707.0	714.0	8,116.8
Cost of goods sold - fixed	425.0	435.0	445.0	455.0	465.0	475.0	485.0	495.0	505.0	515.0	525.0	535.0	5,760.0
Selling, g & a - var.	160.0	161.6	163.2	164.8	166.5	168.2	169.8	171.5	173.3	175.0	176.7	178.5	2,029.2
Selling, g & a - fixed	55.0	55.0	55.0	55.0	55.0	55.0	65.0	65.0	65.0	65.0	65.0	65.0	720.0
Interest	10.3	11.1	13.3	11.5	12.7	11.1	11.2	9.7	8.6	9.1	8.4	8.3	125.4
Profit before taxes	309.7	306.9	302.8	302.7	299.8	299.8	288.0	288.0	287.6	285.8	285.3	284.2	3,540.6
Income taxes	123.9	122.7	121.1	121.1	119.9	119.9	115.2	115.2	115.1	114.3	114.1	113.7	1,416.3
Net Income	185.8	184.1	181.7	181.6	179.9	179.9	172.8	172.8	172.6	171.5	171.2	170.5	2,124.4
Net Income % of Sales	11.6%	11.4%	11.1%	11.0%	10.8%	10.7%	10.2%	10.1%	10.0%	9.8%	9.7%	9.6%	10.5%

Loan Amortization

	Jan	Feb	Mar	Apr	May	Jun	Jul	Aug	Sep	Oct	Nov	Dec	Total
Principal - beginning bal.	1,346.1	1,330.6	1,315.1	1,299.4	1,283.6	1,267.7	1,251.7	1,235.5	1,219.3	1,202.9	1,186.4	1,169.8	
Interest	9.5	9.4	9.3	9.2	9.1	9.0	8.9	8.8	8.6	8.5	8.4	8.3	107.0
Principal payment	15.5	15.6	15.7	15.8	15.9	16.0	16.1	16.2	16.4	16.5	16.6	16.7	193.0
Principal - ending bal.	1,330.6	1,315.1	1,299.4	1,283.6	1,267.7	1,251.7	1,235.5	1,219.3	1,202.9	1,186.4	1,169.8	1,153.1	1,153.1
Interest on line of credit	0.8	1.7	4.0	2.3	3.6	2.1	2.4	0.9	0.0	0.6	0.0	0.0	18.4

Exhibit A.5 Jack B. Nimble Company
Cash Flow Projection For 20x3

	Jan	Feb	Mar	Apr	May	Jun	Jul	Aug	Sep	Oct	Nov	Dec	Total
Cash Flow													
A/R coll. - current month	160.0	161.6	163.2	164.8	166.5	168.2	169.8	171.5	173.3	175.0	176.7	178.5	2,029.2
A/R coll. - prior month	869.0	880.0	888.8	897.7	906.7	915.7	924.9	934.1	943.5	952.9	962.4	972.1	11,047.8
A/R coll. - 2d prior mo.	538.2	545.1	552.0	557.5	563.1	568.7	574.4	580.2	586.0	591.8	597.7	603.7	6,858.4
Total Receipts	1,567.2	1,586.7	1,604.0	1,620.1	1,636.3	1,652.6	1,669.1	1,685.8	1,702.7	1,719.7	1,736.9	1,754.3	19,935.5
Cost of goods sold	937.5	950.9	964.4	977.9	991.5	1,005.1	1,018.9	1,032.7	1,046.5	1,060.5	1,074.5	1,088.5	12,148.8
Selling, gen. & admin.	210.0	211.6	213.2	214.8	216.5	218.2	229.8	231.5	233.3	235.0	236.7	238.5	2,689.2
Interest	10.3	11.1	13.3	11.5	12.7	11.1	11.2	9.7	8.6	9.1	8.4	8.3	125.4
Taxes	396.0			367.7		241.0			350.3				1,355.0
Other - capital investment	125.0	700.0	175.0	200.0	200.0	200.0	200.0	200.0	200.0	200.0	200.0	200.0	2,800.0
Debt principal	15.5	15.6	15.7	15.8	15.9	16.0	16.1	16.2	16.4	16.5	16.6	16.7	193.0
Total Disbursements	1,694.3	1,889.2	1,381.6	1,787.8	1,436.6	1,691.4	1,476.1	1,490.1	1,855.1	1,521.0	1,536.2	1,552.0	19,311.4
Net Cash Flow	-127.1	-302.5	222.5	-167.7	199.7	-38.8	193.1	195.7	-152.4	198.7	200.7	202.3	624.1
Beginning cash	-91.7	-218.8	-521.3	-298.9	-466.6	-266.9	-305.7	-112.6	83.1	-69.3	129.4	330.1	-91.7
Available cash	-218.8	-521.3	-298.9	-466.6	-266.9	-305.7	-112.6	83.1	-69.3	129.4	330.1	532.4	532.4
Line of credit borrowing	228.8	531.3	308.9	476.6	276.9	315.7	122.6	0.0	79.3	0.0	0.0	0.0	0.0
Ending Cash	10.0	10.0	10.0	10.0	10.0	10.0	10.0	83.1	10.0	129.4	330.1	532.4	532.4

Exhibit A.5 Jack B. Nimble Company
Cash Flow Projection For 20x3 (continued)

2. The granting of credit terms of 30 days to customers, which means a month's worth of sales for which the company will not receive immediate cash. In the meantime, it has to expend money ahead of time for the materials and labor that go into the products to be sold
3. Debt service—loan repayment and interest payments—that have been incurred to handle previous tight cash situation but were not adequately planned for by Nimble in his projections
4. Investment in fixed assets—property, plant and equipment—that Jack feels is necessary to achieve his goals. These investments require payment (from cash or borrowed funds) when they are purchased but provide returns only over the lives of the assets acquired. The timing differences have to be financed by the company, and Nimble has not taken this into account.

An examination of the Cash Flow Projection for 20X3 quickly shows that the company looks to be in very good shape by the end of that projection year. While encouraging, this alone does not make the problem go away. As of the beginning of the projection year, Nimble Company is out of cash and has several months of negative cash flow to handle. It is this immediate problem that needs to be handled. Additionally, there are lots of opportunities that would make the cash flow situation even better than it looks in the projection, and these should be considered and implemented if feasible. Finally, even with the favorable projection, there are numbers of operational and financial problems that should be addressed to improve the overall company financial performance.

The suggested solution attempts to point out some of the key financial and operational areas that should be addressed, but the reader should recognize that there are many other areas that deserve attention as well.

Financial Issues

The company's financial structure is seriously out of alignment. The short-term line of credit has been used not only for working capital needs, but also for capital investment requirements. Using short-term money for long-term needs creates a repayment problem since the benefits of those capital investments will accrue only over the long-term. Since repayment requirements are immediate having adequate funds to make them is difficult and in the case of Nimble Company, virtually impossible. That is the major reason the company has been unable to zero out the line of credit as demanded by the bank.

To solve this problem, it will be necessary to reshape the capital structure of the company and, more immediately, to take care of the line of credit problem. One quick and dirty, though temporary, way to deal with the line of credit issue would be to ask the bank for a waiver of the requirement to zero out the loan. The bank might say, "No", in which case the company is no worse off than before. Or they might say, "Yes" to the request, in which case the problem goes away until a more permanent fix is devised. In this particular case, given the very favorable picture in the forecast for the end of year 20x3, it seems likely that the bank will have little choice but to go along with the request for a limited period of time. To refuse the request and call for immediate repayment of the loan will put the company into default and will thereby leave the bank as the owner/operator of the company, a position no bank wants to get into. Since its best option for getting repaid is to help the company get out of its difficulty, an affirmative response to the request is likely, unless there are other factors that cause the bank to feel the loan is a lost cause.

Once the line of credit problem is handled, Nimble Company can then work with the bank to create a more appropriate capital structure consisting of long-term loans, collateralized by the fixed assets it already owns. This reduces immediate cash requirements by deferring the loan payments over a longer period of time, albeit with greater interest payments. But the goal is to get through the immediate cash crunch, and anything that can be deferred is likely to be a good thing. Further, a more properly balanced capital structure is necessary and desirable for the company. As part of the refinancing structuring, the existing line of credit should be extinguished, solving the zero balance problem, and replaced with a new line of credit to be used for working capital needs only. Any new long-term assets should then be financed by appropriate long-term debt.

Operational Issues

An immediate and obvious concern has to be the collection of existing accounts receivable. Sales for the last quarter of 20X2 were $4,426,100 or $48,100 per day. 12/31/X2 accounts receivable were $2,029,600, making Jack's collection period 42.2 days – 12.2 days more than his terms. That 12.2 days calculates out to be $586,800 in unavailable cash. Calculated on an annual basis, his sales were $15,073,400 or $41,300 per day. On that basis, his collection period is at 49.1 days, which represents $788,800 in overdue cash the company is owed. Jack appears to be doing little or nothing to collect his overdue accounts receivable, and he needs to be pushed into going after the slow payers. Failing to pay attention to this type of behavior on the part of his customers will only cause them to take more advantage of him and extend payment times still farther out. A vigorous follow-up program on the overdue accounts is likely to bring in a substantial sum of money.

A second immediate issue is his planned expenditures for capital investments, which total $2,800,000 for the 20X3 projection period. Of particular concern is the $700,000 projected for February. This should be cancelled if possible, deferred if not cancelable, or financed if not deferrable. After that Jack's $200,000 per month projection from April through December needs to be examined closely to eliminate those planned expenditures that are not essential to the basic growth and profitability of his business. It is too easy for production/engineering trained managers to think that all they need to get their jobs accomplished is more equipment. In this case Nimble can simply not afford to spend that much money, and it also seems likely that even without a cash problem there is much more projected than can be justified. In any event, that line item needs to be scaled back significantly both to save cash and avoid becoming over-committed to fixed-asset investment.

Arguably the most significant area of concern is the month-by-month decline in the company's profitability through the 20X3 projection period from 11.6 percent of sales to 9.6 percent. Something is wrong! According to the Financial Forecast Information, fixed costs of goods sold are increasing at $10,000 per month for the entire 12 months. That amounts to nearly $800,000 for the year. Nimble's reasons for these increases must be questioned, and such a review will undoubtedly point out savings of considerable magnitude in the projected cash flow. The profitability decline is a huge red flag, caused principally by the increase in fixed costs of goods sold, and this problem needs to be fixed, again not only to save cash but also to improve company operations and profitability. Any self-respecting bank will be very leery of lending money to a company with declining profitability of this magnitude.

Additional operational areas to review for the purpose of improving both cash flow and profitability are

- Variable costs of goods sold at 40 percent of sales (these should be decreasing to reflect the improvements in efficiency he should be experiencing because of investment in equipment)
- Selling, general and administrative expenses, both fixed and variable, to see if they can be reduced
- Taxes, a look at which might result in the opportunity to defer or reduce some of those payments as well

Finally, Nimble should be looking at his inventory. While his inventory has not increased appreciably since he took over the company and therefore has not been a direct contributor to his cash flow problems, there is still a potential for improved operations. Nimble's inventory turnover for 20X2 (cost of goods sold divided by the inventory balance) is approximately 4.1 times—not bad, but certainly not exciting. The best way to determine if this number is satisfactory or not is to examine industry statistics for the industry. We do not have that information available, so a definitive determination cannot be made. However, if his inventory turnover could be increased to five times, it would free up about $455,000 in cash; if the turnover could be increased to six times, the amount of cash freed up would be about $800,000. Those numbers will be even larger as the business expands. For that kind of potential cash saving, inventory is worth looking into, even though an improvement would take some time to implement—too long for it to be an immediate solution to his existing problem.

If we had more information about the company it would be plausible that other areas for improvement could be found (up to and including the possibility of having Jack replaced by a more effective manager). But the idea presented here is that most of any cash flow saved and profitability gained will come about as a result of operational issues rather than financial issues. This does not mean the financial issues should be ignored or minimized, but that operational issues should be recognized as the principal causes of cash flow problems and the principal sources of cash flow improvement.

APPENDIX B

Cash Conservation Checklist

ASSETS	Yes	No	N/A
Cash			
1. Conserve what you have and invest any excess.	___	___	___
2. Utilize float on disbursements.	___	___	___
3. Negotiate with bank for quicker availability of deposited funds.	___	___	___
4. Use lockboxes if they make economic sense.	___	___	___
5. Centralize cash and use sweep accounts or like devices.	___	___	
6. Invest as early and as long as possible.	___	___	___
7. Don't spend unless you must.	___	___	___
8. Use electronic transfers for incoming cash whenever possible.	___	___	___
9. Offer discounts for cash sales.	___	___	___
10.	___	___	___
11.	___	___	___
Accounts Receivable			
1. Get invoices out no later than time of shipment.	___	___	___
2. Establish and stick with credit terms.	___	___	___
3. Age and monitor your receivables.	___	___	___
4. Follow up regularly and persistently on overdue accounts.	___	___	___
5. Consider (but do not automatically implement) cash discounts or other incentives to pay.	___	___	___
6. Consider shortening payment terms to customers.	___	___	___
7. Control your accounts receivable to sales ratio.	___	___	___
8. Measure and control accounts receivable collection period over two or three months rather than a full year.	___	___	___

ASSETS	Yes	No	N/A
9. Factor receivables if not collateralized.	____	____	____
10. Use collection agencies if necessary.	____	____	____
11. Implement penalties for late payments.	____	____	____
12. Get cash payment for invoices where cost of invoicing exceeds amount of the invoice.	____	____	____

Inventory

	Yes	No	N/A
1. Stay out of the inventory business as much as possible.	____	____	____
2. Buy for customer orders rather than for stock.	____	____	____
3. Use vendor consignment inventory.	____	____	____
4. Negotiate blanket purchase orders with flexible delivery schedules.	____	____	____
5. Consider effective disposal of obsolete inventory for cash.	____	____	____
6. Stratify your inventory (ABC system) and control strata independently.	____	____	____
7. Improve inventory turns.			
8. Consider unloading dead or dying inventory for cash (e.g., fire sales, parking lot flea markets, etc.).	____	____	____
9.	____	____	____

Prepaid Expenses

	Yes	No	N/A
1. DON'T!!	____	____	____
2. Get your deposits back.	____	____	____
3. Avoid salary advances.	____	____	____
4. Consider monthly, quarterly, or semiannual insurance premium payments rather than annual payments.	____	____	____
5. Do not overpay or prepay taxes.	____	____	____
6.	____	____	____
7.	____	____	____
8.	____	____	____

Fixed Assets

	Yes	No	N/A
1. Buy what you need, not what would be nice.	____	____	____
2. Consider used equipment.	____	____	____
3. Rent out extra space.	____	____	____

ASSETS	Yes	No	N/A
4. Consider leases to conserve cash.	____	____	____
5. Sell off idle assets.	____	____	____
6. Refurbish rather than buy new.	____	____	____
7. Use outside contractors for temporary excess manufacturing requirements.	____	____	____
8. Use excess capacity to do contract work for others.	____	____	____
9. favorable payment or financing terms with suppliers of new equipment.	____	____	____
10. Defer purchases.	____	____	____
11. Borrow to finance purchases (chattel mortgages).	____	____	____
12. Build rather than buy.	____	____	____
13. Check plant layout for efficiency.	____	____	____
14. Consider making employees responsible for maintaining their own equipment.	____	____	____
15.	____	____	____
16.	____	____	____
17.	____	____	____

LIABILITIES AND EQUITY	Yes	No	N/A
Accounts Payable and Accrued Expenses			
1. Pay only what you owe (price and quantity).	____	____	____
2. Don't double pay invoices.	____	____	____
3. Pay only properly authorized invoices.	____	____	____
4. Don't pay early except for very good reasons.	____	____	____
5. Take advantageous discounts even if you have to borrow.	____	____	____
6. Negotiate better terms with suppliers.	____	____	____
7. Use computer to schedule and manage payments.	____	____	____
8. Establish plans/budgets for payments; review and analyze variances.	____	____	____
9. Pay slow if you must, but communicate with your suppliers about your plans.	____	____	____
10. Use bartering.	____	____	____

LIABILITIES AND EQUITY	**Yes**	**No**	**N/A**
11. Slow down spending—spend only what you have.	_____	_____	_____
12. Pay off small invoices on time to reduce amount to be managed.	_____	_____	_____
13. Pay cash for small invoices where cost of processing exceeds amount of invoice.	_____	_____	_____
14.	_____	_____	_____

Borrowing

	Yes	**No**	**N/A**
1. Negotiate for lowest interest rate and best terms.	_____	_____	_____
2. Get deferrals on interest and/or principal.	_____	_____	_____
3. Analyze totality of loan costs —interest, compensating balance requirements, restrictive covenants, repayment terms, etc.	_____	_____	_____
4. Borrow as little and as late as practical.	_____	_____	_____
5. Match long-term needs with long-term borrowing.	_____	_____	_____
6. Don't use long-term debt for seasonal, cyclical, or other short-term needs.	_____	_____	_____
7. Roll interest into principal.	_____	_____	_____
8. Convert to longer term repayment schedule.	_____	_____	_____
9.	_____	_____	_____
10.	_____	_____	_____

Equity

	Yes	**No**	**N/A**
1. Consider if it makes sense to pay dividends.	_____	_____	_____
2. Consider if dividend payments are consistent with cash availability.	_____	_____	_____
3. Use stock in lieu of cash dividends.	_____	_____	_____
4. Issue new stock.			
5. Sell stock at discount to employees.	_____	_____	_____
6. Initiate (or promote) dividend reinvestment program.	_____	_____	_____
7.	_____	_____	_____
8.	_____	_____	_____
9.	_____	_____	_____

INCOME AND EXPENSES	Yes	No	N/A

Sales

1. Sell to the company plan.

2. Sell to customers who pay on time.

3. Sell profitable products.

4. Emphasize sales of higher margin products/services.

5. Negotiate advance payments and/or progress payments.

6. Remember that only the margin represents increase in cash.

7. Raise prices (or lower prices).

8. Increase unit sales.

9. Provide volume discounts.

10. Emphasize cash sales.

11.

Expenses

1. Establish budget of expenses to assure positive cash flow.

2. Review and control actual expenses to budget.

3. Establish authorization controls and limits on purchase orders and/or requisitions.

4. Use blanket orders with flexible delivery schedules.

5. Negotiate for cash discounts.

6. Establish an atmosphere of cash conservation among all employees.

7. Control cash disbursements at purchase order level as well as actual expenditures.

8. Each dollar of cost saved equals a dollar of cash improvement.

9. Reappraise assets to reduce taxes.

10. Hiring only when and as needed.

11. Initiate expense reduction program.

12. Competitively bid contracts.

13. Consider less expensive production methods.

14. Reduce or eliminate non-value-added activities.

INCOME AND EXPENSES	Yes	No	N/A
15. Prepare budgets that reflect only essential expenditures.	_____	_____	_____
16.	_____	_____	_____
17.	_____	_____	_____

OTHER	Yes	No	N/A
1. CASH IS KING! Manage your business accordingly.	_____	_____	_____
2. Build cash awareness into your organizational culture.	_____	_____	_____
3. Prepare cash budgets in addition to profit budgets.	_____	_____	_____
4. Pay any bonuses, commissions, etc. based on cash flow criteria.	_____	_____	_____
5.	_____	_____	_____
6.	_____	_____	_____
7.	_____	_____	_____
8.	_____	_____	_____

Index

A

ABC, *see* Activity based costing
ABM (Activity Based Management), 156
Accounting, responsibility, 229, 231–232
Accounting function, 177–238
  activity-based costing applications for, 211–213
  areas of, 179–181
  basic business principles in, 183–184
  budget analysis in, 200–202
  cash management analysis survey for, 188–198
  cost analysis of, 202–206
  developing recommendations for, 213–214
  financial reporting in, 185–188
  goal identification in, 182–183
  goals of, 11
  operations analysis of, 206–211
  organizational issues with, 198–199
  and organization recommendations, 232–234
  prioritizing activities in, 184–185
  review of, 234–237
  specific recommendations for, 214–232, 234–237
Accounts payable, 8, 182, 206–207, 215–216, 235
Accounts receivable, 4, 7, 16, 39–43, 45–47, 182, 207–209, 216–217, 235–236
Accounts receivable-based financing, 252, 255–256
Accrual-based accounting, 19, 20, 186, 188
ACHs (automated clearinghouses), 23
Acquisitions (of new businesses), 316
Activity based costing (ABC), 152–174
  accounting function applications of, 211–213
  case study in, 168, 169, 171–174
  cost assignment view of, 162
  functional cost controls in, 167–170, 172
  levels in, 163–166
  objectives of, 153
  and organizational concerns, 152, 154–157
  overhead considerations in, 164, 166–167
  process view of, 163
  traditional costing vs., 157–161, 165
Activity Based Management (ABM), 156
Adjusted Net Income method, 288–289
Administration, 5, 167
Aging, accounts receivable, 42–43, 46
American Institute of Certified Public Accountants (AICPA), 264
Amortization, 186
Assets, 12, 18, 251
Assumptions, 292–293, 297–298
Audit checks, 60–61
Automated clearinghouses (ACHs), 23
Automatic balance accounts, 66
Availability float, 24–26

B

Backlogs, 4
Balance sheets, 36–39
Banks/banking, 21–23, 28–33, 66–67, 252, 254–255, 258–259
Bank accounts, 66–67
Bankers' acceptances, 256
Basic business principles, 5–6, 183–184
Batch level activities, 163
Benchmarking, 124–151
  case study of, 148–150
  and comparative analysis, 145–148
  employee comparisons for, 141–144
  external, 126–127, 150–151
  internal, 126–130, 148–150
  measures by function for, 133–134
  and organizational structure, 130, 134–141
  qualitative, 132
  quantitative, 131
  and stakeholders, 124
  strategic concepts for, 125–126
  targets of, 150–151
Best-in-class benchmarking, 127
Billing, 7
Board of Directors, 242
Bonds, 257

Borrowed statistics, 146
Borrowing, 12, 251–262
  interest rates for, 21, 23
  and leverage, 259–262
  management of, 258–259
  medium- and long-term, 256–258
  short-term, 253–256
  sources for, 252–253
Bottom-up systems, 80
Budgeting systems:
  analysis of, 200–202
  and cash balances projections, 272, 273
  and cash disbursements projections, 270–272
  and cash flow planning, 267–275
  and cash receipts projections, 268–270
  and corporate planning, 71–74
  and forecasting sales, 268
  recommendations for, 223
  and sales function, 100–103

C

Capital expenditures, 315–316
Capital investments, 155, 248–250
Capital leases, 258
Case study, 325–340
Cash, sources of, 12–14
Cash-based accounting, 186, 188
Cash conservation checklist, 341–346
Cash conversion and expansion, 3, 12
Cash discounts, 47–50, 60
Cash flow(s), 12–23
  classifications of, 286–287
  considerations for, 244–245
  costs of, 38–39
  decisions affecting, 153
  and Federal Reserve System, 21–23
  historical perspective on, 21
  objectives of managing, 17–18
  planning for, see Planning cash flow
  process of, 14–17
  and profitability vs. liquidity, 18–20
  profits vs., 12–13
  statements of, see Statements of cash flows
Cash flow analysis, 285–322
  and controls, 299–312
  and FASB 95, 285–287
  and interpretation, 300, 305, 307–309, 312–322

projections methodology for, 287–298
  and reporting, 293
Cash gap, 12–13
Cash generation cycle, 14, 15, 17
Cash management, 9–11, 17–18, 95–96, 156, 188–192
Cash management services, 29
Cash on delivery (COD), 42, 43, 47
Cash processing systems, 52–56
Cash surrender value (of life insurance policies), 256
Centralization of payables, 59
CEO (Chief Executive Officer), 242
CFO (Chief Financial Officer), 242
Check-clearing process, 22–26
Checking accounts, 29
Chief Executive Officer (CEO), 242
Chief Financial Officer (CFO), 242
Clearing time, 25, 26
COD, see Cash on delivery
Collection float, 24–26
Collection periods, 39–41
Collection systems, 7, 43–53, 109, 110
Commercial paper, 256
Commissions, 109
Commitment, lack of, 81
Commitment fees, 254
Common-size financial statements, 221
Communication, 33, 62, 111
Comparative analysis, 145–148, 221
Compensating balances, 29–30
Compensation, 97, 109–110, 143–144
Competition, strategies for, 74–76
Competitive analysis, 77
Competitive benchmarking, 126–127
Competitive pricing, 106
Compounding, 242, 244
Concentration accounts, 55–56
Contractors, 3
Contracts (with customers), 256
Controls, 167–170, 172, 299–312
Controlled disbursement funding, 63–65
Conversion, 3, 12
Correspondent banks, 25, 29
Costs, 8
  of banking services, 29–31
  of cash flow, 38–39
  of goods sold, 226
  noncompliance, 158
  nonfinancial, 157
  of overhead, 164, 166–167
  of personnel, 141–144

traditional, 159–161
unit, 164
Cost analysis, 202–206
Cost assignment view, 162
Cost performance, 154, 155
Cost reductions, 123–175
  activity based costing method for, 152–174
  benchmarking method for, 124–151
  targets of, 154
  techniques for, 123
Credit policies, 44
Credit terms, 56–58
Currency, 22
Customers, 3, 124, 156, 252
Customer analysis, 77
Customer service, 2–3, 109

D

Days' sales outstanding (DSO), 270
DCF, *see* Discounted cash flow
Debentures, 257
Deliveries, 51
Demand deposit accounts, 29, 66
Demand notes, 255
Depreciation, 186, 245
Detail operating plans, 90
Determination of strategic options, 78
Differentiation strategy, 74
Direct clearance, 25
Direct method planning, 280–282
Disbursement funding, 63–65
Disbursements float, 23, 24, 26, 63
Disbursements systems, 58–67, 270–272
Discounts, cash, 47–50, 60
Discounted cash flow (DCF), 242, 244
Discount rates, 23
Dollars per item, 105–106
DSO (days' sales outstanding), 270

E

Economic conditions, 21
Economic float, 26–28
Electronic funds transfers (EFT), 23, 54–55
Employees, 72–73, 124, 134–135, 141–144, 230, 314–315
Employee Retirement Income Security Act (ERISA), 253
Environmental analysis, 78

Equipment, *see* Property, plant, and equipment
Equipment financing, 257
Equity, 12, 251
ERISA (Employee Retirement Income Security Act), 253
Estimated funding disbursement systems, 63–65
Excess cash, 13, 16, 272–275, 278. *See also* Investing excess cash
Expenses, 8, 186
External analysis, 76–78
External benchmarking, 126–127, 150–151

F

Facility level activities, 163
Factoring, 255–256
FASB 95, *see* Statement of Financial Accounting Standards Board No. 95
Federal Deposit Insurance Corporation (FDIC), 30
Federal Reserve clearance, 25
Federal Reserve System (Fed), 21–23
Finance charges, 51
Finance leases, 258
Financial objectives orientation, 80
Financial ratios, 222
Financial reporting, 183, 185–188
Financial stability (of bank), 30
Financing activities, 313–314, 316
Financing sources, 250–251
Flexibility, 254
Float, 23–28, 59, 62
Focus strategy, 75
Forecasting, 103–104, 264–265, 268
Franklin, Benjamin, 8

G

Gap, cash, 12–13
General ledger, 183, 210–211, 218–219, 236–237
Goals, 69–70, 72, 88, 99, 182–183
Goldilocks Cash Management Principle, 16
Government, 3, 22, 124
Government securities, 23
Guaranties, 256

I

Imprest accounts, 66
Income statements, 226, 228
Incremental cash flows, 244
Indirect method planning, 282, 283
Industry analysis, 77–78
Industry benchmarking, 127
Information systems, 111
Integrated systems, 223
Interest-bearing options, 28
Interest rates, 21, 23
Internal analysis, 78
Internal benchmarking, 126–130, 148–150
Internal disbursements, 60–61
Internal operations, 223, 224, 226–231
Internal rate of return (IRR), 246, 247, 249
Internal statements, 219–227
Internal transfer, 25
Interpretation of cash flow, 300, 305, 307–309, 312–322
Inventory, 4, 7–8, 16, 186
Inventory-based financing, 252, 256
Investing activities, 313, 315–316
Investing excess cash, 21, 239–250
Investments, capital, 155, 248–250
Investment brokers, 252
Investment services, 29
Invoicing, 45
IRR, *see* Internal rate of return

J

Just In Time (JIT), 156

L

Leasing, 257–258
Lenders, 124
Leverage, 259–262
Life insurance, 252, 256
Liquidity, 18–20
Loans, 257
Location (of bank), 31
Lockboxes, 52–54
Long-range planning, 82
Long-term borrowing, 256–258
Long-term investing, 242, 244–247, 249
Low cost strategy, 74

M

Mail time, 25
Management, 3, 5, 62–65, 104–105, 124, 258–259. *See also* Top management
Management by exception, 85
Manufacturing, 7, 10–11, 223
Market pricing, 106
Measurement, performance, 90, 91, 93–94, 154, 299
Medium-term borrowing, 256–258
Mission statements, 72, 88
Monetary policy, 22–23
Money, making, 3
Money supply, 22
Mortgages, 257

N

Net present value (NPV), 246, 247
Net sales, 226
Noncompliance costs, 158
Nonfinancial cost measures, 157
Non-value-added functions, 176–177. *See also* Accounting function
Notes, 255
NPV, *see* Net present value

O

Objectives, 70, 88–90, 153, 266
Open line of credit, 254–255
Operating activities, 308, 309, 312, 314
Operating expenses, 226
Operating indicators, 316–319
Operating leases, 257–258
Operational ratios, 222
Operations analysis, 206–211
Organizations:
   and accounting function, 198–199
   activity-based costing concerns of, 152, 154–157
   benchmarking and structure of, 130, 134–141
   building, 140
   goals of, 2–5, 10
   recommendations for, 232–234
   sales function and planning for, 98–100
Organizational charts, 136–139, 198–199
Organizational planning, 81–83
Overhead considerations, 164, 166–167
Owners, 3, 12, 124

P

Payables, 16, 59
Payment policies, 61–62
Payments/payment systems, 8, 62
Payroll, 182–183, 209–210, 217–218, 230, 236
Pension plans, 253
Percentage markup, 105
Performance, 31, 222
Performance analysis, 78
Performance measures, 130
Personnel, 11, 233–234. *See also* Employees
Planning, corporate, 69–94
    and budgeting, 71–74
    competitive, 74–76
    and sales function, 100–103
    short-term, 81–94
    strategic, 76–81
Planning cash flow, 263–284
    benefits of, 275–276
    and budgeting, 267–275
    considerations for, 265–266
    direct method approach to, 280–282
    and forecasting, 264–265
    indirect method approach to, 282, 283
    and managing cash balances, 276–279
    objectives of, 266
    preparation for, 264
Planning rigidity, 81
Planning systems, 223
Plant, *see* Property, plant, and equipment
"Playing the accounts payable float," 59
Potential for survival, 222
Preemption strategy, 75–76
Prefunding disbursement systems, 62–65
Price-sensitive strategy, 107
Pricing strategies, 105–107
Priorities, 154, 184–185
Processing time, 25
Process view, 163
Product analysis, 100–103, 107–108, 222
Production of services, 7, 10–11
Productivity benchmarking, 141–144
Product level activities, 163
Product-line reporting, 227–229, 231
Profits, 12–13, 186
Profitability, 16, 18–20, 110, 250–251
Projections methodology, 287–298
Property, plant, and equipment, 4, 16, 186, 315
Providing services, 223
Purchasing, 7–8, 11

Q

Qualitative benchmarking, 132
Quality strategy, 106–107
Quantitative benchmarking, 131

R

Ratios, 222, 319–322
Reasonableness, 146–148
Receipts and disbursements forecasting method, 288–292
Receipts systems, 39–58
    and accounts receivable, 39–43, 46
    and cash processing systems, 52–56
    and collection systems, 43–45, 47–51
    and credit terms, 56–58
    projections for, 268–270
Reinvesting profits, 12
Remote collections, 52, 53
Remote payment locations, 62
Reporting, 111, 183, 219–227, 280–283, 293
Reserves, cash, 22, 276–278
Residual values, 244
Responsibility accounting, 229, 231–232
Return on assets (ROA), 18
Return on equity (ROE), 18
Return on investment (ROI), 18
Rigidity, planning, 81
Risk, 248–250
ROA (return on assets), 18
ROE (return on equity), 18
ROI (return on investment), 18

S

Salary, 110
Sale(s):
    of assets, 251
    of equity, 12
Sales function, 4, 6–7, 95–122
    and accounts receivable, 40–42
    accrual- vs. cash-based accounting of, 186
    analysis of, 111–121
    analysis work program for, 117–121
    and cash management study, 95–96
    desirable operating practices of, 113
    forecasts in, 103–104, 223
    goals of, 10
    information/reporting systems for, 111
    initial survey form for, 114–116

Sales function (*cont'd*)
    management/responsibilities of,
      104–105
    and methods of compensation,
      109–110
    and methods of sales, 108–109
    and organizational planning systems,
      98–100
    and planning/budget systems,
      100–103
    pricing strategies for, 105–107
    and product analysis, 107–108
    purpose of, 96–98
Second-day availability rule, 25
Secured borrowing, 255
Security-based financing, 256
September 11, 2001 terrorist attacks, 21
Services:
    bank, 30–31
    production of, 7, 10–11
Service charges, 29
SFAS 95, *see* Statement of Financial
    Accounting Standards Board No. 95
Shareholders, 3, 124
Shortfalls, cash, 272–275, 279
Short-term borrowing, 253–256
Short-term investing, 239–240
Short-term notes, 255
Short-term operating plans, 85–88
Short-term planning, 81–94
    budgeting step of, 87
    detail plans/programming step of,
      86, 87
    evaluating step of, 88
    implementing step of, 87–91
    key results in, 91–93
    and measurement techniques, 93–94
    planning step of, 86
    underlying theory for, 83–85
Size (of bank), 30
"Sleep insurance," 17, 278
Special-interest groups, 3, 124
Spreadsheet driven process, 80
Stability (of bank), 30
Stakeholders, 2–3, 124
Statements of cash flows, 12, 286, 287,
    305, 307–309, 312–316
Statement of Financial Accounting
    Standards Board No. 95 (FASB 95)—
    Statement of Cash Flows, 280,
    285–287, 292
Statistics, borrowed, 146

Stock, company, 12
Stockholders, 253
Strategic planning process, 76–81
Strengths, weaknesses, opportunities,
    and threats (SWOT) analysis, 86
Subcontractors, 124
Suppliers, 3, 124, 314–315
Survey form, cash management analysis,
    188–192
Survival, 3, 222
SWOT (strengths, weaknesses,
    opportunities, and threats)
    analysis, 86
Synergy strategy, 76

T

Tax considerations, 245
Terms, *see* Cash discounts
Time frame (for cash planning), 265–266
Time value of money, 245–246
Top down systems, 80
Top management:
    benchmarking role of, 130
    planning role of, 72–73, 81–82, 84
    sales function role of, 104, 105
    sales study role of, 95–96
Total business float, 26–28
Total Quality Management (TQM), 156
Trade credit, 253–254
Traditional costing, 157–161, 165
Trend percentages, 221

U

Unique niche, 106
Unit level activities, 163
Unsecured borrowing, 255
U.S. Postal Service, 25
U.S. Treasury, 22

V

Vendors, 3, 124, 252–253

W

Wire transfers, 54

Z

Zero balance accounts, 66, 67